Modern Political Culture
in the Caribbean

Modern Political Culture in the Caribbean

Edited by

Holger Henke
and
Fred Reno

UNIVERSITY OF THE WEST INDIES PRESS
Barbados • Jamaica • Trinidad and Tobago

University of the West Indies Press
1A Aqueduct Flats   Mona
Kingston 7   Jamaica

© 2003 by The University of the West Indies Press
All rights reserved. Published 2003

07 06 05 04 03   5 4 3 2 1

CATALOGUING IN PUBLICATION DATA

Modern political culture in the Caribbean / edited by Holger Henke
and Fred Reno.
p. cm.
Includes bibliographical references.
ISBN: 976-640-135-7

1. Caribbean Area – Politics and government. 2. Political culture – Caribbean Area. 3. Democracy – Caribbean Area. 4. Civil society – Caribbean Area. I. Henke, Holger. II. Reno, Fred.

F2183.M628 2003   327.729'2

Cover illustration: Detlef Henke, untitled (acrylic on canvas), 2002.
Book and cover design by Robert Harris
Set in Sabon 10.5/14.5 x 24
Printed in Canada.

To J.A. George Irish – for your example of personal and scholarly integrity, your many years of dedicated work on behalf of Caribbean communities throughout the Caribbean and its diaspora, and your support for new generations of students and scholars.

Contents

Introduction
Politics and Culture in the Caribbean / *xi*
Holger Henke and Fred Reno

Part 1: Elements of Political Culture in the Caribbean

Chapter 1
Is There a New Political Culture in the Caribbean?
Challenges and Opportunities / *3*
Fred Constant

Chapter 2
"Racing" Caribbean Political Culture:
Afrocentrism, Black Nationalism and Fanonism / *21*
Anton L. Allahar

Chapter 3
The Race-Class Problematic and the Caribbean Left / *59*
Perry Mars

Chapter 4
Cultural Identity versus Political Identity
in the French West Indies / *90*
Jacky Dahomay

Part 2: The Ab/Uses of History

Chapter 5
Freedom Ossified: Political Culture and the
Public Use of History in Jamaica / *111*
Holger Henke

Chapter 6
Presenting the Past: The Construction of
National History in a Jamaican Tourist Site / 141
Anita M. Waters

Chapter 7
Icon and Myth in a Caribbean Polity:
V.C. Bird and Antiguan Political Culture / 181
Douglas Midgett

Chapter 8
Imagined Communities: Articulating a
Return to Mythical Homelands in the African
and Indian Diasporas / 212
Simboonath Singh

Part 3: Civil Society and Changes in the Political and Economic Sphere

Chapter 9
Global Culture and the Politics of Moral
Deregulation in Jamaica / 239
Obika Gray

Chapter 10
The Frontline: Valentino, Pablo Moses and
Caribbean Organic Philosophy in the 1970s / 276
Brian Meeks

Chapter 11
Cuba: Civil Society within Socialism –
And Its Limits / 302
Bert Hoffmann

Chapter 12
Fidel Castro's Heirs: Obstacles to and Perspectives
on a New Political Culture in Cuba / 322
Hans-Jürgen Burchardt

Part 4: The Politics of Confrontation and Fragmentation

Chapter 13
Guyana's Dominant Political Culture:
An Overview / *351*
David Hinds

Chapter 14
The Dutch Caribbean: Studies in the Fragmentation
of a Political Culture / *370*
Edward Dew

Chapter 15
Rethinking Democracy in the Post-Nationalist State:
The Case of Trinidad and Tobago / *395*
Percy C. Hintzen

Chapter 16
Democratic Transition and Authoritarianism:
The Case of Haiti / *424*
Fred Reno

Contributors / *452*

Introduction

Politics and Culture in the Caribbean

Holger Henke and Fred Reno

What became evident already in the week following the terror attack on the World Trade Center in New York City is that within a few short hours the political culture of the United States noticeably changed. Clearly and without exaggeration, 11 September 2001 marked the end of the twentieth and the beginning of the twenty-first century – or, as one observer called it more dramatically, the end of the end of History (Zakaria 2001). While the twentieth century was the century of global wars between nations, of totalitarian regimes, of concentration camps and finally of the cold war, the US public and government were cured of their lingering fears of communism in a matter of hours.[1] Without doubt, after about two decades of emphasis on free-market rhetoric, the primacy of politics and culture has re-emerged with an unimagined vengeance. The idea that compared to the unmitigated immediacy of economics in almost all aspects of life, the state, government and politics would wither and become inconsequential now appears to be absurd.

For the Caribbean there have been no such cataclysmic events that would redefine the region's central political concerns and values in such a short time. Nevertheless, even a casual observer will notice that culture and politics in the region are, despite similarities, negotiated differently than, say, in Italy or France, Afghanistan or Egypt, Chile or Singapore. Indeed, many scholars and political commentators, in their attempts to grapple with various issues under investigation, regularly refer, explicitly or implicitly, to the cultural idiosyncrasies of Caribbean people and societies. On the other hand, many observers outside of the region make assumptions about Caribbean people(s), societies and polities which reflect more their own embeddedness in cultural, sociopolitical traditions and moral value systems that, because of the region's colonial history, may not necessarily be foreign to the region but that are definitely not reflective of its public opinion/s, political epistemology/ies, and cosmology/ies (see also Henke 1996, 1997). Both groups – those who sense the cultural differences and those who do not – acknowledge, therefore, the existence and relevance of distinct political cultures.

While over the years there have been many "egg–hen" debates over the exact nature of the relationship between values, political attitudes and behaviour (culture) on the one side and institutions and processes (the political) on the other, the consensus is now more or less that "there are persistent and stable components, such as basic political beliefs and value commitments, and primordial attachments that affect and constrain our political behavior and our public policy" (Almond 2000, 17). Rational-choice theorists and game theorists almost always ignore cultural variables even if they should occasionally pay lip service to them. In addition, most of the scholarly political culture literature focuses on three geographical regions: the developed West, communist countries and developing Asian countries. Apart from Archie Singham's important but clearly outdated *The Hero and the Crowd in a Colonial Polity* (1968), one is hard pressed to find a sustained debate about political culture in the Caribbean.[2] To the extent, then, that the existence of distinct political cultures is acknowledged, there is a challenge to draw a map of some of the cultural idiosyncrasies affecting the different countries and subregions of the Caribbean. Maintaining the metropolitan institutions or importing them from the former motherlands after gaining independence, for example, has more decisively affected the relative political stability in the region than it has on the African or Asian continents.

There are not (yet) many books focusing on the Caribbean that group all language areas and subregions in this diverse region together and treat them – contrary to their historical fate – as one unit, that is, as a political universe of related historical experiences with (for the most part) similar ethnic compositions, similar economic bases and a comparable situation within the global economy. This volume is one of the few that are trying to escape this late consequence of colonial divide-and-rule geopolitics. A price had to be paid for gaining this larger, "de-colonialized", if you will, discursive approach. Thus, while other books focusing on politics in one, two, or a very small group of Caribbean countries are usually able to cover a much greater scope and paint a much broader picture, the chapters in this volume focus of necessity on particular aspects. Nevertheless, grouping them together in four parts addressing comparable phenomena allows readers to draw their own conclusions and comparisons. In addition, several contributors have chosen to address issues in the same country (Jamaica, Trinidad or Cuba), which also enhances the comparativeness and completeness of analysis.

The editors of and contributors to this book are also concerned with another aspect that has dominated in many writings about political culture. The influence of the behaviourist theoreticians (for example, Gabriel Almond, Lucian Pye and Sidney Verba) has reduced political culture to empirically observable attitudes, beliefs and political values. One of the consequences of this approach is that political culture has come to be regarded as autonomous from the other social spheres. In contrast, the interest of this work is to show the limits of such reductionist epistemology. Through its history and through its contemporary challenges, the Caribbean has revealed a great complexity of social relations and the influence of such variables as race, ethnicity, migration and multifaceted dependency (for example, of institutional mimicry, strategies of reproduction of metropolitan models by the local elites, socio-economic conditions, popular culture) on politics.

The cases of Trinidad and of Guyana, analysed by various contributors to this book, illustrate to a certain extent how race, ethnicity and politics can interact. Indeed, we would argue that the factor "race" (or, more accurately, skin colour) intersects significantly with the "classical" political culture factors mentioned above: political behaviour, value systems, beliefs and attitudes. In the context of the Caribbean it appears hardly possible to fully grasp these factors unless their specific connections to "race" and colour are reflected upon. Classical political-culture theories do not facilitate this analytic lens and, therefore, scholars and policy makers trained within the parameters of these theories find it more difficult to understand the overarching and encompassing nature of "race" and colour as determinants, markers and discursive cornerstones of social interaction in the region. Indeed, depending on the particular historical and geographical context, both factors may act either as social glue or as dividers. However, only the specific analysis can reveal their respective importance in the unfolding of historical events and in social or political processes.

In this book, several authors make an implicit link between the recurrent ontological question and the political question. In doing so, they go beyond the classical conceptions of political culture to introduce a semiotic dimension, which in the editors' view renders a better account of the complexity of the social game in the region. This perspective appears to foreground questions about what meaning(s) the actors give to politics in the Caribbean today rather than to confine itself simply to political opinion or values.

The basic question – unspoken but implicit – undergirding all the chapters in this volume is, therefore, "What does it mean to be a Caribbean person, and how does it relate to the contemporary politics in this region or country?" Many specific inquiries spin off from this larger question. What role do race, historical experience, ethnic fragmentation and economic conditions play? How do popular culture, artists and organic intellectuals express or influence political perceptions? How can civil society – and, thus, the people – come to play a greater role in the political process? These are some of the issue areas into which different contributors to this volume break down the larger question of political culture.

From the topics chosen and the approaches with which the authors venture to explain different political phenomena in the Caribbean, it becomes patently clear then that Almond's definition, quoted earlier, can be only a starting point, which in the case of this specific region has to be filled with contextualizing modifications. Indeed, given the depth of class and ethnic divisions in the region – discussed, for example, in chapters by Anton Allahar, Perry Mars, Jacky Dahomay, Holger Henke, Percy Hintzen and Fred Reno – it becomes quite obvious that an understanding of Caribbean political culture needs to break out of the consensus model implied in the writings of such political-culture theorists as Gabriel Almond, Samuel Huntington, Seymour Lipset or Sidney Verba. Thus, in the context of developing regions, a political-culture approach is required which takes local and transnational power constellations into account to a greater extent. Thus, John Gibbins appropriately reminds us that

> a culture is not immediately natural nor determined by the economy or social class, but is a response to "current relations of force" and is the effect of political power conflicts. A society always witnesses a plurality of conflicting hegemonies seeking, but rarely achieving, dominance. The study of political culture is then the historical account of their emergence, a critical analysis of the political and economic forces they represent, a study of their internal character and a rigorous critique or negation of their logic and effect. (1989, 5)

Perhaps nowhere in this volume is the immediate importance of this perspective more salient than in Brian Meeks's contribution.

In addition to supplying evidence that the political Caribbean does indeed exist, this volume is therefore also meant to make a small contribution to the sadly lacking study of political culture in the developing world.[3] Thus, by virtue of its comparability to other literature on political culture in developing countries (for example, the inquiry into the role of Confucian values in the Asian model), the scope of this volume also transcends its narrow geographical focus. The critical engagement of many authors with the effects of colonialism, ethnic strife, globalization and so forth also inserts this book into what Richard Swedberg (2000) has termed the "battle of methods". Because of their implicit or explicit focus on non-economic issues and the relative weight of these issues in policy processes and Caribbean public life, most authors in this volume would come down on the side of the socio-economic approach described by Swedberg, which involves – among other insights – a recognition that " 'culture' should . . . be understood first of all in terms of intersubjective meanings – meanings constructed and communicated between people in and around economic interaction" (Swedberg 2000, 390; see also Geertz 2000).

The book's opening chapter, by Fred Constant, elaborates on the effect of economic globalization on the political culture of the region. Constant considers the new global environment "as a driving force of change in the Caribbean". He elaborates how governability and leadership styles are affected by new international political regimes which lead to the emergence of clinical politics and of more pragmatic leaders than those of the past. Constant expresses concern that the new political culture has "tended to distract many Caribbean governments from the traditional goals of responsiveness to the people's demands".

Anton Allahar introduces the reader in chapter 2 to the two most important variables of political culture in the Caribbean: "race" and class. He does so by discussing them through the lens of popular culture, in particular by demonstrating how the British colonial practice of divide-and-rule promoted racial and class divisions within the subordinate populations. Allahar concludes that the political cultures "exist in the service of . . . foreign and locally dominant capitalist classes".

In the subsequent chapter Perry Mars explains how the Caribbean Left has failed to creatively grapple with the issues introduced by Allahar. In particular, Mars posits that the attempts of the Caribbean Left to capture the imagination of Caribbean masses were "undermined by racial, ethnic and narrow communal divisiveness in the process of change within Caribbean societies". Like Allahar, Mars comes to the conclusion that in Caribbean society, class issues are "neither invariably dominant nor uniform in character or impact".

In chapter 4, Jacky Dahomay juxtaposes cultural identity with political identity, using the specific example of the French West Indies. Echoing some of the issues treated in the chapters immediately preceding his contribution, Dahomay explores issues such as the survival culture, *creolité*, and the impact of the French Revolution, to make the interesting and challenging suggestions that the Haitian peasant masses were "fighting for liberation, indeed, but not for liberty" and that the subsequent "cultural identity never took the direction of a quest for nationalist political identity". It is his position that in the French West Indies "class struggle inherited from the time of slavery has taken a turn towards a desire for assimilation into the French Republic".

The first four chapters in this volume are grouped under the heading "Elements of Political Culture in the Caribbean". The section that follows offers some specific examples, which attempt to shed light on the uses and abuses of history in the Caribbean. Holger Henke's chapter asserts that a cleavage has emerged during the years between Caribbean ruling classes and the majority of the population. While this proposition is neither new nor necessarily unique to this region, Henke intends to point to the increasing dysfunctionalities that have emerged because of this cleavage. Using the example of Jamaica's Port Royal, Anita Waters's analysis in chapter 6 is concerned with the construction of a national history in a Jamaican tourist site. She is able to show that over the years various development plans for one archaeological site presented the significance of the site in quite different terms. Waters's detailed research demonstrates how these examples of "presentism" are indicative of the ways "in which contemporary political issues, some partisan, some gender-, class- or ethnicity-related, are articulated". In chapter 7, Douglas Midgett offers a fascinating analysis of the political strategies and mythology used by V.C. Bird to establish and hold on to his power. Midgett shows, in his detailed analysis, how certain events in Antigua's history were deliberately reinterpreted to suit the needs of the political directorate. In the next chapter, exploring the construction of self, community and "other" in the region, Simboonath Singh compares the mythical homelands in the African and Indian diasporas of the Caribbean. Without any doubt, these issues have played and continue to play a great role in the imagination of Caribbean peoples. Both in corner-shop discussions and among writers and intellectuals in the region, references to homelands – be it Africa or India – are made frequently. At times the connections felt to these homelands have been not only of cultural significance, but also influential in domestic and foreign policy. As Singh emphasizes, " 'vote for your own kind' . . . became the dominant factor in voting patterns and behaviour in countries such as Guyana and Trinidad". Contrasting the African and Indian diasporas in the region, Singh points out that the latter showed "no indication of a 'homing desire' ".

In the first chapter of the section "Civil Society and Changes in the Political and Economic Sphere", Obika Gray poses a number of important theoretical questions regarding the relation between global and local spheres of action. In particular, his chapter attempts to demonstrate how within the emerging world system "counter-tendencies among the urban poor challenged the cultural logic of the interstate system". Subtle connections with and complementary perspectives to Henke's chapter are established here. Most interesting is Gray's observation that "deregulation of capitalist markets and the weakening of the interstate system have brought with them the correlative deregulation of norms and values". Without doubt, many authors in this volume would agree with this perspective.

In his chapter about Caribbean organic philosophy in the 1970s, Brian Meeks does not only rehash some of the cultural-political developments in that time period; more important, he also engages in a dialogue across the decades about issues pertaining to Caribbean philosophy or "world view". In contrasting Caribbean organic philosophy with the more recent writings of Caribbean scholars, Meeks is making a case for the notion of community as a "metaphor for the recognition of alternative cultural forms and communities". Just as in Gray's chapter, Meeks's contribution makes important theoretical observations about counter-hegemonic scripts and practices.

The two chapters that follow take issue with recent developments in Cuba's civil society. For a number of years considerable academic interest about Cuba has existed in Europe, and a number of studies have resulted from it. For the most part, these studies – despite all the talk about global villages and globalization – are ignored, and often writers of North American provenance are cited instead. This volume departs from this practice by introducing two German scholars and their perspectives into the debate. Bert Hoffmann, working at the Latin America Institute of the Free University of Berlin, focuses in chapter 11 on the different types of non-governmental organizations (NGOs) in Cuba – their role, their limits and their significance in the current phase of transformation. Hoffmann warns that a failure of the Cuban state to allow greater autonomy for civil-society involvement is likely to result in "growing erosion of its own social legitimacy – a high price for the Cuban Revolution and with uncertain consequences in the long run". Hans-Jürgen Burchardt, working at the University of Hannover, critically evaluates recent changes in Cuba and the chances for a new political culture in the post-Castro era. Burchardt identifies considerable potential in the local economy, local political system, local culture and environmental conditions for greater democratization and greater involvement of civil society in matters of policy and economy. Beyond this immediately available arena, however, Burchardt states the need to "reassess the levels of autonomy and interdependence of various actors in the state, market and society".

Fragmentation and confrontation have for a long time been important aspects of "Third World" and Caribbean political culture. The last four chapters in this book address some of these issues. For the specific case of Guyana, an ethnically divided country, in chapter 13 David Hinds finds the existence of two competing political cultures: a dominant state-sponsored culture and a radical non-state culture or counterculture. Connecting to the first chapters in this volume, Hinds concludes that in Guyana's case, "racial considerations . . . supersede class considerations at the political level".

Perhaps even more fragmented than Guyana are the societies of Suriname and the Dutch Caribbean. Edward Dew's chapter demonstrates just how deep ethnic divisions are in these countries and how these differences are playing out at the level of "race", religion and politics. It could be argued that although Trinidad and Tobago has an ethnic composition similar to that of Guyana, political conflict is not as endemic there as in Guyana. Quite possibly the presence of a large, stabilizing middle class accounts for this relative absence of political violence.

Percy Hintzen's chapter on the political culture in Trinidad and Tobago therefore offers a welcome comparison to Guyana. In Hintzen's analysis of postcolonial elites in Trinidad, "racial politics . . . have jeopardized and undermined the collective interests of the black population in whose name nationalism was represented".

Fred Reno's closing chapter takes a closer look at another island in the French-speaking Caribbean, Haiti. Reno is particularly concerned with the question of democratization and authoritarianism. Considering the current situation as a reflex reaction to global impulses, Reno questions its effectiveness when the principles themselves are not fully adhered to.

All the chapters in this book explicitly or implicitly make a statement about the intrinsic duality of Caribbean existence. Indeed, many writers have observed the existence of two distinct value systems in the region. Without oversimplifying it, one can be called the colonial mindset, while the other could be regarded as the creolized and hybrid voice of the people. In contrast to other regions, including Latin America, the hybridization process of these two traditions is the most advanced, and almost impossible to break down along class, race, gender or other traditional lines.[4]

David Scott recently pleaded for the cultivation of "a critical black tradition – of a black tradition of criticism" (1999, 127) in the region. While we believe that this is a necessary quest, it would seem that, taken together, the chapters in this book are pointing to a broader "tradition". Indeed, it appears that political culture in the Caribbean is influenced by an extremely dense, contradictory, almost intractable web of contending ethnicities, creolized value systems, hybrid cultural traditions, global life trajectories, international connections and discontinuities. These contending and often antithetical tendencies are mirrors of necessity, keeping each other in tense suspension even while they are constantly questioning the binary notions on which they rest.[5] If and to the extent that this is true, it might not make good sense to speak of one (or the other) political culture in the Caribbean. Rather, it would seem that is it important for students of the region to understand that political culture in the Caribbean is a constant process and movement, resembling a game – trophies and all – with more than only two teams constantly playing with and against each other. Far from being clear and level, both the rules and the fields on which this game is played are themselves subject to negotiation and change. The symbols and meanings which circumscribe them are culturally rooted in Europe, Africa and India (and, to a much lesser extent, China) and fraught with the historical ballast of centuries of historical encounters, shackles of conquest, pangs of oppression, shifty subordination, suggestive temptations, cries of pain, rumours of war, resistance and rebellion, as well as all kinds of psychological and rhetorical strategies of coping with the stress levels residing in the interstices of the events and stories from which this history originates. Often more important than the symbols, however, are the real day-to-day economic necessities. Political culture in the Caribbean is not a singular place, not a "position", not even a space, but rather akin to a last summer night's dance of fireflies seemingly aspiring to ascend to the deceitful constancy of the stars lighting the firmament above them.

If the reader of this book perceives that some of this has been plausibly demonstrated through scholarly arguments, all credit for this has to go to its authors and their contributions. Without their constancy, this book would not have been possible.

Notes

1. Thus, there were early reports that the George W. Bush administration had started talks with Cuba for help in its fight against international terrorism. Subsequently, however, the administration revived some of its cold war reflexes and added Cuba to its list of countries sponsoring terrorism.
2. More recently published and useful contributions include Knight (1990) and Allahar (2001).
3. We are obviously playing here on Inglehart and Carballo's (2000) provocative question "Does Latin America Exist?"
4. Ebel, Taras and Cochrane (1991) observed a similar duality of value systems in the case of Latin American political culture. However, the contrast between both systems is not as stark as in the Caribbean, nor have these value systems merged into a homogeneous whole, which perhaps explains the higher incidences of *caudillismo* and other autocratic forms of rule in Latin America.
5. An excellent treatment of the contradictory origins of symbolic nationalism and nationalistic symbols in the Caribbean can be found in Mohammed (2002).

References

Allahar, Anton. 2001. *Caribbean Charisma: Legitimacy and Political Leadership in the Era of Independence.* Kingston, Jamaica: Ian Randle.

Almond, Gabriel A. 2000. "The Study of Political Culture". In *Culture and Politics: A Reader,* edited by Lane Crothers and Charles Lockhart, 5–20. New York: St Martin's.

Ebel, Roland H., Raymond Taras and James D. Cochrane. 1991. *Political Culture and Foreign Policy in Latin America: Case Studies from the Circum-Caribbean.* Albany: State University of New York Press.

Geertz, Clifford. 2000. "Deep Play: Notes on the Balinese Cockfight". In *Culture and Politics: A Reader,* edited by Lane Crothers and Charles Lockhart, 175–201. New York: St Martin's.

Gibbins, John R., ed. 1989. *Contemporary Political Culture.* London: Sage.

Henke, Holger. 1996. "Mapping the 'Inner Plantation': A Cultural Exploration of the Origins of Caribbean Local Discourse". *Social and Economic Studies* 45, no. 4: 51–75.

———. 1997. "Towards an Ontology of Caribbean Existence". *Social Epistemology* 11, no. 1: 39–58.

Inglehart, Ronald, and Marita Carballo. 2000. "Does Latin America Exist? (And Is There a Confucian Culture?): A Global Analysis of Cross-Cultural Differences". In *Culture and Politics: A Reader,* edited by Lane Crothers and Charles Lockhart, 325–47. New York: St Martin's.

Knight, Franklin W. 1990. *The Caribbean: The Genesis of a Fragmented Nationalism.* 2nd ed. New York: Oxford University Press.

Mohammed, Patricia. 2002. "Taking Possession: Symbols of Empire and Nationhood". *Small Axe,* no. 11: 31–58.

Scott, David. 1999. *Refashioning Futures: Criticism after Postcoloniality.* Princeton: Princeton University Press.

Singham, Archie. 1968. *The Hero and the Crowd in a Colonial Polity.* New Haven: Yale University Press.

Swedberg, Richard. 2000. "Socioeconomics and the New 'Battle of Methods': Toward a Paradigm Shift?" In *Culture and Politics: A Reader,* edited by Lane Crothers and Charles Lockhart, 381–92. New York: St Martin's.

Zakaria, Fareed. 2001. "The End of the End of History". *Newsweek,* 24 September, 70.

[Part 1]

Elements of Political Culture in the Caribbean

[1]

Is There a New Political Culture in the Caribbean?
Challenges and Opportunities

Fred Constant

Introduction

A spectre is haunting Caribbean countries, that of a new political fault line and a new political culture. Like the rest of the world, Caribbean states have found it necessary to try to come to terms with the new international environment with its stress on globalization and competitiveness. The Caribbean has found that it can no longer continue to rely on non-reciprocal preferential access to European and North American markets for its export commodities. Nor will it be possible to protect its assembly-type industries for indefinite periods from competition with imports by means of licences or high tariffs. The wind of economic change blowing the world over has made its presence felt in the Caribbean. Given the openness of its economies, there is little room for shelter.[1]

In the past two decades, exceptions to the traditional model of Commonwealth Caribbean politics have mounted in number and importance. The traditional left/right issues have lost their dynamic force. Polarization of parties over class conflict or ethnic cleavages explains less and less. We do not suggest that traditional right-wing or left-wing parties have disappeared, or that class politics and clientelism are dead. The emerging new style of politics competes with this past types of politics; indeed, much of politics is debate over whose rules to follow. Different fault lines and issues are emerging, some new, some not. They combine in a "New Political Culture" (NPC),[2] which is becoming a major new force on the political scene in the Caribbean as in many locations around the world. Consider these matters:

- The Washington Consensus, with its stress on globalization, privatization, deregulation, structural adjustment, fiscal discipline and public spending reduction, is now becoming dominant in policy formulation, with few exceptions (Williamson 1990). Many Caribbean governments have been converted to the "virtues" of that consensus at the level of rhetoric, despite the slow-moving reforms they have implemented so far.
- New-style leaders are coming to office, ones who break with established programs or parties. Some are national leaders (P.J. Patterson, Patrick Manning, Owen Arthur) who are challenging the old nationalist orthodoxies to which their respective political parties became wedded in the 1970s.
- Performance criteria (effectiveness) are taking over in political survival. Rather than playing any nationalist legitimacy chord, pragmatic and sometimes colourless leaders have to show effectiveness in dealing with economic and social issues or risk being put out of power quickly. Charisma is no longer enough to ensure legitimacy.
- Consequently, class politics and clientelism are declining as new rules of the game for politics emerge in most national insular political scenes. This is not to say that these two old political traditions no longer have any political impact; however, they are losing the centrality they once enjoyed in political mobilization.

Clearly, it is impossible to know how entrenched this NPC will become, how successful it will be as an economic or political cornerstone of global national and international relations, or whether there will be a return to more traditional patterns (Stone 1985). However, it is a driving force of change in the Caribbean as the region cries out for new ideas and new approaches to dealing with the problems and opportunities presented by the unfolding global transformation.

What is certainly true of the Caribbean as a whole is particularly true of Barbados, Jamaica, and Trinidad and Tobago, three countries that have consciously embraced the new liberal orthodoxies. An interesting similarity, despite the changes in political power in these countries, was the convergence of parties in their economic agendas. In large measures, the economic thrust of the Caribbean programmes in the late 1980s and 1990s was quite independent of the specific ruling parties of the day, even in Jamaica, where previously there was a clearer demarcation of economic agendas along either supposedly socialist or capitalist lines. The main concern of this chapter is to understand what is new in order to contrast it with the old. The NPC brings together elements of tradition and elements of modernity to make something that is more than either, and it adds new concerns, such as making governments more efficient and helping average citizens understand and genuinely participate in policy making. Therefore, the point of departure here is a concise examination of the Commonwealth Caribbean model of politics, identifying some indicators of crisis. The chapter will then expose some of the elements that give rise to this ongoing cultural transformation, revealing a process of transition towards new political predicaments. Finally, it will look at some critical consequences of the sweeping adoption of those new norms of governance in selected Caribbean developing islands.

Governability in Crisis: Declining Nationalist Orthodoxies and Irrelevant Styles of Leadership

The anglophone Caribbean has generally been regarded as an area of the colonial world where liberal democracy has been successfully transplanted.[3] There are, however, voices inside and outside the Caribbean debating the question of whether or not this generalization is true and, if so, whether such gains are sustainable in the context of structural adjustment and economic globalization. It has become more and more common to argue that "Caribbean democracy is under pressure and that it may not survive the challenge of global economic restructuring" (Ryan 1999, 29). From the perspective of political culture, two levels of concern can be distinguished: the decline of the old nationalist orthodoxies and its corollary, the irrelevance of traditional styles of leadership.

Old Orthodoxies, New Challenges

Westminster-style democracy has had a lasting influence on the political belief systems of the critical elites of the region.[4] With few exceptions, these elites hold fast to the view that notwithstanding its imperfections, the majoritarian British political model is superior to all others. These political values and predispositions of the Caribbean people were buttressed by the economic system which obtained in the years just prior to independence and which was carried over into the post-independence period. That system was patterned on the Fabian welfare-state model inherited from the British Labour Party government in the postwar era. That system involves a close link between the Trades Union Congress in the region and the Labour Party. In most cases, the leaders of the leading trade union movements became the political leaders of parties which led their countries to independence, full of promises as to what they would do in terms of welfare to the masses when the political kingdom was won. The newly independent states thus became vast dispensaries of patronage – jobs, housing, free secondary and university education, scholarships, petty contracts and much else that the masses believed had been denied to them under the colonial system. Labour accepted the logic of capitalist profitability in exchange for a sustained rise in living standards for their memberships, access to the corridors of power and influence, and the exercise of political rights.

The political system thus became an arena in which rival political and trade union elites promised the moon and sought to outbid each other to dispense patronage to their followers. For the first decade after independence, the resources and opportunities available to most Caribbean states made it possible for populist-style democratic systems to be maintained. Given the worldwide expansion of trade and commerce, resources were available in the form of investment inflows into the tourist industry, into the mining enclaves of Trinidad and Tobago (oil) and Jamaica (bauxite), into the banana industry in Jamaica and, for a while, into the sugar industry. Import-substitutive industries also attracted both foreign and local investment, which helped to provide jobs in the modern sector, which in turn helped to absorb some of the many people who were leaving the rural areas in search of opportunity and betterment in the urban sector. Investors were induced to locate in the islands by generous tax holidays, import duty exemptions on plant and raw materials, rapid depreciation allowances, subsidized utility rates and infrastructure, protected domestic markets and assistance in marketing traditional products internationally and regionally. Both labour and capital were thus part of the patronage system. This populist-corporatist formula formed an essential pillar of the Caribbean democratic system.

The ability of the state, and by extension the political parties controlling the state, to service its clientele was greatly assisted by inflows from various metropolitan countries in the form of aid, price supports and preferential access for sensitive labour-intensive commodities such as citrus, sugar and bananas. The recruitment of farm and domestic labour by the United States and Canada and the massive migration to Britain in the 1950s and the 1960s and to North America in the 1970s and 1980s also helped to drain off much of the potential belligerence that might have exploded in the system if escape were not an option. Migration also meant that remittances were available to sustain families who were left behind.

The statist system was structured so that the elites of both labour and capital had a vested interest in its maintenance. Trade unions had something to offer their new members, while capitalists accepted the welfare state as a sine qua non for the maintenance of social and industrial peace. To quote Carl Stone,

> Both parties, the Jamaica Labour Party and the People's National Party, had more features in common than differences over the period between the 1940s and the 1960s. What they share is a belief that the state should provide aid and welfare to the poorer classes through social policies and public spending programs; a view that the state should provide overall economic policy leadership for the private sector and assume a central role in promoting economic development through state-funded projects; a perception of the need for state regulation of the economy in the national interest; a broadly held consensus that the state must provide social service for the citizens and economic services and infrastructures for those engaged in production through social reforms and legislation; and a common commitment to political patronage whereby scarce benefits that flow from government policies and expenditure (jobs, housing, contracts, etc.) are allocated to party supporters.... To a large extent, this push towards wide-ranging social policies designed to benefit the poorer classes was facilitated by the rapid growth and diversification of the Jamaican economy over the period between 1950

and 1970. This economic expansion provided the income base from which an enlarged role for the state in social and economic services to the poor could be financed. (1989, 21–22)

Much of what Stone says in relation to Jamaica also applies to many other island states of the region. What is evident is that this developmental paradigm, driven by the old nationalist orthodoxies, is no longer dominant. It has been challenged by another vision, that of an economy almost completely open to foreign investment and technology, arguing that the alternatives are not feasible even if they might be emotionally satisfying. The imperatives of generational change combined with the changed global climate have clearly pushed the Caribbean away from the old rhetoric of nationalism as well as from the traditional pattern of political leadership.

Irrelevant Styles of Leadership

Another dimension of concern is the growing alienation from traditional leadership, that of a personalist, paternalist, charismatic style. Lloyd Best (1985), drawing on Archie Singham's seminal work (1968), early distinguished three types of leader: "Sunday School Doctors", produced in the mature plantation colonies where there was no escape for potential leaders from organizing labour, where education came chiefly from Sunday school and the rhetoric was biblical (for example, Vere Bird in Antigua, Eric Gairy in Grenada, Robert Bradshaw in Saint Kitts); "Public School Doctors", where a local ruling class arose after the end of slavery, imbued with the values of their English counterparts (for example, Norman Manley and then Michael Manley, Grantley Adams and then Tom Adams); and "Grammar School Doctors", emerging in the new plantation colonies where education, rather than property, has been the medium of advancement (for example, Eric Williams in Trinidad, Forbes Burnham in Guyana). "Those postcolonial leaders," writes Jacqueline Braveboy-Wagner,

> took advantage of their legitimacy (formal and informal), garnered from their nationalist role, popular prestige and efforts to modernize their societies, to entrench themselves in power and put institutions in place (primarily parties and patronage systems) that would ensure the continued rule. Charisma was enough to ensure legitimacy, even though over time the peo-

ple themselves began to demand more, and charismatic leaders began to look suspiciously like old autocrats (whether benign or despotic). (1994, 7)

These leaders, who share a common messianic leadership tradition, failed not only to adapt to the binding imperatives of change but also of itself to generate functional change. In the great project and process of decolonization, heroic leaders such as Sir Grantley Adams, Dr Eric Williams or Alexander Bustamante had to lead; the people's responsibility was to follow. One positive aspect has been popular arousal against colonialism and injustice of all forms. One negative aspect was, and still is to a lesser extent, the absence of a concept of popular empowerment, with its corollary, the dependence on a Messiah. To quote Trevor Munroe,

> The citizen as elector cannot be expected to have the attitude to reclaiming power from politicians, if as a worker he or she has no rights in relation to parent (or to teacher); if as a woman she has no real equality in relation to man; and if as a church member he or she has no power in relation to priest/parson/archbishop. (1991, 95)

This religio-conceptual background and its contradictory impact on popular political culture should not be underestimated. To one degree or another, the quality of Caribbean political tradition and the process of popular empowerment have both benefited and suffered from this tradition. There has been much analysis of this hero–crowd relationship in the political culture of the Caribbean. What has been less noticed and little understood in terms of its implications for political transformation is the extent to which this popular mentality has not encouraged the search for more sophisticated and complex solutions.

Leaders of that generation, with few exceptions, failed even more than their followers to reject old ways of simplistic thinking, old ways of packaging simplistic solutions to complex problems. They also failed to recognize that the reality of the twenty-first century is increasingly complex, defying single causal explanations of difficulties and, even more, defying simple remedies to the problem of the debt, to the need to increase production, and to the imperatives of human development, environmental depredation, more equitable distribution of income and property, power across ethnic groups, social classes and gender gaps, within nations as well as on a global scale – imperatives of human resources development.

Given the unfolding economic transformation of our global environment, with its stress on liberal orthodoxies, it is not surprising that the imperatives of generational change combined with the changed global climate have clearly pushed this category of political leaders out of power. A new generation of leaders is thus emerging, many of them only in their forties, replacing older autocratic leaders and their personal entourages. In a few cases, political longevity depends on the leader's capacity to adapt to the new international norms. Jamaican prime minister Michael Manley adapted to these new norms successfully. He assumed that in the modern world of competitive global corporations, the national state and concepts of sovereignty as known had become increasingly irrelevant. Caribbean policy makers, he insisted, now had to dismantle the logjammed state and replace it with a more cost-effective alternative which emphasizes deregulation and privatization. In his views at the end of his career, the politics of distribution give way to a new kind of politics which emphasizes growth, a politics in which hard choices have to be made as to which groups have to suffer as a result of those choices and strategic priorities. Most Caribbean leaders are being converted, intellectually or not, to the "virtues" of a set of new international norms very often referred to as the Washington Consensus.

Recovering Governability? Towards a New Political Paradigm

The prevailing mood in the Caribbean is one in which there is an acceptance rather than rejection of the Washington Consensus. This acceptance does not always mean a naive endorsement of all the requisites of the Washington Consensus, but most of the governments in question have been advocating for improvements within this policy framework rather than for its fundamental revision (see, for example, Benn 1997). With one exception, Cuba, the new international era has thus provided the context for perfecting, not rejecting, the new global policy guidelines promoted by international financial institutions such as the World Bank or the International Monetary Fund (IMF).

In defining the emerging new political paradigm, I propose to combine two levels of concern: first, the predominance of "managerial politicians", with its corollary, the wide spread of a clinical approach to economic and social issues; second, the political consequences of the new paradigm in terms of governance, legitimacy and stability.

Pragmatic Leaders, "Clinical Politics"

In most Caribbean countries, a new style of politics, related to new political issues, is becoming dominant. From Trinidad and Tobago to Jamaica or Barbados, to name a few, managerial leaders are taking over, promoting economic success as a basis of achievement and trading upon Western international support as a sign of acceptability. These heads of government assiduously cultivate a reputation for managerial efficiency and offer themselves to the electorate as better able to face up to the harsh international economic environment than any of their rivals. The general thrust of the Caribbean in the first decade of the twenty-first century was reflected quite clearly some years ago by Prime Minister Patrick Manning of Trinidad and Tobago when he noted,

> The world today is in a situation where structural adjustment is the order of the day.... From the standpoint therefore of policy formulation, I think we have a general agreement. We have an agreement on the need for structural adjustment. It is not so much what policy you pursue since we agree on structural adjustments and their approach, but how to do it. (1993)

To some extent, Manning's words echoed Michael Manley's late political testimony when, in a reflective and somewhat pessimistic mood, he had come to believe that

> in the modern world of the competitive global corporations, the national state and concepts of sovereignty had become increasingly irrelevant... and that Caribbean policy makers now had to dismantle the "log-jammed" state and replaced it with a more "cost-effective" alternative which emphasised decentralisation and deregulation. (1993; see also Henke 1998)

There is growing evidence that competitive politics as known in the Caribbean, with all its "tribal" dimensions and its commitment to party alternation after one or two terms, could hardly survive in the new international economic environment, where it was becoming increasingly difficult for party elites to find revenues to keep their followers satisfied. The recent attempt to maintain this practice by borrowing had led to many policy errors which had now served to mortgage future generations. The politics of distribution is no longer relevant. It is giving way to a new kind of politics which emphasizes growth, a politics in which hard choices have to be made as to which groups would be identified to generate that growth and which groups would have to suffer as a result of those choices and strategic priorities.

Nowadays, the emerging new political paradigm defines new rules of the game for politics, challenging three older traditions: clientelism, charismatic leadership and Fabian ideological predicaments. Its advocates include, among others, Percival J. Patterson, Edward Seaga and Bruce Golding in Jamaica; Manning, A.N.R. Robinson and Basdeo Panday in Trinidad and Tobago; and Tom Adams, Erskine Sandiford and Owen Arthur in Barbados. These men have been contributing to changing the politics of their respective countries by embracing, partially or not, NPC issues. These issues include the national deregulation of economies, previously characterized by varying degrees of state involvement and import barriers; the "right-sizing" of economies overburdened by bureaucracy and subsidies and other inefficiencies; export promotion; enhanced regional co-operation; and, globally, efforts to preserve preferential arrangements now in place with the European Union and with Canada and the United States while preparing their phasing out, especially for accession to the North American Free Trade Agreement.

Today, effectiveness, based on economic development, is a crucial variable in determining the political longevity of the ruling elite of the Caribbean. The managerial leader, faced with today's international complexities, rules with a technical approach to economic issues. Political skills are not absent, of course: getting into a position of leadership still demands political skill, good strategizing and the ability to win substantial party support. However, people skills are not necessarily an important criterion for winning a prime ministership today. Therefore, the managerial leader generally has a weaker popular base for legitimacy than the charismatic leader (in terms of the relationship with the people as well as the strength of the institutional base). Yet the pressures for accountability are greater, stemming from greater popular scrutiny of a leader's effectiveness.

According to IMF standards, the mixed picture of the economic outlook makes it more important now than ever for the Caribbean to tackle head on the policy challenges that confront it (see, for example,

Hilaire 2000; Ramsaran 1997). The challenges which the Caribbean faces in the coming years make it all the more critical for countries in the region to pursue the sort of sound macroeconomic and structural policies which the IMF advocates for its members across the world. Only then are these challenges supposed to become opportunities. As noted in a recent address by an IMF official,

> Sound policies are especially important in the Caribbean, because economies here are more vulnerable to external shocks than most. . . . In face of these vulnerabilities, what are the key challenges policymakers face on the threshold of the new millennium? Let me briefly mention three: bolstering domestic financial systems, strengthening fiscal policies and boosting competitiveness. . . . One way to bring the performance of the domestic financial system closer to international best practice is to monitor the system and its performance in light of international codes and standards, accelerate the privatization of state-owned financial institutions, and remove barriers to the entry of foreign players. . . . A second challenge is to maintain sound fiscal policies . . . because traditional sources of external earnings are likely to diminish in the near term. Preferential access to EU markets is being eroded. Competition is intensifying in the tourist sector. Offshore financial centers are under pressure because of money laundering concerns. Frequent natural disasters also necessitate the maintenance of an adequate fiscal cushion. . . . On the spending side, countries should make a greater effort to privatize, close or restructure loss-making public sector enterprises. In order to protect people during a process of painful economic adjustment, it is far better to invest in equipping them to take other skilled jobs than to prop up uneconomic employers. (Sugisaki 2000, 3–4)

These IMF recommendations provide the policy framework for most Caribbean governments. Of course, it is misleading to generalize, and these trends mask big differences from country to country. In Trinidad, the government's challenge is to reduce poverty through a consolidation of macroeconomic gains and through use of oil and gas rents to improve the quality of human development and safeguard the environment while limiting the role of the state in the economy. There are five ongoing policy issues in particular: increasing economic rents from the oil and gas sectors; facilitating employment generation led by the private sector and entrepreneurship in non-oil sectors; increasing human capital through investment in education and social programmes;

improving the delivery of public services to support economic diversification led by the private sector; and ensuring environmentally sustainable growth.

In Jamaica, the economy contracted by 0.4 per cent in 1999 following a 0.5 per cent decline in 1998, thereby marking the fourth consecutive year of decline. Among the factors that hamper growth have been the consistently high real interest rates and weak competitiveness. Although Jamaica has made measurable progress in stabilizing the economy since the mid-1990s, the economy has not yet returned to a path of sustainable growth. Furthermore, the financial crisis of 1995–96 and its aftermath have presented significant new challenges. Five ongoing adjustment policies are currently being implemented: restoring macro-financial indicators, fiscal and monetary adjustments, financial-sector restructuring, rationalization of the public sector, and environmental protection.

In Barbados, after an impressive growth performance in the 1980s, growth in the 1990s slowed to approximately 2 to 3 per cent per year. This volatile growth rate is linked to the dependence of the economy on external flows which have been declining rapidly in the 1990s. Prospects for GDP growth have improved somewhat, mainly because of the expansion of the tourism sector and other services to substitute for the banana industry as the main foreign exchange earner. Here again, there are five ongoing policy issues: reducing vulnerability to external shocks and the burden of economic transition on the poor, economic and risk diversification, development of institutional capacity, human development for long-term growth and developing tourism while protecting the island's natural resources.

What is evident is that the developmental paradigm, driven by the old nationalist orthodoxies and informed by a concern to retain state control of industries and utility services, is giving way to an alternative model of development, opening economies almost completely to foreign investment and technology, following the recommendations of the international financial organizations such as the IMF and the World Bank. There is no longer any government criticism of these recommendations; most of the governments concerned prefer to negotiate their implementation on the best terms possible.[5] The critical problem, then, is whether the Caribbean masses, raised as they have been on state-dispensed patronage, will be accepting the choices which have to be made as beneficial to their long-term interests or whether they will firmly oppose these changes. Beyond the technical aspects of the policy issues under consideration, what is at stake here is nothing less than the survival of Caribbean democracy in the face of global economic restructuring (Duncan 1994).

Caribbean Democracy under Stress

It has become increasingly common in academic circles to debate the general crisis of democracy in the Caribbean, questioning whether the political machinery uniquely implanted there in the ex-colonial world would survive in the context of structural adjustment and economic globalization.[6] The economic recovery programmes (ERPs) inspired by the IMF and the World Bank and pursued by the governments of the Caribbean have been socially painful. Even if there are certainly sound and convincing reasons for these structural adjustment policies (SAPs),[7] they have been producing negative social consequences, even where a marked improvement in traditional indicators was to be recorded. As noted in one Caribbean Development Bank report,

> The generally weak regional performance has . . . contributed to mounting unemployment, with several of the larger BMCs (Borrowing member countries) reporting rates in excess of 20%, reinforcing the view that unemployment is one of the most critical issues for the region over the medium term. Given the weak state of the public sector and, in some cases, an ongoing programme of reforms to improve performance, BMCs were unable, as in the past, to expand public investment as a means of boosting economic activity and employment. In fact, those countries undertaking economic adjustment programmes, in particular Barbados, Trinidad and Jamaica, implemented sizeable cuts in public sector employment, thus exacerbating the already chronic unemployment situations. (2000, 12)

In addition to unemployment, the number of people thrown into what the United Nations defines as "absolute poverty" has also increased across the region, and with increased poverty has come an alarming rise in crime in most countries. Labour unrest has also generated social instability as unions organize against structural adjustment policies. There is clearly a contradiction between the goal officially pursued by these ERPs and their social consequences in the short run. This paradox continues to be of critical importance since the existence of increased levels of poverty and social deprivation and the potential for social instability serve as major social disincentives to the objective on which the whole model is premised, that of stimulating increased private sector investment.

Consequently, a careful review of the experience of adjustment in the selected countries suggests further modification of the policies implemented so far. The excessive reliance on policy instruments as a stimulus to private sector investment has tended to distract many Caribbean governments from the traditional goals of responsiveness to the people's demands. Will the price of economic recovery still be reasonable if it includes a growing disjuncture between grassroots citizens and the political elite on the ground of social equity? What would be the gains of dismantling democracy in the name of restoring economic performance?

This issue relates to the conception of the role of the government in the context of a development strategy which places primary emphasis on private sector participation and an increased reliance on the market system. Minimalist theories of government are too simplistic and indeed quite inappropriate to the reality and circumstances of developing countries, such as most of those in the Caribbean, where the production structure is in many areas still not fully developed and where the private sector would need to overcome a number of problems to become genuinely export oriented and competitive in external markets. In this perspective, Caribbean governments should keep at least three strategic functions in order to consolidate democracy while promoting economic recovery in the context of global economic restructuring. According to Dennis Benn,

> a primary responsibility of government is to provide the broad policy framework to guide economic activity. In this sense, the government should provide a broad regulatory and supportive framework with a minimum of red tape instead of a controlling framework in which bureaucratic procedures frustrate or detract from the efficiency of genuine private sector operations. Secondly, in light of the experience of significant levels of poverty and social deprivation which exist in the society, the government has a major responsibility to guarantee welfare objectives at an acceptable level. Programmes in this area will therefore need to be effectively coordinated in order to increase their efficiency and overall impact. The third area in which the government

can play a critical role is in the definition of strategic production possibilities, although such a function should be carried out in close cooperation with, or, preferably, jointly with, the private sector. (1994, 6)

In sum, liberalism is now the priority for almost all countries. While the technical approach to liberalization is certainly important, there is a growing preoccupation with the effectiveness of government and the type of institutional arrangements necessary for ensuring an optimum process of governance. This preoccupation relates not only to the conception of the overall role of government in the economy, but also to its specific structure and organization with regard to the requirements for the effective delivery of services. The requirements would also necessitate that the political elite remain closer to the people's demands, bearing in mind that in the new dispensation, technical competence in managing economic issues will never be enough to ensure any government both political legitimacy and social stability. Despite the improved performance in some areas, there are still questions about whether the social costs of the reformed policies have been too high for what has been achieved.

Therefore, SAPs should be more carefully adapted to each specific context, taking into account the critical necessity to maintain social cohesion and promote a new partnership between the state and the private sector. The region's democratic leaders have rightly modified their views from a philosophy based on state-directed economic management to one that relies more on the market's ability to allocate resources. The mood of the regional leadership has swung from a fear of foreign investment to anxiety about the lack of it. Now the time has come to consider a proper Caribbean path of development within the global economic restructuring process. Ultimately, the fate of Caribbean people lies in the hands of their own governments, in the extent to which they wish and succeed to promote a vision of their own, despite the policy prescriptions shaped by the IMF and the World Bank. Only then can the challenges of the NPC become opportunities to find a Caribbean path towards sustainable, equitable growth.

Notes

1. For useful reports, see Pastor and Fletcher (1991) and Ramsaran (1997); see also Braveboy-Wagner and Gayle (1997).
2. The New Political Culture (NPC) is the conceptual outcome of an international comparative urban research program directed by Terry Nichols Clark under the Fiscal Austerity and Urban Innovation (FAUI) Project over a period of fourteen years and concerning approximately seven thousand cities around the world. This is not to promote NPC as morally good or technically more efficient but to attempt a positive analysis rather than a normative assessment.
3. See Clark and Hoffman-Martinot (1998).
4. Among the criteria usually associated with this system are a competitive party system, free and fair elections, the concept of a loyal opposition, a neutral bureaucracy, freewheeling interest groups, a free press, recognition of the rule of law and an independent judiciary.
5. Here it is important to mention the efforts of the World Bank and the IMF to take into account the necessity of state regulation in some critical areas:
   > Put simply, governments need to do less in those areas where markets work, reasonably well. . . . At the same time, governments need to do more in those areas where markets alone cannot be relied upon. Above all this means investing in education, health, nutrition, family planning, and poverty alleviation; building social, physical, administrative, regulatory and legal infrastucture of better quality; mobilizing the resources to finance public expenditures; and providing a stable macro-economic foundation without which little can be achieved. (World Bank 1991, 9–10)
6. See, among others, Benn (1994), Braveboy-Wagner (1994), Ramsaran (1997) and Ryan (1994, 1999). Following Ramsaran, I would like to avoid the impression that all the current problems have somehow been caused by SAPs, whether self-inflicted or imposed by foreign aid agencies. Economic difficulties are often a combination of domestic policies and external shocks, and the weight of the respective factors is not easy to identify. This is not to deny that "adjustment policies" cannot worsen the situation if improperly thought out and implemented.
7. For example, the public sector is too large, inefficient and even corrupt; the private sector is lacking in vitality and competitive edge because of a long tradition of protective policies; the governments have been relying on a clientelistic practice or patronage incompatible with liberal democracy.

References

Benn, Dennis. 1994. "Beyond Adjustment: Towards a New Development Paradigm (The Jamaican Case)". Occasional Paper. Kingston, Jamaica: United Nations Development Programme.

———. 1997. "Global and Regional Trends: Impact on Caribbean Development". In *Caribbean Public Policy*, edited by Jacqueline Braveboy-Wagner and Dennis Gayle, 15–34. Boulder, Colo.: Westview.

Best, Lloyd. 1985. "West Indian Society 150 Years after Abolition: A Re-examination of Some Classic Theories". In *Out of Slavery: Abolition and After*, edited by Jack Hayward. London: Frank Cass.

Braveboy-Wagner, Jacqueline. 1994. "Caribbean Performance in a New International Era: Some Thoughts on Criteria for Political Survival". Paper presented at the 19th Annual Conference of the Caribbean Studies Association, Merida, Mexico, 23–28 May.

Braveboy-Wagner, Jacqueline, and Dennis Gayle, eds. 1997. *Caribbean Public Policy*. Boulder, Colo.: Westview.

Caribbean Development Bank. 2000. *Annual Report 1999*. St Michael, Barbados.

Clark, Terry Nichols, and Vincent Hoffman-Martinot, eds. 1998. *The New Political Culture*. Boulder, Colo.: Westview.

Duncan, Neville C. 1994. "Structural Adjustment and the Legitimacy of the State in the Commonwealth Caribbean". Unpublished paper, Faculty of Arts and Social Sciences, University of the West Indies, Cave Hill, Barbados.

Henke, Holger. 1998. "Drugs in the Caribbean: The 'Shiprider' Controversy and the Question of Sovereignty". *European Review of Latin American and Caribbean Studies*, no. 64: 27–47.

Hilaire, Alvin D.L. 2000. *Caribbean Approaches to Economic Stabilization*. IMF Working Paper. Washington, DC: International Monetary Fund.

Manley, Michael. 1993. Speech to the 18th Caribbean Studies Association annual meeting, Ocho Rios, Jamaica, May.

Manning, Patrick. 1993. Speech to the 18th Caribbean Studies Association annual meeting, Ocho Rios, Jamaica, May.

Munroe, Trevor. 1991. "The Impact of the Church on the Political Culture of the Caribbean: The Case of Jamaica". *Caribbean Quarterly* 37, no. 1: 83–97.

Pastor, Robert, and Richard Fletcher. 1991. *The Caribbean in the 21st Century*. Washington, DC: World Peace Foundation.

Ramsaran, Ramesh. 1997. "Structural Adjustment in the Commonwealth Caribbean". In *Issues in the Government and Politics of the West Indies:*

A Reader, edited by John Gaffar Laguerre, 75–102. St Augustine, Trinidad: University of the West Indies, School of Continuing Studies.

Ryan, Selwyn. 1994. "Caribbean Performance in the Next International Era: The Trinidad Case". Paper presented at the 19th Annual Conference of the Caribbean Studies Association, Merida, Mexico, 23–28 May.

———. 1999. "The Crisis of Governance in the Anglophone Caribbean". In *Politique et Développement dans les Caraïbes,* edited by Fred Constant and Justin Daniel, 29–50. Paris: L'Harmattan.

Singham, Archie. 1968. *The Hero and the Crowd in a Colonial Polity.* New Haven: Yale University Press.

Stone, Carl. 1985. "A Political Profile of the Caribbean". In *Caribbean Contours,* edited by Sidney Mintz and Sally Price, 13–33. Baltimore: Johns Hopkins University Press.

———. 1989. "Power, Policy and Politics in Independent Jamaica". In *Jamaica in Independence: Essays on the Early Years,* edited by Rex Nettleford, 19–53. Kingston, Jamaica: Heinemann.

Sugisaki, Shigemitsu. 2000. "Challenges and Opportunities: The IMF and the Caribbean". Address by the Deputy Managing Director of the IMF, High Level Seminar on the Caribbean, St Peter, Barbados, 8 February.

Williamson, John. 1990. "What Washington Means by Policy Reform". In *Latin American Adjustment: How Much Has Happened?* edited by John Williamson, 5–38. Washington, DC: Institute for International Economics.

World Bank. 1991. *World Development Report.* New York: Oxford University Press.

[2]

"Racing" Caribbean Political Culture
Afrocentrism, Black Nationalism and Fanonism

Anton L. Allahar

Introduction

This chapter examines some of the elements of Caribbean political culture and focuses on the twin dynamics of race and class. I will show how the British colonial practice of divide-and-rule is relevant to an understanding of that culture. Specifically, I will highlight those aspects of colonial practice that promoted racial and class divisions within the subordinate populations. Domination, however, can be expected to yield unintended consequences, and in the post-independence Caribbean those consequences have become manifest in the region's political culture. The race and class inequalities that were so crucial to the stability and effectiveness of colonial rule have mutated into the contemporary period, and although the colonizers are no longer present, the political consciousness of the wider population continues to be raced and classed.

As is known, while some elements of the colonized population came to identify with and accept the colonizers' definition and characterization of them (the Euro-Creoles and Afro-Saxons), others attempted to completely reject the colonizers' definition. Ironically, however, the vehicles of that rejection were the very same vehicles of their initial domination: structured inequalities based on race and class. Whereas being "black" and African were once the symbols of inferiority and impotence, in the lead-up to independence black people began to invert that understanding of themselves and to proclaim pride in and derive strength from their colour and ancestral land: Afrocentricity. Unsure or unconvinced of the "race" response, others sought to reject not so much the colour aspects of colonial domination in general but the economic and political dimensions: class. This all comes to a head in the person of Frantz Fanon (1925–61), whose supremely powerful black Caribbean voice some say vindicated the race argument and others claim is Marxist and hence underlines the essential correctness of the class perspective on social inequality. Caribbean political culture today continues to mirror this debate over race and class, albeit under changed circumstances.

The Point of Departure

The modern Caribbean, by which I mean the Caribbean of Christopher Columbus and after, was born of war, genocide, colonialism, slavery and racism. Whether examining the situation within one Caribbean country or among several, the divisions and conflicts associated with these historical processes have endured and are keenly reflected in various political cultures. However, since no two of these countries are alike, individual nuances are bound to characterize different countries (Allahar 1997), and any generalizations about the nature of Caribbean culture, political or otherwise, must be carefully qualified. So along with my general observations concerning political culture in the English-speaking Caribbean as a whole, I will also make specific reference in elucidating my argument to Trinidad's political culture.

Like its peoples, Caribbean cultures came more or less quickly to reflect a process of creolization, a two-way dialectic of exchange that saw the blending of European and African ways of living (Bolland 1997) and, depending on place and time, a smattering of indigenous cultural survivals along with injections from India and China. Owing to the expansionist features of colonial empire-building and to fairly common internal migrations of Caribbean peoples, whether forced or voluntary, many colonies changed colonial masters on various occasions, so in many of today's English-speaking Caribbean countries there are cultural elements of a Spanish, French, Portuguese or even Dutch past. As a consequence of its modern history, then, the Caribbean is to be understood initially as a class project of various European actors, onto which other class concerns were later appended. Further, in pursuit of definite class ends the assorted actors employed a variety of economic and political mechanisms that have remained with us until today. Among these, "race" or racism figured prominently and managed to leave an indelible mark on the societies in question.

In other words, the political culture of today's Caribbean is both class-based and racialized, for the roots of their history are firmly planted in colonialism and slavery, and latterly in neocolonialism and global capitalism. While I do not wish to minimize the question of sex or gender in this appreciation of Caribbean political culture, which remains highly patriarchal, the fact is that sex and gender concerns were never as problematized as were class and race in the distribution of the political spoils at the regional or the various national levels. Of course the general invisibility of women in the public life of colonial and postcolonial Caribbean societies is evidence of their virtual exclusion from politics, and I do not intend in any way to understate that fact, but in the present analysis I am unable to give this phenomenon specific attention.

In what follows I seek to assess the nature of Caribbean political culture as that culture has been shaped by the twin phenomena of race and class. As such, the present analysis is meant to complement the argument I have developed elsewhere (Allahar 2001b), which examined the politics of sport (cricket) and of popular culture (steelband and calypso). My contention is that as dependent capitalist class societies, the countries of the Caribbean betray the classic features of many other similarly situated countries. But the empirical realities of the Caribbean as a region set these countries apart from the non-Caribbean, just as the unique situations of each Caribbean country will necessitate empirical treatments of its specific realities.

The Caribbean as a Creolized Region

Colonization, slavery, sugar, plantations and racism are some of the essential ingredients that went into the construction of the modern Caribbean and that have served to fashion today's political realities in various Caribbean countries. Importantly, what was created was a set of hybrid Creole cultures that did not become fully fused at all the various national levels, let alone regionally. Thus, the celebrated Jamaican anthropologist M.G. Smith (1965) spoke of a "multiracial creole complex" which contained a dominant Creole European tradition that existed alongside an African Creole culture. But even this description is too simple, for in the years that followed conquest and slavery, the Creole complex came to comprise much more than Europe and Africa. Indeed, the very African cultures that were introduced by slaves taken from diverse parts of that vast continent were as many and varied as were the cultures brought by the various European planters and administrators, the Irish convicts and poor whites, the Portuguese labourers, the East Indian Brahmins and untouchable Dalits, the kidnapped Galician peasants, the Chinese coolies and all the other class-bound cultures associated with regimes of slave and indentured labour. As I have shown elsewhere (Allahar 1997), these other cultural infusions have come to pose a serious challenge to the Afrocentric claims that Caribbean culture *is* African culture and that following the granting of political independence to the countries of the region, those of African descent are the rightful heirs of those countries.

While the colonial authorities may not have formally recognized the class and status differences among the servile populations, the latter were keenly aware of them; upon emancipation, formerly clandestine cultural practices reasserted themselves publicly among the liberated groups, while new hybrid cultures that reflected various degrees of socio-ethnic combinations of the above-mentioned European, indigenous, Chinese, East Indian and African elements were also in evidence. These are crucial points to be borne in mind when speaking about the political cultures of the Caribbean. Each such culture represented different combinations and proportions of these elements and could not be expected to yield the same final cultural product in every island.

A Creole culture is much like a rum punch. While individual tastes may vary and some will include cloves or cinnamon, there are several key, indispensable ingredients in any rum punch: rum, sugar, water, lime and nutmeg. Of course, the proportions of these ingredients will differ depending on the preference of the maker. Thus, if one person uses two parts rum to one part water and another uses two parts water to one part rum, the result is still rum punch, albeit different tasting. It is the same with creolization, except that the ingredients are the various "bloods" that constitute the Creole product: some will have more African blood (ancestry), others more Indian, and yet others more European. The end result, however, is still a Creole, and it is up to the political culture of the particular country in question to determine, for example, how much African, Indian or European ancestry makes one African, Indian or European.

With the passage of time, and right into the contemporary period, as political and economic conflicts increasingly assumed racial, ethnic, cultural, religious and linguistic dimensions, different Caribbean countries came to witness pronounced divisions along those very lines. Recently, for example, some Indo-Trinidadians claimed racial persecution at the hands of the Afro-Trinidadian population and requested that the country be partitioned to create a separate state, Indesh, for those of East Indian descent. The situation is by no means unique, since this group of Trinidadians is merely following the earlier example of their Guyanese East Indian brethren who have fled to the imperialist metropole, where they seek refugee status based on the claim that they face political persecution at the hands of their Afro-Guyanese counterparts owing to their racial, religious and cultural distinctiveness. For their part, many "local whites" in the various Caribbean countries, who have traditionally enjoyed privileges based on their skin colour, have also been fleeing the region in the wake of populist political movements such as Black Power, which asserts an Afrocentric or black cultural nationalism.

Class and Race

One of the marvels of the colonial system and the political culture it imparted was the ease with which it simplified the most complex of relations. In reference to the twin questions of class and race, colonial societies came to be seen as those in which the various classes were colour-coded. Certainly at the outset (and in many ways to the present), to be "white" – that is, having a light skin pigmentation, straight hair, slim-bridged nose and other Caucasian phenotypical features, even a certain non-Creole, "cultured" accent – came to be synonymous with high class: a certain measure of material comfort, privilege, power and general social approval. As one descended the class ladder, one became darker and possessed fewer of these social amenities. Among the lighter- or brown-skinned middle classes, those who represented the top of the local society, who had acquired a fair measure of colonial education and who received positions, salaries and social status above their darker-skinned compatriots, there grew a clear fascination with, and embrace of, things British. These are the ones Edward Brathwaite derisively referred to as Afro-Saxons, a term as revealing as it is descriptively accurate: "The educated middle class, most finished product of unfinished creolization; influential, possessed of a shadow power; rootless (eschewing the folk) or Euro-oriented with a local gloss: Creo- or Afro-Saxons" (1971, 311). So hegemonic and so complete was the system of British political domination and indoctrination that major segments of the subordinated populations themselves came to measure their own worth, whether racially, socially or culturally, by white British standards.

In other words, so thorough was the project of colonial domination, both physical and ideological, that even those on the lowest rungs of the class-race ladder came to see themselves as less deserving of the social fruits. As colonial societies became more liberalized and democratized, colonial subjects increasingly bought into the liberal-individualist ideology, which led them to embrace liberal democratic politics, capitalism, class inequality and race inequality as "natural" facets of social life (Allahar and Côté 1998). So when the political system of liberal democracy is tacked onto the economic base of dependent neocolonial capitalism, the result is a more or less stable social order in which the most disenfranchised come to identify with their oppressors and acquiesce in their subordination. In the process they internalize liberal-individualist notions of freedom and success, and consequently accord the system an important degree of social and political legitimacy that permits it to endure. Totally rejecting the idea of structured inequality, they see social mobility as the result of individual hard work along with some measure of good luck.

As the buffer between the colonial masters and the bulk of the working masses, it is the middle-class Euro-Creoles along with some of the elevated Afro-Creoles (Smith 1965) who assumed the reins of government when the colonizers left the colonies. However, government was a role for which they were ill prepared. They were the hand-picked pawns of the departing masters, a class about which C.L.R. James said,

> I do not know of any social class which lives so completely without ideas of any kind. . . . It is such a class which has the government of the West Indies in its hands. In all essential matters they are, as far as the public is concerned, devoid of any ideas whatever. (1980, 134 and 137)

As a class that was supposed to lead the West Indies to political independence, James laments, they were fated to failure. They had no base in the economy, no economic know-how. Nor did they have a history or tradition of political involvement and experience – except for doing as they were told by their masters. They did not even think as a class with a mission. Instead they were an assorted bunch of self-seeking and opportunistic individuals, some professional politicians, some small businessmen, civil servants and petty administrators on whom the colonial and neocolonial masters could count to do the right thing.

These are the ones who led the West Indies into independence and whom James described as politicians who "carry into politics all the weaknesses of the class from which they come" (1980, 132). Principal among these weaknesses were lack of a political vision and will to challenge the content (as opposed to the form) of the colonial order; a virtual absence of knowledge regarding development economics; no real preparation for the independent conduct of foreign affairs; a commitment to (dependent) capitalism (Dupuy 1991); and a flawed system of liberal democracy (Allahar 2001a) that enshrined all manner of social inequalities. Most important, they perpetuated the very class and race prejudices and patterns of social exclusion that the British had exercised so thoroughly against them.

One ideological consequence of embracing liberal democracy is that it does not permit one to see beyond its assumptions. Thus, as citizens become imbued with the notions of individual liberties, equality of opportunity and freedom of choice, they find it very difficult to think structurally. The idea that the class or race structure might limit or impede an individual's ability to move up in society is firmly discarded in favour of a more voluntaristic appreciation of the situation – for in a society where all are supposedly free it is only the lazy or the unlucky who are not mobile. This was and continues to be the position of the Euro-Creole and Afro-Saxon elites in the Caribbean when called upon to discuss poverty and inequality in the region.

A more critical view seeks to link class and race and has no difficulty understanding why in such a society one was rich because one was white, not to mention the temptation also to argue the reverse. Indeed, in *The Wretched of the Earth,* the Martinican-born psychiatrist and race theorist Frantz Fanon was unequivocal in his claim that in the colonies "you are rich because you are white, you are white because you are rich" (1963, 40). In an earlier book, *Black Skin, White Masks,* Fanon charged that those Martinicans "who are not too pure racially but who are often rich" did nevertheless derive colour benefits from their wealth: "it is understood that one is white above a certain level" (1967a, 43).

Unlike the United States with its simple black-white racial divisions, then, the Caribbean boasts a very sophisticated hierarchy of racial classifications, a pigmentocracy that goes beyond colour as such and targets shade. As Gordon Lewis tells us, "it is the degree of skin color, not the possession of 'negro blood', that has been the criterion of social acceptance" (1985, 237). This leads to what has been referred to as "social colour", a designation which recognizes the socially constructed nature of race. Hence, Lewis continues, "In U.S. society, money talks; in Caribbean society, money whitens. It is possible to be black in physiognomy yet white in social terms" (p. 237). Thus, wealth can cause one to be perceived as less black than one actually is; money can rescue one from "the epidermalization of inferiority" (Fanon 1967a, 13).

As a consequence, the political cultures of the Caribbean were (and continue to be) deeply classed and raced. Traditional patterns of racial inclusion and exclusion still prevail (Cummings 1990), and in an economic arrangement where colour is currency, family connections were effectively class connections. Throughout the colonial period the fact that whites or light-skinned people dominated business and commerce and literally financed the established churches, which controlled the best schools, meant that the class-colour hierarchy of (dis)privilege was virtually self-sustaining. The richer one was, the lighter in complexion, and vice versa. But in all of this one must not be distracted from the fundamental class nature of all other divisions. For in spite of the fact there has been some mobility among the so-called coloured classes consisting mainly of blacks and East Indians, the "general condition of the non-white majorities remains effectively untouched, particularly because of continuing racial prejudices, but even more because the neo-colonialist economic order still requires a large reservoir of cheap, unskilled labour" (Lewis 1985, 238).

So in the last analysis, regardless of how compelling racial or ethnic factors may appear to account for the picture of social stratification in Caribbean societies, it is class that holds the key to understanding the political structures and cultures of those societies. However, one must be careful not to trivialize the "race question", for at the levels of popular culture and populist politics the irrational, primordial pull of race outweighs any rational appeal to class identity or consciousness. The challenge, then, is to theorize the link between class and race with a view to understanding better how political culture feeds into political mobilization. C.L.R. James said it best: "The race question is subsidiary to the class question in politics, and to think of imperialism in terms of race is disastrous. But to neglect the racial factor as merely incidental is an error only less grave than to make it fundamental" (cited in Gilroy 1987, 15). This message seems to be totally lost on the Afrocentric political entrepreneurs of today's black diaspora, particularly in its Caribbean version, where political consciousness has become so racialized.

Racialization of Political Consciousness

I have discussed elsewhere (1998) the "racialization of political consciousness" in Trinidad and Tobago. This is a term which speaks to the tendency for racial differences to be perceived as crucial in determining political actions, economic opportunities, social standing, even cultural legitimacy or authenticity. Race is invoked as the prime cause and explanation of behaviour, whether of something as public as political party allegiance or as private as the choice of a marriage partner. Race is also assumed to be biologically fixed and immutable (primordial), so that any attempt to treat it as a social construction is resisted vigorously by those who have a great deal of emotional investment in notions of racial purity and the associated concept of cultural superiority (Allahar 1996).

Although most are unwilling publicly to acknowledge it, lighter skin colour is seen as more socially acceptable across all colour segments of the Caribbean population: "If you white you all right; if you brown stick around; if you black stay back!" Trinidadians have also developed fine distinctions of colour and hue that are widely accepted as meaningful descriptive markers in everyday speech: white, near-white, half-white, white by association, brown-skinned, dark-complexioned, real black, light-skinned, red-skinned, sapodilla brown, *béké rouge*. There is also the notion of having "good skin" (lighter complexion), but this too is nuanced, as indicated when Trinidadians speak of "locally assembled whites" who are distinguished from "true" whites, who are from abroad. These concerns with skin are coupled with a host of other desirable and undesirable phenotypical attributes associated with hair type, thickness of lips, nose shape and so on. But through it all, so hegemonic is the notion of race that even members of the most shunned or despised groups are known to harbour sentiments that define them as or contribute to their definition as inferior.

Owing to the very highly developed racialized consciousness that exists in Trinidad (and no doubt in other Caribbean countries too), one finds a general tendency to minimize the importance of class as a political or even an analytical category. That racialization is linked to the country's history, to the times and conditions under which the various waves of immigrants (forced or voluntary) arrived, to their relationship to capital, to their differential access to and use of power and to the various adaptations they made to their new environment. Thus whites, even poor ones, were made to feel superior to enslaved blacks; freed blacks also felt superior to their enslaved brethren, though inferior to the whites, even the poor whites; Indians came with their caste and religious divisions but arrived after the end of slavery and were regularly viewed with suspicion, at times even disdain, by the recently freed slaves; Portuguese, Syrians and Chinese had their own niches, setbacks and triumphs, and so on. However, in the context of the present argument,

> when the Indians began settling in the society, they did so on terms most unfavourable to themselves. Not only did they occupy the lowest-paid sector of the economy but they were also placed by the other social groups in the lowest position in the system of social stratification operative in the society. (Singh 1974, 48–49)

By the middle of the twentieth century, when the Indians pressed for the construction of schools of their own cultural and religious persuasions, we are told that this idea was firmly resisted by the "still dominant planter and commercial classes" and certainly did not "meet the approval of the westernised Negro and coloured middle-class professionals whose dislike of the Indians was an already established tradition in the society" (Singh 1974, 59).

In the case of the African-Indian encounter in Trinidad, while there was ample evidence of amicable and co-operative living arrangements, length of stay in the new society and the different material circumstances that attended each community's daily social transactions were such that separation and xenophobia were more the order of the day: "The two races did not mix: they lived in uneasy but mainly nonviolent, coexistence" because "neither felt that their existence was threatened by the other, or that the other way of living was dangerous or oppressive to their own" (Brereton 1974, 37). After emancipation, the Africans opted for moving to the towns in search of non-plantation jobs, while the terms of indentureship that bound the Indians to the land confined the latter largely to the rural way of life. Thus as late as the 1950s, mutual feelings of xenophobia persisted and the prejudices and stereotypes which were developed by both groups towards one another during the colonial period "are still strong today" (p. 38). Since the Africans were there longer and boasted greater numbers, the logic of "first come, first served" – which today characterizes aboriginal claims to patrimony all over the world – clicked in, and they came to feel they were more rightfully entitled than the Indians to be the inheritors of the land (Deosaran 1987; Warner 1993). As will be seen presently, this has been an important source for Afrocentric beliefs and politics in Trinidad.

Race versus Nation

During the period of decolonization and transition from Crown colony and of the rise of nationalist politics, it was apparent that when formal political independence came to Trinidad and Tobago (1962), it was "black in complexion". For example, David Trotman writes of the mood during the independence celebrations and the somewhat transparent attempt to create the image of Trinidad and Tobago as a racial paradise: "in listing the cultural achievements of this racial paradise it is steelband, calypso and carnival – the national cultural triumvirate – which are given prominence, with no mention of any Indian cultural contribution. In this portrait the Indian is painted out" (1991, 394).

The early 1960s was an emotional time for Trinidadians and Tobagonians: decolonization, independence, choosing a national anthem, agreeing on a national flag and national colours, electing their own prime minister – in short, they were witnessing and participating in the birth of a nation. But in all of this the black presence and the black voice were more in evidence than the Indian. Indeed, in the whole exhilarating celebration that was independence, the Indian voice was often muted.

For the birth of the nation was an urban phenomenon, and as a population the blacks were far more urbanized than the Indians. The fact also that the first prime minister, Eric Williams, the father of the nation, was intellectually brilliant, culturally urbane, charismatic, black and strong could not help but define the colour or racial tone of the new nation. So despite the fact that the leaders of the independence movement and the political party that led the way "considered themselves . . . committed to a multiracial society, the movement could not help but be considered by both Africans and Indians as an African party with its political leader as a living symbol of African vindication" (Trotman 1991, 386). Hence, Williams's African-dominated party, the People's National Movement (PNM), which held uninterrupted political power for almost four decades, served to condition the climate of racial consciousness in Trinidad, where "the political battleground seemed irrevocably drawn along racial lines" (p. 386). This is a point with which Kelvin Singh would agree, having written earlier that in the lead-up to independence the existence of a "numerically larger" and more united "Negro and Coloured population . . . allowed the PNM to be organised on an essentially Negro basis, and to use race as a basis for winning power by electoral means" (1974, 64)

Situating Afrocentricity

The granting of political independence to India in 1947 signalled the beginning of the end of the British Empire. Shortly thereafter winds of political change swept the vast African continent, and they would soon produce favourable echoes in the Americas, including the Caribbean, where earlier, in the 1930s, struggles for freedom and independence had come to be couched in racial terms (Allahar 2001c). As suggested above, the colonial strategy of domination relied heavily on the idea of "race", and it was not surprising that along with much else that the British brought and left in the Caribbean when they departed, a racialized consciousness was most evident. That consciousness continues to inform the political culture today. One central manifestation of this legacy is the politics of Afrocentrism, which now colours much of the political culture of the region.

The central, directing motive of Afrocentricity and Negritude is to be found in the attempt to reclaim history for all Africans and persons of African descent living in the diaspora. According to David Caute, Negritude constituted "the collective project of the Black peoples" and is best seen as an attempt to romanticize "the forgotten richness of Negro-African history" (1970, 18–19). Furthermore, the sense of uprootedness and socio-cultural dislocation occasioned by colonialism led African and African-Caribbean scholars to embrace the philosophy and practice of Negritude as a

> combination of nostalgia for African primitivism, political radicalism, and intellectual sophistication. . . . The notion of Négritude, for all its outward ferocity, yields a small but vital concession to the prevailing white culture. The white man, master of the world, never bothered to create a literary ideology around his whiteness. (Caute 1970, 21)

This provoked the Nigerian poet Wole Soyinka, a most outspoken critic of Negritude, derisively to quote a Nigerian proverb by way of dismissing the whole black nationalist dream. He wondered why, since "a tiger does not proclaim his tigritude", black people had to run around trumpeting their Negritude (1999, 141). For Soyinka, the tiger's "tigritude" is obvious: it just pounces.

Afrocentrists make two key claims: (1) the combined histories of colonialism, capitalism and imperialism have served to rob Africans and their descendants in the New World of their past; and (2) for political reasons, the recording of those histories has been hopelessly distorted. These are important affirmations because a central tenet of Afrocentric thinking holds that who one is today and who one will become tomorrow are inextricably bound up with one's past. If a people's past is not known, they are fated to suffer what Fanon labels "serious psycho-affective injuries", which will eventually lead to a nation of "individuals without anchor, without a horizon, colorless, stateless, rootless" (1963, 218). To reclaim one's history, then, is at once a political and an intellectual act: it is political because it will empower those concerned, in this case Africans at home and in the (Caribbean) diaspora, and it is intellectual because it addresses and seeks to correct an erroneous writing and reading of history. Intuitively, as Greg Thomas writes, because of the almost universal entrenchment of anti-black racism it is

> hardly a surprise that many young blacks are attracted at whatever level to Afrocentricity. The story line of the great African civilization rising, falling and ascending phoenixlike on the wings of Ethiopia is epic and thrilling, and they obviously find it empowering psychologically and philosophically – if not, as yet, materially. (1995, 27)

Given the claim that history and memory are crucial to a people's sense of identity and self-worth, Afrocentrists charge that a major technique of colonial domination was to be found in the colonizers' distortion of African history. In line with George Orwell's observation that "who controls the past controls the future, and who controls the present controls the past" (1948, 34), the colonial authorities and their historians were bent on (re)writing the history of African peoples in such a way as to deny that it contained any major accomplishments of an intellectual or cultural sort, any moments of true grandeur or phases of notable glory. Instead Africans were portrayed as uncivilized, uncultured and generally inferior to the European colonizers. Thus, Robert Miles notes that whether German, French or British, the Europeans who went to Africa were convinced that the "Teutonic or Anglo-Saxon 'race' had an inherent capacity and desire for democratic institutions" (1989, 114), while the African, though viewed as human, "was nevertheless defined as an inferior human being" (p. 30). Throughout the colonial period, as European hegemony took hold, this pattern of thought conditioned the development of a collective psyche of inferiority among the Africans. Thus, in the same way that "Europeans were superior by virtue of their 'civilisation' and achievements" (p. 24), the Africans were imagined as the opposite: savage and wild. This "incarnation of the wild man was also distinguished by skin colour, permitting a conception of the Other as 'black' and therefore definitely distinct from the European who was 'white' " (p. 25).

According to Fanon, because colonialism "turns to the past of the oppressed people, and distorts, disfigures and destroys it", it is politically expedient for the oppressed, in this case the black African, to become aware of the historical lie and to discover "that there was nothing to be ashamed of in the past." For the truth was that their past was filled with "dignity, glory, and solemnity" (1963, 210). Here Fanon is exhorting black people, whether at home or in the diaspora, to snap out of the erroneous, manufactured images of them and to affirm or assert their rightful place in history. In order to do so, their history must be reclaimed and rewritten with two goals in mind: correcting the distorted historical record that has led others to view Africans negatively and developing in black people themselves a more positive appreciation of their past accomplishments and future promise. To this end Malcolm X said it most clearly when he affirmed that for black people, "what is necessary is that we have to go back mentally, we have to go back culturally, we have to go back spiritually, and philosophically, and psychologically" (1970, 146). For when all is said and done,

> History is a people's memory, and without a memory man is demoted to the level of the lower animals. When you have no knowledge of your history, you're just another animal; in fact, you're a Negro; something that's nothing. (Malcolm X 1970, 55–56)

Self-Esteem and Achievement

One of the central assumptions of this claim concerns group psychology and the fact that if a group of people think positively about themselves, they will likely achieve great things, whereas on the other hand, a poor self-concept will lead to low self-esteem and is conducive to a low level of aspiration and achievement. This is based on the understandable impression that among children and adults alike, self-esteem is a key variable in predicting or explaining success and high social achievement. In other words, common sense would seem to dictate that those who feel good about themselves would be more likely to perform better at a variety of social endeavours than those who feel less positively.

This idea is echoed by many commentators, some Afrocentric, some not, some activist, some academic. Thus in the early 1970s, the radical Black Power advocate Stokely Carmichael spoke of the "need for psychological equality" among blacks, for that is the basis of "black consciousness" and "political strength", both of which are the sine qua non of black community survival: "The reality of black men ruling their own nations gives blacks elsewhere a sense of possibility, of power, which they do not now have" (Carmichael 1968, 68). In *Black Power*, Carmichael wrote of the need to preserve the "racial and cultural personality of the black community", for therein lies the "cultural integrity" of black people. For him, cultural integrity includes "a pride in being black, in the historical attainments and contributions of black people. No person can be healthy, complete and mature if he must deny a part of himself" (Carmichael and Hamilton 1967, 55). Bernard Moitt is in full agreement "because Blacks in the diaspora face a constant identity crisis and must inevitably seek answers and inspiration from their past" (1989, 360).

What this means is that political identity, culture and psychology are all wrapped up in history, which is in turn the repository of self-esteem. Citing Fanon, William Van Deburg notes that for colonized people, culture was at the very heart of the freedom struggle. Indeed, revolution itself was a cultural undertaking, with national consciousness constituting "the most elaborate form of culture" (Van Deburg 1992, 58). Black African feelings of inferiority and inefficacy are directly contrasted with white European arrogance, which is based on the fact that Europeans are the developers of culture and civilization. According to Martin Bernal, it is thus necessary to "lessen European cultural arrogance" by countering with a positive (if not superior) image of Africa and Africans (1987, 73). To this end, treating Egypt as black and Greece as white, Stephen Howe writes that "the two main claims involved in Afrocentric views of the world of Antiquity" hold that "ancient Egypt was a black African civilization, and ancient Greece an ungrateful, derivative legatee of Egypt's achievements" (1998, 195). Viewing Egypt as the cradle of all human civilization, the Afrocentric reading of its history seeks to realize Bernal's exhortation.

Myth and History

What is crucial to bear in mind is that history, particularly revisionist history, is replete with myth. Not that anything is wrong with myth as such, for much of daily living depends on the willingness of people to construct myths, to believe in them and even to live by them. Whether it is the myth of God (religion), of race (biology), of the nation (politics) or of market democracy (capitalism), human beings have shown tremendous inventiveness and an equal preparedness to engage in self-delusion. In the human search for meaning and belonging, whether to a clan, a tribe, a race or a nation, the species has shown itself to be remarkably adept at creating myths of belonging and rootedness. As Anthony Smith has written, "no national movement and no persisting ethnic identity can emerge without a bedrock of shared meanings and ideals", for all such rootedness "must come to terms with the basic myths and symbols which endow popular perceptions of ethnic boundaries and identities with meanings and sentiments" (1984, 95). Often these are myths of a pristine, heroic past when leaders or elders were brave and virtuous and when ethnic or tribal communities were politically and socially undifferentiated and united in peace. Smith writes, "The community, according to this mode of myth-making, is descended from a noble and heroic ancestor, and for that reason is entitled to privilege and prestige in its own and other peoples' estimations" (p. 96). In the present context, A.G. Hopkins's notion of "the myth of Merrie Africa" is quite appropriate:

> On this view the pre-colonial era was a Golden Age, in which generations of Africans enjoyed congenial lives in well-integrated, smoothly-functioning societies. The means of livelihood came easily to hand, for foodstuffs grew wild and in abundance, and this good fortune enabled the inhabitants to concentrate on leisure pursuits . . . of interminable drumming and dancing. (1973, 10)

Thus, Anthony Smith (1988) and Walker Connor (1992) wrote about the myth of the modern nation, while Benedict Anderson spoke of nations as "imagined communities" (1983) and Eric Hobsbawm and Terence Ranger (1983) argued that "traditions" are and can indeed be "invented". The mythical and fictional aspects of ethno-national identity notwithstanding, Connor has cautioned, "The fault lines that separate nations are deeper and broader than those separating non-kindred groups, and the tremors that follow those fault lines are more potentially cataclysmic" (1992, 55).

The point is that even if imagined or invented, the political consequences of identities thus constructed are very real. In the context of the present argument, the myths propagated by the Afrocentrists are no less instructive. However, the motives of Afrocentrists, as ethnic political entrepreneurs, must not be confused with the responsibilities of serious intellectuals or scholars even if some of the former do indeed believe that theirs is the correct view of history and that what they are claiming is proper. If an Afrocentric approach to the world were to "have positive confidence-building or identity affirming functions", Howe writes, that would be, "if it were true, the strongest defence of the movement" (1998, 5). Unfortunately, however, as the prominent black historian Wilson J. Moses has argued, "Like most mythologies, it is only half believed and simply represents an attempt on the part of respectable, *honest people* to create a positive folk mythology" (cited in Thomas 1995, 27, emphasis added). This much is clear and noncontentious, but Howe's critique of this aspect of Afrocentric thinking is powerful:

> One can certainly accept that more-or-less honest people, in their capacity as political activists, might seek to build a positive folk mythology which encourages those they wish to mobilize – even if they do not wholly believe in the propositions they advance. It is less clear whether honest *intellectuals* can properly behave in such a way, using their university posts, editorships, classroom or media access and apparatus of scholarship to do so. . . . I do not think that the faith in the political or psychological benefits of false "folk mythologies" is justified. (1998, 5)

Afrocentricity and Black Cultural Nationalism in Trinidad

The idea of Afrocentricity is alive in the context of Trinidad's political culture. One example of this as manifested at the level of popular political culture is Carnival, which for many is the national festival of the country (Hill 1972). In this section I will focus on a single example of Afrocentric thinking as contained in a book of readings titled *Ah Come*

Back Home: Perspectives on the Trinidad and Tobago Carnival (Smart and Nehusi 2000). While it is difficult to assess how widespread the position represented by these writers is, they do reflect an increasingly strong direction of thinking in influential circles of the black intelligentsia (lawyers, doctors, politicians, civil servants, even corporate managers) as well as among black intellectuals (scholars, artists, teachers and journalists). These are the people who "engage in the production of ideas and the manipulation of cultural symbols" (Gagnon 1987, 5–6).

Afrocentric commentators on Trinidad equate Carnival with the country's national festival and insist that Carnival is an African cultural product belonging entirely to Africans (Smart and Nehusi 2000). Such an approach, which draws heavily on the idea that ethno-racial attachments are primordial (Allahar 1996), serves very clear political ends. It also implies that the so-called Indo-Trinidadians, who for whatever reasons do not see Carnival as their national cultural marker, are denied a place to call home:

> For Caribbean people and many others, the ultimate representation of home is carnival . . . we know that we will be understood there. It is the dwelling place of some of our deepest affections; the place of familiarity and of family that reminds us of the ancestors because of the material markers of their presence there. (Nehusi 2000a, 1)

For both Smart and Nehusi, the terms "black" and "African" are loosely treated as synonyms, and as will be seen, Nehusi's use of the term "Caribbean people" is meant to signify "black" or African-descended people.

While there are many Indo-Trinidadians who participate in Carnival and many who choose not to do so, there are also many Afro-Trinidadians who participate and many who do not. This notwithstanding, several commentators continue to see the annual Carnival as Trinidad's national festival and as the country's flagship cultural event. As early as 1972, for example, Errol Hill (1972) saw in Carnival the potential for developing a *national* theatre; the recent contributions of Peter Minshall's *mas* bands, among others, have gone a long way in making that potential seem even more real. In the minds of black nationalists, however, the national festival that is Carnival is racialized and has become synonymous with African history and traditions. In other words,

Carnival, which they claim was born in Africa, is the supreme African festival and belongs entirely to black people (Smart and Nehusi 2000), who, regardless of where they were born, are Africans – Africa is *home* for all Africans. Ian Smart, for example, depicts Trinidad Carnival as "the quintessential African festival" (2000a, 72). In the estimation of his co-editor, Kimani Nehusi, the street parade segment of the celebration is symbolic of the Africans' reclaiming their physical, spiritual and cultural freedom: "Possession of the streets was a sign of Afrikan possession of self, a spiritual reconnection with ancestors through millennia of cultural practice, a liberation through expression of impulses *carried in genes* for uncounted generations" (2000b, 96; emphasis added).

It is my contention that the foregoing constitutes only part of the larger agenda of those black nationalists who want to define Carnival in racial terms. Thus Smart declares, "Trinbagonians can then rightly claim their festival as 'we thing' only because it is a 'black thing'" (2000a, 72). However, the loose invocation of the royal "we" must not be taken as referring to all Trinidadians and Tobagonians, for Smart has a very definite idea of who "we" are and precisely what "black" means. The intention is clearly one of racial inclusion and exclusion, for those who are not defined as "black", which in this context means "African", are not part of "we".

Nehusi apparently does not realize the racist implications of claiming that behaviour, whether economic, political, cultural, or social, is genetically coded. His statement, quoted earlier, smacks of the same kind of essentialism, if not racism, reflected in Smart's declaration that "the African mind is one that deals with the big picture. The African mind is driven by and towards holism" (2000a, 51). It would seem as though there is some secret that the African mind alone has been able to uncover, and also that all Africans are possessed of this special gift. In a manner reminiscent of those who propagated the myth of a merry Africa, according to which all Africans in Africa loved one another and got along beautifully before the advent of the white slave masters, the contributors to the volume in question can be seen as endorsing the mythical aspects of ethnic and national belonging. In the context of the United States and the Black Power movement there, Black Panther leader Bobby Seale referred to black disenfranchisement and the various demands of his party when he wrote that "these things are directly related to the things we had before we left Africa" (1970, 62).

Afrocentrists are known to spin tall tales of racial identity and solidarity among Africans the world over. Thus, Smart and Nehusi are unequivocal in their claim that Africa is the cradle of human civilization and the source of ancient human history. To their minds, contemporary history is written and produced by white supremacist barbarians bent on denigrating the signal contributions of Africans (see, for example, Nehusi 2000a, 13; Smart 2000a, 38).

This theme is also picked up by other contributors to the volume, who see white racism and white supremacist ideology as the bedrock of black disenfranchisement. Patricia Alleyne-Dettmers, for example, essentializes "barbaric Europeans" (2000, 139) and both Smart (2000b) and Patricia Moran (2000) condemn what they refer to generally as "European barbarism", while Olaogun Adeyinka speaks more specifically of the "heroic struggles of Africans" to liberate themselves "from Spanish, French and British barbarism" (2000, 111). Thinking specifically of the Trinidad Carnival, Moran sees all of this as a conspiracy on the part of what she calls "white bandits" and those "Aryan marauders . . . the vast hordes of starving Aryan barbarians", who, even today, would steal "we thing", which is Carnival and steelband (2000, 175). As noted earlier, however, to the extent that "we" is African, it does not include those non-African segments of the Trinidadian population.

It is the same unspecified use of the word "we" by Vonulrick Martin, who, in speaking of Carnival in the diaspora, refers to "this thing we call mas, we thing, we Carnival" (2000, 180). Similarly, where syntax demands, the personal pronoun "our" is interchanged with the royal "we". So Smart, who appears uncomfortable with the traditional idea of white tourism from North America and Europe to the Caribbean, eschews any attempt at class analysis and charges, "After all it is our sun, and our sea, and our sex and our fun that those hungry visitors from the North come seeking" (Smart 2000a, 36). As with the "we" discussed earlier, there is no attempt to specify just who the "our" is. Is it all Trinidadians, or all Africans, or what Smart, Alleyne-Dettmers and Moran term "African-ancestored" Trinidadians (Smart 2000a, 35, 37; Smart 2000b, 202–3; Alleyne-Dettmers 2000, 132; Moran 2000, 174)? And just how does one go about defining "African" in Trinidad? Do we use the same racist criteria as the colonial masters – skin colour, hair texture, nose shape and penis size? In a system of widespread "race" mixing, are so-called African-ancestored people not also simultaneously European-ancestored, Indian-ancestored and so on? On what basis, then, does one privilege the African over the other elements? Such an uncritical understanding of the term "Trinidadian" makes no sense to me. For above all else, the term signifies a rich historical and ethnocultural mixture of a polyglot people. That rich mixture should therefore be the necessary starting point for any discussion of who or what constitutes a true, true Trinidadian.

We all know that in no system of logic do two wrongs make a right. Thus, if in principle Eurocentricity is wrong, how in principle can Afrocentricity be right? Nevertheless, another contributor, Pearl Eintou Springer, the director of Trinidad's National Heritage Library, seems to think that there is no contradiction to be found in the simultaneous condemnation of Eurocentricity and promotion of Afrocentricity. Hence, she declares that Trinidad's "society needs really to lose its hatred and fear of the word African and of Afrocentricity" (2000, 25). The contradictions also mount when she writes of her own participation in the 1970 Carnival street parade, which coincided that year with the Black Power mobilizations in Trinidad. Here she writes, "We marched and pranced to the music of the African drums. No tourists joined that band" (Springer 2000, 23). In the same paragraph she notes that all the revolutionary icons were present in the same band, which supposedly featured no tourists, "from Che Guevara to our own Kwame Turé, from Huey Newton to Malcolm X" (p. 23). Apart from the fact that Kwame Turé (Stokely Carmichael) was born in Trinidad and declared by the government a persona non grata there, one is left to wonder whether she is aware of the fact that Che was a white man from Argentina, or whether she is oblivious to the fact that both Huey Newton and Malcolm X, if they had attended Carnival in the flesh, would have had to have been issued tourist visas.

Essentialization of Africa and Africans

When Moran affirms that "It cannot be overstated that we, Africans, invented civilization" (2000, 174), it is clear she makes no distinction between or among Africans from the north, south, west, east or even central parts of that vast continent. This essentialization of the Africans as comprising a single, undifferentiated community is also evident in a second piece by Smart in the same volume, in which he writes that "Africans all over the globe who have been subjected to white supremacy must be engaged unremittingly in the struggle for liberation in order to be made whole again" (2000b, 199). It is clear that he is referring not only to Africans in Africa, but also to black people all over the world who choose to claim some African ancestry.

The tendency to essentialization is common in such Afrocentric approaches to history and their explicit acceptance of primordially based identity politics (Allahar 1996). In this chapter, reference to "Africa" and "Africans" use the notions of community, "race" and ethnicity as their main units of analysis. The authors of the studies contained in Smart and Nehusi (2000) speak ideologically to what supposedly binds the community together, for example, common blood lines, common ethno-cultural experience, common collective memory, common African origins and so on. I say "supposedly", for much of this idea of community cohesiveness is rather mythical or fictional. It is part of the essentialization and homogenization of Africa and Africans to which I have alluded. In the process, those social and structural factors that divide the community are ignored. I am thinking here of internal class, colour, economic and political inequalities within, say, the so-called African diasporic community, not to mention ideological cleavages related to religion and inter- and intra-ethnic rivalries. These divisions are real but are generally masked by sentimental and ideological appeals to a diasporic unity and identity in which co-ethnic brothers and sisters are easily accepting of one another.

Such readings of history and their related approaches to society, and the ethnic entrepreneurs who promote them, deliberately revise certain historical facts, such as the capture and sale of Africans by Africans to slave traders, ethnic cleansing within the "black" communities of Rwanda and Burundi, or black-on-black violence within the African American community in the United States. For these reasons it is easy to see why any facile appeal to community cohesion on the basis of "race" is unlikely to withstand critical scrutiny – hence my scepticism. In other words, whether we are dealing with the economic entrepreneurs of the business sector, who use "race" to divide workers and pay low wages, or political and ethnic entrepreneurs, who seek to promote the idea of community cohesion along lines of common "race", colour and culture, the ideological functions of political distraction and social control are unmistakable.

In sum, then, the primordial argument is troubling, for it seeks to essentialize Africa and Africans. We all know that Africa is a continent and not a country, and we also know that African societies and peoples vary widely among themselves in terms of phenotype, culture, social structure, political institutions, systems of religious belief, economic practices and so on. To this we must also add that African countries, like those of the West, are deeply internally divided along lines of class, economics, politics, ethnicity and all the other lines that we are so familiar with in the West generally. The idea that one can identify an African diaspora which transcends the divisions of which I have spoken and which implies class and political consensus and fraternal goodwill just does not square with reality. To my mind such a notion of diaspora is ideological, and it tends to raise more questions than it answers.

Although African traditions and heritage are a part of Carnival, this does not mean that Carnival is an exclusively African tradition. Yet this is not the interpretation or perception that many people within Trinidad and Tobago, as well as tourists who visit, seem to hold. In this regard, Indo-Trinidadians have traditionally been seen as out of place, even as intruders, in the Carnival experience. This image of the Indian "invader" is not held only by some African participants in and spectators of Carnival; it has also been internalized by segments of the Indian population. In a society as ethnically divided as Trinidad, this lack of participation by some East Indians in Carnival festivities has interesting and important social implications that are tied to national identity and that also mirror the larger racialized political culture of the country.

Frantz Fanon

I turn now to the work of Frantz Fanon, who has been invoked by black nationalists as their "patron saint" (Carmichael, quoted in Caute 1970, 103) but who also, depending on one's reading of him, might just suggest a class-based corrective to the exclusive racial focus of some commentators, thus leading Stephen Howe to assert that Fanon's ideas were poles apart from "Afrocentric and cultural nationalist thought"

(1998, 77). However, to say Fanon was not a cultural nationalist does not automatically imply that he was a Marxist or that he was committed to a rigorous class understanding of the Caribbean reality. For as David Caute wrote much earlier, Fanon "was not a communist, or indeed an orthodox Marxist. . . . Fanon was not a Marxist in any traditional sense. He regarded the Western proletariat as neither revolutionary nor sympathetic to the colonial peoples. The Western workers were, in his opinion, the beneficiaries and accomplices of latter-day colonialism" (1970, 65 and 76).

My decision to focus on the work of Fanon is based on the importance accorded to him by leading scholars of emancipatory politics, and specifically by scholars of "black liberation". Much of the renewed interest in Fanon's work came with the development of cultural studies, the reading of postcolonial literatures and the whole postmodern turn within the academy. For example, in his preface to Fanon's *The Wretched of the Earth,* Jean-Paul Sartre challenges the reader to "have the courage to read this book, for in the first place it will make you ashamed, and shame, as Marx said, is a revolutionary sentiment . . . you will find that Fanon is the first since Engels to bring the process of history into the clear light of day" (in Fanon 1963, 14). In one stroke of the pen, then, Sartre places Fanon in the company of two of the most important intellectuals and revolutionary theoreticians of the nineteenth and twentieth centuries, if not of all time.

Then there is Harvard University sociologist Henry Louis Gates, Jr, who sees Fanon as a true "global theorist" who is central "in the rereadings of the Renaissance" (1999, 251). The renowned University of Chicago Distinguished Professor of English Homi Bhabha, for his part, notes that in some circles Fanon is "revered as the prophetic spirit of Third World liberation". Bhabha's description is carefully measured: "Heir to the ingenuity and artistry of Toussaint and Senghor, as well as the iconoclasm of Nietzsche, Freud and Sartre, Fanon is the purveyor of the transgressive and transitional truth" (1999, 179–80). To this list of leading postcolonial theorists we can add Columbia's preeminent Edward Said, who describes Fanon as "penetrating, visionary and innovative" (1993, 268–69), while also comparing him to Freud, Nietzsche and Marx. For Said, Fanon is both revolutionary theorist and tactician, and his claim to prominence in this area is to be found in the fact that he "more dramatically and decisively than anyone . . . expresses the immense cultural shift from the terrain of nationalist independence to the theoretical domain of liberation" (pp. 268–69).

Of course this list could be greatly expanded, but my intention at this point is simply to show the continuing relevance and importance of Fanon. To this end, I chose a few world-renowned scholars who have placed Fanon at the centre of the discussion that relates to political identity and the postcolonial condition. Indeed, there is actually an academic field of Fanon Studies (Robinson 1993), just as there is a "Fanonian tradition" (Prasad 1992, 87–88) of scholarship and analysis that one commentator has labelled "a Fanon industry" (Howe 1998, 79). Fanon's distinction goes even further than this, for he was not merely an observer, analyst and detached critic of colonialism, he actually got his hands dirty and participated in the Algerian revolution. Thus, as Edouard Glissant, the celebrated scholar from Martinique, has noted, "of all the French Caribbean intellectuals, he is the only one to have acted on his ideas . . . to take full responsibility for a complete break" (cited in Gibson 1999, 10). And as if to sum up the entire question of Fanon's relevance, Bhabha ends his essay "Remembering Fanon" quite starkly: "The time has come to return to Fanon" (1999, 195).

Fanon's Works

The work of Fanon sits squarely in the centre of the debate over black emancipation and the extent to which political mobilization along lines of race can be of service in the struggle for emancipation in postcolonial, capitalist society. Fanon suggests that the European colonial project, which was conceived with a view to plundering the riches of "other" peoples, lands and cultures, came to use the idea of race to legitimize the plunder. The implication was that certain inferior peoples, who were not quite capable of civilization, had to be led by other superior peoples. The latter saw it as their duty, for some even God-ordained, to rescue the inferior races, and they felt no compunctions about buying, selling and owning slaves as part of the rescue mission.

Among black nationalists in the Caribbean (and elsewhere), Fanon's work is seen as a call to action to both colonized and recently decolonized peoples. He invokes the need for a pursuit not only of economic and political freedom from ties to colonizing countries, but also individual and psychological liberation from the racialized chains of Europe. According to Fanon, black men are trapped in the artifice of a dominant construction of blackness in dialectical opposition to the identity of the white colonizer: "For the black man there is only one destiny. And it is white" (1967a, 12). Only by releasing themselves from this ideological bind can black men and women be free to develop stronger senses of national and community identity beyond the confines of domination and inequality embedded in colonized and decolonized systems.

What Fanon intended when he wrote and what his ideas have become in the hands of subsequent interpreters of his writings are separate matters. I am reminded here of Marx, who, when he saw how his ideas were being distorted by others in the name of "Marxism", declared, "I am not a Marxist." Were he alive today Fanon might well want to make the same declaration, but for what it is worth I will attempt to assess the impact of his ideas on contemporary Caribbean political culture. I will focus on two themes in his work: his failure to specify rigorously the question of class, and his legitimization of an illegitimate concept – race – and the consequent essentialization of people into "races". In other words, while Fanon makes an important contribution by sensitizing us to the psychological reality of capitalism in both colonial and postcolonial contexts, his work remains largely descriptive and prescriptive, short on explanation.

Fanon and Marx

To begin, there is no doubt that Fanon saw himself as a Marxist, as a man of praxis. He was not content with merely understanding the nature of colonial oppression and violence; rather, once understood, he was set on engaging the oppressor in physical struggle. To this end one needs only to recall Marx's Eleventh Thesis on Feuerbach and his general condemnation of the German philosophers – his contention that those "philosophers have only interpreted the world, in various ways; the point, however, is to change it" (Marx and Engels 1959, 245). To this Fanon says, in *Black Skin, White Masks*, "What matters is not to know the world but to change it" (1967a, 17). Fanon claims a certain affinity with Marx, but he parts company with him on the central issue of revolution and which class holds the future in its hands. For Marx and Engels (in *The Communist Manifesto*), that class was the industrial proletariat in the urban centres of the then industrially advanced countries. They reasoned that the overall conditions of life under capitalism, the alienation brought on by the factory system, the harsh exploitation of workers by capitalists and the consequent development of consciousness by the working class would lead sooner or later to the outbreak of revolutionary violence and the ultimate overthrow of capitalism. Hence they wrote, "Of all the classes that stand face to face with the bourgeoisie today the proletariat alone is a really revolutionary class"; on the other hand, given the empirical situation they face, the peasants "are not revolutionary but conservative. Nay more, they are reactionary" (Marx and Engels 1955, 20).

Focusing on pre-independence Algeria in *The Wretched of the Earth*, however, Fanon directly reverses Marx and Engels and declares, "it is clear in the colonial countries *the peasants alone* are revolutionary, for they have nothing to lose and everything to gain" (1963, 61, emphasis added). And he goes on to charge that

> in the colonial territories the proletariat is the nucleus of the colonised population which has been most pampered by the colonial regime. The embryonic proletariat in the towns is in a comparatively privileged position. In capitalist countries the working class has nothing to lose; it is they who in the long run have everything to gain. In the colonial countries the working class has everything to lose. (Fanon 1963, 108–9)

What Fanon fails to realize is that the capitalist countries are not distinct from the colonial countries, since the latter are also capitalist (Allahar 2001b, 232). This is a crucial sociological point that he misses, one that speaks to the difference between dependent capitalism in the colonies and advanced capitalism in the imperialist centres. The failure to appreciate this distinction is what leads Fanon to presume that the colonies are homogeneous in class and race, and as for the black nationalists who have embraced him, this further conditions the erroneous assumption that colour or race could then serve as a rallying point for colonized peoples. So in *Toward the African Revolution*, Fanon views racism as "only one element of a vaster whole: that of the systematised oppression of a people" (1967b, 43). His use of the term "people" here is entirely uncritical and carries no hint of class differentiation among the colonized populations themselves.

However, on this matter Fanon is also very inconsistent. For while at times he seems to lean towards class analysis, he is far more comfortable with the notion of racial solidarity. So whereas a Marxist approach would emphasize the opposition of class and economic interests within both the metropolitan capitalist and the colonial capitalist populations, Fanon opts instead for a more descriptive rendering of the situation. In his essay "French Intellectuals and Democrats in the Algerian Revolution", he appears to reject imperialism and colonialism without seeming to touch capitalism. Indeed, he continues to speak uncritically of "colonised people" and challenges the Marxist notion of proletarian internationalism in favour of an imagined class and political solidarity among colonial peoples: "In a colonial country, it used to be said, there is a community of interests between the colonised people and the working class of the colonialist country. The history of the wars of liberation waged by the colonised peoples is the history of the non-verification of this thesis" (Fanon 1967b, 82).

At other points it is not entirely clear that he accepts this idyllic view of a homogeneous colonial citizenry, for his analysis and condemnation of the national bourgeoisie in the colonies are most poignant. His definition of class seems based more on politics than on economics; thus he provides little by way of an economic description of the national bourgeoisie, that is, its economic behaviour, choosing instead to paint it in dependent political terms merely as "the bourgeois fraction of the colonised people" (Fanon 1963, 109). He is most cynical about nationalist politics and sees all attempts at national independence as fated to failure. Indeed, the national bourgeoisie, sometimes referred to as the "national middle class" (which betrays his sloppy understanding of the term "class"), is criticized for being bourgeois! He can thus be seen as setting up a straw man by asking the national bourgeoisie to act as its own executioner, to put its knowledge, skills and capital in the service of an anti-colonial revolution. Presumably, also, this would be a bourgeois revolution – Fanon is deafeningly silent here on the question of socialism. In his own words,

> It would seem that the historical vocation of the national middle class in an underdeveloped country is to repudiate its own nature in so far as it is bourgeois . . . very often the national middle class does not follow this heroic path; rather, it disappears with its soul set at peace into the shocking ways

... of a traditional bourgeoisie, of a bourgeoisie which is stupidly, contemptibly, cynically bourgeois. (1963, 150)

But Fanon is not alone in expecting the national bourgeoisie to commit class suicide. One of his foremost interpreters, Irene Gendzier, also speaks of "the inability of the bourgeoisie to act in the national interests" and of the bourgoisie as exhibiting "a total indifference to the needs of the mass of the population; and worst of all, an economically ineffectual and pretentious minority" (1973, 218). What both Fanon and Gendzier (and others in this vein) miss entirely is the fact that capital has no nationality, class, race or sex. In the economic pursuit of the bottom line and the political drive to domination, capital will exploit wherever it can and whoever stands in its path. So there is no reason to expect that the bourgeoisie would develop nationalist sentiments if those sentiments impaired its historical mission of expanded capital accumulation. It amounts to wishful thinking and even naive politics, for if the bourgeoisie were to do as these thinkers seem to expect, then it would not be acting as a bourgeoisie at all. In the contemporary Caribbean this is precisely the managerial bourgeoisie of which Alex Dupuy (1991) speaks, a mere junior partner of the international corporate bourgeoisie. Generally speaking, as junior partners, the bourgeoisies at the helms of post-independence Caribbean countries are neither revolutionary nor nationalist, for their principal mandate is to preserve the conditions for the expanded reproduction and accumulation of capital. This leads them to adopt anti-nationalist economic policies and non-progressive political alliances (Allahar 1995). In other words, the black leaders of these countries are committed to the retention of capitalism; at times they have even been known to espouse a black nationalist rhetoric to distract the popular masses from the class realities of dependent capitalism.

Fanon's differences from Marx and Engels are also evident here. For while the latter were firmly convinced that the petit bourgeoisie, what Fanon sloppily calls the "national bourgeoisie" or "national middle class", sometimes referred to as the "middle class", was fundamentally reactionary, they did nevertheless concede to it the possibility of acting progressively at certain historical junctures. Thus, for example, Marx and Engels note that when the writing is on the wall and "the class struggle nears the decisive hour, a small section of the ruling class cuts itself adrift and joins the revolutionary class that holds the future in its hands" (1955, 20). This "small section" they refer to as "bourgeois ideologists" (p. 20) and reason that they are ideally suited to provide political leadership to the vanguard of the socialist revolution. So instead of charging the entire bourgeoisie with the obligation to commit class suicide, Marx and Engels focus on a fraction of that class and credit it with a certain degree of consciousness and foresight. They acknowledge that given the privileges of its class position, this class was able to achieve a superior intellectual development that could be put in the service of the proletarian revolution.

Because of his tendency to homogenize and essentialize key social actors, Fanon is led to make descriptive statements that are of little political utility in a struggle for liberation. Thus, he writes that "in the colonies the economic substructure is also a superstructure. The cause is the consequence; you are rich because you are white, you are white because you are rich. This is why Marxist analysis should always be slightly stretched every time we have to do with the colonial problem" (1963, 40). But whenever something is stretched, however slightly, a certain amount of distortion follows. And in attempting to stretch Marxism, Fanon renders it less than Marx intended. As a consequence, Fanonism, as a "stretched Marxism", is unable to capture fully the exigencies of an anti-colonial struggle because it leaves out of the equation that part of the progressive forces which, though bourgeois and white, is not classist, racist or sexist.

Related to this idea of stretching Marx one might also refer to Fanon's treatment of the lumpenproletariat as a revolutionary force in the anti-colonial struggle. While in the colonies and the ex-colonies this class is almost entirely black, it cannot be assumed to be class conscious. Marx and Engels were not talking of the working poor when they designated this class as *lumpen,* or scum. The lumpenproletariat is not merely a class of unemployed women and men; its ranks are made up of unemployable drunks, drug addicts, ruthless pimps, diseased prostitutes, violent murderers and the like, whose passions revolve around their vices. Theirs is a world of violence and brutality, routinely unleashed on one another. To the extent that they are employable at all, they are more like mercenaries, except that they will work for far less: a quick drug fix, a few dollars, even a bottle of rum. Fanon recognizes the mercenary element of this class when he describes its "ignorance and incomprehension" as weaknesses and says that if it "is not immediately organised by the forces of rebellion, it will find itself fighting as hired soldiers side by side with the colonial troops" (1963, 109). But exactly what kind of appeal does one make to such a class? On this score Fanon appears both naive and confused, and this stems directly from his non-analytical understanding of class:

> Fanon's critical analysis of the colonial proletariat foundered on his failure to distinguish between genuinely proletarian elements such as dockers and miners, and petty-bourgeois groups such as taxi drivers and clerks. . . . [He also] fails to distinguish between the hard-core, corrupted *Lumpenproletariat* and the migrant peasants who move to and fro between the town and village, and who are more capable of the revolutionary activity he describes and desires. (Caute 1970, 78 and 80)

None of this, however, dampens the highly positive reception of Fanon in certain black nationalist circles, where he assumes guru-like status, and his work continues to shape political options for many who see "race" as real. Thus, Molefi Asante, the leading Afrocentric thinker today, "insists on the centrality of Fanon's ideas to his intellectual formation" (quoted in Howe 1998, 78–79). Then there was the entire leadership of the Black Power movement in the United States (which had a loud echo in the Caribbean), who, in the words of Caute, sought to make Fanon their patron saint: Fanon "the black psychiatrist was canonized by Afro-American activists" (1970, 103). Eldridge Cleaver dubbed *The Wretched of the Earth*, which had sold more than 750,000 copies by the end of 1970, "an historical event", the "Bible" of the black liberation movement (1969, 18 and 20). According to Black Panther Bobby Seale, who claimed to have read the book six times (1970, 25), it served as a guide in distinguishing "jive" cultural nationalists from those militants who would correctly utilize culture in the service of black liberation (p. 34). One of the leaders of the Student Non-violent Coordinating Committee (SNCC), James Forman, saw Fanon's ideas as lying at the root of modern black nationalism (Van Deburg 1992). Finally, there was Dan Watts, editor of *Liberator* magazine, who in an interview with the *Chicago Sun-Times* told the interviewer that the black activists, especially those who were armed and poised to take the struggle to the streets, were prepared to die for their cause. Watts was quite convinced that the activists had also done their homework, by which he meant,

"They all read. Read a lot. Not one of them hasn't read the Bible."
"The Bible?"
"Fanon . . . You'd better get this book. Every brother on a rooftop can quote Fanon." (Quoted in Zolberg and Zolberg 1967, 50; Van Deburg 1992, 61)

Conclusion

David Caute writes, "Fanon agreed: to enslave men it was necessary to divest them of their humanity by systematic mystification" (1970, 11–12). In agreeing, however, Fanon did not realize that the reverse might also have been true. In other words, as I have attempted to demonstrate, systematic mystification in the form of systematic myth-making has informed Afrocentric thinking and has served to empower those descendants of slaves who claim still to be denied their freedom in the Western world. Thus, following Hopkins (1973), Robin Cohen speaks of the "Merrie Africa" myth as a "tendency for uncritical celebration of the African past, and the exaggeration of the degree of communal solidarity in pre-industrial societies" (1979, 7). As has been shown above, this myth-making is a crucial aspect of Afrocentricity and black nationalist ideology, and it has been embraced by many black people in the so-called African diasporas throughout the Caribbean. To understand that embrace I have used the Caribbean, and Trinidad in particular, as an example, but the phenomenon is by no means restricted to that area.

In sum, then, I charge that the Caribbean region as a whole is creolized, while Trinidad itself is a "douglarized" nation (that is, in racial terminology, a nation that is defined predominantly by the mixing of African- and Indian-descended people). The various political cultures of the region were all forged in the fires of colonization, slavery, racism, indentureship and dependent capitalism. As a consequence they betray the scars of these historical processes. There is certainly no democracy of races anywhere in the Caribbean, just as there is no class democracy, if by democracy one understands an equal access to and sharing of the social fruits. Indeed, what one finds is liberal democracy, which enshrines the inequalities of dependent capitalism. The various political cultures thus exist in the service of those foreign and locally dominant capitalist classes and the protectors of the dependent capitalist order, the postcolonial state (Dupuy 1991). To this extent race, ethnicity, religion and other social divisions will serve very clear class interests, conditioning the political cultures of the region and its various member countries. But one must not be distracted, for even though divisions may appear on the surface to be ethnic or racial, they remain fundamentally of a classed economic and a political nature.

Acknowledgements

The author would like to thank Diana Caitlin Savage for her most able assistance in securing library sources and in the preparation of the manuscript according to the UWI Press style sheet.

References

Adeyinka, Olaogun Narmer. 2000. "A Carnival of Resistance, Emancipation, Commemoration, Reconstruction, and Creativity". In *Ah Come Back Home: Perspectives on the Trinidad and Tobago Carnival*, edited by Ian I. Smart and Kimani S.K. Nehusi, 105–29. Washington, DC, and Port of Spain, Trinidad: Original World Press.

Allahar, Anton L. 1995. *Sociology and the Periphery: Theories and Issues*. Toronto: Garamond.

———. 1996. "Primordialism and Ethnic Political Mobilisation in Modern Society". *New Community* 22, no. 1: 5–21.

———. 1997. "History and the Genesis of Fragmented Caribbean Identities". *Journal of Social Sciences* 4, no. 2: 3–31.

———. 1998. "Popular Culture and Racialisation of Political Consciousness in Trinidad and Tobago". *Wadabagei: A Journal of the Caribbean and Its Diaspora* 1, no. 2: 1–41.

———. 2001a. "Framing of Political Culture in the English-Speaking Caribbean: Cuban Socialism vs US Imperialism". *Canadian Journal of Latin American and Caribbean Studies* 26: 223–43.

———. 2001b. " 'Race' and Class in the Making of Caribbean Political Culture". *Transforming Anthropology* 10, no. 2: 13–29.

———, ed. 2001c. *Caribbean Charisma: Reflections on Leadership, Legitimacy and Populist Politics*. London: Lynne Rienner.

Allahar, Anton L., and James E. Côté. 1998. *Richer and Poorer: The Structure of Inequality in Canada.* Toronto: Lorimer.

Alleyne-Dettmers, Patricia. 2000. "Beyond Borders, Carnival as Global Phenomena: 'Going Bananas, Food for the Devil' ". In *Ah Come Back Home: Perspectives on the Trinidad and Tobago Carnival,* edited by Ian I. Smart and Kimani S.K. Nehusi, 131–62. Washington, DC, and Port of Spain, Trinidad: Original World Press.

Anderson, Benedict. 1983. *Imagined Communities: Reflections on the Origin and Spread of Nationalism.* London: Verso.

Bernal, Martin. 1987. *Black Athena: The Afroasiatic Roots of Classical Civilization.* Vol. 1: *The Fabrication of Ancient Greece.* London: Free Association Books.

Bhabha, Homi. 1999. "Remembering Fanon: Self, Psyche, and the Colonial Condition". In *Rethinking Fanon: The Continuing Dialogue,* edited by Nigel Gibson, 179–96. Amherst, NY: Humanity Books.

Bolland, O. Nigel. 1997. *Struggles for Freedom: Essays on Slavery, Colonialism and Culture in the Caribbean and Central America.* Belize City, Belize: Angelus.

Brathwaite, Edward. 1971. *The Development of Creole Society in Jamaica: 1770–1820.* Oxford: Clarendon.

Brereton, Bridget. 1974. "The Experience of Indentureship". In *Calcutta to Caroni: The East Indians of Trinidad,* edited by John La Guerre, 25–38. London: Longman.

Carmichael, Stokely. 1968. "Power and Racism". In *The Black Power Revolt,* edited by Floyd Barbour, 61–72. Boston: Extending Horizons Books.

Carmichael, Stokely, and Charles V. Hamilton. 1967. *Black Power: The Politics of Liberation in America.* New York: Random House.

Caute, David. 1970. *Frantz Fanon.* New York: Viking.

Cleaver, Eldridge. 1969. *Post-Prison Writings and Speeches.* Edited by Robert Scheer. New York: Random House.

Cohen, Robin. 1979. "The Making of a West African Working Class". In *The Politics of Africa: Dependence and Development,* edited by Timothy M. Shaw and Kenneth A. Heard, 5–21. New York: Africana.

Connor, Walker. 1992. "The Nation and Its Myth". *International Journal of Comparative Sociology* 33: 48–57.

Cummings, Christine. 1990. "The Ideology of West Indian Cricket". *Arena Review* 14, no. 1: 25–32.

Deosaran, Ramesh. 1987. "The Caribbean Man: A Study of the Psychology of Perception and the Media". In *India in the Caribbean,* edited by David

Dabydeen and Brinsley Samaroo, 81–118. London: Hansib/University of Warwick.

Dupuy, Alex. 1991. "Political Intellectuals in the Third World: The Caribbean Case". In *Intellectuals and Politics: Social Theory in a Changing World,* edited by Charles C. Lemert, 74–93. Newbury Park, Calif.: Sage.

Fanon, Frantz. 1963. *The Wretched of the Earth.* Translated by Constance Farrington. New York: Grove.

———. 1967a. *Black Skin, White Masks: The Experiences of a Black Man in a White World.* Translated by Charles Lam Markmann. New York: Grove.

———. 1967b. *Toward the African Revolution: Political Essays.* Translated by Haakon Chevalier. New York: Grove.

Gagnon, Alain G. 1987. "The Role of Intellectuals in Liberal Democracies: Political Influence and Social Involvement". In *Intellectuals in Liberal Democracies,* edited by Alain Gagnon, 3–16. New York: Praeger.

Gates, Henry Louis, Jr. 1999. "Critical Fanonism". In *Rethinking Fanon: The Continuing Dialogue,* edited by Nigel Gibson, 251–68. Amherst, NY: Humanity Books.

Gendzier, Irene L. 1973. *Frantz Fanon: A Critical Study.* New York: Pantheon.

Gibson, Nigel C., ed. 1999. *Rethinking Fanon: The Continuing Dialogue.* Amherst, NY: Humanity Books.

Gilroy, Paul. 1987. *There Ain't No Black in the Union Jack: The Cultural Politics of Race and Nation.* London: Hutchinson.

Hill, Errol. 1972. *The Trinidad Carnival: Mandate for a National Theatre.* Austin: University of Texas Press.

Hobsbawm, Eric, and Terence Ranger, eds. 1983. *The Invention of Tradition.* Cambridge: Cambridge University Press.

Hopkins, A.G. 1973. *An Economic History of West Africa.* London: Longman.

Howe, Stephen. 1998. *Afrocentrism: Mythical Pasts and Imagined Homes.* London: Verso.

James, C.L.R. 1980. *Spheres of Existence: Selected Writings.* London: Allison and Busby.

Lewis, Gordon K. 1985. "The Contemporary Caribbean: A General Overview". In *Caribbean Contours,* edited by Sidney Mintz and Sally Price, 219–50. Baltimore: Johns Hopkins University Press.

Malcolm X. 1970. *By Any Means Necessary.* New York: Pathfinder.

Martin, Vonulrick. 2000. "Coming Back Home to Take Home Back". In *Ah Come Back Home: Perspectives on the Trinidad and Tobago Carnival,*

edited by Ian I. Smart and Kimani S.K. Nehusi, 179–95. Washington, DC, and Port of Spain, Trinidad: Original World Press.
Marx, Karl, and Frederich Engels. 1955. *The Communist Manifesto*. New York: Appleton-Century-Crofts.
———. 1959. *Basic Writings on Politics and Philosophy*, edited by Lewis S. Feuer. New York: Doubleday.
Miles, Robert. 1989. *Racism*. New York: Routledge.
Moitt, Bernard. 1989. "Cheikh Anta Diop and the African Diaspora: Historical Continuity and Socio-Cultural Symbolism". *Présence Africaine*, nos. 149–50: 349–60.
Moran, Patricia. 2000. "Experiencing the Pan-African Dimension of Carnival". In *Ah Come Back Home: Perspectives on the Trinidad and Tobago Carnival*, edited by Ian I. Smart and Kimani S.K. Nehusi, 163–77. Washington, DC, and Port of Spain, Trinidad: Original World Press.
Nehusi, Kimani S.K. 2000a. "Going Back Home to the Carnival". In *Ah Come Back Home: Perspectives on the Trinidad and Tobago Carnival*, edited by Ian I. Smart and Kimani S.K. Nehusi, 1–16. Washington, DC, and Port of Spain, Trinidad: Original World Press.
———. 2000b. "The Origins of Carnival: Notes from a Preliminary Investigation". In *Ah Come Back Home: Perspectives on the Trinidad and Tobago Carnival*, edited by Ian I. Smart and Kimani S.K. Nehusi, 77–103. Washington, DC, and Port of Spain, Trinidad: Original World Press.
Orwell, George. 1948. *Nineteen Eighty-Four*. New York: Penguin Books.
Prasad, Madhava. 1992. "The 'Other' Worldliness of Post-Colonial Discourse: A Critique". *Critical Quarterly* 34, no. 3: 74–89.
Robinson, Cedric J. 1993. "The Appropriation of Frantz Fanon". *Race and Class* 35, no. 1: 79–91.
Said, Edward. 1993. *Culture and Imperialism*. New York: Knopf.
Seale, Bobby. 1970. *Seize the Time: The Story of the Black Panther Party and Huey P. Newton*. New York: Random House.
Singh, Kelvin. 1974. "East Indians and the Larger Society". In *Calcutta to Caroni: The East Indians of Trinidad*, edited by John La Guerre, 39–68. London: Longman.
Smart, Ian Isidore. 2000a. "Carnival, the Ultimate Pan-African Festival". In *Ah Come Back Home: Perspectives on the Trinidad and Tobago Carnival*, edited by Ian I. Smart and Kimani S.K. Nehusi, 29–76. Washington, DC, and Port of Spain, Trinidad: Original World Press.
———. 2000b. "It's Not French (Europe), It's Really French-Based Creole (Africa)". In *Ah Come Back Home: Perspectives on the Trinidad and Tobago Carnival*, edited by Ian I. Smart and Kimani S.K. Nehusi,

197–221. Washington, DC, and Port of Spain, Trinidad: Original World Press.

Smart, Ian Isidore, and Kimani S.K. Nehusi, eds. 2000. *Ah Come Back Home: Perspectives on the Trinidad and Tobago Carnival*. Washington, DC, and Port of Spain, Trinidad: Original World Press.

Smith, Anthony D. 1984. "National Identity and Myths of Ethnic Descent". *Research in Social Movements, Conflict and Change* 7: 95–130.

———. 1988. "The Myth of the 'Modern Nation' and the Myths of Nations". *Ethnic and Racial Studies* 11, no. 1: 1–26.

Smith, M.G. 1965. *The Plural Society in the British West Indies*. Berkeley: University of California Press.

Soyinka, Wole. 1999. *The Burden of Memory, the Muse of Forgiveness*. New York: Oxford University Press.

Springer, Pearl Eintou. 2000. "Carnival: Identity, Ethnicity and Spirituality". In *Ah Come Back Home: Perspectives on the Trinidad and Tobago Carnival*, edited by Ian I. Smart and Kimani S.K. Nehusi, 17–27. Washington, DC, and Port of Spain, Trinidad: Original World Press.

Thomas, Greg. 1995. "Multiculturalism versus Afrocentricity: The Black Studies War". *Village Voice*, 17 January, 23–29.

Trotman, David V. 1991. "The Image of Indians in Calypso: Trinidad 1946–1986". In *Social and Occupational Stratification in Contemporary Trinidad and Tobago*, edited by Selwyn Ryan, 385–98. St Augustine, Trinidad: Institute of Social and Economic Research.

Van Deburg, William L. 1992. *New Day in Babylon: The Black Power Movement and American Culture, 1965–1975*. Chicago: University of Chicago Press.

Warner, Keith Q. 1993. "Ethnicity and the Contemporary Calypso". In *Trinidad Ethnicity*, edited by Kevin Yelvington, 275–91. London: MacMillan.

Zolberg, Aristide, and Vera Zolberg. 1967. "The Americanization of Frantz Fanon". *The Public Interest*, no. 9: 49–63.

[3]

The Race-Class Problematic and the Caribbean Left

Perry Mars

Introduction

This chapter revisits the issue of the relationship between race and class posed in debates among Caribbean academics on the one hand and radical political activists on the other, particularly during the postcolonial period. This debate is still relevant today, despite the dominant dismissive mood in major sections of Caribbean academia since the destabilization of the Caribbean Left in the 1980s. The currency of this race-class issue in the Caribbean relates to the fact that the critical concern that inspired it in the first place, the problem of economic and political inequalities in our midst, is still not resolved. Also, the issue of inequality has become even more problematic today given the current asymmetrical and deadly impact of increasing economic globalization in the region as elsewhere in the Third World. The central notion of the resolution of man-made inequalities has been a major theme on the Left agenda throughout the world (see Anderson 1998; Bobbio 1996, 1998; Giddens 1994), and the varied approaches to it in the Caribbean have left a legacy of controversy and conflicts over what is in this chapter called "the race-class problematic".

Although the race-class problematic does not represent the totality of the Left agenda in the Caribbean, the issue is fundamental to understanding much of the scope and limitations of the Caribbean Left in terms of its role in the contestation for hegemony or political power. But if basic to the shortcomings of the Caribbean Left was its overemphasis on an unadulterated class analysis of the Caribbean reality, Caribbean academics have generally been culpable for largely ignoring or minimizing the salience of economic class altogether in attempts to grasp the reality of Caribbean conditions. Very little clarification or reconceptualization of the issue has been forthcoming by way of debate or discourse, whether in practical or academic terms, in the Caribbean regional context within recent times, particularly since the debacle that befell the Caribbean Left in the 1980s. Advocates of postmodernism and globalization contend that the old class and race divisions of yesterday, along with the Left that is concerned with these issues, are now obsolete or irrelevant in the wake of the supposed colour-blind "level playing field", fragmented identities and universal economic uplifting processes being introduced by global market forces and modern technological developments. Yet the growing economic, political and racial disparities caused by these very globalizing forces in the Third World (see Moody 1997; Petras and Veltmeyer 2001; Thomas 2000), including the Caribbean (see McAffee 1991), make resolution of the problems and conflicts posed by race and class relations all the more crucial today if the world is to be made a more livable space for the majority of humankind.

One major problem that has long plagued progressive political thought and practice in the Caribbean is the absence of adequate theory generating fundamental understanding of the critical interrelationships between race, ethnicity and class in the region. Perhaps the most significant consequence of this void has been failure of activist politics, particularly of the Caribbean Left, to attain any appreciable degree of hegemonic sway over the Caribbean masses. This failure is manifested in the fact that the essential class project of the Left (which involves uniting the working and subordinate classes) usually becomes undermined by racial, ethnic and narrow communal divisiveness in the process of change within Caribbean societies. The objective here, therefore, is to critically re-examine the intellectual and practical development of this race-class problematic, with a view towards gaining appropriate insights into the resolution of the types of conflicts which tend to inhibit democratic and transformative politics in the region. The particular interest here is the extent to which race, ethnicity and class, separately or conjointly, explain the dynamics of the Caribbean political process.

The bulk of earlier attempts at explaining the Caribbean conflict process can be divided into two streams. The first, associated with the cultural pluralist argument, suggests a mutually exclusive relationship between race or ethnicity on the one hand and class considerations on the other (Kuper 1971a, 1971b; Smith 1960, 1965). The second, usually derived from a Marxist historical perspective, accepts the political significance of both class and race but assumes an inverse or contradictory relationship between the two, in the sense either that class is always dominant or that one (say, class) advances at the expense of the other (say, race or ethnicity). In other words, in multi-ethnic Caribbean societies such as Guyana and Trinidad and Tobago, race-based politics tend invariably to undermine class politics in the process of struggle towards change (see Jagan 1997; Rodney 1979, 19). The problem with these two approaches, however, is their failure to see or highlight the dynamic and often symbiotic interrelationship between race, ethnicity and class, and the possibility that understanding this symbiosis can generate insights into creative approaches to peaceful conflict resolution and political development. Both approaches tend to ignore or talk past each other, and they fail to examine closely the wealth of empirical or historical evidence of political conflicts in which both race and class played significant roles (often competitive, often interchangeable).

Closer examination of the patterns of political conflicts in the Caribbean suggests, first, that the intensification of race- or ethnicity-based conflict does not necessarily imply the diminution of class conflict or vice versa; second, that it is difficult to extricate class configurations from particular levels of intensity of ethnic conflict; third, that much of the intensity of ethno-political (class and ethnic) conflict is produced by extrinsic factors such as state response to protest and foreign instigation of domestic divisiveness; and fourth, that the almost invariable coerciveness of state responses to ethno-political conflicts is usually counterproductive to peaceful conflict resolution and democratic political development.

The main argument here is that debates and discourses on the relationship between race and class in the Caribbean have so far generated little insight into the actual process of conflict resolution and meaningful democratic participation, mainly because academics and political activists have shunned learning from each other and have failed to conceptualize race and class in the context of actual historical events that demonstrate active political conflict and violence in the region. A reconceptualization of the issue is needed, which takes into consideration the increasing international significance of race and class, as well as of the comparative and historical dimensions of political conflict, as important for guiding initiatives towards conflict resolution and successful democratic transformations in the region. By understanding how the race-class dimensions operate within the course of particular conflict activities or "events" (such as riots, strikes, boycotts and demonstrations), one is better equipped to understand the relative impact of race, ethnicity or class on the longer-term processes or cycles of change and transformations which these events themselves might have inspired or influenced in Caribbean societies as a whole.

Caribbean Social Science

Caribbean social science studies on the issues of race and class range from the earlier conceptualizations of cultural pluralism and social stratification to the later developments of the plantation society model and a variety of hemispheric Marxist scholarship, including the recently emerging, although inchoate, interest in Gramscian concepts of political legitimation, hegemonic struggle and ideological practices.

For the cultural pluralists, independent cultural sections of Caribbean societies represent the principal agents of conflict and what is considered the very remote possibility of social change. Cultural pluralists explicitly reject Marxist attribution of significance to social or economic classes in explaining the Caribbean social and political processes (Smith 1960, 1965). These cultural sections are usually exemplified by ethnic groups such as East Indians, Africans and Chinese in such multi-ethnic societies as Guyana, Trinidad and Tobago, and Jamaica. Two basic factors within the cultural pluralist model would seem to inhibit the prospects of social change: the necessity for the political dominance of a single cultural section (or white colonial elite, in M.G. Smith's time) with the capacity to repress or firmly control conflict between subordinate groups; and the difficulty or near impossibility of individual mobility out of a person's own cultural section within a single lifetime, as Smith asserts (1960). The negative implications here for peaceful conflict resolution and participatory democracy lie in the assumption that social structural change must necessarily involve extreme or violent conflicts between groups and that in the context of a plural society the demand is usually for either forceful or charismatic, as distinct from consensual, leadership (Smith 1965).

A rival "social stratification" approach introduces Weberian class considerations to describe Caribbean society as based more on the criterion of occupational status hierarchies than on purely ethnic or cultural sections (Braithwaite 1960; Smith 1962; Stone 1972). However, the social stratification approach admits the possibility of overlaps between these occupational hierarchies and cultural or ethnic sections of particular Caribbean societies like Guyana (Smith 1962). Within this system, political conflicts are thought to be mitigated or avoided both by the prospects of upward mobility of individuals within the system and by the existence of what is assumed to be a kind of consensual adherence of all groups to the single dominant value of the white European ruling elite. This adherence to white value consensus becomes the principal mechanism of conflict resolution and the guarantee of political integration and stability.

One innovation in the cultural pluralist argument, suggesting the use of a cross-cutting mechanism that presumes to mitigate the conflict situation in Caribbean societies such as Guyana, is Leo Despres's notion of "broker institutions" (1967). These broker institutions include trade unions, religious organizations and educational institutions which, according to Despres, act as a kind of bridge between the various plural sections at both the national and local levels of the Guyanese society, and so are placed in a position to broker peace and reconciliation between rival groups in the system.

Although a credible counterweight to cultural pluralism, the plantation society model, developed mainly during the 1970s, is equally one-sided in its conceptualization of the social structural and conflict problem. In this model, the internal dynamics of both race and class become absolutely subordinated to the machinations of international economic relations, which sees the nation state as the principal actor in the process. Only in relatively few cases, however, is marginal recognition given to the dynamic interrelationship between the domestic elements of race and class within the plantation society model (Beckford 1972; Beckford and Witter 1980). On the whole, however, the plantation society approach in explaining Caribbean socio-economic development ends up subsuming both race and class within state and international relations.

During the 1980s an alternative Marxist political economy literature emerged (Ambursley and Cohen 1983; Jacobs and Jacobs 1980; Marable 1987; Post 1978; Thomas 1988) which emphasizes the fundamental role of economic class forces. But much like the plantation society school, this new Marxist approach tends to subordinate or even exclude racial and ethnic considerations as critical to the understanding of Caribbean social and political processes. Also, the Marxist conceptualization of classes here tends in most cases to be rigid and static, as it seems to attempt more to classify structural characteristics of the Caribbean reality than to explain the dynamic, fluid and complex processes of political conflict and social change. Conflict resolution within this perspective either is not discussed or is ideally contemplated as occurring only at the end of revolutionary struggles, when an egalitarian universe has been attained and class divisions have disappeared.

The 1990s would seem to have represented something like a shift from the more orthodox Marxist approach towards the incorporation of Gramscian and critical theoretical insights into analyses of race and class relations in multi-ethnic societies in the Caribbean (Bakan 1990; Mills 1987). However, most of these works focus on the African American and black diaspora experiences (Gilroy 1993; Omi and Winant 1994; San Juan 1992). In these works the analytic shift is essentially away from preoccupation with the distinctive or exclusive impact of either class or racial structures in relative isolation from each other to considerations of the dynamic interplay between class, ethnic and often gender relations. Here class or race relations are perceived in terms of the struggle for identity and hegemony within a highly competitive, conflictual and increasingly global capitalistic universe. But it is important to note that while the American literature is preoccupied with explaining how racial domination takes place and with the oppressive implications of this domination for African Americans in general, the Caribbean literature focuses on counter-hegemonic class struggle and on rebellion against oppressive conditions.

By clearly establishing that both race (or ethnicity) and class are indispensable in formulating theories of socio-political conflicts and change in the Caribbean context, Caribbean social science, both pluralist and Marxist, has provided useful insights for understanding related political activism in the region. Both race and class are closely bound up in the Caribbean experience today, mainly because of the historical significance of the ideology of domination which is cast in both class and racial terms and which is responsible for the subjugation of Caribbean peoples since the periods of slavery and colonialism. The major problem with most of the Caribbean social science approaches would seem to be their insistence on dichotomizing the two concepts of race and class, either by totally negating the relevance of class, as in the cultural pluralists' perspective, or by absolutely subordinating race to class, as in the orthodox Marxist approach. Similarly, the discernment of an inverse linear relationship between race and class – that is, the assumption that the salience of one decreases to the extent that the salience of the other increases, as in the case of the more recent Gramscian and neo-Marxist studies of the black diaspora experience – is equally problematic.

The notion that race and class at times work together as a unified, relatively autonomous movement, as in the form, for example, of what Gramsci termed a "historic bloc", or in his words, "the unity of opposites and distincts" (Gramsci 1978, 137; see also Bocock 1986), is significantly absent from these studies. Modified to suit Caribbean and black diaspora conditions, the concept of a historic bloc, which generally addresses the issue of multi-class alliances and coalition building within a unified political movement or party, is equally important to the recurring issue in Caribbean multi-ethnic societies, that is, the need for bridging ethnic or racial boundaries or for conflict resolution within a single class, as in the cases of the black and white working classes in the United States and the East Indian and black workers in Guyana and the Caribbean.

What also tends to be neglected in Caribbean social science theories, unlike in some of the discourses of the Caribbean Left, is comprehensive and sustained study of the two main class formations that have played perhaps the most decisive role in the determination of political conflicts and change involving race-class mobilizing patterns in the region: the middle classes and the lumpenproletarian elements. The Caribbean middle classes are critical in terms of their greater access to political and economic power, their tendencies towards ideological and political faction, their interest in the preservation of colonialist values based on colour and status, and their dogged efforts towards upward mobility in the social and political system. The lumpenproletariat elements are derived from the extremely high degrees of both urbanization and unemployment in the region and have been historically most instrumental as major participants in much of the public social and political protest, ranging from the most peaceful to the most violent in the region. This lacuna in Caribbean social theories would seem to follow from the general neglect of studying the actual conflict events themselves and the prospects for conflict resolution in the modern Caribbean.

The Caribbean Left, therefore, in their popular mobilization strategies and in their struggles to influence the national political agendas, operated largely within a theoretical void as far as knowledge of the race-class interaction dynamics in the region is concerned. Their own efforts to develop some theoretical framework for understanding Caribbean political conditions and processes were equally limited by their reluctance to draw on the strengths of existing social theories, by their reliance on precepts deduced almost exclusively from foreign theoretical and ideological frames and influences, by their frequent assumptions about the dispensability of racial and ethnic factors in the pursuit of political power and fundamental social change, and to a large extent by their general neglect of theory construction, for which exclusive dependence on decontextualized foreign ideology and preoccupation with constant political agitation are often substituted.

Caribbean Left Perspectives

Attempts by the Caribbean Left to reconcile race and class in their analysis of capitalist relations go back to the 1920s among Caribbean intellectuals in Harlem, who organized themselves under the banner of the African Blood Brotherhood (ABB). While their Marxist persuasion dictated their theoretical commitment to economic class analysis as a basis for understanding capitalist society in America, their experience with American racism compelled, also, a racial interpretation of the overall structure of white domination. An early flirtation with Garveyist pan-Africanism by the ABB was, however, soon abandoned in favour of an even more rigid and militant class determinism, influenced largely by their admiration for Stalinist Russia in the 1930s (see Cruse 1984; Tillery 1992).

C.L.R. James, in the 1940s, also attempted to link Marxist class analysis with racial considerations relating to his experiences in America and the black diaspora. James concluded that the unique conditions of blacks in America, who are placed in the double bind of both racial and class subordination and oppression, propels this group into a necessary role of vanguard leadership of the racially diverse working classes in America and beyond (James 1996). He also complemented Frantz Fanon in the 1960s in his strong criticism of the lighter-skinned middle classes in the Caribbean and throughout the Third World and the black diaspora as being incapable of leadership of the working classes since they were seen to represent appendages of the white colonial ruling classes. In addition, the middle classes were seen to be interested only in upward mobility within a system that absolutely disadvantages the usually darker-skinned working and subordinate classes in these parts (Fanon 1964; James 1962).

An early attempt to relate such a race-class analysis to specifically Caribbean conditions emerged with the Marxist "inner circle" of the People's National Party (PNP) of Jamaica, founded in 1942 on the issue of Garveyist black consciousness within the Jamaican Marxist movement (Munroe 1990). Richard Hart, for example, contends that most of the members of the inner circle were Garveyists, and that Garveyism had been the foundation on which the PNP and, indeed, most of the modern anti-colonial political movements in Jamaica were built (cited in Munroe 1990). However, the inner circle itself was more convinced by the strict class perspectives of classical Marxism than by considerations of racial determinism such as those in the Garveyist perspective.

The reception of Garveyism within the early Jamaican Left was somewhat different from its reception by the ABB and radicalized African Americans. The PNP inner circle's failure to discern the basic contradictions between its Marxist objectives and Garveyism could be attributed to three things. The first is the absence in the Caribbean of either a white majority population or a white working class, so that the question of a black-white working-class alliance did not apply as it did in the case of the struggle in the United States. The second is Garvey's anti-colonialism, an ideology which largely influenced the emergence of the Leftist-led decolonization movement throughout the region during the 1950s. The third is that the Garveyist movement remained largely minuscule throughout the Caribbean, and therefore its race-centred theory posed very little competitive threat to the newly emerging, class-oriented leftist movements in these parts.

Nevertheless, the general Caribbean leftist reception of Garveyism did not go quite beyond the recognition of the possible complementary relationship between the two movements. In fact, the early pre-independence Caribbean Left, in its analysis of struggle and strategies for change, appeared to have completely abandoned considerations of race and ethnicity in preference for more orthodox Marxist class analysis, often applied wholesale from the works of Lenin, Stalin and other classical Marxist texts (see Munroe 1990). At the ideological and propaganda level, at least, this strict Marxist orthodoxy applied not only to the inner circle in the Jamaican case during the 1940s and 1950s, but equally to the People's Progressive Party (PPP) in Guyana between 1950 and 1970.

The contradiction posed by the PPP's class-reductionist perspective soon became clear when, between 1953 and 1955, the party needed wider mass unity in a nationalist resistance against colonialism. This contradiction gave rise to the 1955 ideological-cum-racial split in the PPP-led nationalist movement. The split was initially characterized as a contest between "extremist" Marxists led by Cheddi Jagan and "moderate" socialists led by Forbes Burnham. Thus, the nationalist multiracial alliance of 1953, when the PPP swept the polls in the first democratic elections in the country, was short-lived, as evidenced not only by the split, but more significantly by the violent dismissal of the PPP government from office by the British, who saw as intolerable a Marxist-led regime in a British colonial territory (British Guiana Constitutional Commission 1954; Jagan 1997). The 1955 PPP split later culminated in a spate of racial and political violence throughout Guyana, mainly between 1962 and 1964. Similar race-political violence in Trinidad in the early 1960s also threatened Trinidad's nationalist response. These racially violent experiences helped to stimulate among the Caribbean Left a more serious quest for understanding this rather enigmatic relationship between race and class in the region.

Despite the racial characteristics of political violence in Guyana during the 1960s, the PPP still insisted on a fundamental class-analytical perspective, contending, as Jagan continually put it, that "race is only skin deep". In practice, however, the race card was liberally used by both the PPP and its People's National Congress (PNC) rival as a mobilizing strategy in the contention for political power. The PNC's perspective on this issue was even more superficial: it sought to avoid its own racial contradictions by presuming to have finally solved the racial problem mainly through bureaucratic and legal fiat and through a commitment to what it termed "cooperative socialism". In fact, the PNC's slogan of "Peace, not Conflict" between 1964 and 1985 represented a thinly disguised tactic of racial domination through political repression, including the selective use of coercive state force.

The postcolonial period, particularly the 1970s, saw the emergence of a new wave of Caribbean leftist movements, mainly in response to an increased repressiveness on the part of Caribbean regimes, and influenced in part by the Black Power movement in the United States. Among these new groups, only the Workers' Party of Jamaica (WPJ) remained ideologically orthodox in the Stalinist tradition, with a very classic Marxist class analysis of Jamaican and Caribbean conditions. Other newer Left Caribbean groups, such as the Working People's Alliance (WPA) in Guyana and the National Joint Action Committee (NJAC) in Trinidad, made serious attempts to reconcile their class interpretations of Caribbean politics with the race relations issue at both the national and international levels.

Imperialism, or international capitalism, was perceived by this newer Left as being structured along both race and class lines, and therefore the main source of both class and race conflicts in the region. Thus, economic exploitation became synonymous with institutionalized racism under imperialist operations in peripheral capitalist societies like those in the Caribbean. NJAC, for example, defined imperialism as white or European racist domination (NJAC 1981). Although the political leadership of Caribbean states and parties tends to be black in general complexion, this ostensibly black leadership is thought to be, in the intellectual tradition of C.L.R. James and Frantz Fanon, a mere extension of, and in service to, a white-dominated imperialist system. Within this logic, both external capitalists and internal political elites are thought to constitute a distinct ruling class in opposition to the coloured masses of Caribbean peoples. It follows, therefore, according to this newer leftist logic, that strategies for political power and social transformation should be based on multiracial mass alliances against the oppressive Caribbean state and imperialism.

Walter Rodney's contribution to this analysis is most significant. He redefines the race-class conflict situation to include multiracial strategies against imperialism and oppressive Caribbean states, leading towards eventual socialist transformation. While many social theorists and practical politicians at the time viewed East Indians and blacks as mutually opposed and perpetually hostile racial contenders for political domination in such multiracial countries as Guyana and Trinidad, Rodney argues that the main race-class contradiction was the one between white imperialism and the black Caribbean masses, which comprise peoples of both East Indian and African descent (1970). Rodney's position on this issue undoubtedly influenced NJAC's political platform during the 1970s. Blacks and East Indians, being the most exploited working and peasant classes, therefore become, in Rodney's logic, natural allies in the anti-imperialist struggle towards socialism. In addition, Rodney defined white imperialism as embracing not only white European domination, but also the collaboration of the lighter-skinned "races" such as the Portuguese and Chinese (1970). As such, Rodney discerned a clear race-class divide, or conflict situation, between the politically and economically dominant lighter-skinned races, and the more exploited, subordinate, darker-skinned masses in the Caribbean region. The thrust of these arguments was, however, to be significantly modified by Rodney when he became more directly involved in Guyanese politics during the 1970s.

By the latter part of the 1970s the WPA in Guyana, led by Rodney at the time, projected a shift in the main problematic of struggle, that is, a shift from imperialism to the domestic state apparatus as the primary source of oppression, given the extreme repressive tactics of the Burnhamite PNC regime during that time. The WPA position then was that under Burnhamist PNC rule, an emerging black "bourgeoisie" supported by an East Indian "bourgeoisie" dominated both black and East Indian working classes; consequently, imperialism was to be regarded as a possible source of appeal for protection or support against undemocratic domestic dictatorship. In keeping with this modified class-race perspective, the WPA, in a later electoral manifesto, advocated what it called a "multiracial democratic republic" (WPA 1992), a call which recognized the need for some kind of mass alliance to include the lighter-skinned races and middle-class elements in a coalition against the Burnhamite dictatorship.

By 1979 Rodney seemed to have moved fully away from a focus on distinctive racial categories as the precipitants of political conflicts in Guyana towards an almost total negation of race and a class analysis that revealed little of the Marxist polarization between capital and labour. As he saw it in these later years, first, the national capitalist and middle classes became allies of the working classes since the former also suffered deprivations under international capitalism and imperialism; second, the masses of working peoples (comprising both urban workers and rural peasants), together with other elements of the more oppressed middle classes, were being driven into unity against the oppressive Burnhamist dictatorship; and third, the anti-dictatorial alliances necessarily become multiracial in character since all racial groups similarly suffered under the Burnhamist republic (Rodney 1979). These WPA modifications echoed the earlier important modifications made to the theoretical position held in the 1960s by Eusi Kwayana, one of the WPA's founder-leaders, that is, a shift from a very strident black nationalist, or separatist, advocacy and support for Burnhamism during the 1960s to a position which equally applauds both the accomplishments of the East Indian working classes and multiracial political alliances during the 1980s (see Kwayana 1988).

By the 1980s the WPA's position represented, perhaps, the most advanced thesis on the race-class issue among the Caribbean Left, and could well have been viewed as a standard for comparison with other significant leftist positions on the issue throughout the region and beyond. The WPA was among the earliest of the Left parties in the region to confront the problem of race in relation to class in terms both of a conscious and concerted theoretical effort and of sustained practical political struggle. Comparatively, mention should be made of the short-lived United Labour Front (ULF) in Trinidad and Tobago, which surfaced during the 1970s, envisaging a multiracial, multi-class alliance as reflected in its origins in the labour movement, comprising mainly East Indian sugar workers, black oilfield workers and mixed urban middle-class elements in the island. However, despite its unique opportunity, the ULF failed to develop any concerted theoretical position of its own, as it soon became absorbed within the more middle-class-oriented and equally short-lived governing coalition, the National Alliance for Reconstruction (NAR), during the 1980s.

In general, the Caribbean Left settled for an interpretation of the Caribbean conflict situation as one driven basically by class forces, with race consistently playing a subordinate role in the process. This interpretation is reflected in both the orthodox Marxist minimizing of race, as in the case of the PPP, and the more amorphous subsuming of racial categories within some form of nationalist multiracial alliance, as in the case of the more ideologically flexible WPA and ULF. In practice, however, a major portion of the Left often recognized the strategic importance of race-based political mobilization, particularly in countries where significant racial concentrations either coincide with extreme class exploitation (as in the United States) or can make a difference in the contest for political power (as in Guyana and Trinidad and Tobago). For the Caribbean Left, therefore, the resolution of the race issue is thought to be bound up with the prior resolution of the class issue and the ultimate attainment of socialism in these parts.

Much of the Left's conceptualization of the race-class dynamic is derived from theoretical or ideological positions elaborated either in classical Marxist texts, which influenced the older Left, or by Third World revolutionary intellectuals such as Fanon, Amilcar Cabral and Black Power advocates in the United States, who influenced the newer radical Left in the region. But unlike Fanon (1964), Cabral (1970) and James (1962), the Caribbean Left has largely neglected serious consideration of the role of the middle classes in the political conflict process, or more specifically the possible contradictions of middle-class leadership of the working-class or Left struggle in the region. Considerations on this issue within the Caribbean Left movements are often confusing, as with the case of WPA leaders contending both that the middle classes in general suffered deprivation under the Burnham regime in Guyana (Rodney 1979) and that the Burnhamite regime actually created a new, enriched petit bourgeoisie from among Burnham's typically black supporters (Thomas 1983).

A critical problem thus remaining with the various attempts by the Caribbean Left at theorizing this race-class problematic resides in both their failure to pursue systematic empirical research, much of which could be drawn from Caribbean social science, and their neglect of the history of struggle reflected in the events that actually demonstrate political conflict. For it is in these events that both racial and class politics are directly played out. What is critically needed, therefore, is a careful historical and cross-national comparative analysis of the patterns of political conflicts throughout the region, as a basis for a better theory and understanding of the Caribbean race-class dynamics.

Patterns of Political Conflicts

To more fully understand the specific or interrelated roles of race, ethnicity and class in Caribbean conflict situations, it is important to look more closely at the patterns underlying the varieties of events that demonstrate active conflicts between groups in the political process. Earlier attempts at the explanation of conflict patterns and impact in the Caribbean have either concentrated on particular events, usually at the higher extremes of political violence such as rebellion or revolution (Bakan 1990; James 1963; Meeks 1993), or examined a series of events at the level of strikes and riots, with very little if any systematic analysis of the role of race and class in the process (Chase 1964; Henry 1972; Lewis 1939). What is needed is a more systematic focus on a series of events within specific historical periods, whether domestically or cross-nationally, ranging from non-violent to violent action, to discern underlying patterns of behaviour in the cases of class, ethnicity or race in the conflict process, and ultimately to relate that pattern to ongoing longer-term trends or "change processes" in the society as a whole (see McAdam and Sewell 2001).

Political conflict events in the Caribbean, particularly in the larger multiracial territories, reflect a very complex admixture of economic, political, cultural and ideological considerations which make it extremely difficult to separate or specify the relative significance and levels of involvement of either race or class in the process. If we go back in history to Caribbean slave revolts, for instance, we notice that although distinctive and mutually opposed racial categories (black/white) were involved, the demands for material and tangible rewards – land, wages, freedom and so on – on the part of the black slaves at the bottom of society became the basic stimuli for the events (Bakan 1990; Rodney

1981; Williams 1964). Similarly, the often violent protests of East Indian indentured servants against a predominantly white planter establishment and colonial state demanded the same type of economic or material benefits, which highlights the essential class nature of the indenture protests (see Jagan 1997; Rodney 1981).

However, at the ideological level, notions of race, ethnicity or religious convictions became inextricably bound up with the class conscious demands of the rebellious slaves (Bakan 1990; James 1963; Moore 1987). The idea of race in rebellion became much more pronounced in the post-emancipation period, particularly after the immigration of other races and ethnic groups (Portuguese, Chinese and East Indian) in the region. The most prominent examples in this respect were the series of anti-Portuguese riots in the urban centres of Guyana in the second half of the nineteenth century. In these riots, particularly the so-called Angel Gabriel Riots of 1856, the class-related project of escape from poverty on the part of the black ex-slave population coincided with an almost scapegoating frenzy of violent attacks against people of a particular ethnicity, the Portuguese, who became identified with business and wealth in an otherwise economically depressed society (Rodway 1946). The elevation of race at a conscious level in these periodic events led to a recognition of both the relative autonomy of race in relation to class and the difficulty of conceptually separating race from class in the Caribbean conflict process.

The Caribbean-wide labour unrest of the 1930s was also affected by racial and ethnic considerations, as in the case of mass opposition to the Italian invasion of Abyssinia (now Ethiopia) and the play upon religious and racial epithets by the populist leader Uriah Butler in his nationalistic mass appeals in Trinidad and Tobago during that decade of crisis (see Lewis 1939). The 1930s was, however, most significant for inspiring the development of labour and political organizations, as well as precipitating the massive region-wide decolonization struggle of the 1950s and 1960s. A major demand of the 1930s uprising was for the instituting of self-government, which inspired the political movements engaged in the later decolonization struggles. These decolonization struggles themselves represented a most volatile period of intricate race-class political confrontations and violent conflicts throughout the region. The political unrest of the later decolonization period was thought to have provided verification of the cultural pluralist thesis, which discerned the occurrence of interracial violence on the eve of the withdrawal of the white-dominant section (colonial authorities) and the succeeding struggle for dominance on the part of the two major racial-cultural sections (East Indians and Africans) in Guyana and Trinidad and Tobago. At the same time, however, the Marxist Left saw obvious class involvement in the form of British imperialist domination and its classic divide-and-rule policies, which were clearly aimed against the nationalist, Marxist and working-class political movements in the region (Chase 1964; Jagan 1997; Reno 1964; St Pierre 1999).

There is much substance on both sides of the argument. In Guyana, for example, racial and ethnic elements often took on a life of their own quite independently of the declared positions – the peaceful overtures and joint appeals – of the political leaders, organizations and movements, particularly during the political and ethnic violence of 1962–64. In this instance the relative autonomy of race and ethnicity was reflected in largely spontaneous roving ethnic gangs targeting individuals and property of rival ethnic groups for violent mutual destruction, with the disintegrating consequence of entrenching racially polarized communities throughout Guyana. However, these ethnicized realities obscured a deeper, bitter class conflict waged between the big business sector (represented most prominently by the Georgetown Chamber of Commerce), with much help from British and US imperialism, and the Leftist-inspired labour-political movement led by the Marxist PPP under Jagan. It was Jagan's attempts to tax capital and democratize the labour movement in Guyana that brought his movement into direct violent conflict with the economically dominant classes and the colonial authorities at the time. But even more important was the specific role of the middle classes, not only in fanning the antagonism between foreign capital and local labour in the interest of their succession to political leadership and control of state power, but in deliberately mobilizing numerically advantageous ethnic constituencies in their support, with the consequence of a zero-sum mutual-elimination contest between groups.

The postcolonial period also witnessed periodic political conflicts reflecting the relative autonomy of racial and ethnic formations throughout the region. However, it becomes difficult to eliminate class activism in the process since both the class and ethnic dimensions of the conflict groups tend to be mutually legitimizing and reinforcing in the process of political mobilization. The 1965 riots in Jamaica, involving blacks against Chinese populations, provide an example. For although racial confrontations in this particularly violent conflict might have been obvious, working-class elements in downtown Kingston suggested that the events represented "resentment against particular Chinese business men and anger towards the wealthier classes in general" (New World Associates 1965, 4). In similar terms, both the ethnic-racial and class dimensions were observable in several other major political conflict events in the region, including the 1970 Black Power uprising in Trinidad and Tobago; the continual "tribalistic" violence involving armed supporters of the two major political parties, the Jamaica Labour Party (JLP) and the PNP, in Jamaica throughout the 1970s and early 1980s; the periodic electoral violence in Guyana involving black supporters of the PNC and East Indian supporters of the PPP, lasting for about half a century and continuing even today; and the Black Muslim (Muslimeen) attempted coup in Trinidad and Tobago in 1990.

The 1962–64 period of ethno-political violence in Guyana laid a strong foundation for continuing racial divisiveness and acrimony into the 1990s, as exemplified during the Guyana elections of 1992 and 1997. These events were undoubtedly outstanding examples of the conditional dominance of the racial-ethnic variable, and perhaps of the temporary priority of race over class in explaining the political conflict process in Guyana. The recurrence of strong ethnic voting and conflict patterns in the 1992 and 1997 elections is a strong indication against the arguments of both the PNC and the WPA that the racial conflict situation had been resolved during the 1970s either because of the "cooperative" and law-and-order policies of the Burnhamite regime, as in the PNC argument, or because of the alienation and consequent alliances among the multiracial masses in response to Burnhamist oppressiveness, as in the WPA argument.

At the cross-national comparative level, the Caribbean experience reflects certain distinctive patterns and trends which could shed further light on the race-class political conflicts in these parts. The most prominent features of these comparative trends are, first, the overwhelming instances of foreign involvement in the events (Mars 1995a); and second, the relatively high frequency of events involving political-factional conflicts within the middle classes and reflected at the level of partisan rivalries for political power. Correspondingly, there is a relative rarity of conflicts that could be characterized as spontaneous mass or group events during the postcolonial period (Mars 1995b). As regards labour-derived conflicts which might involve working-class militancy, racial divisiveness is usually reflected in the frequent failure to organize solidarity strikes across the racial divide, as evidenced, for example, in the general strike led by the Guyana Agricultural Workers Union (GAWU) in 1977. Usually, spontaneous working-class political protests in the Caribbean are soon co-opted by middle-class political leadership in the pursuit of political power.

A third feature is that race-based or race-conscious participation seems to concentrate mainly at the higher, more violent levels of political conflicts, particularly those involving greater degrees of state intervention or repression. For example, in Guyana, relatively non-violent events such as in the 1955 split, the 1977 GAWU general strike and the 1989 anti-IMF labour unrest involved more ideological or economic demands, while the more violent events in the 1962–64 political upheaval, the 1969 Amerindian uprising and the 1992–2001 national elections, in addition to material demands, reflected near-genocidal ethnic violence in the first case, the threat of ethnic-geographic secession in the second and the deliberate targeting of ethnic-political rivals in the third. This observation should suggest that the race factor becomes instrumental mainly in the *escalation* of class conflict into political violence, rather than as the principal motive force determining the events.

A fourth observation, therefore, is that collaboration or alliances across race boundaries become more difficult to realize than collaboration across class boundaries. The failures of collaborative efforts between the WPA and the PPP, of the Patriotic Coalition for Democracy (PCD) or of the general strike led by the Federation of Independent Trade Unions of Guyana (FITUG) during the 1989 anti-IMF labour unrest were in large part because of racial suspicions and distrust among the participating organizations. By contrast, alliances or collaboration between middle-class elements (such as intellectuals and professionals) on the one hand and the labour movement reflecting working-class interests on the other have always been prevalent and pervasive in the Left experience – indeed, in the general political experience – throughout the Caribbean.

The evidence also suggests that women's role in the struggle was not necessarily unequal to that of men. From the times of slavery, women were in the forefront of resistance or rebellion against domination, whether as spies for or against the master classes or as direct participants in the resistance efforts. Nanny was a remarkable example of a female rebel leader of the Jamaican Maroons, and it is said that by 1800 women outnumbered men in Jamaican Maroon colonies established in opposition to planter-class domination in Caribbean slave society (Momsen 1996). The more modern periods also saw women in the forefront of anti-colonial struggle, as in the cases of Janet Jagan, Jessie Burnham, Winnifred Gaskin and Jane Phillips-Gay in Guyana during the 1950s and 1960s, and in anti-dictatorial struggles, in which the women's arms of both the PPP and the WPA in Guyana played a leading role. In 1998 and beyond, women's leadership in the sometimes spontaneous, sometimes PNC-led post-election protests against the PPP regime has been very prevalent in Guyana.

Reconceptualizing the Race-Class Problematic

The race-class problematic is concerned with establishing the extent to which racial and class configurations, separately or conjointly, influence the Caribbean conflict situation and the prospects of realizing ethno-political conflict resolution and meaningful democratic changes in the region. What needs explanation in peripheral capitalist societies is the extent to which racial and ethnic considerations intrude into the historical class project of the Left and consequently undermine efforts towards mass or working-class mobilization, particularly in multi-ethnic societies such as Guyana, Trinidad and Tobago, and Jamaica. The historical class project of the Left relates to the consistent conceptualization of struggle and change in terms of what are conceived to be the interests of the subordinate classes who constitute the basic constituencies for leftist political mobilization. For this reason also, Caribbean Left political organizations perceive themselves as having an organic relationship with the labour movement, despite fundamental contradictions within the Caribbean labour movement itself today.

An adequate theory of Caribbean race-class relations should take into consideration specific insights gleaned from systematic empirical research as exemplified in much of Caribbean social science, in leftist theoretical and practical struggles and in the history of political conflicts in the region. The objective here is to build from the observation or discernment of patterns of interaction between groups – particularly their propensities for both conflictual and co-operative interaction – a program for the incorporation of greater mass or popular involvement in developmental projects. The contributions of Caribbean social science to this issue pertain to its elevation of the race-ethnicity problem into prominence in the analysis of Caribbean political and social processes, in its attribution of some form of relative autonomy to these categories and, in more recent instances, relating the racial-ethnic impact to hegemonic forms of control and struggle.

We also learn from the history of Caribbean political conflicts that both class and racial forces are largely interdependent and interchangeable in the process; that conflict occasionally produces discernable opportunities for co-operation or resolution; that organized resistance or struggle often supersedes spontaneous eruptions, in which case co-optation of working-class struggle by middle-class leadership plays an important part; that class and racial-ethnic conflict situations become extremely vulnerable to external (foreign) manipulation and intervention; that racial and ethnic involvements become more obvious at higher, escalating levels of political violence; and that women's role in the conflict process is no less significant than that of men.

Largely ignored by previous theories of Caribbean race-class relations has been the necessity of specifying the contexts and conditions in which, as is usually asserted, racial-ethnic configurations become relatively independent of class forces. The observed interchangeability between race and class in Caribbean conflict processes should suggest, for example, that the almost absolute autonomy attributed to these categories by cultural pluralists and theorists of racial hegemonic formation in the United States seems unjustified. Unlike the situation in the United States, as asserted by racial formation theorists, those at the bottom of the class pyramid in the Caribbean, in the absence of middle-class leadership, do not necessarily struggle with a conscious or exclusively racial paradigm in view. Most groups usually deny or submerge their own racial agendas while attributing possible racism to the other, rival (particularly dominant) group. However, in this scenario the dominant group is more often perceived as oppressive for reasons going beyond racism itself, in which case economic and political forms of exclusion or oppression would seem to predominate in the levels of consciousness of these subordinate groups, as suggested by their specific political-demand profile.

Class relations in the Caribbean, therefore, cannot be construed simply as a function of race relations as might be probable in the case of the United States, as the racial formation theorists (Omi and Winant 1994; San Juan 1992) suggest. In the Caribbean, the conditions which tend to determine when racial configurations become predominant seem to relate to particular situations of crisis and levels of conflict in the system, that is, situations of perceived threat or danger to the existence, survival or development of particular racial-ethnic groups. Such crisis situations usually stem from drastic economic deprivations, escalating levels of political violence, ideological conflicts, foreign destabilizing pressures and middle-class factionalism; very rarely do they stem from purely or spontaneously racial or ethnic identity considerations.

The specific impact on the Caribbean conflict situation of both the foreign dimension and middle-class propensities has so far been inadequately theorized in the social science and leftist literature in the region. The basic undertheorized issue here is the specific intervention of foreign forces in the domestic conflict situation, not only in terms of divide-and-rule policies, but more specifically in the systematic subversion of the Left political forces in these parts (see Mars 1998). A more systematic and rigorous approach to understanding the nature of destabilization would be better able to specify the extent to which the class affinities between the foreign destabilizing forces and Caribbean middle-class political leadership maintain power through the use of ethnic-based (and other kinds of) support. Undoubtedly, the consolidation of middle-class rule represents a fundamental dimension of Caribbean politics. But unlike Ken Post's assumptions about the Jamaican middle classes (1978), which are echoed in the presuppositions of racial formation theorists in the United States, that race invariably represents the predominant means of articulating the hegemony of the ruling classes, it could be argued that in the Caribbean context, these racial, ethnic and colour considerations compete with often more salient interests such as economic property, wealth, and educational or intellectual capabilities in legitimizing the political dominance of the Caribbean middle classes.

It is necessary also that theories of race-class relations in the Caribbean context come to grips with the nature of political conflict and violence. The more fruitful approach here, for a proper understanding of the race-class problematic, involves focusing on a series of contentious "events" (such as strikes, riots, protest demonstrations and the like) which demonstrate inter-group or collective conflicts within a specified time frame (see McAdam and Sewell 2001). The idea here is to discern patterns and trends which generate insights into the variable or interlocking roles of race, ethnicity and class in the conflict process within Caribbean societies. This "events data analysis" is informative for the creation of theory that is relevant to the prospects of peaceful conflict resolution.

Approaches to successful resolution of ethno-political conflicts in the Caribbean must also proceed by way of interrogating several assumptions or hypotheses suggested in both the Caribbean social science and the leftist perspectives on this issue. Firstly, there is the fallacy of what could be termed the "spontaneity" assumption accepted by Rodney, the WPA, NJAC and most of the radical Left elements during the 1970s – that is, the conviction that the various ethnic elements of the Caribbean masses and working classes will automatically and spontaneously unite either because of their similar level of class consciousness or as a response to common oppression by either a domestic power elite or foreign capital penetration. It was this spontaneity assumption which led Rodney and the WPA to unconditionally reject any notions of including the autocratic Burnhamite ruling party, the PNC, within their proposed national programmes for resolution of the ethno-political conflict problem in Guyana, despite the fact that the PNC commanded the loyalty of the vast majority of the black Guyanese population. The WPA's conviction that the PNC was increasingly losing black support because of political oppression was found to be wishful thinking, particularly in the light of the continued ethnic polarization and violent conflicts in all of the 1992–2001 national elections in Guyana.

Two further contentions to be re-examined are what could be called the "coercive state" and the "withering away of race" hypotheses. The "coercive state" thesis, advocated by M.G. Smith and implemented by the Burnhamist PNC in Guyana, is based on the assumption that inter-ethnic unity and peace are fostered or maintained through the employment of force by a dominant cultural section or a coercive state apparatus. The "withering of race" hypothesis, advocated by classical Marxist intellectuals and political parties like the PPP and WPJ, assumes that ethnic divisiveness and conflicts will disappear when the perceived class conflict is finally resolved in the conquest of state power by the Left political forces and working classes. The overwhelming evidence, however, based on close observation of the history of Caribbean political conflicts, suggests that neither of these hypotheses can be fully substantiated. The "coercive state" thesis, for example, did not quite prevent violent ethno-political conflicts in Guyana, and might well have contributed to the escalation of conflicts into higher levels of intensity, as in the cases of the 1969 Amerindian uprising and the 1992–2001 black–East Indian electoral violence in Guyana. The "race withering" hypothesis still remains idealistic, as suggested in the very difficulty of organizing working-class struggles (for example, solidarity strikes) across ethnic lines in Guyana and Trinidad and Tobago. In any case, the coincidence of both class and ethnic forces in political conflicts in the Caribbean suggests that, if adequate conflict resolution is to be realized, the one cannot satisfactorily be addressed in total isolation from the other.

In general, the Caribbean Left has failed to grasp the complexities of transformative politics, which implies not simply struggle for state power – which has been tremendously costly to the Left in the past – but, more important, hegemonic struggle on the part of a mass-based multi-ethnic coalition of forces. Hegemonic struggle here entails persistent efforts to institutionalize and disseminate a Left agenda which focuses on democratic inclusiveness and economic redistribution and a mass-based, practically oriented political education program geared to reach the widest cross-section of the population, particularly those who have been hitherto marginalized or excluded from the political process. For the Caribbean Left, exclusive preoccupation with the conquest of centralized state power has led largely to neglect of mass work, including campaigning in opposition-controlled constituencies – with the consequence of increasing its already precarious marginalization and isolation in relation to the Caribbean masses and subordinate classes. In short, a reconstructed theory should look beyond vanguardist notions of organized struggle, which give a fixed privileged position of leadership to a particular domestic class or group, towards giving greater priority to mass-based, internationally oriented political alliances and hegemonic, as distinct from partisan, power struggle.

It should be recognized that, in the light of the increasing economic globalization and international hegemonic control by dominant capitalist powers, real political power resides beyond the immediate reaches of the Caribbean state itself, while at the same time control of the state institutions remains confined to a limited (professional-commercial) sector of the middle classes. For this reason, state or political power remains outside the immediate reaches of the Caribbean working and subordinate classes. It is also within the hegemonic struggle that a gender-inclusive strategy, providing equal space for the always reliable initiative of Caribbean women in class politics, should be facilitated. To be addressed here also is how to resolve the contradiction whereby the frequency and high proportion of women's participation in political protests and demonstrations are not similarly reflected at pivotal leadership levels, whether of political parties or of the Caribbean state.

An adequate race-class theory also facilitates a thoroughgoing understanding of the relationship between conflict, violence and co-operation as necessary for ethno-political conflict resolution. The major issue for conflict resolution is the observation that, in addition to inequitable distribution of economic and political resources, much of Caribbean political conflict stems from middle-class factionalism and instability. Perhaps the most feasible approach to conflict resolution in the Caribbean context, therefore, is middle-class or state initiative in the development of new institutional arrangements which facilitate constructive mediation and negotiations between mutually opposed ethno-political formations. Such political interventions should be aimed at bridging racial or ethnic divisions, or at rewarding interracial co-operation among the masses and subordinate classes throughout the region.

The modification or transformation of existing state forms might also be necessary for the reduction of ethnic tensions and the promotion of sustainable interracial projects, particularly within the working and subordinate classes. Perhaps the best form the modified state should take is one involving hegemonic control by multiracial mass-based alliances, coupled with a more decentralized democratic process of political participation and decision making. The concept of multiple "people's assemblies" advocated by most of the radicalized Left in the Caribbean during the 1970s can be readily accommodated within this transformed state concept. Also, the Caribbean Left should pay more attention to social research and theory construction based on their own experiences of struggle. It is on this foundation that they are better able to avoid the kind of total dependence on decontextualized ideological preoccupations which helped to decapitate the New Jewel Movement in Grenada, along with the socialist experiments throughout the Caribbean, during the 1980s.

Conclusion

Clarifying the Caribbean race-class problematic is critical for the advancement of leftist or transformative political theory and projects in the region. A study of this issue in the context of historical and comparative patterns of political conflicts grounds leftist political theory in the concrete reality of Caribbean conditions. This approach is fundamental to a critical aspect of the Caribbean Left agenda: what has been called "working-class unity and democracy". The focus here, therefore, is more on the participatory aspect of the Caribbean Left agenda, to complement or reinforce the redistributive aspect. The Caribbean experience reveals that although the class issue is consistently significant, it is neither invariably dominant nor uniform in character or impact. At critical historical moments – usually moments of intense economic insecurities and political conflicts – racial, ethnic or tribalistic activism intrudes either to escalate middle-class factional conflicts into higher levels of mass political violence or to stymie inter-class alliance strategies, mainly by fragmenting the subordinate classes in multiracial Caribbean societies such as Guyana, Trinidad and Tobago, and Jamaica.

The Caribbean experience suggests that several of the traditional presumptions about necessary leftist strategies for political power and revolutionary transformation in multiracial societies can no longer be taken for granted – assumptions such as that the working and subordinate classes are inherently cohesive and revolutionary; that political organization and mass mobilization always increase the cohesiveness and capability of movements towards change; that long-standing popular discontent is sufficient to spontaneously propel mass mobilization and unity; that ignoring the race issue necessarily increases the potential for easy mobilization of the working classes; or that political mobilization of the masses or subordinate classes is sufficient to eventually resolve the racial or ethno-political problem.

The principal lessons from observation of the actual conflict situation in the Caribbean relate not only to the level of theory construction, but equally to leftist struggles for power and change and to the prospects for ethno-political conflict resolution. For theory construction, we are forced to come to grips with a revised conceptualization of the role of class or race in the spectrum of power struggles, in which case a conflation of the two into singular units of analysis, or "historic blocs" (preferably called "ethno-political units"), would seem more compelling as agency in the conflict process than either class or race considered separately. In terms of leftist struggles, we learn that race or ethnicity becomes significant as an agent mostly in the escalation of rather than in the precipitation of political conflict and violence in Caribbean societies. As regards conflict resolution, we understand that since most divisive conflicts stem directly from middle-class factional politics, successful conflict resolution is best approached by a more inclusive strategy, to facilitate and enhance the involvement of the working classes and women in the political leadership structures and decision-making processes throughout the region.

It is on looking closely at patterns of political conflict in historical and comparative perspective that we develop a clearer understanding of the international and middle-class pressures on working-class unity. Mainly because of these external pressures, the idea of working-class unity, although pivotal to the overall Left agenda, tends to be illusive, particularly because of the fragmentation (ethnic and otherwise) of the working classes that attends economic globalization processes. In addition, distortions in the increasingly globalized capitalist economy and labour market, resulting particularly in the numerical reduction of permanent labour forces and the reduction in scope of labour recruitment and mobilization, also contribute significantly to the problem. For this reason it would appear that under the assault of capitalist globalization, commitment to the idea of working-class unity is simply ideological or even mythical.

But far from being merely ideological or mythical, the idea of working-class unity is rooted in the practical and material considerations of human survival, which is most significant today in the globalized world of increasing economic inequality both within and between nations. The idea of working-class unity assumes its utility and practicality in the very struggle towards its realization; such working-class unity can contribute to the resolution of mutually destructive conflicts and violence, and, to that extent at least, further the mass democratization process in divided societies like those in the Caribbean.

References

Ambursley, Fitzroy, and Anthony Cohen, eds. 1983. *Crisis in the Caribbean.* New York: Monthly Review.
Anderson, Perry. 1998. "A Sense of the Left". *New Left Review,* no. 231: 73–81.
Bakan, Abigail. 1990. *Ideology and Class Conflict in Jamaica.* Montreal and Kingston: McGill-Queens University Press.
Beckford, George. 1972. *Persistent Poverty.* London: Oxford University Press.
Beckford, George, and Michael Witter. 1980. *Small Garden . . . Bitter Weed: Struggle and Change in Jamaica.* London: Zed Press.
Bobbio, Norberto. 1996. *Left and Right: The Significance of a Political Distinction.* Chicago: University of Chicago Press.
———. 1998. "At the Beginning of History". *New Left Review,* no. 231: 82–90.
Bocock, Robert. 1986. *Hegemony.* New York: Tavistock.
Braithwaite, Lloyd. 1960. "Social Stratification and Cultural Pluralism". In *Social and Cultural Pluralism in the Caribbean,* edited by Vera Rubin. *Annals of the New York Academy of Sciences* 83: 816–36.
British Guiana Constitutional Commission. 1954. *Report of the British Guiana Constitutional Commission.* London: Colonial Office.
Cabral, Amilcar. 1970. *Revolution in Guinea: Selected Texts.* New York: Monthly Review.
———. 1973. *Return to the Source: Selected Speeches.* New York: Monthly Review.
Chase, Ashton. 1964. *A History of Trade Unionism in Guyana.* Georgetown, Guyana: New Guyana Company.
Cruse, Harold. 1984. *The Crisis of the Negro Intellectual.* New York: Quill.
Despres, Leo. 1967. *Cultural Pluralism and Nationalist Politics in British Guiana.* Chicago: Rand McNally.
Fanon, Frantz. 1964. *The Wretched of the Earth.* Translated by Constance Farrington. Middlesex: Penguin.

Giddens, Anthony. 1994. *Beyond Left and Right: The Future of Radical Politics*. Stanford, Conn.: Stanford University Press.

Gilroy. Paul. 1993. *The Black Atlantic: Modernity and Double Consciousness*. Cambridge: Harvard University Press.

Gramsci, Antonio. 1978. *Prison Notebooks*. Translated by Joseph A. Buttigieg and Antonio Callari. New York: International Publishers.

Henry, Zin. 1972. *Labour Relations and Industrial Conflict in Commonwealth Caribbean Countries*. Port of Spain, Trinidad: Columbus Publishers.

Jacobs, Richard, and Ian Jacobs. 1980. *Grenada: The Route to Revolution*. Havana: Casa de las Americas.

Jagan, Cheddi. 1997. *The West on Trial*. London: Hansib.

James, C.L.R. 1962. *Party Politics in the West Indies*. Port of Spain, Trinidad: Vedic Enterprises.

———. 1963. *The Black Jacobins*. New York: Random House.

———. 1996. *Special Delivery: The Letters of C.L.R. James to Constance Webb, 1939–48*. Edited by Anna Grimshaw. Oxford: Blackwell.

Kuper, Leo. 1971a. "Political Change in Plural Societies: Problems in Racial Pluralism". *International Social Science Journal* 23: 594–607.

———. 1971b. "Theories of Revolution in Race Relations". *Comparative Studies in Society and History* 13, no. 1: 87–107.

Kwayana, Eusi. 1988. "The Indo-Guyanese Contribution to Social Change". Paper presented at the Genesis of a Nation Activity, Georgetown, Guyana, May.

Lewis, Arthur. 1939. *Labour in the West Indies: The Birth of a Workers Movement*. London: Fabian Society.

Marable, Manning. 1987. *African and Caribbean Politics*. London: Verso.

Mars, Perry. 1995a. "Foreign Influence, Political Conflicts and Conflict Resolution in the Caribbean". *Journal of Peace Research* 32: 437–52.

———. 1995b. "State Intervention and Ethnic Conflict Resolution: Guyana and the Caribbean Experience". *Comparative Politics* 27: 167–86.

———. 1998. *Ideology and Change: The Transformation of the Caribbean Left*. Detroit, Mich.: Wayne State University Press.

McAdam, Doug, and William H. Sewell, Jr. 2001. "It's about Time: Temporality in the Study of Social Movements and Revolution". In *Silence and Voice in the Study of Contentious Politics*, edited by Ronald R. Aminzade et al., 89–125. Cambridge: Cambridge University Press.

McAffee, Cathy. 1991. *Storm Signals*. Boston: South End.

Meeks, Brian. 1993. *Caribbean Revolutions and Revolutionary Theory: An Assessment of Cuba, Nicaragua, and Grenada*. London: Macmillan.

Mills, Charles W. 1987. "Race and Class: Conflicting or Reconcilable Paradigms?" *Social and Economic Studies* 36, no. 2: 69–108.

Momsen, Janet. 1996. "Gender Roles in Caribbean Agricultural Labour". In *Caribbean Freedom: Economy and Society from Emancipation to the Present*, edited by Hilary Beckles and Verene Shepherd, 216–24. Kingston, Jamaica: Ian Randle.

Moody, Kim. 1997. *Workers in a Lean World: Unions in the International Economy.* London: Verso.

Moore, Brian L. 1987. *Race, Power and Social Segmentation in Colonial Society: Guyana after Slavery, 1838–1891.* Philadelphia: Gordon and Breach.

Munroe, Trevor. 1990. *Jamaican Politics: A Marxist Perspective.* Kingston, Jamaica: Heinemann.

National Joint Action Committee (NJAC). 1981. *An Analysis of the Economic System.* Port of Spain, Trinidad: NJAC.

New World Associates. 1965. "Disturbances in Kingston". *New World Fortnightly,* no. 24 (1 October).

Omi, Michael, and Howard Winant. 1994. *Racial Formation in the United States.* New York: Routledge.

Petras, James, and Henry Veltmeyer. 2001. *Globalization Unmasked: Imperialism in the Twenty-first Century.* London: Zed Books.

Post, Ken. 1978. *Arise Ye Starvelings.* The Hague: Martinus Nijhoff.

Reno, Philip. 1964. *The Ordeal of British Guiana.* New York: Monthly Review.

Rodney, Walter. 1970. *Groundings with My Brothers.* London: Bogle-L'Ouverture.

———. 1979. *People's Power: No Dictator.* (Mimeograph). Georgetown: n.p.

———. 1981. *A History of the Guyanese Working People.* Baltimore: Johns Hopkins University Press.

Rodway, James A. 1946. *History of British Guiana.* 3 vols. Georgetown, Guyana: J. Thompson.

San Juan, E., Jr. 1992. *Racial Formations/Critical Transformations: Articulations of Power in Ethnic and Racial Studies in the United States.* New Jersey: Humanities Press.

Smith, M.G. 1960. "Social and Cultural Pluralism". In *Social and Cultural Pluralism in the Caribbean,* edited by Vera Rubin. *Annals of the New York Academy of Sciences* 83: 1–15.

———. 1965. *The Plural Society in the British West Indies.* Berkeley: University of California Press.

Smith, Raymond T. 1962. *British Guiana.* London: Oxford University Press.

Stone, Carl. 1972. *Class, Race, and Political Behaviour in Urban Jamaica*. Mona, Jamaica: Institute of Social and Economic Research.
St Pierre, Maurice. 1999. *Anatomy of Resistance: Anti-Colonialism in Guyana, 1923–1966*. London: Macmillan.
Thomas, Caroline. 2000. *Global Governance, Development and Human Security*. London: Pluto Press; Kingston, Jamaica: Arawak.
Thomas, Clive Y. 1983. "State Capitalism in Guyana: An Assessment of Burnham's Co-operative Socialist Republic". In *Crisis in the Caribbean*, edited by Fitzroy Ambursley and Anthony Cohen, 27–48. New York: Monthly Review.
———. 1988. *The Poor and the Powerless*. New York: Monthly Review.
Tillery, Tyrone. 1992. *Claude McKay: A Black Poet's Struggle for Identity*. Amherst: University of Massachusetts Press.
Williams, Eric. 1964. *British Historians and the West Indies*. Port of Spain, Trinidad: PNM.
Working People's Alliance (WPA). 1992. *Elections Manifesto*. Georgetown, Guyana: Working People's Alliance.

> # [4]

Cultural Identity versus Political Identity in the French West Indies

Jacky Dahomay

Introduction

The question of identity, as raised by democratic modernity, is being critically reassessed today. Suffice it to quote the names of Paul Ricoeur, John Rawls, Jürgen Habermas, Charles Taylor, Michael Walzer and many others who have contributed to this debate. I would like to examine the relationship between cultural identity and political identity through one particular exemplary historical case, that of the French-speaking West Indian societies. Philosophical thought is always situated, and this "situation", far from being an epistemological obstacle, can have a heuristic function. The following questioning is therefore that of a West Indian who happens to be a French citizen and whose analysis stems from the striking uniqueness of the societies which came into being at the dawn of modern times in the slave-holding colonies of America, as if clocks had been set at zero (to quote Claude Lévi-Strauss) and we had witnessed the birth of a culture.

A Culture of Survival

Let us take what Edouard Glissant names "le transbord" of the African-born peoples over here as a starting point. I use that word because there was no core continuity between, on the one hand, the previous cultural and ethnic identities which had defined the living environment and all the symbolic forms that established the world for the Africans and, on the other hand, their plight as slaves in America. Of course, the West did not invent slavery, but while in ancient and traditional slavery the cultural divide between master and slave was not total, in modern-day slavery, as it became established in the American colonies, the acculturation was almost complete. Not only did the Africans find themselves in situations of extreme alienation and inequality, their status that of mere commodities, but they were to go through a process of de-Africanization – creolization, so to speak – as a new Weltanschauung was forced on them.

This loss of identity is all the more tragic since everything was done to prevent the building of a common world with other slaves, as the colonists regrouped (more by circumstances than by choice) Africans of various ethnic origins who did not speak the same native languages. As chattels, the slaves were not entitled to a cultural identity, that is, a collective identity, and even less to a common world that could be fashioned into a political space. Should they, individually, seek to make sense out of their new lives, recreate some symbolism in relation to the memory of their lost community, they would be doomed thereby to a deep solitude, to the futility of individual strategies that could result only in despair or death. It is a case of the atomization of the individual such as history had never produced prior to slavery. The slave plantations, amid fledging modernity, were the first to experiment with "la vie nue", as Agamben (1997) calls it.[1] Undoubtedly, this system is an early indication of what the concentration camps were to be.

We must take this into account if we are to grasp the peculiarities of the cultures that emerged then and that still affect our relationship with culture and politics today. The majority of slaves had no real choice but to cope with their new plight, to create a new meaningful world with a new set of symbolic values. We may note that death – as Hegel had clearly understood – remained the essential reference for the slaves, and in case they forgot it, the master was there to remind them constantly with terrifying methods. That was how a culture of survival was born. It was no longer a time-honoured culture based on age-old traditions, even if some elements had been borrowed from the various original cultures; the slaves had to come up with new symbolic forms that would allow them to survive. This they could accomplish only within an all-encompassing social framework (including the simplest techniques of production, which were imposed on them by the master) over which they had little control. They had access neither to the public space nor to what could be called the civil society. They did not even have control over primary functions such as parenthood or family, since their partners and children did not belong to them. Their culture, as a culture of survival, had to be one of minimal existence, and any attempt at building an identity culminating in cosmogony was difficult if not impossible.

The Birth of *Créolité*

The notion of "culture of survival" was the root element in the genesis of *créolité* ("creoleness"), for the slaves could survive only by becoming creolized. The fact is that the gradual creolization of blacks in the Caribbean was to mean going beyond the early culture of survival. Yet Creole culture was forever, despite its evolution, to bear the mark of this initial stage of social restructuring. We will see, in reference to Gérard Barthélémy's views (1996), how in Haiti the so-called *bossale* culture has resisted the Creole culture, while in the French West Indies, because of the belated abolition of slavery, *créolité* has prevailed. But first I will try to point out the essential features of this original Creole culture.

For my purpose, I will leave aside the characteristic elements of this culture – kinship and sexuality, the cult of the dead, religion and the development of the Creole language, and so on (see, for example, André 1987) – which have already been highlighted by Caribbean anthropology. What I am mainly interested in here is the relationship with political identity, and what is relevant to a common world view. What characterizes the culture developed by blacks in the Caribbean during slavery is that it is pre-modern, not quite archaic but still reactive and elaborated in a space ruled by politics. It is a different context from that of the Greeks, where the *polis* had evolved from a tribal culture as well as from a new approach to the quest for meaning in public politics. Creole culture had to grow up against an imperial Western culture which was itself being modernized and weaned from the traditional theological and political foundations of Europe. The Americas had already witnessed a kind of radicalization of modernity, which itself probably affected the revolutionary events that shook Europe in the late eighteenth century (the American Revolution being a case in point). If the logic of the imperial Western culture was to disrupt the world of the colonized, the logic of the early Creole culture was to re-create coherence in opposition to this process of disruption. Therefore, unlike other traditional cultures, *créolité* has been essentially polemic.

Meanwhile, the white slavemaster's culture developed a public space far removed from the habitual forms of monarchical legitimacy. But the political identity among slavemasters was never to match the civil religion associated with the French revolutionists, and the colonists were affected quite differently by the French Revolution, as suggested by C.L.R. James: "The coarse San Domingo whites had no spark of that exalted sentiment which drove the revolutionary bourgeoisie elsewhere to dignify its seizure of power with the Declaration of Independence or the Rights of Man" (1983, 58). What the masters really wanted was a minimal civil identity that would guarantee their rights and security, and the continuation of slavery through denying blacks any civil equality or participation in public life. As for the mulattos, they were more interested in securing equality with the whites for themselves than in equality for all.

Most traditional cultures function within the framework of a comprehensive world view. Inside these cultures, social ties are based on a coherent interpretation of reality that precedes politics. At the same time, these cultures often develop identity concepts and practices that are compatible with the emergence of a public space. In this respect, unfortunately, Creole cultures are concerned only with partial identities. As Gérard Barthélemy points out, such cultures are born of a crisis in the organization of society; they appear because "ni la famille, ni le village, ni le clan, ni l'Etat n'était en mesure, dans un premier temps, d'apporter de cadre social indispensable" (1996, 187). Maybe the success of "rhythm" in Afro-American cultures can be accounted for through this production of partial identities; this is Barthélemy's point when he asserts that rhythm generates "des phénomènes d'accord et de simultanéité sans communication véritable" and leads to "des phénomènes de groupes sans structures collectives" (p. 187). Thus, the original Creole culture results from dysfunctional social ties in its definition both of a community identity and of a political identity. This is what caused me to name it a "tragic culture", to the extent that the tragic, as Yves Barel says (1987), results from the tension between traditional communitarian identities and a new civic identity required by the emerging *polis*. By the same token, Creole culture remains a culture open to both assimilation and archaic introversion.

In its assimilationist version, Creole culture can be grafted onto modern forms of republican political identity, while in its archaistic version it may parasitize any attempt at grounding social ties in the public space. But in either version, Creole culture is forced to feed on and be determined by what it is not. Within the framework of Creole culture, *I* is bound to be *another person*, neither a being determined by a solid community nor an actor required by the public space. That is why the quest for identity in the West Indies has been dramatic and still raises issues totally unknown to the history of human societies.

There remains the need to show how, originating in this cultural framework, the process of creolization was to reach down to our times and render the cultural identity–political identity relationship extremely complex. To that end I will compare the evolution of Haiti with that of the French West Indies.

The Impact of the French Revolution in Haiti

The key event that was to alter the evolution of francophone Caribbean societies was undoubtedly the French Revolution. In its deepest finality, it accomplished the demise of the former theological and political foundation and helped set up the republican public space. What characterized the French revolutionists was their enthusiasm, akin to a civil or a republican religion, which sought to recapture the very ethos of ancient civility and reintroduce it into modernity. The revolution was also an attempt at disembodying the power structure and de-institutionalizing social ties; in this respect, it has been claimed that by sweeping away all forms of social foundation, the revolutionists were ushering in the mask of death and the strategies of the Terror. However, after many vicissitudes, French society managed to establish and then strengthen the republic, owing to an (at least theoretical) separation between cultural identity and political identity, the former being pushed into the private sphere while the latter summoned the individual to become an active subject in the public sphere.

The West Indian revolutionists did not act upon similar impulses. This is what Alejo Carpentier conveys when he has Victor Hugo say, as he is sailing to the isles, "la Révolution devient plus schématique et plus simple, à mesure qu'on s'éloigne de la France" (cited in Perotin-Dumont 1985, 121). The various populations present felt committed in very different ways to the new process. After the abolition of slavery by Léger Félicité Sonthonax in 1793, then by the Convention of 1794, a period of upheaval began that ended with Napoleon's re-establishment of slavery in Guadeloupe in 1802 and Haiti's independence in 1804.

In Haiti we have to distinguish between the African-born *bossale* blacks and the colony-born mulattos, or black Creoles. While the Creoles (some, like Toussaint l'Ouverture, also slave owners) were to seize power and try to reproduce the plantation system, the *bossale* blacks, who were former slaves and overwhelmingly in the majority, were to form the Haitian peasantry. But they also were to rebuild a cultural identity which Barthélémy (1996) shows to have a clearly archaic underpinning, a strong egalitarian impulse, the permanent rejection of all forms of accumulation – in a word, all that makes up the "counter-plantation", as the Haitian sociologist Jean Casimir (1991) puts it – a definitely anti-capitalist and anti-modern culture with all the features of those societies that, as Pierre Clastres (1974) suggests, deny the state.

This process led to a deep division between the minority Creole elite and the peasantry. The former became the ruling class and set up a system of internal colonial domination, the popular classes allowing them to hold power on the condition that they could continue to enjoy an "archaistic" lifestyle abounding in strategies of non-development. It was as if there were two systems, the *bossale* one and the Creole one – so much so that even today, the visitor is struck by the social apartheid that exists in Haiti and that causes social ties to be very fragile. Nonetheless, the coherence underlying the two systems, which I think Barthélémy pays little attention to, has not been sufficiently underlined.

If we accept that the Haitian peasantry developed strategies of cultural identity based on an anti-state model, we still need to point out that this strategy, unlike what happened in archaic societies, evolved within a nation state, and therefore inside a space ruled by politics. In this case, the state had to, as it were, govern a society that denied the state, the latter being closer to a colonial state than to a state in charge of a civil society (which in fact supposedly allows for a diversity of private cultural identities but recognizes in return the state's right to rule a public space). This, conversely, accounts for the idiosyncrasies of the Haitian state, which has continually demonstrated little concern for the *res publica* and whose only relatively stable institution has always been the army, a reality that has precluded the building of a common world. It appears that the Haitian state, by relying on a culture of survival, has made death its main instrument of power. Such is, in my view, the essence of Macoutism, as Haitian totalitarianism is called.

As paradoxical as it may seem, while of all Caribbean and even Third World countries, Haiti is the one with the most original past, the most glorious history of routing out slavery, it is actually a nation in which political identity and the public and civic spaces are particularly weak, civil society is hardly emerging and cultural identities, although they seem strong, have actually been exhausting themselves trying to reduce the quest for identity to an almost archaic communitarianism. Besides, the latter does not have the solidity of a tribal or ethnic identity; Haitian sociologist Franklin Midy calling it "une identité quasi-ethnique". Be that as it may, for the past ten years the system has been going through a crisis, mainly because the identity based on the peasant community has proven obsolete and the popular classes have now been trying to make new sense of the political space, demanding democracy and the rule of law.

The Specificity of the French West Indies

The French Antilles have followed a quite different path from that of Haiti. Though Napoleon's plans to re-establish slavery in Guadeloupe were carried out successfully, it remains difficult to comprehend this success. Apparently, the black troops led by Louis Delgrès and Jean Ignace waged in vain a classic war against those of Antoine Richepanse, while Jacques Dessalines's army in Haiti (Santo Domingo) owed its triumph to the guerrilla tactics of the *bossale* peasants, who had had previous experience of Dessalines's repressive measures. Why Delgrès and Ignace's troops did not receive the same popular support in Guadeloupe is still a mystery. But, no doubt, it can be partly explained by the cultural distance which separated and isolated a man like Delgrès, motivated by revolutionary faith and the ideals of the Enlightenment, from a peasant mass of former slaves who, although they were more creolized than those of Haiti, proved unable to display the kind of resilience and readiness to fight that is normally required for revolutionary action.

Despite the criticism directed at me by historian Florence Gauthier (1997), I still firmly believe that the vast majority of the Haitian peasant masses were not motivated by the ideals of the Enlightenment.[2] They were fighting for liberation, indeed, but not for liberty. Liberty, as explained by Hannah Arendt in her *Essay on Revolution* (1963), requires public institutions and can be conquered only through public action in the public space. The Haitian masses were longing for a way out of slavery and towards liberation, but this longing did not correspond to an explicit demand for a public space and democratic public institutions. This is probably the reason that the Haitian Declaration of Independence, unlike the French and American ones, contains no references to "the Rights of Man and Citizen", and the regime established in 1804, whether as an empire under Dessalines or as a kingdom under Henri Christophe, was a republic only in name.

It remains that, following this failure of the black troops in Guadeloupe, the second high point in the history of the French West Indies was 1848, the date of the second abolition of slavery. From then on, the French islands were to implement a logic that still affects today's society. New strains were added to Creole identity (for example, the Hindu culture), and a civil society of sorts began to appear with the launching of numerous associations related to dancing, of benefit societies and above all of trade unions. The surprising thing is that this cultural identity never took the direction of a quest for nationalist political identity, whereas in many other colonized countries the movements fighting for cultural identity did often turn into political organizations leading to national independence. It was not until the 1960s that an independence movement took root here in the French West Indies, and it ended, as we all know, in failure. On the contrary, right after 1948, the claim for citizenship took the form of a demand for republican assimilation to metropolitan France, which resulted in the granting of departmental status in 1946.

Creole Identity

My hypothesis is that this specificity in the history of the French West Indies results from the fact that the pre-colonial societies of Africa and Asia had experienced socially comprehensive forms of cultural identities; like West Indian societies, they developed strategies of cultural identities which were hard put to meaningfully define the totality of experience. This is not simply because we are dealing here with what Edouard Glissant calls an "identité rhizome" (1981). It is true that Creole cultures have displayed a great ability to assimilate new, multifarious contributions, but what matters most is that Creole cultures can use numerous – even contradictory – strategies in the social sphere. Creole cultures have been forever trying to express the impossibility of building social ties, as conveyed by sayings like "Niggers' schemes are bound to fail" or "Even back in Africa niggers already hated niggers." At the same time, concrete actions seek to fit into the political sphere. This divorce between cultural identity and political identity has caused Haiti to become a "non-republic", and it has also prevented the French West Indies from establishing an independent republic, leading them therefore to seek integration into the French Republic.

In fact, Creole identity cannot fall back on any one specific institution, be it the church or the state, for historical reasons that I have already delineated. From the very beginning, Creole identity evolved by circumventing institutions, leaving it to the Other to set up all institutions and hierarchies, in other words, all the collective structures that make the public space possible. Such is the cornerstone of assimilation.

On the whole, Creole identities are neither simply archaic nor purely narrative. Within them, concepts of good and evil and other values have not been transmitted by tradition but have been reinterpreted, reconstructed in record time. They are quasi-reflexive or quasi-reconstructive identities. They are not produced by an actor involved in the political space and therefore cannot be assimilated to political or pre-political identities – hence their originality. Though fathered by modernity, there is something anti-modern (akin to Freudian "fusion", almost holistic) even postmodern, about them. We could say they are "partial identities", since they find it so difficult to elaborate a coherent view of society and the cosmos. Myth is noticeably absent from these cultures. They are therefore, by necessity, open, in as much as they take their cue mostly from the Other, from the colonizer's culture (although the latter had not yet, during slavery, been unified into a common political space). Psychologists agree that paranoia is, so to speak, the distinguishing feature of our cultures, in which individuals function in accordance with the persecution principle and not the guilt principle. It must be added that because of their openness, though they are evolving outside politics and the public space, these cultures question politics and the meaning of the social order, which are reliable indicators of their future evolutions.

The Evolution of Creole Cultures

Creole cultures (Haitian culture less than the others) have progressively evolved an awareness of universality. In fact, the questions that slaves had to answer concerned their accession to the order of humanity. In other words, it was a questioning of their generic identity. Edouard Glissant, in *Le Discours antillais,* severely criticizes the "ideal repúblician", the "légalité repúblicain" and the "école laïque et obligatoire" as being inculcated ideals. He writes that "l'idéal repúblicain est une idéologie de dissolution dans l'autre" (1981, 141 and 154). In view of their historical conditions, the slaves themselves were bound to raise the issue of the universal. This was not imposed from outside but sprang from an ineluctable logic – in a word, that of modernity – in the sense that the logic of recognition can be enacted only within the dimension of universality. The result is that Creole cultures have also become cultures – seeking an impossible synthesis – that are beset by identity crises.

Nowhere in the history of humanity has identity been so dramatically staged. Frantz Fanon used the phrase "culture d'alienation", meaning that fragmentation and schizophrenia characterize it. Glissant was undoubtedly the first to insist on the exceptional originality of the cultures reconstituted in the American space at the time of colonization. While Aimé Césaire, the Negritude poet, expressed the black people's painful quest for universal humanity, Glissant was to make a return to the extremely peculiar circumstances of West Indian identity formation. In this regard, Glissant makes a distinction between what he calls "cultures ataviques" (such as Islam and Christianity) – that is, cultures in which filial bonds, legitimacy, territory obsession and the will to conquer are prevalent – and "cultures composite" (like those of the Creole societies of America); the latter do not generate "une Genèse (adoptant les mythes de création venus d'ailleurs), et cela pour la raison que leur origine est évidemment d'ordre historique et non mythique" (Glissant 1997, 36). Hence, when speaking of "Creole cultures", it is necessary, according to Glissant, to use the word Creole in its fullest sense: a mode of cultural reconstruction absolutely original in the history of humanity, which Glissant calls *créolisation* in his *Traité du tout-monde:* "La créolisation est la mise en contact de plusieurs cultures ou au moins de plusieurs éléments de cultures distinctes, dans un endroit du monde, avec pour résultat une donnée nouvelle, totalement imprévisible par rapport à la somme ou à la simple synthèse de ces éléments" (1997, 37). Breaking away from a multiculturalist problematics, Glissant claims to bypass the paradoxes of modern identity politics by insisting that creolization is the process in which identity is not the "root", but the "rhizome", in which Creole identity does not necessitate a certain "territory", but simply the land, thus prefiguring the world of tomorrow, inhabited by a multifaceted, diverse humanity that will accept itself as such and live in accordance with a new poetics of relation.

Seductive though it may be, Glissant's theory is far from satisfactory. When one considers the different expressions of *malaise antillais*, whether through poetry (Negritude, *créolité*) or political nationalism, one realizes their failure to synthesize the three dimensions of identity: cultural identity, political identity and universality. This is what I would like to discuss; this is what makes the quest for political and administrative status in the West Indies extremely complex.

From Cultural Identity to Political Status

What is remarkable in the case of the French West Indies is that no theory or ideology of cultural identity has ever succeeded in producing a coherent political agenda or acted as a catalyst to set off the political practices necessary to bring about effective transformations in the present political status of these countries. It is also remarkable that the school of thought that first took the problem of cultural identity into consideration, Césaire's Negritude movement, did so by championing assimilation. Césaire was one of the principal originators of the 1946

Law of Assimilation. His later evolution, as deputy and mayor of Fort-de-France, towards a demand for self-government reflected more a position of principle than the implementation of political practices really aimed at that goal. The various nationalist movements which met with some success here and there, especially in Guadeloupe, did manage to reformulate the question of cultural identity but were unable to convince the majority of the populations of the French overseas departments to decide to leave the French Republic. Today, the most widely accepted concepts of identity politics, to be found notably in artistic and literary circles, are based on Glissant's notions of *créolité* and are defended by such writers as Patrick Chamoiseau and Raphaël Confiant. However, one must observe that even if the ideology of *créolité* poses, with Glissant, the problem of cultural identity in relevant and renewed terms, it too has failed to put forth a coherent political project for the future of Guadeloupe, Martinique and French Guiana. How can one explain this difficult and complex articulation between political identity and cultural identity in our regions?

The error on the part of the nationalist movements is twofold: on the one hand, nationalists confuse cultural identity with political identity, which one may argue is the problem with nationalism in general. On the other hand, if, in other cases, nationalist projects (for example, in Algeria) effectively led their colonized populations to independence, the mistake of French West Indian independence movements has been to underestimate the attachment their fellow citizens have to their status as French citizens. Césaire has been by far the most successful politically because he led his likes out of the colonial framework by making a success of the overseas departmental status. The poet had clearly understood that after slavery was abolished, the sole political demand that was appealing to the French West Indian people was integration into the French Republic.

Nonetheless, the fact remains that these various political movements' demands for cultural identity have not gone unheeded. Today, overseas departmental status is eroding, and the question of its obsoleteness is more topical than ever. Yet the issue has been confused as never before if one considers the recent suggestion by Lucette Micheaux-Chevry (political leader of the Right and a once virulent proponent of departmentalization) that a new status be adopted, but still *within* the French Republic. What is disconcerting is that Micheaux-Chevry is backed in this effort by the independence parties, which are renouncing, for the moment, their official party line of independence. Writers such as Glissant, Chamoiseau and Confiant seem to support the political leader's initiative, as they themselves offer no alternative political agenda. Whatever the reasons, very few political parties do promote independence pure and simple these days.

The Neglect of Political Identity

Glissant is absolutely correct in defining Creole cultures as "composite" cultures, because they are not bound to territory. Even the islands of the anglophone Caribbean were granted an independence that was not the result of violent struggles for "national" liberation. Nevertheless, Glissant's theoretical framework of Creole identity development is short-sighted in that it overlooks the role of the political space in the process of identity formation. While Césaire has sought to base the recognition of West Indian identity on the universalist component (that is why little importance has been attached to forming an independent political space), nationalists have assumed that cultural identity would automatically take its cue from political identity. In the works of Glissant and his epigones, Chamoiseau and Confiant, the role of political identity in the process of identity formation seems to have been short-circuited. What all these theories fail to analyse is how the Antillean and Guianese people's access to a public political space has affected their identity formation. J.G.A. Pocock, in his *Vertu, commerce et histoire,* writes that

> le domaine public, à la différence du domaine social doit être perçu comme institutionnalisé et formalisé, sans quoi la distinction entre public et privé ne peut être maintenue. Or, l'institutionnalisation du domaine public entraîne l'institutionnalisation de l'expérience sociale, des modes d'apparition de cette expérience et par conséquent, l'institutionnalisation et la différenciation de la temporalité ainsi appréhendée. (1998, 120)

In other words, the access to politics granted the slave descendants is one structured by these same French Republican institutions, which, needless to say, have profoundly affected their experience of identity.

Historically, the egalitarian impulse within Creole identity and its desire for recognition have found expression in the importance bestowed upon the fight for French citizenship. Glissant, along with certain West Indian historians, considers this coveting of French nationality as the effect of a form of alienation or, to quote Glissant himself, "dissolution dans l'Autre". The actual paradox is that in slavery days the slaves preferred to be governed by the *Code Noir* (Negro Code) segregation laws, as inhumane as they were, rather than find themselves in direct confrontation with the white master. It seems that French West Indian slaves were always suspicious of claims for autonomy as voiced by the colonists in their relations with the authority of the king, namely with what they called "ministerial despotism", as if a modicum of "equality" could mean protection from the master's direct authority. Thus the image gained acceptance of a "Benevolent France" which was working for black emancipation. The First Republic in 1794, then the Second in 1848, had actually abolished slavery. But the *békés,* the descendants of the colonists, have fiercely maintained their opposition to the political and civic emancipation of blacks by denying them access to public affairs and public education. It is therefore necessary to bear in mind that in the French Antilles, the class struggle inherited from the time of slavery has taken a turn towards a desire for assimilation into the French Republic.

Republican Integration and Cultural Emancipation

As is the case in all democratic republics where political identity is supposed to transcend cultural identities, secular education has played a fundamental role in forming political identity throughout the French West Indies. Despite its being an undeniable factor of alienation, with its mandatory references to "our ancestors the Gauls", the republican school system has played a major role in the former slaves' social as well as well as cultural liberation. The white planters, known as the *békés,* allied under the circumstances with the clergy, wanted to keep the slave descendants in a position of inferiority, treating them as if they were inferior by nature and constantly denigrating their cultural features, while at the same time hindering their participation in public affairs. The blacks responded by demanding not only equality, but also their rightful place within republican citizenship, which in fact fostered a "suspicion" of all notions of differentiated citizenship. A case in point, worthy of mention, is the introduction of East Indians to the French West Indies after the abolition of slavery. This population could not refer to a slave past in their identity formation and consequently completely abandoned all notions of returning to India. Thus, East Indians had no choice but to become creolized and seek access to public education. All these elements produced a common unification within Creole identities as transformed by the republican public space. It may be added that in continental France itself, the republican ideal was developed in the nineteenth century with the participation of people of colour from our region. Therefore, Victor Schoelcher bridged the gap between republicans from both sides of the Atlantic. His being the most popular political figure in the francophone Caribbean (except for Haiti) is food for thought. It is clear that political identity in this case was affirmed by elaborating an "original" citizenship, resulting from the Creole egalitarian impulse and taking the form of a quest for the recognition of a generic universal identity.

The relationship between political identity, cultural identity and universality (the three components of modern identity) is therefore extremely complex, and ignoring it when attempting to elucidate Creole identities might be cause for political confusion. The 1946 Departmentalization Law, by generalizing the metropolitan administrative political institutions in the French territories of America, modified the process of identity formation, and by excluding ethnic-based classifications rendered it "reflexive", to use a word borrowed from Habermas, making room for "un contexte intersubjectivement partagé d'entente possible" (1977, 155). All this has greatly weakened all notions of independence in the French West Indies, added to the fact that "tant que tous les citoyens ont les mêmes droits et tant que personne ne souffre de discrimination il n'existe pas de raison normativement convaincante de faire sécession de la communauté existante" (p. 134). It is precisely because the desire for republican integration is strong throughout the populations that all the pro-independence movements, regardless of their orientation (Marxist, nationalist or culturalist), have thought it appropriate to freely criticize universalist ideals and democratic politics. However, this has had no effect other than to contribute to the isolation of these movements from majority public opinion. In order to make themselves more credible in the eyes of the masses, it has not occurred to these same nationalists to develop a higher conception of democracy and the republic.

The malaise continues. How can one be at the same time West Indian and French, let alone European? This discontent can be ascribed to the need for recognition of our cultural identity as well as to a serious crisis in civic consciousness. The first point has been emphasized mostly by French West Indian and Guianese intellectuals. This discontent finds its legitimacy in the denunciation of the false universalism evidenced in some forms of French republicanism. The latter, in fact, in abstractly postulating a universalistic political identity, neglected the peculiarities of all cultures. In doing so, it touted as universal what was only the culture of the "majority" of the French population. By the same token, France's minority cultures had no choice but to voice demands for a policy of recognition in the long run. France's ambiguity in this case was patently obvious: while claiming to defend universalist ideals, France simultaneously shut out the otherness of minority cultures and, worse, embarked on enterprises of colonial domination. It is significant that Jules Ferry, the legendary founder of the French public school system, was nicknamed "Tonkinois" (the Tonkinese) for his support of the colonial project. It is also equally revealing that the French Republic has not yet recognized the necessity of commemorating the abolition of slavery, an anniversary which is observed only in the French West Indies. Even now, the commemoration of the abolition of slavery is not a national holiday on an equal footing with 14 July. How can one not realize that under these conditions numerous French schoolchildren are bound to be ignorant of this part of the history of France, which corresponds to the history of colonial France and its slave practices? Herein lies the injustice: that in the construction of history, republican memory chooses what historical events to commemorate. These wounds and these sufferings in Creole identity formation have not been recognized by the Republic. A formal legal and political recognition of the equality of citizens is not sufficient. It is French cultural identity and politics which should open up to the question of recognition. From a moral standpoint, Paul Ricoeur asserts,

> Le passé ne laisse pas seulement des traces inertes, des résidus, mais aussi des énergies dormantes, des ressources inexplorées qu'on assimilerait plutôt à des promesses non tenues, lesquelles fondent la mémoire, comme il a été dit par Paul Valéry, parlant du futur du passé. Le caractère dormant des poten-

tialités non déployées est ce qui permet les "reprises", les "renaissances", les "réveils" par quoi le nouveau enchaîne avec l'ancien. (1998, 31)

There exists a "cultural injustice" towards the populations of the overseas departments that a republic worthy of the name should seek to redress.

The second point characteristic of the *malaise antillais* is concretely evidenced today in a serious deficiency in civic consciousness. It is as if the law had no transcendental value, as if the notions of public good and public space were void of meaning. Departmentalization, despite the developments of institutions, did not know where to draw the line between the public and private spheres. This partly explains the actual political practices of the French state in the Antilles and Guiana. Departmentalization never really ended practices inherited from the colonial past. Everything was done here to encourage political corruption, if not lawlessness pure and simple. But this lack of distinction between the public and private spaces originates partly in the nature of the cultural identity that has been historically elaborated here, as I have explained, outside the public space. Moreover, Creole identities, whose anthropological analysis shows them to be strongly "mother-centred", are identities with weak "superegos".[3] Politics often reduces itself to its purely instrumental aspect because neither the state nor the historical cultural tradition, in spite of the assimilation of French institutions, offers an alternative image of politics. Thanks to republican integration, political institutions and the public space of citizenship have definitely modified Creole cultures, making them more reflexive and determining the ways the individual forges his or her identity. However, the insufficiencies mentioned earlier also render these identities more fragile. Should the problem be solved by reinforced integration, by a redefinition of the place of the citizen in the French Republic or by independence?

To conclude, let me simply say that reflecting on the articulation between cultural identity and political identity in the French West Indies as well as the latter's political future is a mind-boggling task. I just wanted to underscore the complexity without proposing any statutory solution. The most widely accepted solution would imply a specific place within the French Republic. In my view, this solution is worth examining. Unfortunately, the risk is for French West Indians and

Guianese to implement it simply as part of a calculating or instrumental logic. If being French entails no goal other than to ensure material rights and advantages, then the real risk is to witness continued degradation of all ethics of citizenship. The question remains, how can one be a republican in the tropics? I hold a purely instrumental republicanism to be totally unacceptable. The state cannot continue to simply be a legal reference, defining only what is right and disregarding what is good. This would lead to a loss of community values along with a destruction of social ties. If liberalism tolerates only "acceptable" conceptions of the common good, it is because liberalism also rests on a certain idea of what is good. It is up to each minority culture to define the values that allow individuals to build their identities. If the liberal democratic state cannot define these values, the state, if it wants to remain republican, must make sure that there continues to exist a political public space, permitting the participation of all in a common political culture, which should be elaborated intersubjectively – of course not to the point where a ready-made transcendental definition of what the common good would be offered, but through the collective search for that common public good. The question remains, Is independence necessary to achieve this goal?

Acknowledgements

The author would like to gratefully acknowledge the assistance of Guy Lubeth and Sydney Sene-Reece, who translated the original French version of this chapter.

Notes

1. I do not necessarily go along with all of the author's views.
2. I developed those ideas in the article "L'esclave et le droit" (Dahomay 1995). Florence Gauthier discussed my article in a critical review she did for *Chemins Critiques* (January 1977).
3. We can only refer the reader to the already quoted essay by Jacques André (1987).

References

Agamben, Giorgio. 1997. *Homo sacer.* Paris: Seuil.

André, Jacques. 1987. *L'Inceste focal: dans la famille noire antillaise: crimes, conflits, structure.* Paris: Presses universitaires de France.

Arendt, Hannah. 1963. *On Revolution.* New York: Viking.

Barel, Yves. 1987. *La Quête du sens: comment l'esprit vient à la cité.* Paris: Seuil.

Barthélémy, Gérard. 1996. *Dans la splendeur d'un après-midi d'histoire.* Port-au-Prince, Haiti: Henri Deschamps.

Clastres, Pierre. 1974. *La Société contre l'Etat.* Paris: Ed Minuit.

Dahomay, Jacky. 1995. "L'Esclave et le droit". In *Les Abolitions de l'esclavage: de L.F. Sonthonax à V. Schoelcher, 1793, 1794, 1848,* edited by Marcel Dorigny, 67–86. Saint Denis, France: Presses universitaires de Vincennes; Paris: UNESCO.

Fanon, Frantz. 1952. *Peaux noires, Masques blancs.* Paris: Seuil.

Glissant, Edouard. 1981. *Le Discours antillais.* Paris: Seuil.

———. 1997. *Traité du tout-monde.* Paris: Gallimard.

Habermas, Jürgen. 1997. *Droit et démocratie: entre faits et normes.* Translated by Rainer Rochlitz and Christian Bouchindhomme. Paris: Gallimard.

James, C.L.R. 1989. *The Black Jacobins.* New York: Vintage.

Perotin-Dumont, Anne. 1985. *Etre patriote sous les tropiques: la Guadeloupe, la colonisation et la Révolution: 1789–1794.* Basse-Terre, Guadeloupe: Societé d'histoire de la Guadeloupe.

Pocock, J.G.A. 1998. *Vertu, commerce et histoire: essais sur la pensée et l'histoire politique au XVIIIe siècle.* Translated by Hélène Aji. Paris: Presses universitaires de France.

Ricoeur, Paul. 1998. "Le Fondamental et l'historique". In *Charles Taylor et l'interprétation de l'identité moderne,* edited by Guy Laforest and Philippe de Lara, 19–34. Paris: Cerf; Laval, Que.: Presses de l'université de Laval.

[Part 2]

The Ab/Uses of History

[5]

Freedom Ossified
Political Culture and the Public Use of History in Jamaica

Holger Henke

Free yourself from mental slavery,
none but ourselves can free our minds.
  – Bob Marley

There will be no peace,
till men get equal rights and justice.
  – Peter Tosh

Liberty is not the ability to do what you want,
but the desire to be what you can.
  – Jean-Paul Sartre

Introduction

At the current historical conjuncture, state apparatuses, political parties and processes in many countries and even entire regions are experiencing a massive crisis of delegitimization. Confidence in political institutions has declined in high-, middle- and low-income countries, and in all major regions of the world voter turnout has been falling since the

1980s (cf. Munroe 2000). While the phenomenon certainly cannot be accounted for by monocausal explanations, some blame can be put to the rapidly increasing processes of globalization and its concomitant effects of cultural homogenization and commercialization of almost all aspects of life, including politics. For many developing countries, sharply increasing social inequalities are an additional factor. Jamaica and much of the rest of the Caribbean region have been located at the vortex of the restructuring of global political economy ever since Cristobal Colon's presumed discovery of the region. Since then the region has always provided a good indicator of the state of affairs in capitalism and in the hegemonic projects sustaining its existence. In this chapter I attempt to provide a critical perspective on the current processes of democratic delegitimization in the English-speaking Caribbean.

In 1991, during the late Michael Manley's second period as prime minister of Jamaica, then president of South Africa Nelson Mandela graced Jamaica with a visit. It is hard to describe in words what this visit meant for Jamaicans, but suffice it to say that the visit seemed to turn the island, or at least its capital, Kingston, into a major holiday. Actually, the public mood was even more aroused than on a holiday like Christmas or Emancipation Day, when many people tend to stay at home, visit family or friends, or go to the beach. The atmosphere of euphoria, pride and delight among the country's elites and "common" people was so thick and obvious, it could almost be touched by hand. Nobody received presents or anything material, but, unlike on national holidays, large crowds were on the streets along which Mandela and his then wife, Winnie, were expected to travel. People climbed fences, trees and roofs to catch a glimpse or take a picture of this living legend. Even the police were caught by the brotherly, blissful and ecstatic mood that was so tangibly in the air. When Mandela visited the campus of the University of the West Indies, the police appeared, to a more detached (yet similarly enthusiastic) observer, completely inattentive to what was going on in the crowd that surrounded Mandela as he made his way to the main assembly hall, where an honorary doctoral degree was bestowed on him. In terms of crowd control they were not in charge of the situation, nor did they need to be.

Later that day Mandela was supposed to be "presented to the people" who had gathered in the National Stadium, which was packed to maximum capacity. Prior to Mandela's arrival in the stadium, a tragic event happened, which completely marred his visit and – had it by chance turned out to be different – might have left the author of this chapter unable to ever write it. Apparently, some spectators in the stadium's bleachers were trying to slip through holes in the fence in order to join some other, "more equal", people who had the privilege of being in the stadium's arena and in front of a podium that had been erected for Mandela and the honoraries accompanying him. In fact, police and soldiers were busy preventing more people from disappearing into the crowd of privileged viewers and were catching those that were trying. At one point, apparently frustrated by their fruitless attempts to prevent a growing exodus from the bleachers, they started beating people back through the hole in the fence. When some people, in a display of disapproval, began to throw soda cans and bottles at the security forces, at least one soldier completely lost his nerve and started shooting into the crowd seated in the bleachers. I will not forget my absolute horror at seeing this soldier kneeling down and firing his rifle, a horror tempered only by a subconscious relief that he was not firing quite into the section I was seated in. One person died and several were injured. By any standard, this was a major tragedy and an enormous blemish on a state visit, which had the same – if not even greater – symbolic significance to the people of this country than had the state visit by the Ethiopian emperor Haile Selassie in the early 1960s.

Mandela later claimed that he had not been aware of the incident when he entered the arena and, in fact, believed that the explosions to be heard throughout the stadium had come from firecrackers. The next day Jamaica's minister of national security, K.D. Knight, publicly announced that he would have the incident investigated.

To this day, I marvel at this political decision and the apparent hesitation of the minister in charge to assume responsibility for the death of a civilian in a situation which clearly did not justify the use of deadly force and for the thoroughly negative light it shed internationally on Jamaica as host to such an illustrious visitor. I use this decision for comparison when there are similarly consequential situations in other countries, both in the Caribbean and elsewhere, which call for a person in authority to take responsibility for scandalous actions by people under their authority, and I always seem to arrive at the conclusion that to merely investigate this incident was insufficient and was clear evidence of a lack of preparedness by the political directorate in Jamaica to assume responsibility. Wherever anybody else may stand on this issue, it ought to be clear that this event speaks loudly to fundamental questions of authority and power, of the representation of the public good, of the presentation of politics to the public and of the responsibility and democratic accountability of the political class in Jamaica. In short, the question of Jamaica's political culture has to be answered and put into the context of political developments in the history of the Caribbean region.

The basic thesis of this paper addresses three distinct, yet related, historical developments. First, the democratic promise of freedom for the people of the Caribbean which gave rise to the emancipation period was not fulfilled, as the planter class was not prepared to renounce their power. Second, when they were no longer able to hold on to their power during the labour unrest of the 1930s and during the independence movement, political responsibilities were given to the middle classes, which celebrated this transition as a major achievement.[1] However, the actual arrangements that were made still kept the majority of the people from meaningful participation in the political process and from access to economic resources. Nevertheless, this majority bought into the celebratory notion of a freedom which they continued to be denied. This became quite obvious in the 1970s when a fundamentally ambivalent middle class temporarily seemed to fulfil the promise of freedom but ultimately failed to deliver it. Third, in the current period of globalization and neoliberal economics, the discrepancy between the democratic promise in the notion of freedom and the socio-economic realities is thrown into a particularly strong focus. I argue here that (1) this ethos has now attained a quasi-mythical status in many anglophone Caribbean countries and (2) at the very same time, the notion of freedom is stripped of its practical meaning and has in many instances become counterproductive. In short, Caribbean freedom has become ossified.

Political Culture as a Theoretical Concept

Far too often, political analysts confine themselves to the study of either structures (such as government) or decision-making processes. In contrast to this, the study of political culture attempts to uncover (the sociogenesis of) values, attitudes and judgements (sometimes prejudices) which inform the political process in a particular country, region or population. Political culture is a concept that is difficult to grasp and define. There is hardly any agreement on the definition of, methods for or paradigms of political culture. As a research agenda, however, it is probably as old as politics itself. In most early civilizations we can find ideas about the connections between political institutions and the consciousness of the society. Is the political system supported by the people and, if yes, why? If not, why not? Do the people trust their leaders, the elites and the institutions? Which forms and areas of socialization serve the political legitimacy of the system? In his famous funeral oration, Pericles contrasts the virtues of the Athenian republic with the restrictive nature of Sparta:

> The freedom which we enjoy in our government extends also to our ordinary life. There, far from exercising a jealous surveillance over each other, we do not feel called upon to be angry with our neighbour for doing what he likes, or even to indulge in those injurious looks which cannot fail to be offensive, although they inflict no positive penalty. But all this ease in our private relations does not make us lawless as citizens. Against this fear is our chief safeguard, teaching us to obey the magistrates and the laws, particularly such as regard the protection of the injured, whether they are actually on the statute book, or belong to that code which, although unwritten, yet cannot be broken without acknowledged disgrace. (www.fordham.edu/halsall/ancient/pericles-funeralspeech.html)

Particularly interesting in this passage is the idea of the balance between freedom and a sense of obligation towards the community. Thus, Pericles makes a distinction between the private individual and the public individual (that is, the citizen). This is a point to which I will return later in the discussion. At this point, the close connection between private freedom and public liberality has to be emphasized.

Using political culture as a conceptual approach to the comparative study of a particular context within which political attitudes and opinions unfold and operate may well reveal unpleasant and even disturbing aspects of a national ethos by explaining how these aspects have served to twist public opinion and policy into a particular, often negative, shape or direction. Thus, the sociologist Norbert Elias attempts to explain why in Germany the people tend to submit to such a large extent to the authority of the state and the political leaders while de-emphasizing the voice of their own consciences:

> The traditions of German society often created a rather weak individual conscience. Even in the case of adults, the functioning of the individual conscience – at least in the case of the expanding sphere of public affairs – remained dependent on the existence of an external control and the coercion and discipline one had not the determination to impose on oneself. Among the external institutions many Germans relied on for the restraint of their selfish impulses in these spheres of life, the state and its representatives played a particularly important role. Thrown back on their own conscience, they were not strong enough to build stable constraints against disallowed, outlawed and dangerous impulses. . . . Particularly in times of national emergencies and war, many Germans happily shed the burden of self-control and responsibility for their own life. (Greiffenhagen 1997; my translation)

The implications of this analysis for the explanation of the Holocaust are immediately obvious. Too many Germans simply turned their head the other way instead of speaking out and thereby allowed the rule of the mob to become the policy of the state. A tradition of Prussian military-style obedience succeeded in twisting the collective psyche of this nation to combine political acquiescence and personal *Gemütlichkeit* (that is, comfort) and to hold both higher than moral outrage and ethical calls for resistance.[2]

Elias's work is also relevant to other aspects of the concept of political culture. In his seminal work "On the Process of Civilization", he reminds us that concepts central to an understanding of a particular society undergo a process. As he puts it,

> The process of their social genesis may well be long forgotten – one generation passes them on to the other without the entire process of change remaining present with it, and they live as long as the echo of past experiences and situations maintains an actual value, a function, in the actual existence of society, as long as succeeding generations are able to recognize their own experiences embedded in the sense of these words; *they will wither if in actual social life no functions, no experiences relate to them anymore.* (Elias 1999, 94–95; emphasis added)

This is an important reminder, which points to the fact that collective symbols, national myths and even collective historical traumas are – contrary to conventional wisdom – not fixed for eternity but indeed subject to constant reinterpretation. They are both agents of and subject to change. This is precisely one of the main points argued in this paper.

It is important to note that the concept of political culture has gone through several stages in its use in political science. While the concept was already implied in earlier discourses and notions, it was Gabriel Almond who introduced it in the early 1960s into political science. Subsequently, the concept was used by leading authorities in political science such as Seymour Lipset, Sidney Verba and Samuel Huntington. A number of approaches that applied the the concept – emphasizing psychological accounts, comprehensive sociological accounts, anthropological definitions, heuristic definitions providing ideal-type constructs, or objective definitions which define culture in terms of the consensual or dominant values in a society – competed with each other. The "civic culture" paradigm evident in much of the political culture literature presented in the 1960s posited "a mix of subject-participant cultures combining trust and a strong deference to authority with a positive attitude to the goods of active participation" (Gibbins 1989, 7). This approach, which became the basis for many of the so-called modernization theories, was justly criticized as presenting naively ethnocentric Anglo-American confidence in liberal democracy. In addition, the civic culture paradigm was not able to demonstrate a necessary relationship between certain attitudes and activities, on the one hand, and liberal democracy, on the other.

In contrast to formal structural or psychological studies of politics, the political culture concept focuses on the embeddedness of the political system in, as Lucian Pye expressed it, "an intelligible web of relations" constituted by "the traditions of a society, the spirit of its public institutions, the passions and the collective reasoning of its citizenry, and the style and operating codes of its leaders" (1965, 7; see also Verba 1965; Dewey 1963).[3] In Verba's view (1965), the concept usually emphasizes values that transcend particular groups or classes of a society, but – equally important – there often is a notable contrast between elite values or beliefs and those of the wider society.[4] However, while Verba repeatedly notes such differences, he does not seem to pay sufficient attention to the possibility that the elites may manipulate common beliefs to their own advantage. Precisely this possibility is being explored and corroborated in this chapter. The example of Jamaica and the anglophone Caribbean may therefore also serve as a case study with implications for the theory of political culture.

Having come under severe criticism, the concept of political culture fell out of fashion in the 1970s, but it has recently re-emerged as a conceptual approach to the systematic and comparative understanding of political systems in and across different societies and regions.[5] In recent times, consumerist and postmodern interpretations of (political) culture have given the concept a new slant. While there is greater appreciation today for the cultural idiosyncrasies and traditional resources in different parts of the world, the recent thrust towards globalization also serves as an extremely powerful conveyor belt for Western notions of political culture and values.[6] Without immersing myself too deeply in a discussion about the contending definitions of the concept, my own view is in favour of an understanding of political culture which emerges from the dynamic interplay of various social forces within a given society. Such a view seems best represented in the hegemonic theory of political culture, which John Gibbins describes the following way:

> A culture is not immediately natural nor determined by the economy or social class, but is a response to "current relations of force" and is the effect of political power conflicts. A society always witnesses a plurality of conflicting hegemonies seeking, but rarely achieving, dominance. A study of political culture is then the historical account of their emergence, a critical analysis of the political and economic forces they represent, a study of their internal character and a rigorous critique or negation of their logic and effect. (1989, 5)

Only such a definition focuses sufficiently on the specific contexts each society constitutes as parameters of political thought and praxis. Although this definition may seem overly reliant on voluntary consent and instrumentality (see Gibbins 1989), it is clearly less static and decontextualizing than Verba's and Pye's definitions.

While I do not wish to suggest that political culture of necessity has to develop into a Western-style democracy coupled with a legal system premised on individualism and private property, I would argue that the people of the modern Caribbean in most instances have pursued an egalitarian, de-racialized and inclusive political culture. Pursuing this political ideal in both theory and political praxis, they have advanced it as the logical development of the Enlightenment promise enshrined in European and Anglo-American constitutions. For the purpose of this chapter, political culture is therefore also regarded as a normative concept partially overlapping with the notion and concept of democracy. As a measure of civil society, it involves three essential aspects: (1) uncensored public discourse, (2) the selection of political leaders in a process of free choice and broad participation and (3) the accountability and assumption of responsibility by private and public sector leaders.[7] However, as already indicated, a comprehensive discussion about the historical development and contemporary application of these concepts also requires the consideration of psycho-social themes, historical traditions and language, and may even include discussions about seemingly mundane things like architecture. Implicit in the concept is that different nations have a different economy of emotions (Elias's *Affekt-Ökonomie*). The debate about the symbolic or public use of history in the anglophone Caribbean is not simply a matter of political style or in the interest of an analysis of political discourse; it also carries fundamental theoretical implications for the nature of democracy in the region, as well as practical implications with regard to an understanding of how Caribbean societies or polities operate.

Freedom and Caribbean Political Culture

As Anthony Giddens points out, "traditions of behaviour have their own moral endowment, which specifically resists the technical power to introduce something new" (1991, 146). This observation is of immediate importance to the argument I would like to advance in this section. The fundamental idea is that many Caribbean societies have come into their own on the basis of the notion of freedom. It is well known and does not need to be repeated here that chattel slavery (and later indentured labour) was the dominant mode of existence for the majority of people in the majority of territories in the region. Caribbean existence had from the very beginning been defined in terms of resistance to this oppression, and emancipation and independence were important turning points and have ever since remained important points of reference to the individual and collective psyche of the region's people. In essence, these notions – or, to use Verba's term, this fundamental "evaluative mode of orientation" (1965, 519) – have become, justifiably, the cornerstone of the collective "truth" in these societies. In addition, there are very tangible arguments which speak in favour of the celebration of liberation and liberty in these parts.

Having acknowledged the overriding significance of freedom in the collective psyche of Caribbean people, I argue here that what Jürgen Habermas has termed the "public use of history" (1998) has given the notion of freedom in Jamaica a particular twist. In late modernity and under the current circumstances of globalization, the individual and collective ethos of freedom has taken on such a high level of political sacrosanctity that it regularly becomes an obstacle to meaningful communication between the political leadership and the people. For while an ethos of freedom has become the national canon in many Caribbean countries, it is important to keep in mind that – probably as a matter of colonial heritage – the middle and upper classes in the region always considered themselves to be a little freer than the majority of the people. Thus, whenever the ruling classes invoke the canon of freedom, they can be rather certain that they will find a large resonance among the people. However, this equation does not work the other way around, and it appears that the ruling classes from the beginning did not find themselves answerable to the electorate and responsible by standards of democratic conduct. The constraints and changes wrought upon Jamaica in the late twentieth century have led to the paradoxical situation that the national ethos of freedom has become counterproductive even before it had the chance to fulfil the democratic promise or challenge implied in it.

We need to take a step back, however, and realize that freedom in the anglophone Caribbean is not of a generic nature, but rather is a historically specific and socially constructed phenomenon.[8] Thus, Thomas Holt points out that there are two important dimensions to what he calls the "problem of freedom" (1992, xxii). First, slavery was supplanted by a new system, free labour, which had its own embedded forms of coercion. Second, freedom was an important facet of the political relations and tended to challenge privileges of the ruling class. The contradiction between these dimensions imposed an overwhelming need to be negotiated, and this could be achieved only by prescribing new rules of inclusion and exclusion:

> Critical to sustaining social structures founded on blatant inequalities, within the terms of such an ideology, was the notion that some people – because of their fundamental natures – should be restrained, should not be free. In the West Indies racialist ideologies came to be essential to sustaining the overarching ideology of freedom. (Holt 1992, xxiii)

By moving away from plantation labour and establishing a black peasantry, Afro-Jamaicans established a different vision of freedom – a freedom that rejected the inclusion of its own antithesis. When it became obvious after emancipation that the apprenticeship arrangement was not substantially different from work under slavery, the freed slaves understandably soon retracted from it, and complaints by the authorities about "a general appearance of sullenness & bad disposition", as the Jamaican governor Peter Howe, Marquess of Sligo, put it, were voiced.[9] As Franklin Knight aptly summarizes, "political reconstruction in the Caribbean had immediate meaning only for a small, privileged sector of the society" (1990, 160). That there was little headway achieved on the road to freedom can also be seen when we study the labour and socially discriminating arrangements of the so-called indentured labourers who were imported from India and China (see, for example, Sue-A-Quan 1999).

In the transition from slavery to freedom, the resident white ruling class often proved to be the greatest obstacle of all parties involved. Quite frequently they refused to implement orders from the colonial government and thereby undermined the transition process. Holt described the Jamaican situation correctly, writing that "the black majority should have power but could not, the large colored group could have the power but should not, the white minority should not have power but will" (1992, 109; see also Rodney 1981).

The historical trajectory of this birth hour of freedom in the Caribbean continued right to the workers' unrests in the 1930s. At this point and in the following years, certain quarters of the middle class supported the call for greater self-determination and independence (from the colonial government) uttered by the majority of working people, but they did so in order to save their own social position and to deflect possible challenges to their own privileges that grew out of the post-emancipation arrangements. In other instances, such as that of Portuguese immigrants in Guyana, the middle class helped to organize and voice opposition to the planter class (Rodney 1981). In both Trinidad and Jamaica – to cite just the largest two anglophone Caribbean islands – the transition to independence was managed by a handful of middle-class representatives who were led by a charismatic leader (Alexander Bustamante in Jamaica, Eric Williams in Trinidad) who embodied both the hopes – and *only* the hopes – of the majority of the people and the political expectations of the middle and upper classes.

An example of what the middle class's half-hearted attitude towards genuine independence specifically meant to the political development of the region's societies is the process of constitutional decolonization in Jamaica. As Munroe pointed out in his 1984 study of the decolonization process in this country, the incorporation of a Bill of Rights into the Constitution was contested on a number of counts. Decisions about the political future of the post-independence Caribbean, however, were to a large extent the prerogative of elements of the middle classes. More often than not, they were concerned that their short- and medium-term political privileges remain untouched. As A.W. Singham emphasized in his seminal work about political culture in the region, the political elites "are willing to adopt and adapt quickly any idea of cultural form superficially, so long as it does not unleash tension and insecurity or threaten their positions" (1968, 96). The same may be said for their readiness to adopt different economic programmes. Supporting the political legitimization of middle-class rule in many anglophone Caribbean countries, penal codes were introduced that were strict enough to allow the state to effectively thwart public challenges (see, for example, Harriott 1999; Mars 1998; Nanton 1983).

To the extent that this analysis applies, one has to take note of the overriding importance of the public interpretation, display and celebration of history. Without too much simplification one can say that the history of the post-emancipation period is one of class or colourist oppression and simultaneous struggle for freedom from external rule and dependency. Interestingly, though, in the quest for national independence the (domestic) ruling elites focused almost exclusively on the latter aspect.[10] In fact, one could argue that the pursuit of political independence almost served to reject a broader interpretation of freedom – one that would address fundamental questions of equality and self-realization. Rather than address this aspect of the struggle for freedom, by their ostentatious display and celebration of liberty the middle classes tended to reinterpret the comprehensive concept of freedom and replace it with a significantly narrower version, that is, the struggle against foreign, white, British, colonial, racist rule. In doing so, they institutionalized a particular public use of history, one that, in Foucaultian terms, would produce a very specific truth.[11] There can be little doubt that this production of a symbolic history or truth was a conscious and deliberate political course they embarked upon, one which significantly aided their efforts to legitimize their rule. While the aspect of contemporary oppression in the national discourse is muffled, the notion of freedom is the official national ethos.[12]

Having said this, it important to point out that this official national ethos is already a chloroformed version of what the notion really signifies. Very often the imagery which informs the symbolic politics of Caribbean elites has been sterilized of its inherently more radical aspects. For this reason, one of the most authentically indigenous creations of Caribbean diasporic culture, Rastafarianism, with its symbols of liberation, has never obtained any significant official endorsement. This observation is underlined by a recent study by Charles Carnegie of the symbolism of Marcus Garvey and his movement in the early twentieth century. As Carnegie points out, in the official iconography of the Jamaican state, Garvey, a national hero, almost never appears as the plumed, gold-braided commander-in-chief of his visionary African empire or in his robes of an honorary doctor of Civil Laws, which are much more impressive images of this supreme freedom fighter:

> In images of him produced by the Jamaican state, Garvey appears the carefully groomed black banker, perhaps, not the fiery orator, or the supreme statesman. His image is carefully *contained* by symbols of the Jamaican state. . . . While the Jamaican state has skilfully appropriated Garvey – anointing him a national hero, commissioning and installing statues of him, regularly reproducing and circulating his image on currency notes, coins and postage stamps – it has done so with discernible ambivalence and nervousness. (1999, 50–51)

The significance of this observed practice is immediately clear. Not only is this a prime example of the officially manipulated public use of history, it is also a clear indication of the exploitation of the emblems and prophets of Caribbean freedom by a ruling class which is struggling hard to justify its rule over an impoverished and often politically disenfranchised citizenry.

In Jamaica, four of the seven national heroes would be regarded as unambiguously black, and all seven were leaders of resistance movements. However, because of the long-term psychological pervasiveness of the colonial racist ideology and practice, framing the liberation project as a race-based enterprise entails inherent contradictions. If and when used in the international arena, it regularly forces a black nation state on the defensive, and internally "this racialized dominant symbol, with its lower-class associations, generates as many tropes of self-contempt as it does images that might contribute to positive self-worth and motivation" (Carnegie 1996, 501). Where interracial worker alliances appeared to threaten the status quo that secures middle-class privilege, the middle classes were equally prepared to put aside ethnic antagonisms in order to close ranks against this challenge.

The national ethos of freedom is, of course, grounded in the real and palpable aspirations and struggles of its peoples. That struggle was historically directed against colonialism and its oppressive plantation system. A large number of upsurges, rebellions, revolutions (first and foremost the Haitian Revolution) and other forms of resistance has profoundly shaped the culture and nature of the political discourse of the majority of people in those parts (see, for example, Henke 1996b). It is therefore important to recognize that there is a body of resonance for the ethos of freedom. In contemporary Jamaica, however, this notion assumes a more immediate economic and social content and expresses itself as a call for "respect" and "justice". The small Caribbean middle classes have historically developed into an intermediary position in which they assumed a stake in the status quo of the colonial and, later, postcolonial system and the stratification of power and subordination erected by it.

While, therefore, the proliferation of official holidays and official and unofficial references to notions of liberation, freedom, independence and so forth in Jamaica has a real grounding in the country's history and the enormous significance of the concept of freedom therein, the fact that the middle classes have used the very same notion to divert the public's attention from their role as enforcers of a system which actually perpetuates inequality, injustice, and extreme class privileges left the notion of freedom from the very beginning in an awkward and ambivalent position.[13] I argue here that despite the universal aspirations and democratic ideals which generally stand behind the concept of freedom, its public use as a tool for the legitimization of class privilege and discrimination caused this central ethos in Caribbean political culture to be compromised, impure, polluted, tainted – pick your favourite adjective. At a minimum, a consequence of this ambivalence is that the use of the notion is not entirely convincing or credible when uttered by members of the ruling elites or by privileged members of the middle class who identify with the elite. Futhermore, its ambivalent application is one of the reasons that many Caribbean people remain suspicious of political projects which put mobilization for liberation into the centre of their political message.

Change, Identity and Political Culture

To the extent that political culture in the anglophone Caribbean is part of a historical tradition, one will find certain constants. Among these constants are a preoccupation with self-determination and independence, ethnicity or "race"; rejection of undue foreign influences; and quest for liberty and identity – to mention only some of the most obvious. I have discussed several aspects of these elements of political culture in the anglophone Caribbean in the previous section. However, the onus still rests on the remainder of this chapter to analyse the contemporary ways in which these aspects may express themselves. In particular, I will take a closer look at the issue of press freedom, at the evolution of a modern civil society, and at the state's response to popular demands regarding the past involvement of politicians in undemocratic or even criminal activities. It is important to keep in mind that since the early 1980s most Caribbean economic and political systems have faced serious (often externally induced) pressures for reform, transparency or openness, and accountability.

Political culture cannot be understood simply as an immutable and rigid corset of values and behavioural patterns. It also has to be understood as part of a historical process, that is, as evolving and as subject to changes. Giddens appropriately points to this nexus between change, identity and collective psyche in the context of modernity:

> Temporal succession . . . retains little of the resonance of collective processes of transition characteristic of earlier eras. In traditional contexts, the lifecycle carries strong connotations of renewal, since each generation in some substantial part rediscovers and relives modes of life of its forerunners. Renewal loses most of its meaning in the settings of high modernity where practices are repeated only in so far as they are reflexively justifiable. (1991, 146)

With the increasing pace of access to information through travel, telephone, the Internet and migration, most societies of the anglophone Caribbean have experienced higher levels of political awareness, which have translated into a growing articulation of political demands at all levels of society (see, for example, Munroe 1996; Payne and Sutton 1993). In fact, the growing complexity and pace of Caribbean economics and social life affects even deeper levels of the national psyche. Thus, we need to keep in mind Michel Foucault's conceptualization of power as a phenomenon that actually penetrates our bodies. Complementary to this notion is Elias's analysis of the growing complexity of societies and his observation that these processes were directly reflected in the economy of emotions, the social attitudes of people, their thoughts and their complete socio-genetic habits (*soziogener Habitus*; Elias 1999). Parallel to the newly increasing public demand for rights, mentioned above, the continuing denial of these rights has led to greater cynicism and withdrawal from the political process and the system. At the same time, the political class, aware of its value as a source of political legitimacy, continues to promote a generalized notion of freedom – a practice which in effect undermines the essence of its very meaning. A few examples may serve to illustrate this.

Although the either exculpatory or accusatory frameworks of the cold war era are no longer available, in recent months the question of press freedom has resurfaced in several of the islands. This fact alone may already help to convey a sense of the depth of the democratic challenges and political changes in these parts. In the second half of 1999 the Jamaican government proposed a new law ostensibly directed against corruption in – perhaps even of – the public sector. However, the legislation also targeted the investigative functions of the press and was hotly debated, particularly among representatives of the media themselves. Clearly, this suggests that the state (that is, its representatives) feels severely circumscribed in its ability to act and that the public quest for accountability is perceived as a political threat rather than as a democratic right of citizens and the media which act on their behalf. As the *Jamaica Gleaner* put it in a recent editorial about the recently introduced Freedom of Information Act, this piece of legislation "did not start from a base that the people have a right to know, but rather sought to define those areas where the public would be allowed access to information" ("Freedom of Information", 25 February 2000).

Although I do not suggest that there is an automatic model function to the Universal Declaration of Human Rights or the US Constitution, it nevertheless needs to be pointed out that the official reactions cited above do not satisfy the strict meaning of the freedom of speech provision provided in these documents.[14]

In recent years, a plethora of glaring abuses of the human and civil rights of the average Jamaican has been perpetrated by the official organs of the state. It can be argued that these are not only abuses of an anonymous power, or even its individual representatives, against individuals supposedly represented by them. If, indeed, from a more existential point of view, both the prisoner and the guard are in prison, then this abuse really is self-abuse. Or, as Bob Marley rephrased a popular Ewe proverb, "When the rain falls, it don't fall on one man's house" ("So Much Things to Say", *Exodus,* Island Records 1977). As was already mentioned, this (self-)abuse is a remnant of what was introduced in colonial times by the oppressive rule of exterior forces. It may, however, recently have reached a new symbolic level with apparent attempts by the Jamaican government to appropriate land claimed by the Maroons (escaped slaves) as contractually granted by the British colonial power. According to recent reports, the government has intruded on such lands in order to construct a highway of questionable ecological and development impact without establishing the proper land ownership or negotiating with the Maroons, whose ancestors settled in the remote areas of the country, successfully resisted capture by the British and to this day have far-reaching rights (such as community policing). In a significant recent statement of defiance, the president of the Maroon Federal House of Assembly, Meredie Rowe, took issue with the current Jamaican government's quasi-colonial attitude:

> The Maroons reserve the right to apprehend any group or organisation that trespasses on our lands within the bond of the Maroon Treaty and try these persons in our night court as determined by the treaty of 1738/39 that gives the Maroon leader the right to any punitive action, be it person or organisation. (Morais 2000)

Whatever the real or symbolic merits of this recent conflict are for many citizens in this Caribbean nation, their fundamental rights and even their very lives are in jeopardy every day, whether they go on the streets or whether they are in the privacy of their homes.

It has been pointed out that "across-the-board downsizing of the state, including severe cutbacks in expenditure on the social sector, in the context of a private sector at best slow in filling the gap, is a major impediment to the preservation, much less the deepening of democracy" in the region (Munroe 1996, 116). However, while I acknowledge the exploitative tendencies among many foreign investment ventures in the region, Munroe's argument can also cut the other way. Thus, the historical tradition of popular resistance to what is perceived as "the system" has affected the relative work ethic of many potential employees. It is, for example, widely recognized by foreign and local investors that many employees in the region regard their employment more as an entitlement than as a position that entails both rights *and* duties. Thus, many employers find it hard to enforce control mechanisms to improve the quality and quantity of work performance. The problem of theft by employees is recognized and is likely to be among the factors potential or actual investors consider when deciding whether or not to invest in a Caribbean venture. It is suggested here that the general impulse for freedom from oppression has in some instances hindered the development of a co-operative ethos[15] and of internationally competitive levels of work ethic. To the degree that this is true, the use by political elites of the notion of Caribbean freedom as an instrument for the creation of political loyalty and legitimacy has to be considered utterly counterproductive.

Given the discontinuities introduced by the colonial rule, with all its abuses, its cultural deprivation and its introduction of artificial means of pitting people against each other, as well as their persistence in the postcolonial era, it can further be argued that Caribbean democracy and nation building are still faced with the daunting task of creating coherent civil societies guided by a sustainable measure of a *volonté générale* of shared interests and shared objectives which would facilitate rather than obstruct Caribbean freedom. As political philosophers like John Dewey or, earlier, Jean-Jacques Rousseau pointed out, it is only when people perceive that public objectives also reflect their own individual concerns that they experience a culture as a common *political* culture, and only then do they "truly view themselves as interdependent parts rather than as independent wholes" (Barnard 1989, 142; see also Dewey 1963). To the extent that this is a precondition for a successful democratic project, recent developments in Jamaica and other anglophone Caribbean countries have fallen short of the democratic promise celebrated by regional elites. Rather, as the above examples attempt to demonstrate, the public celebration of a history of resistance and struggle for freedom has been used as a legitimating excuse for a one-man, two-party and/or class-based rule of a few over the many, which has often implied political tutelage and has regularly bordered on oppression.[16]

In recent years there have been signs which indicate a strengthening of civil society in the region. There have been clear efforts by both individuals and organizations to demand greater accountability and bureaucratic transparency from governments. There is clear evidence, for example, of the extent to which the "people on the street" recognize and disapprove of the posturing of the political elites when it comes to defending the rights of people. Thus, when the Jamaican prime minister, promoting a Caribbean Court of Justice, recently asked publicly, "Have we no shame that we are continually relying on the UK Judicial Privy Council as our court of last appeal in the administration of justice?" the following letter to the editor confronted him with the above-mentioned cases and then pointed out,

> Mr Prime Minister, this little rock has produced men of the calibre of Marcus Garvey, Paul Bogle and Bob Marley just to name a few who have awakened the consciousness of black people the world over and you, Sir, travel the world on the same notion that you are continuing this enlightenment however, in your neck of the wood these cruel atrocities are still being visited upon us (sic!). (Townsend 2000)

Contrasting the prime minister's responsibility with some of Jamaica's most outstanding advocates for human liberty serves, of course, a double purpose. It elevates the letter's author to a moral level presumably equal to these eminent individuals and, at the same time, a level (at least) equal to the presumed irreproachability of the prime minister himself. However, using these advocates as a point of reference also clearly draws the line between their actions and the prime minister's perceived failure to take responsibility for the state of affairs.[17] Clearly, this speaks for a well-developed political consciousness which is aware that freedom, equal rights and justice are the pillars of both the theory and the practice of democracy. Increasingly this awareness also translates into collective action.

Caribbean political elites are generally well aware of the limits of their legitimacy and get nervous about any possible political trespassing. Since the summer of 1999 the civil rights group Jamaicans for Justice (JFJ) has pursued an issue of great symbolic political significance which relates to the question of whether a truth commission similar to the South African model would help the nation to come to terms with the political violence and the involvement of political parties and individual politicians in it.[18] The issue arose when a veteran politician publicly voiced what sounded like a confession of guilt for a well-known execution-style killing of political opponents during the 1970s. Following this, another politician (of what was then the opposition), who is now the radio talk-show co-host on whose show the initial statement was made, announced that he would be prepared to tell what he knows about political violence in Jamaica if he was granted immunity from prosecution. The mere proposition sparked an intense national debate in which voices both for and against could be heard. Interestingly, though, both major parties soon closed ranks in taking distance from the idea for a Jamaican truth commission. About three weeks after the idea began to gather steam, both the prime minister and the leader of the opposition, veterans themselves, in a rare public demonstration of political unity quite predictably rejected the idea. While both hinted at possible mistakes in the past, they were very quick to point out their own efforts in reducing political violence. In a statement fraught with ambivalence, the leader of the opposition, Edward Seaga, said,

> My opponents from the PNP and myself got together and decided that we must make the change. In taking that decision, we were able to transmit it down the line to the persons who would have to implement that change – the people on the corners, the people in all groups. They welcomed the change and they made the change – but from our initiative. Having done so, we have eliminated the tribalism that continues to grow in other areas. ("No to Confessions", *Jamaica Gleaner*, 16 September 1999)

The obvious question which arises from Seaga's statement is this: If you were responsible for implementing peace, were you not also responsible for the violence? Moreover, how much of an opponent is the PNP really if both parties and their leaders implement peace (and violence) among the people by either tacit or explicit agreement? On balance, there would appear to be more benefits from an (albeit painful) purgative process of confession, revelation and forgiveness, which would publicly restore the distorted balance between the symbolic prestige and material benefit of public service, on the one hand, and the assumed ethics of this service, including the preparedness to assume personal responsibility and take consequences for one's own political actions or the actions of subordinates in the state bureaucracy, on the other. However, the statements by the prime minister and the leader of the opposition and their swift boastfulness about inadequate initiatives simply seem to promise new bottles for an old wine.

Political philosophers from Plato to Alexis de Tocqueville to Karl Popper have emphasized the special requirements and responsibilities asked of leaders of communities. Democratic theory in particular has always stressed relations between liberty, morals, ethical conduct and responsibility, both as they are required from the citizens of a community and as they are required from its leaders. Some were more optimistic, others more pessimistic. De Tocqueville, in fact, gives the lawmakers both the authority and the capacity to shape the mores of society (Alulis 1993). Given the historical and current situation, this appears not to be a relationship that exists in Jamaica or much of contemporary anglophone Caribbean. Here, rather, leaders often seem to regard themselves as members of a special anointed caste which is somehow above the law and above the people who elect them into office.[19] One of their most valuable ways of creating the impression that this is not the case is to cast themselves in the light of heirs to previous struggles for freedom. To the extent that this political spectacle continues to work, little real progress in furthering responsible democratic governance and respect for civil rights is likely. C.L.R. James's almost forty-year-old warning still rings eerily true today:

> Has democracy sunk ineradicable roots in us? I say that I see no sign of it and many signs to the contrary. . . . Democratic government does not create democracy. Democracy creates democratic government. . . . I have never known a population claiming to be democratic where so many people (both Negroes and Indians) live in such fear of the whole apparatus of government. (Quoted in Look Lai 1992, 184–85)

In Lieu of a Conclusion: A Call for Passive Resistance (To Be Continued)

It may seem contradictory to argue that freedom unfulfilled now should be considered "freedom ossified". To some extent I concede to this argument. However, the following question arises: If there are no more Cuban experiments, "third paths" and democratic socialisms, or only just land reforms considered possible (and many would make this postmodern argument), is it not time to perhaps foster a new understanding of what freedom is and can be for the people of the region? Is it not perhaps time to redefine a notion of freedom which has come to object to almost every attempt at social engineering or at the imposition of structure or order in a time when the achievement of economic take-off requires an enormous individual and collective work ethic?[20] Would a less celebratory notion of freedom and a greater emphasis on commitment and care (as defining elements of freedom) not also empower society to demand with greater moral force the adherence to democratic ideals from their political leadership? Only if those questions are answered in the negative should the above argument be dismissed a priori as counter-revolutionary or conservative.

As Verba has reminded us, the distinction between ideological and pragmatic politics also applies in the realm of political beliefs and, hence, political culture. While, as earlier mentioned, he points out that more primordial political beliefs can actually stabilize a political system, he also mentions that even where symbolism and ritual play a great role, commitment to these "might be much more in terms of the specific benefits that are perceived as deriving from these symbolisms and political rituals" (Verba 1965, 547). As this chapter has attempted to demonstrate, the notion of freedom (and its various derivatives) in the Caribbean has become exclusively focused on the symbolic-ideological dimensions and has increasingly lost the tangible pragmatic-utilitarian side from which it originally derived. This shift in the meaning of the notion has served the elites of the region, who have actively promoted its use as an ideology.[21] In order to reverse the shift that has occurred, it would appear that a de-ideologizing of the notion's current use ought to be promoted.

It is suggested here, therefore, that credible leaders of Caribbean civil society take the initiative and voice their view that they disallow political leaders to use and celebrate the notion of Caribbean freedom and independence as long as they do not genuinely intend to fill these notions with the life they deserve. By their demonstrative non-attendance of events sponsored by political parties or the government to celebrate national independence, emancipation, national heroes and so on, individuals of high standing in society should demonstrate their conviction that these institutions have little credibility to organize and celebrate Caribbean freedom. Equally, they could publicly return state honours, medals and titles conferred to them in protest against state transgression. By following such a strategy of passive resistance, a forceful statement could be made which severely undermines a critical element of political legitimization and which could become a possible force for positive change in practices of state oppression and symbolic exploitation. As the French philosopher Henri Lefebvre reminded us, each individual may be seen as only a grain of sand and society as "human sand"; taken together, however, "they form a mass – indeed the heaviest and most impenetrable of masses. A sandbag can stop bullets!" (1992, 152).[22] Saying, however, that the notion of freedom in the Caribbean should be somehow devalued might be misconstrued as a reactionary project. Because of the inherent danger of being misunderstood, it has to be made very clear that the goal is not to minimize freedom but, *au contraire,* to make it impervious to classist misuse for the political legitimization of its own antithesis. It is only if the notion of freedom is itself freed from the ambiguities that have historically surrounded it and from the hegemonic interpretations imposed by insincere elites that it will be able to be mobilized for human rights, democratic reform, enforcement of political responsibility and economic empowerment. At the same time, it needs to be stressed that freedom is not in every instance simply a right of every individual, but that it can also be a privilege that has obligations and performance criteria attached to it. As Jean-Paul Sartre explained, it also has to be tempered by the demands of the collective in order to prevent social chaos, and it is as much about potential and aspirations as it is about maximizing individual or collective space.

Acknowledgements

This chapter has been previously published under the same title in *Identities: Global Studies in Culture and Power* 8, no. 3 (2001): 413–40.

Notes

1. It has to be remembered that the middle strata in most Caribbean societies cannot be equated with the European middle classes. Caribbean societies are far too complex and shot through with race and colour contradictions to establish such a simple correlation. As Novella Keith aptly remarked, they never uttered the "cry of freedom" (1982, 30). For brevity's sake, however, we will use this term and designate it to mean the small strata of African and Indian Caribbeans who were able to attain a certain measure of education, wealth, property or social position even before the arrival of independence.
2. This is the reason that all progressive and politically aware citizens ought to emphasize the youthful courage and agitation of the Scholl siblings and hold them in high regard. However, that even in contemporary Germany honouring the resistance to the Hitler regime often resembles more a footnote and a formality of public affairs shows the persistence of Elias's characterization of the German political psyche.
3. Pye, however, seems to put an undue emphasis on the rational or conscious components shaping a particular political culture. In the light of findings from modern communications science, anthropology and postmodern analyses of politics, I would be inclined to give greater credence to subconsciously formed elements of political culture.
4. Using Verba's definition of political culture, however, is not meant to imply that I subscribe to his Eurocentric modernization theory, which uncritically posits European and American political culture as the model to be emulated by developing countries. In fact, Caribbean political culture has been defined by a struggle against racialized European concepts of politics, economics and human rights, which were basically established for Europeans only.
5. Stephen White (1979) deserves credit for being one of the initiators of this renaissance.
6. Together with Ian Boxill (1994), I would argue, however, that a purely postmodern interpretation of political culture is not (yet) a very fruitful approach for the interpretation of most developing societies. Here the imperatives of economic survival, social equality and modern standards

of political participation rule out the postmodern emphasis on shifting identities, deconstructable polyculturalism, unstable definitions and so forth.
7. With Herbert Aptheker (1981), I do not necessarily perceive a contradiction between revolution and democracy.
8. As Aptheker has correctly pointed out, freedom is a historical process that always "must be viewed within its time and place and social context" (1981, 5).
9. Cited in Holt (1992, 61). Of course, here one of my own biases is showing, which is greatly informed by my familiarity with the Jamaican experience. It has to be noted, for example, that the character of the peasantry in the different Caribbean territories varies in different ways (see, for example, Mintz and Price 1986). As the case of Antigua also shows, not all Caribbean countries went through an apprenticeship period. Nevertheless, the net consequence of such variations was the same, since in Antigua the freed slaves were, after emancipation, also forced to remain on the plantation in order to sustain themselves. We would also need to point out that the notion of freedom means different things to different peoples at different times. Basically, however, for most people it refers to a sense of self-determination and justice. Unfortunately, in a chapter of this length not all of the wide variations between different Caribbean societies can be discussed; only the obvious trends can be highlighted.
10. It is interesting to note in this context Dawa Norbu's quotation of G.F. Rudenpo: "The concept 'we', that is, people's idea of themselves as a social community, was secondary to the concept 'They'. 'We' ideas originate from an apprehension of the difference from 'other' " (1992, 102–3).
11. In a lecture delivered on 14 January 1976, Foucault pointed out that "basically, we have to produce truth like we have to produce wealth; indeed, we have to produce truth *in order to be able to produce wealth*" (1978, 76; my translation and emphasis). I am mindful that the questions of property, ownership and persistence of foreign investors play an important role in explaining the motivation for the middle class to produce this particular version of history. However, in this chapter I am more concerned with the technique itself and its consequences.
12. During a demonstration in Kingston in the mid-1990s, this relationship between official and popular ethos was etched into my mind as an emblematic representation when a minister of government (Robert Pickersgill) attempted to address and calm down a sizable crowd of protesters gathered in Half-Way Tree while a juice vendor boldly crossed in

front of him lifting up his product and shouting out from the depth of his lungs, "Bag juice!"
13. There are also a gender and a "race" dimension to this ambivalence. Thus, it has to be recalled that colonial slavemasters granted freedom to girls and women more often than to men. The reason for this preference, of course, was that instead of being formally enslaved, they became sexually enslaved as mistresses and as mothers to illegitimate children. With regard to the question of differential validity of this notion for different ethnic groups, it has to be kept in mind that African-Creole workers in Trinidad, Guyana and Jamaica long regarded the imported indentured Indian workers as "strike breakers", that is, as an ethnic group that negatively affected the quality and extent of their personal freedom.
14. Promoting this argument means, of course, that (in my view) opinions contrary to those of the state or any other organization or authority, as well as the right to publicly express them, are the ones that are to be protected from persecution. Opinions that are in line with the "official truth" do not require protection.
15. This is true even in the pursuit of some foreign policy ventures (see, for example, Henke 1996a, 1998); as Boxill (1993) has demonstrated, insular individualism among the elites has frustrated the development of an "ideology of regionalism"; as James (2000) suggests, there is decreasing acceptance in the region of immigrants coming from Caribbean sister nations. Both observations, and the persistent threat of separatism as in the case of Nevis and Tobago, appear to indicate that co-operation and regionalism have been sacrificed on the altar of an individualistic ideology of "independence". Barbados's prime minister Owen Arthur recently pointed out that "direct investment by the nationals of any Caribbean nation in any other Caribbean state is somewhat perceived as a threat" (2000).
16. Several countries of the region (such as Trinidad and Tobago, Guyana, and Grenada) have developed genuine multi-party systems. Others, such as Jamaica, may have more than two parties, but these have not yet reached a threshold of political viability and may well disappear.
17. Incidentally, in May 2000 the human rights organization Amnesty International charged the Jamaican minister of justice with making damaging and divisive comments about human rights representatives in his country. According to Amnesty, the minister "misrepresented those defending human rights, claiming they care little for police officers killed in the line of duty and labelling them 'human rights wimps' " (Amnesty International 2000).

18. In the Caribbean region such a commission is also currently being considered in Suriname.
19. I am aware that there are inherently undemocratic practices and traditions of intolerance prevalent in sections of Caribbean society. These include issues such as flogging (as disciplinary measure for both children and convicts), gay bashing and domestic violence against women, to mention just a few. However, to include a discussion of these and their possible relation to the choice of leaders cannot be reasonably achieved within the confines of this paper.
20. Work ethic is not to be equated with discipline, although the latter is included in it. By "ethic" I also mean a sense of pride in one's own work, which serves in turn as a natural motivator. To achieve this kind of work ethic requires a national effort in which the working people recognize themselves in their work.
21. Implicit throughout the argument is the view that the majority of Caribbean people experience a lack of participation in the political process, and indeed Verba points out that this alienation is a factor for the relative attractiveness of an ideological approach to politics. Thus, because of the alienation, it becomes more likely that the focus is on distant, more millennial objectives which, despite their apparent unattainability, are likely to be more psychologically rewarding than smaller and more pragmatic goals, which, "since they too are unattainable due to the lack of influence over the government, will appear petty and trivial" (Verba 1965, 558).
22. As I prepared this chapter for its first publication, an echo of the popular revolutions in Eastern Europe reverberated through Serbia as the Yugoslav people were fighting to rid themselves of Slobodan Milosevic, ten years after the fall of communism behind the Iron Curtain.

References

Alulis, Joseph. 1993. "The Promise of Democracy and the Problem of Liberty". In *Tocqueville's Defense of Human Liberty: Current Essays*, edited by Peter Augustine Lawler and Joseph Alulis, 37–61. New York: Garland.

Amnesty International. 2000. "Jamaica: Comments Deriding Those Defending Human Rights – Damaging and Divisive". Press release, 11 May. Available online: http://web.amnesty.org/ai.nsf/Index/AMR380042000?OpenDocument&of=COUNTRIES\JAMAICA, accessed 19 October 2002.

Aptheker, Herbert. 1981. *The Nature of Democracy, Freedom, and Revolution*. New York: International Publishers.

Arthur, Owen. 2000. "Address by Prime Minister Owen Arthur of Barbados at the Third Caribbean Media Conference, Georgetown, Guyana on May 5". *Jamaica Gleaner*, 14 May.

Barnard, F.M. 1989. "Will and Political Rationality in Rousseau". In *Modern Political Theory from Hobbes to Marx: Key Debates*, edited by Jack Lively and Andrew Reeve, 129–48. London: Routledge.

Boxill, Ian. 1993. *Ideology and Caribbean Integration*. Kingston, Jamaica: Consortium Graduate School of Social Sciences, University of the West Indies.

———. 1994. "Globalization, Sustainable Development, and Postmodernism: The New Ideology of Imperialism". *Humanity and Society* 18, no. 4: 3–18.

Carnegie, Charles V. 1996. "The Dundus and the Nation". *Cultural Anthropology*, no. 11: 470–509.

———. 1999. "Garvey and the Black Transnation". *Small Axe: A Journal of Criticism*, no. 5: 48–71.

Dewey, John. 1963. *Freedom and Culture*. New York: Capricorn.

Elias, Norbert. 1999. *Über den Prozeß der Zivilisation: Soziogenetische und psychogenetische Untersuchungen*. 2 vols. Frankfurt: Suhrkamp.

Foucault, Michel. 1978. *Dispositive der Macht: Über Sexualität, Wissen und Wahrheit*. Berlin: Merve Verlag.

Gibbins, John R., ed. 1989. *Contemporary Political Culture: Politics in a Postmodern Age*. London: Sage.

Giddens, Anthony. 1991. *Modernity and Self-Identity: Self and Identity in the Late Modern Age*. Stanford: Stanford University Press.

Greiffenhagen, Martin. 1997. "Norbert Elias und die Politische Kulturforschung". Lecture, Norbert Elias Centenary Conference, Centre for Interdisciplinary Research, University of Bielefeld, 20–22 June 1997. Available online: http://www.uni-bielefeld.de/Publikationen/97-4-Greiffenhagen.pdf

Habermas, Jürgen. 1998. "Über den öffentlichen Gebrauch der Historie". In *Die postnationale Konstellation: Politische Essays*, edited by Jürgen Habermas, 47–61. Frankfurt: Suhrkamp.

Harriott, Anthony. 1999. "Police and Citizenship in Jamaica". Public lecture, John Jay College of Criminal Justice – CUNY, New York City, November 11.

Henke, Holger. 1996a. "Dependency and Foreign Relations: A Comparative Study of the Manley and Seaga Governments in Jamaica, 1972–1989". PhD diss., University of the West Indies, Mona.

———. 1996b. "Mapping the 'Inner Plantation': A Cultural Exploration of the Origins of Caribbean Local Discourse". *Social and Economic Studies* 45, no. 4: 51–75.

———. 1998. "Drugs in the Caribbean: The 'Shiprider' Controversy and the Question of Sovereignty". *European Review of Latin American and Caribbean Studies*, no. 64: 27–47.

Holt, Thomas C. 1992. *The Problem of Freedom: Race, Labor, and Politics in Jamaica and Britain, 1832–1938*. Baltimore: Johns Hopkins University Press.

James, Carl. 2000. " 'Immigrants', Political Culture and the Goal of Integration in the Anglophone Caribbean". Paper presented at the 26th Annual Conference of the Caribbean Studies Association, 29 May–3 June, Gros Islet, St Lucia.

Keith, Novella E. 1982. "Democratic Socialism in Jamaica: Politics of Reform, Transition to Socialism or 'Third Way' of Development?" PhD diss., Rutgers University, New Brunswick, NJ.

Knight, Franklin W. 1990. *The Caribbean: The Genesis of a Fragmented Nationalism*. New York: Oxford University Press.

Lefebvre, Henri. 1992. *Critique of Everyday Life*. Translated by John Moore. London: Verso.

Look Lai, Walton. 1992. "C.L.R. James and Trinidadian Nationalism". In *C.L.R. James's Caribbean*, edited by Paget Henry and Paul Buhle, 174–209. Durham, NC: Duke University Press.

Mars, Perry. 1998. *Ideology and Change: The Transformation of the Caribbean Left*. Detroit: Wayne State University Press and University of the West Indies Press.

Mintz, Sidney W., and Sally Price, eds. 1986. *Caribbean Contours*. Baltimore: Johns Hopkins University Press.

Morais, Richard. 2000. "Maroons Threaten Action". *Jamaica Gleaner*, 16 March.

Munroe, Trevor. 1984. *The Politics of Constitutional Decolonization: Jamaica 1944–62*. Mona, Jamaica: Institute of Social and Economic Research.

———. 1996. "Caribbean Democracy: Decay or Renewal?" In *Constructing Democratic Governance: Mexico, Central America, and the Caribbean in the 1990s*, edited by Jorge I. Dominguez and Abraham F. Lowenthal, 104–17. Baltimore: Johns Hopkins University Press.

———. 2000. "Caribbean Thought and the Political Process". In *Contending with Destiny: The Caribbean in the Twenty-first Century*, edited by Kenneth Hall and Denis Benn, 237–47. Kingston, Jamaica: Ian Randle.

Nanton, Philip. 1983. "The Changing Pattern of State Control in St Vincent and the Grenadines". In *Crisis in the Caribbean,* edited by Fitzroy Ambursley and Robin Cohen, 223–46. New York: Monthly Review.

Norbu, Dawa. 1992. *Culture and the Politics of Third World Nationalism.* London: Routledge.

Payne, Anthony, and Paul Sutton, eds. 1993. *Modern Caribbean Politics.* Kingston, Jamaica: Ian Randle.

Pye, Lucian W. 1965. "Introduction: Political Culture and Political Development". In *Political Culture and Political Development,* edited by Lucian W. Pye and Sidney Verba, 3–26. Princeton: Princeton University Press.

Rodney, Walter. 1981. *A History of the Guyanese Working People, 1881–1905.* Baltimore: Johns Hopkins University Press.

Singham, A.W. 1968. *The Hero and the Crowd in a Colonial Polity.* New Haven: Yale University Press.

Sue-A-Quan, Trev. 1999. *Cane Reapers: Chinese Indentured Immigrants in Guyana.* Vancouver, BC: Riftswood.

Townsend, Rohan. 2000. "Yes, We Are Ashamed!" *Jamaica Gleaner,* 20 March.

Verba, Sidney. 1965. "Comparative Political Culture". In *Political Culture and Political Development,* edited by Lucian W. Pye and Sidney Verba, 512–60. Princeton: Princeton University Press.

White, Stephen. 1979. *Political Culture and Soviet Politics.* London: Macmillan.

[6]

Presenting the Past
The Construction of National History in a Jamaican Tourist Site

Anita M. Waters

Introduction

Beginning well before Jamaica became independent and continuing through the present, a variety of constituencies private and public, local and foreign, have launched plans for the development of Port Royal in Kingston, Jamaica, and each plan encodes specific social and political interests. Each plan reflects the greater or lesser influence of a variety of actors, including academic historians, bureaucrats, entrepreneurs, archaeologists and politicians, as well as the unofficial historians of popular culture and informal social memory. Each embodies a historical narrative with an implicit framework of national identity.

Disputes over the framing of history are not a postmodern development in the case of the postcolonial Caribbean. On the contrary, the history of that region has long been characterized by polarized approaches, sudden rewrites and socially patterned amnesias. Venues for heated debates about the essential features of Caribbean history range from parliamentary assemblies and university classrooms to reggae dance halls and calypso tents. It is no coincidence that one of the most serious public disturbances in Jamaican history, the Rodney Riots of 1968, was touched off by the deportation of a historian, Walter Rodney.

Port Royal's claim to importance as a venue of Caribbean history is indisputable. Located at the tip of the peninsula that forms the Kingston harbour in Jamaica, it was a booming New World city of eight thousand whose association with a variety of pirates and other outlaws led it to be declared the "wickedest city in the world". Then, one June day in 1692, a massive earthquake killed thousands and much of the city sank beneath the sea. Port Royal had a centuries-long history of natural and social drama: besides the earthquake, there were several major fires and innumerable violent hurricanes. In the 1700s a major British naval base was built on what remained of Port Royal; the hero of the Battle of Trafalgar, Horatio Nelson, had his first command there.

After the huge earthquake and other catastrophes, Port Royal was never again a place where well-off civilians took up residence, and with the decline of the naval base in the 1800s and its closure in 1905, Port Royal sank deeply into poverty. In the 1880s yet another hurricane decimated the area; twenty-five years later, many of the damaged houses remained unrepaired (Black 1988, 63). Only in 1936 was a paved road constructed between Kingston and the village. Throughout this time, there has been a continuous presence of a community of one to two thousand people. Tourist books usually characterize Port Royal as a sleepy fishing village.

In this chapter I first discuss the apparently chronic crisis of historical perspective in the Caribbean. Second, I set out a conceptual framework that uses concepts from the social memory literature and discuss texts that spell out key problematics in Caribbean and other production of historical narrative of the postcolonial period. Third, I trace the development of plans for Port Royal that span thirty years in light of the processes that affected the production of history in the intervening years. Finally, I consider the trajectory of meanings that Port Royal has embodied in postcolonial Jamaican political culture.

History in the Caribbean

Richard Price locates one of the strongest images of Caribbean amnesia in George Lamming's novel *In the Castle of My Skin*. A Barbadian schoolboy in the 1930s is learning about slavery from his teacher. Lamming tells us his thoughts:

> He didn't understand how anyone could be bought by another. . . . Slave. . . . Thank God, he wasn't ever a slave. He or his father or his father's father. Thank God nobody in Barbados was ever a slave. . . . [He] laughed quietly. Imagine any man in any part of the world owning a man or woman from Barbados. . . . And nobody knew where this slavery business took place. . . . Probably it never happened at all. (Cited in Price 1998, 167–68)

Lamming is not the only Caribbean intellectual who senses an absence of history. In Derek Walcott's words, the region suffers from an "absence of ruins" (cited in Price 1998, 167), Orlando Patterson writes that "to be a West Indian is to live in a state of utter pastlessness" (cited in Price 1998, 167) and Edouard Glissant notes that history in the Caribbean is characterized by "the loss of collective memory, the careful erasure of the past" (cited in Price 1998, 166). Walcott wrote, "In time the slave surrendered to amnesia. That amnesia is the true history of the New World" (Walcott 1976, 114).

The pervasive sensation that history is forgotten has led some writers towards the deliberative and transformative process of regaining history. One must "lay claim to and take hold of our history" both in order to be fully conscious and to "transform the unjust system we have inherited" (Sylvia Wynter, quoted in Nettleford 1976, 149). But is Caribbean history forgotten, or is it just that one voice is not heard? Sociologist Marie-José Jolivet writes, "To denounce the 'erasure', to denounce collective 'amnesia', is little more than to deplore the fact that collective memory is not what one would like it to be" (cited in Price 1998, 212).

Caribbean history is often seen as polarized in two broad camps. William Green identifies the first as that of "imperial" historians, who see the cultural tensions between segments of Caribbean society as "an enlightened and complex culture struggling to subdue an unenlightened and primitive one in exceedingly difficult circumstances" (1993, 33). The second he calls the "creolization" approach, in which Afro-

Caribbean culture is "elevate[d] to a position of equality in a bipolar struggle" in which Africans in the Caribbean resist the domination of their former colonial masters (p. 33).

Walcott's characterization of the ways that literature serves "the muse of history" is a similar extreme duality. One participates either in "a literature of revenge written by the descendants of slaves" that "yellows into polemic" or in "a literature of remorse written by the descendants of masters" that "evaporates in pathos" (Walcott 1976, 112). Two postures towards history are available to Caribbean people, according to Walcott: "metropolitan cynicism," which leads to a sense that African history is inferior; and a romantic, oversimplifying focus on exotic customs, rituals and gods, a longing "for the ancestral dignity of the wanderer-warrior" (p. 125). Both are problematic.

In Jamaica, the ambivalence about history seemed to have reached a peak from the late 1960s through the 1970s, when many revisionist projects were undertaken. In particular, slave resistance was discovered anew (Mathurin 1975). In 1975, Michael Manley's government named two new national heroes: Nanny, a Maroon folk hero known for clashes with the British, and Sam Sharpe, who led a rebellion in 1830 that deeply shook the slave-holding world. The government's Agency for Public Information published a history of Nanny and Sam Sharpe written by Edward Kamau Brathwaite (1976), and a public square in Montego Bay was renamed for Sharpe. Another manifestation of the urgency with which history was approached was a collection of essays edited by John Hearne and published in 1976 as part of the regional arts festival Carifesta; it included views on Caribbean history from V.S. Naipaul, Brathwaite, Jan Carew and Aimé Césaire, among other accomplished writers and thinkers of the region.

Social Memory

The sociological perspective known as "social memory" challenges a positivist or Rankian view of the past that supposes that the job of the historian is to uncover what "actually happened". Instead, narrative history is seen as "an organic form of knowledge" (Samuel 1994, x) whose content is shaped by social forces. Maurice Halbwachs, the nineteenth-century founder of the field of social memory, recognized that shared memories sometimes served as markers in social differentiation.

Halbwachs used the concept of "presentism" (Olick and Robbins 1998) to denote the observation that contemporary interests and values determine how histories are written. Conflicts over presentations of history are seen as arenas in which contemporary political issues, some partisan, some gender-, class- or ethnicity-related, are articulated. In a good example of presentism, Martha Norkunas's ethnography of Monterey, California, as a tourist destination shows that it presents a "selectively reconstructed history" with clear underlying political and ideological assumptions (1993, 9): "Certain groups in the city claimed their power was based on social evolutionary superiority and substantiated that claim through distortions in historical and touristic texts. History, literature, ethnicity, class, nature and even industrialism were brought under control and integrated into the ideology of dominance" (p. 93).

Jamaican election rhetoric is a clear laboratory in which to observe presentism in historical narratives; politicians' historical references attempt to establish direct continuity between commemorated events of the past and their own contemporary leadership. In the 1976 election, for example, when the People's National Party (PNP) needed to summon support from women voters, it capitalized on its decision to name two new national heroes and claimed in its advertisements that the Maroon leader Nanny would have approved of the PNP's policies towards women.

Numerous authors have pointed out the importance of commemorative rituals and monuments in contributing to national identity (Barthel 1996; Gillis 1994; Hobsbawm and Ranger 1983), including museums (Bennett 1995). History is regularly revised to reinforce the power of the ruling elite, whether by inventing traditions (Ranger 1983), by asserting an official version of past events (Melanson 1991) or by projecting an image of social integration onto a disorganized past (Lewis 1975). In fact, governments are sometimes so blatantly manipulative of public history that, in Raphael Samuel's words, "historians have become accustomed to thinking of commemorization as a cheat, something which ruling elites impose on the subaltern classes. It is a weapon of social control, a means of generating consensus, and legitimating the status quo by reference to a mythologized version of the past" (1994, 16). Instead of accepting such an outcome as a given, Samuel recommends a more open-minded, ethnographic approach in which other possible official motives are considered. Ethnographies of heritage development in the United States have noted, for example, the increasing influence that African Americans have had on the way that history there is framed (Fraser and Butler 1986; Horton and Crew 1989). That approach is especially appropriate in the Caribbean context, where both competition between foreign and local ruling elites and active subaltern narrative production conspire to prevent a single strong official version of national history.

The social memory literature has also developed the idea of conflict in presentations of history, subsumed under the concept of contestation, and rooted in Michel Foucault's notion of counter-memory, memories that "differ from, and often challenge, dominant discourses" (Olick and Robbins 1998, 126). Counter-memories and unofficial histories enter into social memory in competition with the official versions endorsed by ruling elites. History's "sources are promiscuous, drawing not only on real-life experience but also memory and myth, fantasy and desire" (Samuel 1994, x), not just those of the ruling class, but also those of other social groups. One rich source of unofficial memory is popular culture, which depending upon the society may include the works of tapestry weavers, cartoon animators, artefact collectors or street musicians.

Contestation between official memory and counter-memories in national historical narratives is relatively rare, according to James Fentress and Chris Wickham (1992), because elites tend to have a firm grasp on the construction of national consciousness. However, the social memory literature tends to focus on European national histories and has not adequately addressed the specific memory-work that postcolonial nations are engaged in.

Silences in Caribbean History

Michel-Ralph Trouillot, in his book *Silencing the Past: Power and the Production of History,* focuses on the "silences" that enter history as concretely as do the facts that are mentioned. "By silence," he writes, "I mean an active and transitive process: one 'silences' a fact or an individual as a silencer silences a gun" (1995, 48). Trouillot likens the production of narratives about the Haitian Revolution to a play-by-play account of a sports event. The chronicler does not tell everything that happens, only those things that are important to the game. There is a shared framework – the rules of the game – that shapes both what the chronicler says and what the audience understands. The rules derive from the fact that "narratives are premised on previous understandings ... shaped by Western conventions and procedures" (p. 55). In the case of Haiti, privileging literacy and access to French culture limits the ability to produce influential narratives to a tiny elite (p. 55).

According to Trouillot, silences enter history in four "moments": first, the creation of sources (what is mentioned in these sources, and what is not); second, the creation of archives (what is thought to be important enough to save and catalogue, and what is discarded); third, the production of narratives; and finally, the moment when the significance of people or events is judged in the future.

In *The Convict and the Colonel* (1998), Richard Price traces the story of an anti-colonial uprising and consequent massacre in rural Martinique in 1925. The event's clear connotations of colonial domination and resistance have given way to remembering one of its participants, the folk artist Medard Aribot, as the builder of a charming little house that appears on postcards of Martinique. Price wonders how "one generation's powerful historical metaphors could so quickly become the next generation's trivial pursuit" (1998, 157). He calls the process "the postcarding of the past", or "the folklorization of colonialism" (p. 173). Medard is no longer "a symbol of struggle and anticolonial contestation" (p. 174) but instead is associated only with a picturesque and colourful cottage that graces tourist brochures.

Price's critique of "postcarding" history underscores the fact that the silences are not random: they serve specific social, political and economic interests. This is also true of the more specific type of historical narrative production that we are studying here: the development of "heritage" destinations. Commodification and trivialization are frequent charges levelled against developers of heritage tourism destinations (Barthel 1996; Morgan and Pritchard 1998; Pattullo 1996). David Lowenthal claims that historical narratives at some museums are "gross generalizations, entertaining but largely fictitious accounts, a conflating of time periods, and sanitized versions of discomfiting realities" (quoted in Greene 2000, 19).

Furthermore, to make heritage destinations more appealing to the Europeans and European Americans who comprise the majority of tourists, local Afro-Caribbean culture is often sacrificed. "By not displaying the cultural heritage of the majority of the population," said one critic, the destination "has taken from them, by implication, their role as history makers, as active participants in their own past" (Cannizzo 1987, quoted in Cummins 1992, 51). Some tourist culture derives its sensibility more from "white folk memories" of race relations in the US plantation South than from any Caribbean culture (Pattullo 1996). Afro-Caribbean culture is, in Richard Burton's words, "subject to a fatal combination of folklorization, exoticization, and commodification", making the modern Caribbean person "as much a spectator of his or her 'own' culture as the average tourist" (Burton, quoted in Price 1998, 183).

Research Questions and Methods

Port Royal is in many ways an ideal backdrop for an exploration of the issues connecting social memory and present-day social and political interests. Since the 1950s it has sparked the imagination of scores of architects, historians, planners and entrepreneurs who have developed more than a dozen discrete plans for Port Royal, some extremely elaborate and far-reaching. At the same time, almost no actual changes have been made to the physical structures at Port Royal, so each plan has started anew with designs to change nearly the same historical remains into its own vision of a commemorated past. All of the plans offer fresh narratives about Port Royal's long history, and some offer critiques of previous plans. Why Port Royal is so constant an inspiration and why plans to change it almost never materialize are two questions related to this project.

This research addresses other issues as well:

- To what degree do various presentations of history at Port Royal reflect the social and economic interests of those who control the project?
- What were the extant narratives at the points at which plans were developed, and which of these were influential?
- What trends can be discerned in the presentation of colonialism and imperialism, of slavery and resistance, of European and African experience? Is opposition to colonialism "postcarded"?

- What counter-memories or unofficial narratives are evident? Is Port Royal an arena in which official history and counter-memories collide?
- What social, cultural or political groups vie for influence over the framing of Port Royal? Are their contemporary interests evident in their perspective on Port Royal's past?

This chapter is based on materials gathered over the past three years, including five long taped interviews with major stakeholders, informal interviews with eleven other individuals and a study of documents and clippings files at the National Library of Jamaica, the Urban Development Corporation and the branch library in Port Royal. The presentation of Port Royal to tourists was explored in descriptions gathered from nine tourist guides published in the United States, the United Kingdom and Jamaica. Trends in academic interests in specific areas and eras of Caribbean history were charted in *Historical Abstracts* from 1957 onwards and in *Historiography* (Kinnell 1987). Over the past several years I have familiarized myself with the available exhibits and the physical layout of Port Royal. I took many photographs of the historic areas and museum exhibits, and took careful notes about the content of the guided tour of Fort Charles, which was provided to me by one of the regular guides hired by the Jamaica National Heritage Trust (JNHT). While most proposed plans for Port Royal have not come to fruition, displays such as those of the Fort Charles museum are useful crystallizations of the thinking about history that was current when the installations were created.

For each plan to develop Port Royal, I first explored the way Port Royal's history is presented. I also noted what sources were consulted in constructing a plan's narrative about Port Royal's history and what kinds of concerns about authenticity were expressed. In addition, for each plan I explored five other issues:

- What was the intended role for the Port Royal community itself in the proposed project?
- What concerns were addressed regarding the natural setting of Port Royal and the environmental impact of the proposed development?
- Who were the major stakeholders in the plan?
- Who were the intended audiences or consumers of the development?
- What was the role of profit in the plan?

In this chapter, I cannot report in detail about all of these issues. I will instead provide an overview of the trajectory of change in plans over the last fifty years and then return to the theoretical questions posed at the beginning.

Port Royal Chronology

Since the 1950s there has been interest in developing Port Royal, mainly for tourist purposes. In 1951 the British Colonial Office produced a study recommending "official support of neglected historic sites" in hopes of gaining "greater economic returns by opening them to the tourism market" (Ackworth 1951, cited in Cummins 1992, 41). In the same year Port Royal was devastated by a hurricane that left only 10 houses standing out of 260 in the village (Black 1988).

In the hurricane's aftermath, the colonial government of Jamaica made some infrastructural improvements in and around Port Royal, and in the mid-1950s a company owned by English businessman Anthony Jenkinson constructed the Morgan's Harbour Hotel and Beach Club, Port Royal's only hotel. In October 1952 an organization of local residents was formed to rehabilitate the area, "all of which was vested to them" (*Daily Gleaner*, 30 July 1968, 23). The Port Royal Brotherhood, as it was called, was part of the Ministry of Housing. Clinton Black (1988) suggests that there was an intentional connection between the new organization's name and the buccaneer collective the Confederacy of the Brethren of the Coast. If this is true, it is one of the very few instances in which the Port Royal community associated itself with pirates.

The 1965 Plan

The earliest comprehensive plan was produced by the Port Royal Company of Merchants (PRCM), spearheaded by Sir Anthony Jenkinson, the owner of Morgan's Harbour Hotel. Jenkinson submitted proposals to the government in 1964, and a meeting took place with Edward Seaga, then minister of development and welfare, who approved it in principle. The plan is documented in a fifty-four-page feasibility report commissioned by the government and written by the London firm of Robert

McAlpine and Sons, Civil Engineering and Building Contractors, on behalf of the PRCM, to further explore Jenkinson's proposals.

The proposal (PRCM 1965, 48–54) called for two new hotels, one at Fort Charles with 250 rooms, one in the Old Coaling Station with 200 rooms; recreational facilities, including a multi-use swimming pool; and a re-formed shoreline with a newly created 800-foot beach of imported white sand. Also planned were a new marina with apartments, boat- and car-parking facilities and a cruise-ship pier, and the conversion of the old cast-iron Naval Hospital into a terminal with adjacent boutiques, bars, an aquarium, bowling alleys and tennis courts. New construction of seven buildings, replicas of the seventeenth-century pre-earthquake period, would constitute the historical area of the attraction. King's House would replicate "the building in which Sir Henry Morgan lived whilst governor" and was to be "a completely timber built building. Elaborate wooden carvings will emphasize the nautical associations" (p. 50). Governor's House would serve as museum, housing "the more important treasures" (p. 51), and the Goldsmith's Shop would house banking facilities. Other planned replicas were St Paul's Church and tower, the tavern, the inn and the Merchants' Exchange. None of these plans was realized.

The history of Jamaica in general and Port Royal in particular was recounted in the PRCM feasibility report in a little over two pages, half of this devoted to Port Royal as an English town that existed before the earthquake of 1692. Mention was made of the Arawaks, "of whom little or no traces remain" (PRCM 1965, 9) and who disappeared completely within fifty years of Columbus's landing. The report briefly described the settlement of the Spaniards from 1494 to 1655, mostly in Spanish Town. Neither the Arawaks nor the Spanish used the peninsula much. The British took the island in 1655, and construction began on the port at Port Royal the following year.

The word "pirates" was not used in the report. Instead, it pointed to Port Royal's

> notoriety, stemming from the activities of Henry Morgan, who lived in Port Royal from 1668 until his death in 1688, and who was one of the best known buccaneers of this colourful and bloodthirsty period. He later became Sir Henry Morgan and Lieut. Governor, and led many lucrative expeditions against the Spanish possessions in the New World. (PRCM 1965, 9)

The prosperity of the pre-earthquake city was noted, but the focus was mostly on wealth that was seized by buccaneers. However, one of the buildings that was proposed for restoration was a Merchants' Exchange, which would be "re-constructed in accordance with a Lloyd's Coffee House on the first floor, whilst the ground area [would] be available for 'Merchantmen to exchange their wares', as was the case in the seventeenth century" (PRCM 1965, 51).

Port Royal's history as a British naval base was valorized in this 1965 document:

> The early eighteenth century saw the rise of Port Royal as a Naval Station of great importance, reaching its greatest brilliance in the last twenty-five years of the century. Some of the most famous names in British Naval History, Benbow, Vernon, Sir Peter Parker, Nelson, Collingwood, Rodney and Prince William Henry, later King William IV, were all stationed at Port Royal in the eighteenth century.
>
> From 1815 onwards, while still flourishing as a naval station, Port Royal's fame began to fade and in 1905 the Dockyard was closed. (PRCM 1965, 10)

The report saw the value of Fort Charles in the fact that it once housed Nelson; that Nelson was in residence for only a few weeks of Port Royal's three-hundred-year history does not, evidently, diminish the honour.

While others before and after this have suggested a wholesale eviction of the community of Port Royal, in the PRCM plans the members of that community were seen as a potential labour force. In fact, the community's high unemployment rate was seen as "encouraging", in that labour shortages would not impede the project (PRCM 1965, 24).

The sources used for this plan were a description made by an English surveyor in 1688, a maritime exploration report of an expedition organized jointly by the National Geographic Society of America and the Smithsonian Institution, and documents from Jamaican and British institutions, including the British Admiralty. The only concerns about authenticity were for architectural authenticity. The seven planned buildings would be "exact replicas", though outfitted with modern conveniences such as air conditioning and refrigeration (PRCM 1965, 50). No mention was made of the African presence in Port Royal at any point in its history. Nor were any concerns expressed about the environmental impact of this development.

The primary target audience was overseas visitors, especially those arriving by cruise ship. At the time that this plan was written, unlike today, most cruise-ship dockings in Jamaica landed in Kingston. This plan specified that all the new facilities would be open to the public as well as tourists; in the early 1960s there were still tourist facilities in the British West Indies that forbade entrance to local Afro-Caribbeans (Kincaid 1988; Pattullo 1996).

The Urban Development Corporation Plans

When the PRCM plan failed to materialize, development of the site devolved to agencies of the Jamaican government, which had been independent since 1962. One such agency, the Urban Development Corporation (UDC), supported a plan that distinctively expresses the interests of public parks administrators and archaeologists (UDC 1967).

The UDC's plan called for construction of two hotels, a new town commercial centre, marinas and a white sand beach, but omitted the idea of a cruise-ship pier. Historic parks were planned, including a long strip of park along the area called Morgan's Line, linking the remains of Fort Charles with the planned shopping area. One of the UDC's objectives came to fruition seventeen years later when "Nelson's House" in Fort Charles became a museum.

The narration of Port Royal's history that the UDC offered again evoked buccaneers, admirals and the pre-earthquake town. The Hanover Gun Battery was called "the ideal site for the children's Museum of Pirates" (UDC 1967, 17), but that is the only context in which the word "pirate" was used. Instead, the document deferentially referred to Port Royal's "association with the Brethren of the Coast, Buccaneers", and noted that "names such as Morgan, Nelson, Rodney and Benbow have made the name Port Royal internationally famous" (p. 6), interestingly conflating several time periods and linking Morgan with British military officers. In this history, like the one before it, there was no reference to the historical experience of Africans in Port Royal.

The intended audience for these planned facilities was a mixture of Jamaicans and foreigners, mostly day visitors and groups of schoolchildren. Although the plan called for new hotels, the plan said that "it is perhaps wise to discourage overnight accommodation on the strip" (UDC 1967, 15).

In contrast to the entrepreneurial interests of the PRCM, the UDC very directly reflected the social and economic interests of the public administrators, academics and other local and expatriate professionals. The document called for the employment of a contingent of archaeologists and historians in continuous operation for fifty years to come, as well as of managers for the "careful handling" that would be necessary "if we are to create a resort area around and within an historic site" (UDC 1967, 16).

Architects and archaeologists at that time were realizing their professions' potential gain from Port Royal projects. Marine archaeologists, first Edwin Link and then Robert Marx, had explored the underwater city from the late 1950s onwards (see Link 1960; Marx 1967). An article in *Jamaica Architect* suggested that archaeologist Robert Marx's finds would help planners in "piecing together a picture of the town and its buildings in the days of Henry Morgan and his buccaneers" (Concannon *c.*1966).

Archaeology and Revisionism: 1968–1984

In the years after the 1967 UDC plan, the UDC, the JNHT and the Institute of Jamaica, three of the government agencies with authority over Port Royal development, looked towards the United Kingdom for guidance. The JNHT contracted with English archaeologist Phillip Mayes, who established the Port Royal Project at the Old Naval Hospital and undertook extensive excavations seeking seventeenth- to nineteenth-century artefacts. Interest in re-creating the pre-earthquake town of Port Royal led the UDC to hire the London firm Shankland/Cox as architectural consultants in 1970, beginning the long association of architect Oliver Cox with Port Royal development (Aarons 1989).

This period saw the publication of an enduringly influential popular history of Port Royal by former government archivist Clinton V. Black (1988, first published in 1970). The first part of Black's book is a narration of the "Age of the Buccaneers" and the "Age of the Admirals". Black mentions Arawak artefacts which have come to light as unintended benefits of archaeological digs for pirate treasures, but his history of Port Royal begins with Christopher Columbus and remains consistently centred on the uses to which Europeans put the area. Black includes many anecdotes about the exploits of pirates, criminals and admirals. The narration reaches a pinnacle that illustrates its colonial orientation – Prince William Henry's visit to the naval base in 1783,

> the first time in the history of the island that a prince of the blood royal had visited the colony. Salutes rang out as he landed. Once more there were splendid balls and gay parties. His Royal Highness's charm and condescension were on all men's lips, and women's also it would seem, while in honour of his visit Port Royal's newest fort – the Polygon Battery – was renamed Prince William Henry's Polygon. All, in fact, was glitter and charm, as befits the end of an era. (1988, 62)

What follows is a chapter called "Port Royal in Decline". The message is clear that after the Sailor King's visit, Port Royal's historical interest was at an end.

One piece of scholarship from this period is a meticulously researched and detailed history of Port Royal by historians Michael Pawson and David Buisseret (1975), published by Clarendon, an imprint of the Oxford University Press. In this curious volume, no detail about pre-earthquake Port Royal is too trivial. One can find the registry dates of every tavern registered from 1665 to 1685; a virtual yellow pages of residents from architects, bakers and barbers through watermen, wherrymen and victuallers; and house-by-house descriptions of Port Royal's crowded streets. The English residents are the only ones whose lives are recounted in such detail; the authors blame an absence of sources for their inability to describe anything about the way the over eight hundred Africans experienced life in the pre-earthquake town. Nine of the book's twelve chapters deal with the period up to 1692. Its last chapter, "Port Royal Today", offers no information about the existing community. Instead, it describes only what remains from the seventeenth and eighteenth centuries. Contemporary Port Royal is termed a "singularly unspectacular little town" (p. xiv), in stark contrast to its very important past.

The 1970s witnessed a political challenge to the imperial world view by the PNP, which won the 1972 elections under Michael Manley's leadership. The new government lowered the voting age and instituted popular social programmes aimed at helping the poorest Jamaicans, such as free education up to university level, minimum wage for domestic workers and a land-lease programme that made idle land available to small peasants. Some PNP actions dealt blows to the old colonial order: abolishing the Master and Servant Law, which had been the only legal basis regulating employer-employee relations; taxing property; and putting the bauxite companies "under heavy manners" (Manley 1976).

One long-forgotten plan for Port Royal is an interesting example of this transitional period. In the files of the UDC library is a paper prepared by C. Ricky Simmons, a Jamaican businessman living in Miami. It proposed the Jamaican Historic Theme Park and Funland (Simmons 1978). Simmons imagined a Port Royal where the buildings would resemble those of Disney World. Interspersed among them would be "various types of fun-rides such as merry-go-rounds, ferris wheels and roller coasters" (p. 3). At an annual pirate carnival, town residents "would be encouraged to wear costumes of the era" (p. 4). So far, it might seem that Mr Simmons's plan is an easy target for a sociologist's derisive anti-commercialism. However, it is in this proposal that the African presence in Port Royal is recognized for the first time. Simmons proposed an elaborate amphitheatre and a floating stage for live performances such as Jamaica's National Dance Theatre Company "dancing a piece choreographed to depict the landing of the slaves, etc." (p. 3). The image of slaves landing in Port Royal is missing from all previous historic narratives in commemoration plans.

That times were changing is also evident in some changes in focus in the Port Royal Project, which appointed its first trained Jamaican Curator of Museums, Roderick Ebanks, as successor to the British archaeologists who had held the post previously. Ebanks brought an interest in Afro-Jamaican culture to the excavation processes, and Afro-Jamaican earthenware assemblages emerged for the first time as a focus for the archaeological project under his leadership.

Nowhere is the shifting focus more clear than in a 1983 document authored by students at the College of Arts, Sciences and Technology (CAST) course in Physical Planning and Technology. This document is arguably the first truly postcolonial historical account of Port Royal, in the sense that it rejects "European grand narratives of modernization" and begins to reconstruct "the appalling scale of loss experienced by colonized and indigenous peoples" (the definition of postcolonial narratives offered by Green and Troup 1999, 281). The historical focus of the two-volume "Port Royal Development Plan" is squarely on the African-born population of seventeenth-century Port Royal. One of the students, Robert Steele, wrote,

> In most historical studies of Port Royal hardly any mention is made of the numerous Africans that were there and although most of them were slaves, they must have played a major role in Port Royal's development. In some books it has been mentioned that the relationship between African slaves and European masters was a most amicable one, when compared with other areas of the mainland. The evidence necessary to support this argument is lacking. (1983, 22)

Recognizing that Port Royal is "a symbol of colonial and imperialist supremacy", Steele recommends modest development focusing on its archaeological importance with the hope that such an approach would "awaken the consciousness of the world as to the disastrous effects of colonial exploitation" (Steele 1983, 24). Another section of the report, written by Blaize Nichson, describes the period 1722 to 1820 as the "decline of Port Royal to little more than a naval station" (Nichson 1983, 3). This is the same time period described by the PRCM as Port Royal's "greatest brilliance" (1965, 10).

The 1983 CAST document also slams the romantic view of pirates. The admiration of buccaneers is linked here with crime in contemporary society:

> The Buccaneers were a barbarous set of people whose robberies, theftry, and many treacherous, demeaning and other deplorable acts had caused Port Royal to become known as the world's most wicked city. Through the ages Port Royal has become known as the Buccaneer capital of the Caribbean during the mid seventeenth to eighteenth century and even Robert Marx has chosen to call it Pirate Port in one of his books.
>
> Knowing all this it does not seem appropriate to regard Port Royal with any great esteem. Yet still renowned Buccaneers such as Henry Morgan are being labeled as great Jamaicans. It is therefore not surprising that the Jamaican society is so besieged with so many delinquencies. (Steele 1983, 23)

In 1999 JNHT archaeologist Roderick Ebanks echoed this assessment of the pirates. Referring to Hans Sloan's book about Henry Morgan's acts of cruelty and his slaughter of innocent people, Ebanks likened piracy to carjacking and other "crazy, anti-social behavior" that should not be romanticized or glorified (personal interview, July 1999).

The 1984 Installation

In December 1984 Port Royal officially reopened for tourists, with the museum of archaeology housed in the Naval Hospital and new markers of major sites (*Daily Gleaner,* 17 December 1984, 1). An example of the products of this period shows that pirates, wealth, navy admirals and the dramatic earthquake were its main focuses:

> Once called "the richest and wickedest city in the world" Port Royal was also the virtual capital of Jamaica. To it came men of all races, treasures of silks, doubloons and gold from Spanish ships, looted on the high seas by the notorious "Brethren of the Coast" as the pirates were called. From here sailed the fleets of Henry Morgan, later lieutenant-governor of Jamaica, for the sacking of Camaquay, Maracaibo, and Panama, and died here, despite the ministrations of his Jamaican folk-doctor. Admirals Lord Nelson and Benbow, the chilling Edward "Blackbeard" Teach, were among its inhabitants. The town flourished for 32 years until at 20 minutes to noon, June 7, 1692, it was partially buried in the sea by an earthquake. (JNHT sign at Port Royal entrance, *c.*1984)

The reference here to Morgan's "Jamaican folk-doctor" is one of the few references to Afro-Jamaican culture entering the Port Royal narrative. It is notable in that most sources on Morgan's death refer only to his more famous English physician, Sir Hans Sloan, though Black tells of Sloan's having worked with "a black obeahman to whom Morgan sometimes resorted" (1988, 23). Note also that the sign seems to put John Benbow and Horatio Nelson, who are eighteenth-century figures, back in the buccaneer days, and it depends for dramatic effect on the earthquake's unexpectedness and rapidity.

The installation at Nelson's House in Fort Charles was opened in 1977 and updated in 1984. This small museum includes information about the Arawak people, the European military battles in the Caribbean, the earthquake, piracy and buccaneering, the naval base, Columbus, shipping, and slavery.

The museum at Nelson's House represents imperial history in several ways. First, the small building is called Nelson's House because, one sign says, "the building [was] occupied by Lord Nelson when he was commander of the fort". Likewise, the fort's walkway is Nelson's Walkway, and a shrine inside the fort pays homage to his memory. Although the British hero was here only for a few weeks in 1779, his status in imperial history as the hero of the Battle of Trafalgar twenty-six years later sanctifies even the whereabouts connected with his earlier life. Second, even when acknowledging an aspect of history important to Afro-Jamaicans, the English emerge the heroes. For example, the most the exhibit has to say about slavery is contained in one plaque labelled "Ending the Slave Trade". It reads in its entirety,

> The British slave trade was abolished in 1807. The Royal Navy was then ordered to police the Atlantic Ocean to apprehend British subjects who continued to trade in slaves, even in ships flying foreign flags. Royal Navy cruisers were stationed off the coast of West Africa and in the Caribbean for this purpose. Slaves found by such ships were set free.

The installations are different in several ways from the historical narratives that preceded them. First, they acknowledge the community of Port Royalists. For example, a plaque about the Naval Hospital mentions that the "building withstood the 1951 hurricane and served for some time as a refuge for many of the town's residents". Second, they make some references to Afro-Jamaican culture, as in the reference to the "folk-doctor" above. The museum displays some relics from slavery, including shackles, but these all come from plantation areas on the main part of the island. These developments, however, were to become more pronounced in the next major plan developed for Port Royal.

The Cox Plan

In 1984, the Overseas Development Administration of the British government commissioned Shankland Cox, a UK corporation headed by Oliver Cox and Jean Cox, an architect and a social scientist, to work with a steering committee that included representatives of the UDC, the Jamaica National Trust Commission and the Port Royal Brotherhood. The group produced a detailed eighty-page proposal with accompanying maps, diagrams and blueprints. Where previous documents centred on commercial possibilities or archaeological potential, this one used architecture as a starting point. It concerned itself with a mix of renewal, conservation, redesign and restoration of buildings, suggesting materials for street surfaces and designs for signposts and streetlights (Cox 1984).

This plan proposed transformation of Port Royal into "an attractive tourist center" (Cox 1984, 9) through substantial reproduction of buildings that existed mainly in the seventeenth century, including a block of the original Lime Street; refurbishment of various buildings; and development of parkland and new facilities, such as a ferry terminal and an extended beach.

Cox's firm was known for its work in urban London; the strength and purpose of this plan is in its architectural renovations, reconstructions or conversions of sixty-one structures in Port Royal, many illustrated with artists' renderings and detailed floor plans. Oliver Cox had a clear interest in pre-earthquake Port Royal as a quintessentially English town:

> The trading and naval connections between Port Royal and the ports of southern England, in particular that of London, is well established. The only Port Royal resident who built houses . . . was a Londoner, Robert Snead. The design of buildings from about 1678 onwards showed a close correspondence to the famous London post-fire building regulations of 1667. (Cox 1984, 39)

A dense little town of two thousand dwellings and a population of 130 people per acre, Port Royal in 1690 was said to have resembled Cheapside, then the commercial centre of London, replete with four-storey houses ridiculously unsuited to this tropical environment. Cox quoted Pawson and Buisseret with appreciation:

> The English built at the point just as if they had never left some shire town in the old country, putting up especially after the 1670s splendid brick houses of several storeys and building a church which with its battlemented tower and splendid aisles might have come straight from East Anglia. . . . The English, in contrast to the Spaniards, made very little allowance at first for local conditions. (Cox 1984, 40)

Authenticity to early English specifications was valued in Cox's discussion of building projects for Port Royal. Snead's own building specifications would be used to construct exemplary structures of the period. The plan also called for some construction on eighteenth- and nineteenth-century models. Drawings were documented with reference to historical documents, such as "view from HMS Sparrowhawk 1831" or "Maps: Pedron of 1810 and Berne of 1822" (Cox 1984, 49 and 51).

The vision of Port Royal history presented here centred on the European experience in the pre-earthquake period, and the author credited the assistance of Buisseret as well as representatives from the British Museum and the Museum of London. The report did not attempt to summarize the historical literature, but the summary paragraph shows the focus on the English experience as "Jamaica's earliest history" (Cox 1984, 10):

> The Town's use as a springboard for the occupation of Jamaica by the English under Cromwell, its turbulent years as a pirate port, developing into the wealthiest, largest and wickedest city in the western hemisphere, its dramatic eclipse in the great earthquake of 1692 followed by its determined recovery as a military and naval stronghold, all retain their ability to exert a compelling fascination for historians, archaeologists and the general public. (Cox 1984, 9)

The only unusual detail here is Cromwell's name, putting Port Royal more firmly still into the English historical context.

For each plan, I asked whether the natural setting of Port Royal was a concern and whether the environmental impact of the proposed development was assessed. Cox's document considered ways to minimize the risks of natural disasters such as hurricanes and earthquakes by building new structures to a strict code and reinforcing existing buildings if possible. Six buildings would be either built or rebuilt to serve as hurricane refuges for the community of Port Royal, most of whom sat out the 1951 and 1980 hurricanes in St Peter's Church or the Old Naval Hospital. Environmental problems with sewage were seen in the plan as pre-existing and requiring intervention. Beyond this, the Cox plan did not assess the prospective development's effects on the environmental resources of the area.

That said, however, the plan is a relatively low-impact one. It did not call for a cruise-ship pier; it assumed that visitors would continue to arrive by ferry and road. Sturdy concrete buildings such as the former Police Training School Blocks, although discordant with the rest of the plan, were considered too solid to remove, and the plan called for a more modest reuse of the space. New accommodation for visitors would total of 83 rooms over a dozen or so locations. Modest plans for new and converted housing would be for the townspeople themselves.

The most strikingly different aspect of this plan, compared with previous ones, is its affirmation of the Port Royal community. The report pointed out that the people had survived countless disasters and were determined to stay. It was a poor community – 39 per cent were unemployed in 1980 – but Port Royalists were proud of their peaceful and crime-free village, where neighbours and family members chipped in to help the poorest survive. In contrast to the token mention in previous plans, this plan took the community into consideration in its statement of primary objective, that is, to convert Port Royal for tourism "without disrupting the flow of life for its inhabitants and in a manner that captures their enthusiastic support" (Cox 1984, 9). Of six further objectives, three focused on the community. The first of the six read,

> To recognize that the combined loyalty of the inhabitants of Port Royal to the place is the reason why these descendants of the first pioneers have survived, while all their original homes and belongings and much of their land has not. And to respect the strong sense of community they express by treating with respect and care those parts of the present town they use, enjoy and recognize as their town, to resist any attempt to transform what they know and love into an unrecognizable tourist attraction. (Cox 1984, 10)

Other objectives promised to make the town "economically viable for its inhabitants" (p. 10) and to train local residents for jobs resulting from the project. One paid tribute to archaeologists and their work; another promised to look to Jamaicans for an audience as well as to tourists.

The living conditions of the Port Royal community would be improved in this plan in the areas of sewage and drainage, water supply, electricity and street lighting, obviously benefiting community residents as much as visitors. The danger of gentrification was addressed:

> We have assumed that all of the housing within the whole of this area will be for the use of the people of Port Royal. It has thus been of the greatest encouragement to learn that this is the declared policy of the Government, at a meeting on May 21st chaired by the Prime Minister, with the Ministers of Construction and Tourism and the Director of the National Housing Corporation in attendance. (Cox 1984, 71)

If the eight-member steering committee can be accepted as the stakeholders of this plan, their interests seem well represented here. They included two members of the Port Royal Brotherhood, whose presence on the committee was consistent with the attention the plan gave to the community. The other committee members were two representatives from the Jamaica National Trust Commission, two from the UDC, the government town planner and a representative of the United Nations Development Programme. The interests of land and marine archaeologists in continuing their work unimpeded were respected in this plan generally, and architects and planners seem to be the only ones with an economic stake in its execution.

The UNESCO Plan

In 1987 a team consisting of representatives of the International Development Bank, UNESCO and Commonwealth Historic Resource Management produced what Seaga, then prime minister, sees as the most complete development plan for Port Royal (personal interview, July 1999). According to Seaga, financing through the Caribbean Development Bank was in place to implement the plan, but in 1988 when Hurricane Gilbert caused devastating damage to the island, the funds had to be diverted to relief and rebuilding efforts.

The UNESCO plan (UNESCO 1987) called for the development of three interrelated sites: Port Royal, New Seville and Spanish Town. The plan envisioned Port Royal as an archaeological park, to which an admission fee would be charged. The public would see archaeologists at work and would purchase as souvenirs replicas of artefacts that archaeologists had discovered. As at the development at Williamsburg, Virginia, visitors would be able to watch craftspeople at work in small workshops devoted to model shipmaking, ceramics and pewter.

Archaeologists continued to have a strong voice in the planning process. Beginning in 1981 Professor Donny Hamilton of Texas A&M University had established a programme using the area every summer to train students in marine archaeology and providing reports about findings to the JNHT. The conditions under which he conducted his research and training were detailed in the UNESCO report. The government provided living quarters, the archaeological resource and access to JNHT staff, while Texas A&M provided technical expertise, student labour and most of the funding. The result was praised by the UNESCO report as work "of the highest professional quality" (1987, 147–48).

Hamilton's perspective on Port Royal is reflected in the way UNESCO framed the area first and foremost as an archaeological site. Of special interest to "archaeologists and amateur archaeologists" was the area's status as a "'catastrophic' site where cultural features and materials are preserved more or less undisturbed" (UNESCO 1987, 14). The plans called for archaeological excavations of various areas, after which the areas would be "landscaped as archaeological parks, leaving as much as possible of the excavated remains of the buildings exposed for public view" (p. 15). Lime Street would provide both land and underwater archaeological sites for visitors to explore, outfitted by on-site diving and snorkelling facilities.

The narrative history in the UNESCO plan focused squarely on pirates, who were portrayed as titillating and inherently amusing:

> The restoration . . . would provide ample scope for the exploitation of the pirate and buccaneer themes with which it is already associated. Captain Morgan and other boisterous and bawdy characters gave Port Royal its reputation as the Sin City of the Caribbean. Port Royal presents an unusual opportunity to combine serious archaeological research and historical restoration with popular entertainment. A visit to Port Royal would be an educational and fun experience. (UNESCO 1987, 15)

In contrast, the naval history that had been valorized in very early plans disappeared almost entirely. Horatio Nelson was particularly conspicuous by his absence. Even when Fort Charles was discussed, Nelson's name was not invoked. One section of the plan suggested three "significant themes" in Port Royal history:

1. The English period of ca. 1655 to the 1692 earthquake, during which Port Royal was a thriving mercantile center and occasional pirate haven;
2. The disappearance of part of the city beneath the sea and the subsequent preservation as a "sunken city"; and
3. The naval center operations of ca. 1700–1900.

> The first two of these have immense historical and legitimate romantic appeal and are already familiar to a very wide non-Jamaican audience. (UNESCO 1987, 146–47)

The third, by implication, was not considered a draw for visitors. A discussion of the Fort Charles Maritime Museum, which was called Nelson's House at the time that the document was written, never mentioned Nelson, and British Royal Naval activity was almost completely absent in a list of seventeen "Exhibition/Education Themes and Interpretations":

BEFORE 1692:
Creation of Port Royal
The Early Town
The Later Town
The Taverns
Henry Morgan & Company
Earthquake

AFTER 1692:
Survival & Rebuilding
The Naval Dockyard
Tradesmen of Port Royal
Naval Campaigns
The Naval Hospital
The New Technology
Port Royal Today
Piracy & Pickles
Keepers of the Peace
Archaeology of Port Royal
People of Port Royal – Yesterday
(UNESCO 1987, 186–87)

Curiously, no plan was more concerned with marketing than this one. More than 6,300 square feet of retail outlet space was planned, but more could be established "on the initiative of the private sector" (UNESCO 1987, 239). This attention to retail sales may be due to the influence of the Jamaica Labour Party (JLP) government and its investment in the Things Jamaican craft stores that were located in many tourist areas throughout Jamaica. Things Jamaican had developed a Port Royal line of reproductions of pre-1692 artefacts, such as pewter mugs. This report recommends that Things Jamaican reintroduce the line "with an improved marketing strategy" (p. 238). An eight-page appendix by S. Dello Strologo, senior industrial advisor for the United

Nations Industrial Development Organization, consists of a list of historical products, reproductions and handicrafts, including detailed recommendations such as "two-pronged iron fork with bone handle (recently found in Port Royal)" and "Naïve 'Chinoiserie' styles from samples salvaged from Port Royal" (pp. 246 and 245). Dello Strologo's report details suggestions for all three sites (Spanish Town, New Seville and Port Royal), but its only reference to Afro-Caribbean culture, a reference to head-carrying baskets and mats, is suggested specifically for Spanish Town. Artefacts having to do with Port Royal are of English, Dutch and Spanish origin.

The community's well-being was not neglected in the UNESCO report:

> Port Royal is a living community of over 2,000 inhabitants. It is urgently in need of improvement and upgrading of the infrastructure, housing conditions and the local economy. These topics should receive top priority in any development of Port Royal. The preservation and conservation strategy for Port Royal must highlight the rich historical and archaeological remains, be respectful of the present day inhabitants and provide a dynamic and informative attraction for visitors. (1987, 14)

An effort was planned to effect an awareness of historic preservation among the local people. A final recommendation reads, "The local population must be actively involved in the planning of the project and participate in investment-related and labour intensive work" (p. 16).

While environmental concerns were not at the forefront as they are in the Port Royal Development Company (PRDC) plan, discussed below, the UNESCO plan was a relatively low-impact one, with no cruise-ship pier or extensive building plans. The plan did, however, intend that cruise-ship passengers be foremost among visitors to Port Royal. Cruise ships could dock in Kingston, and visitors would ferry over to a newly built visitors' arrival centre in the Old Naval Dockyard. There visitors would see a presentation about Port Royal and its attractions.

The Port Royal Development Company Plan

Pragma Development Limited was incorporated in 1993 with a board of directors comprising ten representatives of private sector businesses (Pragma 1996, 4) under the direction of Robert Stephens, a local businessman and former head of the Jamaica Tourist Board, who had previously organized the Sunsplash concert festivals in Jamaica. After several years of planning, Pragma signed a memorandum of understanding with the Government of Jamaica "to undertake the development of Port Royal as a historical and cultural port of call for cruise ships" (PRDC 1998, 2). At the time, Stephens estimated that the total project budget would be about US$30–$35 million ("Port Royal Project Hailed", *Weekly Gleaner* [North America], 1 November 1996, 4), but it is now estimated at over US$60 million (Stephens, personal interview, July 1999). Almost US$6 million has been spent so far by the newly formed PRDC in extensive planning for the heritage tourism project (PRDC 1998). Some investment has been made in community development and in technical surveys. Leases were signed with the Government of Jamaica, and the project was until recently in the phase of seeking capital investment. With the economic downturns following 11 September 2001, the PRDC office has closed, and the plans seem at the time of writing to be on hold.

The 1998 plan that was developed by the PRDC returns to the idea of building a cruise-ship pier and arrival centre. With a new historical-interpretive master plan, it would restore a dozen or more major areas for use as museums and commercial purposes, all subject to approval by the JNHT. A living-history experience is planned, with "a roving troupe" giving "impromptu performances" throughout the town, and strolling musicians playing seventeenth-century music (PRDC 1998, 18).[1] The plan is unusually broad in scope. For example, it specifies that the village, the adjacent Palisadoes Strip, the mangroves and the offshore cays be designated a protected area and managed by a non-governmental organization designated by the Natural Resources Conservation Authority. Upgrades of basic infrastructural systems such as water supply, wastewater collection, drainage, landscaping and garbage disposal would be the responsibility of the PRDC, while the Government of Jamaica would be responsible for the access road, ferry pier and fire and police services. Sports facilities, housing and the educational needs of the community are addressed as well.

Port Royal's history is presented in the plan in a very conventional way. The preliminary feasibility study, produced three years before the final plan by private sector interests alone, has a one-page history that can only be described as Anglocentric. The "wild and wicked swashbuckling pirates" and "the Lord Protector Cromwell and successive Kings of England" figure prominently (A.V. Plus 1995, 3). Nelson, absent in the 1980s, is back, but his role in history has to be explained: "the great Horatio Nelson, the hero of the battle of Trafalgar" (A.V. Plus 1995, 3). Port Royal is seen as a way to understand Britain:

> The British involvement in Jamaica would reflect several reigns, periods and styles, going from the Stuarts through the Commonwealth, the Restoration period of Charles II, James II, supplanted by William of Orange, on to the Queen Anne period, followed by the Georgian Period, then by the styles of the Regency period, of William I, Victoria and Edward I. (A.V. Plus 1995, 3-4)

This Anglocentrism is toned down considerably in the more recent plan documents. Instead, the historical perspective seems to be more in line with the JNHT viewpoint. One such idea is the conceptualization of Port Royal as part of a "historic triangle" composed of Port Royal, Kingston and Spanish Town. The JNHT would simultaneously develop heritage tourism destinations involving all three points in this triangle (Ainsley Henriques, personal interview, July 1999). The three areas are tied together in a way that includes both the pre-earthquake English town history of Port Royal and its prominence as a naval base in the next two centuries.

Some planned commemorations focus on the buccaneers; in fact Henry Morgan's picture serves as the centrepiece of the PRDC logo. Visitors will be invited to become "Pirates for the Day" by renting costumes upon arrival (PRDC 1999). The plan calls for a Pirates Museum on the upper level of the Naval Hospital, and one existing building at Fort Charles will be "refurbished and redecorated in the style of the pirate's [sic] era" and serve as a pub (PRDC 1998, 10). A statue of Henry Morgan will be erected in centre of the Lime Street reconstruction (PRDC 1998). Outside the Naval Hospital, a platform will serve as a stage for pirate shows, "such as the re-enactment of the capturing of a ship by Pirates" (PRDC 1998, 18).

Natural history becomes part of the attraction in a planned light-and-sound simulation of an earthquake to be housed in the Giddy House. Naval history will be celebrated in restorations of the Victoria and Albert Battery and other gun emplacements, and two existing buildings in the Fort will "house memorabilia of the famous admirals who visited or were commanders of the Fort" (PRDC 1998, 10).

Also evident here is the recognition of the Afro-Jamaican history of Port Royal as well as of the contributions of the current community. One developed area will house an African Market, "of the type that would have been found in 17th or 18th century Jamaica", that will sell "African crafts and foods and Jamaican foods with African influence" (PRDC 1999, 10). "Port Royal style" fish will be available in the food court. One structure may be used "to house statues of Jamaican National Heroes and other persons who have played an important role in the history of Port Royal and Jamaica" (PRDC 1998, 16). Jamaica's national heroes are primarily of African descent. Another clue that this history is one more inclusive of Afro-Jamaican culture is that excursions to the Bob Marley Museum in Kingston are to be organized for cruise-ship visitors from Port Royal, and reggae music, a musical form explicitly associated with working-class Afro-Jamaicans, is part of the planned entertainment.

The PRDC's plan depends for its account of history on Black's *Port Royal*. However, a master interpretive plan has been commissioned from a Canadian museum-design specialist who has worked closely with the developers.

The PRDC plan brings community involvement to a higher level than previous plans. The PRDC contracted with Edu-Tech to establish and equip a learning centre with computer technology and to undertake training programmes for youth and adult residents. During the summer of 1999, three hundred residents participated in a summer camp programme for pre-schoolers through adults. The programme included performing arts, culinary arts (selling "Port Royal Emancipation Punch alongside bammy and ackee for the holiday fête"), computer technology and communication techniques (PRDC 1999, 1).

In no previous plan has the environment been so clear a focal point. The agreement with the Government of Jamaica allowed for the formation of the Port Royal Environment Management Trust (PREMT) to manage and protect the surrounding areas. A local environmental technology firm was employed to study the proposed development's impact on the natural environment, and two social scientists conducted an assessment of its socio-economic impact. Various eco-tourism components have been suggested.

The entrepreneur behind the PRDC plan, Robert Stephens, differs from previous corporate actors because he is a Jamaican educated in

Jamaica and associated with popular culture. He has assembled a wide range of stakeholders for his project. The March 1998 development plan lists fifty-three professionals and consultants and seven major commissioned reports. Financial support has been received from the Caribbean Development Bank, the Inter-American Development Bank, the European Investment Bank, the National Investment Bank of Jamaica and the Government of Jamaica, among others (PRDC 1998, 24).

The proposed cruise-ship pier in this plan makes it clear that overseas short-term visitors are a prime target audience for this project. However, Stephens envisions weekend use of the facility by Jamaicans from Kingston and beyond.

Discussion

Port Royal is a perennial backdrop in Jamaican political culture, inspiring visions ranging from the Disneyesque funland to the staid and sombre memorial park. What is it about the site that has made it so constant an inspiration? While Port Royal is an accessible site with a compellingly dramatic social and natural history, I believe that the answer also lies in its value as a political symbol. Like most successful political symbols, Port Royal has both breadth and ambiguity. It allows the beholder to read into it any of a multitude of possible meanings. For some it might represent the dangers of nature out of control, for others extreme wealth and luxury. For Jenkinson and other members of the PRCM, it was a symbol of British naval glory. For Afro-Jamaican students in the 1980s, it symbolized lawless acquisition by colonial oppressors.

In the paragraphs that follow, I consider Port Royal's meaning as a historical symbol and discuss the silences and socio-economic interests that characterize the narratives and plans.

Piracy as a Political Symbol

The primary theme of Port Royal history is its association with pirates. Standard Jamaican history books (such as Allen 1993; Gleaner Company 1995; Hurwitz and Hurwitz 1971) and tourist guides never fail to make that connection. Ambivalent feelings about pirates date back to their heyday, when British authorities sometimes authorized them to act on behalf of the Crown as privateers in hostilities aimed at undermining Spanish shipping, and at other times condemned and executed them. Morgan was at different times sentenced to hang and appointed lieutenant governor of the colony of Jamaica.

When I first considered the ubiquity of references to pirates in Caribbean popular culture, I hypothesized that pirates might represent opposition to the domination of colonial planters. Sustained conflicts between pirates and the planter class began when indentured servants were lured away from their masters to join piratical ranks (Dunn 1972). In the Bahamas, when planters finally defeated pirate forces and regained control over the islands, they adopted the motto that the Bahamas still has today: "Pirates Expelled, Commerce Restored". Recent scholarship about pirates suggests that allusions to pirates in contemporary culture might reflect anti-colonialism or opposition to neocolonialism in the newly independent nations of the region. Marcus Rediker found that pirate social relations "were marked by vigorous, often violent, antipathy toward traditional authority" (1987, 275). Pirates perceived themselves as "preyed upon" (p. 279), and royal authorities of the period feared that pirates might, as Cotton Mather speculated, "set up a sort of Commonwealth" (quoted in Rediker 1987, 281). Rediker argues that pirates represent what Eric Hobsbawm called "social banditry", those who protested against "oppression and poverty" with "a cry for vengeance on the rich and the oppressors" (quoted in Rediker 1987, 268).

Recent scholarship has also uncovered the fact that that perhaps one-quarter or more of the men on pirate ships were of African descent and that pirates worked against the slave trade by accepting escaped Africans into pirate communities (Kinkor 1995). Coupled with the romantic view of the outlaw in Caribbean culture exemplified by Ivanhoe "Rhygin" Martin, celebrated in the movie *The Harder They Come,* and by "Johnny Too Bad" of countless popular songs, as well as the link between theft and opposition to colonial domination (Burton 1997; Price 1998), piracy seems to be a logical symbolic choice in expressions of opposition to the enduring racial and class hierarchy.

My research in Port Royal, however, uncovered almost no support for this hypothesis. Instead, as Afro-Jamaicans gain control over the framing of Port Royal's history, sympathy or even tolerance for pirates wanes. In general, the more a narrative emphasizes the contributions of Afro-Jamaicans to Port Royal, the less it focuses on pirates. Instead of representing opposition to European colonialism, the lawlessness of pirates is linked with the extraordinary liberties enjoyed by Europeans in the colonies.

The data presented here suggests that the image of unbounded white privilege is the source of the appeal that pirates have for the tourist trade. Repeatedly in the plans for Port Royal, pirates are associated with Port Royal's attractiveness for visitors from the United States and Europe. The 1965 plan, which completely ignores the presence of Afro-Jamaicans in Port Royal, celebrates the buccaneers uncritically and with clear recognition of their appeal to tourists. The 1996 plan, which tries to include something for all constituencies, concentrates its links with pirates in the entryway from the cruise-ship pier to the town rather than in the entryway that local visitors would use.

My interviews with members of the Port Royal community revealed little affinity with the pirates of the town's past. Instead, pirates were vilified as out-of-control criminals. The CAST report of 1983 linked romantic views of pirates with the rise in crime, a perspective echoed by JNHT archaeologist Roderick Ebanks, who says that Henry Morgan's actions were "something you don't want to glorify; . . . it was crazed, anti-social behaviour" (personal interview, July 1999). Ebanks (1996) has also advanced the idea that pirates were in the service of planters, a point of view that further undermines the possibility of pirates as a liberating symbol.

An interesting expression of the link between lawlessness and Port Royal is a column by Morris Cargill, the late white Jamaican columnist whose curmudgeonly wrath was often directed against the majority of Jamaicans. His interesting article about Port Royal (*Daily Gleaner*, 5 April 1998) expressed his approval that the agreement had been reached so that Port Royal can be developed as a port of call for cruise ships, but he had two further suggestions. First, there should be a "really elegant and well-run casino . . . called the Henry Morgan Casino". Morgan was not a pirate; he was "a very successful privateer, which is quite a different thing". Cargill continued:

> I'd like to make another suggestion quite seriously. What about the Bank of Port Royal, specializing in laundering drug money? As I have written before,

I fail to see what is wrong with converting ill-gotten gains into investment in respectable business enterprises.

One subtle change in the approach to pirates is the way their entry to Port Royal is conveyed. The most common view is that the buccaneers happened to use Port Royal of their own volition, but historians long ago established that Governor Edward D'Oyley distributed commissions to members of the Brethren of the Coast to protect the new English settlement from Spanish ships (Pawson and Buisseret 1975). Ebanks, the JNHT archaeologist, stresses the deliberate, indeed contractual, relationship between the English and the buccaneers, as well as the way the pirates' looted goods served to finance the incipient plantation system (personal interview, July 1999). Similarly, a deliberately Afrocentric new history of Jamaica reiterates the idea that the buccaneers were a defence force for the English settlement, calling Port Royal "the Babylon of the West" (Sherlock and Bennett 1998, 85).

The path that British naval history traces in the trajectory of development plans shows that historical revision is not a linear process. In the earliest years, Port Royal's association with the British navy was central to its interest for tourists. The 1965 narrative saw Port Royal "as a Naval Station of great importance, reaching its greatest brilliance in the last twenty-five years of the century" (PRCM 1965, 10), that is, including the time when, a quarter-century before he established his fame as a military personage, the barely post-pubescent Horatio Nelson was put in charge of the cannons around Port Royal for a few uneventful weeks.[2] Nelson's fame as a military personage in European sea battles decades later secured his cult of personality in a nostalgic imperial political ideology, and the wooden platform of Fort Charles, which would be walked by many generations over more than two centuries, was known at least by mid-nineteenth century as Nelson's Quarterdeck.

The UNESCO plan saw no appeal in this history, but Nelson resurfaces in the PRDC plan, which seems to be all-inclusive in its approach. Instead of a move away from British imperial history towards Afro-Jamaican history, the PRDC plan, probably reflecting the wide range of stakeholders and potential investors, includes British naval history, as in its planned "Admirals Museum" at Fort Charles, as well as elements from Afro-Jamaican folk culture, as in the inclusion of a mento band and African crafts.

Silences in Port Royal

Contrasting with the crashing sounds of earthquake meticulously recounted by historians, there are long and deep silences in narratives of Port Royal history. The distribution of silences is not random, of course, but strongly corresponds to Jamaican caste and class hierarchies. Narratives of Port Royal not surprisingly favour the European over the African and the indigenous, the ruling class over the working class and the enslaved.

Silences are evident in the unanswered and sometimes unasked questions of history. Who raided the sunken ruins for their wealth, probably throughout the eighteenth century? Why does no one question the ludicrous impracticality of the old city of Port Royal? Why is piratical loot always presented as Spanish wealth when it was simply the plunder of other European rampages against indigenous people in Central and South America?

The silence about the way the Africans and Afro-Jamaican Creoles lived in pre-earthquake Port Royal is a good example of a silence that enters at the moment that archives are created (Trouillot 1995). Although more than eight hundred people of African descent populated pre-earthquake Port Royal, there seems to be a total absence of accounts of their lives, in contrast to copious documentation of European lives (Pawson and Buisseret 1975).

An example of a silence at the moment of narrative, when facts are retrieved and arranged (Trouillot 1995), is the way the fact of collusion between the English colonial government and the Brethren of the Coast, described in detail by historians, eludes mention in most historical accounts. A recently published and academically reputable history is illustrative. It reads, "a small number of English buccaneers opted to establish themselves in Jamaica in the settlement of Port Royal" (Ferguson 1999, 78). This wording erases the fact of formal English control over who settled in Port Royal, enhances the attractive illusion of pirates' autonomy and exonerates the English colonial government of its complicity with the torture and butchery that the pirates carried out under its protection if not under its orders.

Another moment when silences enter history is in judging the significance of the events about which we have sources, archives and narratives. Exemplary here is the history of the Port Royal community itself, the generations of Afro-Jamaicans who have inhabited the area and eked out a living there. A sentence or two in Black's popular history (1988) relates the fact that hundreds of villagers sought shelter from the 1951 hurricane in the Old Naval Hospital, and some had to reside there for months. This story of survival in the midst of destructive forces would make a dramatic narrative – one can imagine exhibits like those at the museum about the Johnstown flood in Pennsylvania, or in Windsor Castle about the fire that destroyed one wing – but it is an untold story so far.

The Future of the Past

While the social memory literature sometimes implies that commemoration reflects the interests of broad classes of society, the plans under study here show more correspondence with the narrower interests of their producers. The 1965 plan clearly reflects the British entrepreneurial interests of Jenkinson and others like him. The UDC and UNESCO plans favour archaeologists, and professional architects would have been the beneficiaries had so many reconstructions of historic buildings been undertaken under the Cox plan. As mentioned earlier, the all-inclusive nature of the PRDC plan corresponds with the long list of stakeholders. Given its intention to find investors for the final project costs of US$60 million, there was an incentive to include all possible ways that Port Royal could be developed. While the plan is the brainchild of Stephens, a Jamaican with a clear understanding of popular Afro-Jamaican culture, the project requires enormous capital investment. It is likely that if investors are found, their specific interests will shape which parts of the plan are implemented and which fall by the wayside.

The role of the residents of Port Royal has changed dramatically since the 1965 plan, when the community's high unemployment rate was named as an advantage to developers. Each plan since then has called for improvements to infrastructures for the community's benefit, and the PRDC plan has already implemented educational programmes. While future work will further clarify the residents' position, cursory research reveals approval of some of the development plans, disbelief that major changes would actually take place and a complete lack of engagement with the period of history that seems to most interest developers and tourists.

The community has a relatively small voice in the decision-making process. The PRDC plan names Clive Laidley as the representative of the Port Royal Brotherhood on the "Enterprise Committee and Advisors", one voice among twenty-eight members.

Corporate, professional, political and economic interests vie for influence over the packaging of Jamaican history for consumption by local and foreign visitors. Different corporate strategies reveal themselves in the contrast between the Things Jamaican craft-souvenir approach of the UNESCO plans and the stage-show production expertise evident in the PRDC plan. Architects and archaeologists have strong voices in the 1984 Cox plan and the 1987 UNESCO plan respectively. In a July 1999 interview, Seaga used their lack of development of Port Royal as a point on which to criticize the PNP governments of the 1970s and 1990s.

As for competing economic interests, the players so far have come more or less from the middle of the spectrum: émigré businessmen, local bureaucrats and members of the rising Afro-Jamaican middle class. There has been little participation from the two extremes: the stakes are not high enough to interest the very wealthy and powerful, and the poverty-stricken residents of Port Royal can exert little influence. Should the PRDC's plans come to fruition in the form of a US$60-million investor, a global corporate presence would overwhelm all competition. Does the Afro-Jamaican working-class Port Royal community have any hope against such a foe? Could symbolic work, through cultural resistance and historical revision, help it prevail? Given the tendency of Port Royal development plans to evade execution, reinforced by recent world developments, it seems unlikely, however, that the PRDC plan will be able to obtain the high levels of investment sought. One prediction can be made with the most confidence: that Port Royal will continue to inspire new visions of the past in the future.

Notes

1. PRDC 1998 was printed from the PRDC's Web site; page numbers refer to the printout and are therefore approximate.
2. During Nelson's command there was fear of an attack from French ships. Nelson's confidence in the face of the threat is indicated in his having written to a comrade that he might soon be learning to speak French (Walder 1978, 44).

References

Aarons, G.A. 1989. "Port Royal: An Archaeological Adventure: The Last Fifteen Years: 1974–1989". Jamaica Journal 22, no. 4: 32–40.

Ackworth, Angus Whiteford. 1951. *Buildings of Architectural or Historic Interest in the British West Indies: A Report.* Colonial Research Studies 2. London: HMSO.

Allen, Beryl M. 1993. *Jamaica: A Junior History.* Kingston, Jamaica: Carib Publishing.

A.V. Plus. 1995. "Port Royal/Kingston Tourism Project Socio-Cultural and Economic Component". Typescript, Kingston.

Barthel, Diane. 1996. *Historic Preservation: Collective Memory and Historical Identity.* New Brunswick, NJ: Rutgers University Press.

Bennett, Tony. 1995. *The Birth of the Museum: History, Theory, Politics.* New York: Routledge.

Black, Clinton V. 1988. *Port Royal.* 2nd edition. Kingston: Institute of Jamaica Publications.

Brathwaite, Edward Kamau. 1976. *Nanny, Sam Sharpe and the Struggle for People's Liberation.* Kingston, Jamaica: Agency for Public Information.

Burton, Richard D.E. 1997. *Afro-Creole: Power, Opposition and Play in the Caribbean.* Ithaca, NY: Cornell University Press.

Cannizzo, Jeanne. 1987. "How Sweet It Is: Cultural Politics in Barbados". *Muse* 4, no. 4: 22–26.

Concannon, T.A.L. c.1966. "Plans for Port Royal". *Jamaica Architect* 1, no. 3: 82–84.

Cox, Oliver. 1984. "Report on Port Royal Proposals". Unpublished document, National Library of Jamaica.

Cummins, Alexandra. 1992. "Exhibiting Culture: Museums and National Identity in the Caribbean". *Caribbean Quarterly* 38, no. 2: 33–53.

Dunn, Richard S. 1972. *Sugar and Slaves: The Rise of the Planter Class in the English West Indies 1624–1713*. Chapel Hill: University of North Carolina Press.

Ebanks, Roderick. 1996. "A Position Paper on Port Royal". *JNHT Diggings* 3, no. 1: 1–4.

Fentress, James, and Chris Wickham. 1992. *Social Memory*. Oxford: Blackwell.

Ferguson, James. 1999. *A Traveller's History of the Caribbean*. New York: Interlink.

Fraser, Gertrude, and Reginald Butler. 1986. "Anatomy of a Disinterment: The Unmaking of Afro-American History". In *Presenting the Past: Essays on History and the Public,* edited by Susan Porter Benson, Stephen Brier and Roy Rosenzweig, 121–32. Philadelphia: Temple University Press.

Gillis, John R., ed. 1994. *Commemorations: The Politics of National Identity*. Princeton: Princeton University Press.

Gleaner Company. 1995. *The Gleaner Geography and History of Jamaica*. 23rd edition. Kingston, Jamaica: Gleaner Company.

Green, Anna, and Kathleen Troup. 1999. *The Houses of History: A Critical Reader in Twentieth-Century History and Theory*. New York: New York University Press.

Green, William A. 1993. "The Creolization of Caribbean History: The Emancipation Era and a Critique of Dialectical Analysis". In *Caribbean Freedom: Society and Economy from Emancipation to the Present,* edited by Hilary Beckles and Verene Shepherd, 28–40. Kingston, Jamaica: Ian Randle.

Greene, Elizabeth. 2000. "Plotting a Future for History". *Chronicle of Higher Education* 46, no. 34: 18–19.

Hearne, John, ed. 1976. *Carifesta Forum: An Anthology of 20 Caribbean Voices*. Kingston: Institute of Jamaica.

Hobsbawm, Eric, and Terence Ranger, eds. 1983. *The Invention of Tradition*. Cambridge: Cambridge University Press.

Horton, James Oliver, and Spencer R. Crew. 1989. "Afro-Americans and Museums: Towards a Policy of Inclusion". In *History Museums in the United States: A Critical Assessment,* edited by Warren Leon and Roy Rosenzweig, 215–36. Urbana and Chicago: University of Illinois Press.

Hurwitz, Samuel J., and Edith F. Hurwitz. 1971. *Jamaica: A Historical Portrait*. New York: Praeger.

Kincaid, Jamaica. 1988. *A Small Place*. New York: Plume.

Kinkor, Kenneth J. 1995. "From the Seas! Black Men under the Black Flag". *American Visions* April/May, 26–29.

Kinnell, Susan K., ed. 1987. *Historiography: An Annotated Bibliography of Journal Articles, Books and Dissertations.* Vol. 2. Santa Barbara, Calif.: ABC-Clio.

Lewis, Bernard. 1975. *History Remembered, Recovered, Invented.* Princeton: Princeton University Press.

Link, Marion Clayton. 1960. "Exploring the Drowned City of Port Royal". *National Geographic* 117, no. 2: 151–83.

Manley, Michael. 1976. "Not for Sale". Address to the Thirty-eighth Annual Confernece of the People's National Party.

Marx, Robert. 1967. "The Last Day of Port Royal". *Jamaica Journal* 1, no. 1: 16–20.

———. 1973. *Port Royal Rediscovered.* Garden City, NJ: Doubleday.

Mathurin, Lucille. 1975. *The Rebel Woman in the British West Indies during Slavery.* Kingston: Institute of Jamaica.

Melanson, Richard A. 1991. *Reconstructing Consensus: American Foreign Policy since the Vietnam War.* New York: St Martin's.

Morgan, Nigel, and Annette Pritchard. 1998. *Tourism Promotion and Power: Creating Images, Creating Identities.* Chichester, England: Wiley.

Nettleford, Rex. 1976. "Melody of Europe, Rhythm of Africa". In *Carifesta Forum: An Anthology of 20 Caribbean Voices,* edited by John Hearne, 139–54. Kingston: Institute of Jamaica.

Nichson, Blaize C. 1983. "History". In "Port Royal Development Plan". CAST Physical Planning Technology Course, supervised by Rose-Marie Brown. Unpublished report. Urban Development Corporation Library, Kingston, Jamaica.

Norkunas, Martha K. 1993. *The Politics of Public Memory: Tourism, History and Ethnicity in Monterey, California.* Albany: State University of New York Press.

Olick, Jeffrey K., and Joyce Robbins. 1998. "Social Memory Studies: From 'Collective Memory' to the Historical Sociology of Mnemonic Practices". *Annual Review of Sociology* 24: 105–40.

Pattullo, Polly. 1996. *Last Resorts: The Cost of Tourism in the Caribbean.* London: Cassell.

Pawson, Michael, and David Buisseret. 1975. *Port Royal, Jamaica.* Oxford: Clarendon.

Port Royal Company of Merchants (PRCM). 1965. "Plan: Proposed Development at Port Royal, Jamaica". Unpublished document, National Library of Jamaica.

Port Royal Development Company Limited (PRDC). 1998. *The Port Royal Heritage Tourism Project Development Plan.* Available online: http://portroyal-jamaica.com/Devplan3htm, accessed March 1998.

———. 1999. *Physical Improvements*. Available online: http://portroyal-jamaica.com/physical.htm, accessed 29 December 1999.

Pragma Development Limited. 1996. *Port Royal/Kingston Tourism Project: Project Summary and Status Report*. Kingston, Jamaica: Pragma Development Ltd.

Price, Richard. 1998. *The Convict and the Colonel*. Boston: Beacon.

Ranger, Terence. 1983. "The Invention of Tradition in Colonial Africa". In *The Invention of Tradition*, edited by Eric Hobsbawm and Terence Ranger, 211–62. Cambridge: Cambridge University Press.

Rediker, Marcus. 1987. *Between the Devil and the Deep Blue Sea: Merchant Seamen, Pirates and the Anglo-American Maritime World, 1700–1750*. Cambridge: Cambridge University Press.

Samuel, Raphael. 1994. *Theatres of Memory*. Vol. 1. *Past and Present in Contemporary Culture*. London: Verso.

Sherlock, Philip, and Hazel Bennett. 1998. *The Story of the Jamaican People*. Kingston, Jamaica: Ian Randle.

Simmons, C. Ricky. 1978. "Jamaica Historic Theme Park and Funland". Unpublished proposal. Urban Development Corporation Library, Kingston, Jamaica.

Steele, Robert. 1983. Part 1.2. In "Port Royal Development Plan". CAST Physical Planning Technology Course, supervised by Rose-Marie Brown. Unpublished report. Urban Development Corporation Library, Kingston, Jamaica.

Trouillot, Michel-Ralph. 1995. *Silencing the Past: Power and the Production of History*. Boston: Beacon.

UNESCO. 1987. *Feasibility Study for Conservation and Restoration of Cultural Heritage of Jamaica*. Vol. 1.

Urban Development Corporation (UDC). 1967. "Port Royal: Existing Conditions". Report Number 4002116PR. Kingston, Jamaica Urban Development Corporation.

Walcott, Derek. 1976. "The Muse of History". In *Carifesta Forum: An Anthology of 20 Caribbean Voices*, edited by John Hearne, 111–28. Kingston: Institute of Jamaica.

Walder, David. 1978. *Nelson*. New York: Dial.

[7]

Icon and Myth in a Caribbean Polity
V.C. Bird and Antiguan Political Culture

Douglas Midgett

> The people in a small place cannot give an account,
> a complete account of themselves.
> – Jamaica Kincaid, *A Small Place*

Introduction: On the Historiography of Small Places

The small place about which Jamaica Kincaid writes with such candour and compassion is, of course, Antigua. It does not have to be Antigua; there are numerous places like it. But the legacy of venality, of material and intellectual poverty, of corruption of trust and spirit, is, in this case, Antiguan. Of all that she has to say – and she has much to say that merits our attention – perhaps the most profound and disheartening is her account of a people whose relationship to their own history is tenuous and unenlightened – at least this is the thread I pursue in this chapter. Listen to Kincaid: "When the future, bearing its own events, arrives, its ancestry is then traced in a trancelike retrospect, at the end of which, their mouths and eyes wide with astonishment, the people in a small place reveal themselves to be like children being shown the secrets of a magic trick" (1988, 54). But what if this ancestry has been already packaged for their consumption, the conjuring accomplished as a factor of their political experience, an ideological construction that is part of a national myth?

We know, almost as an article of faith in this postmodern age, that history is, after all, a story, someone's story – written or told from their point of view and reflecting their peculiar interest. Until very recently, for people in the West Indies the history that was told them was about someone else, and it was told from someone else's perspective. Other peoples had history, and some of this was learned by generations of West Indians. And even when it was about the places in which they lived, and so in some way must have concerned them, it was not about them. That is because it was a colonial history, one that, insofar as it served any purpose for them at all, served to locate them in their proper place in the colonial scheme of things. So one might understand why the situation that Kincaid describes so eloquently has come about. And one might understand the nature of the case I relate here and appreciate the confusion in the experience of the people who have lived it.

V.C. Bird: A Political Life

When the Antigua Labour Party (ALP) was re-elected as the government in the 1989 general election, the electoral career of V.C. Bird, prime minister of Antigua and Barbuda, was extended to nearly five decades.[1] It was an extraordinary career, not just in longevity but in terms of the political and social epochs that Bird witnessed and helped shape during his tenure of public service. It was an extraordinary ride for him and his constituents, who watched him pass through transformations from a young, resolute labour stalwart, to leader of a powerful political movement which, for nearly twenty years, was scarcely challenged for control of the island's government, and finally, to a living representation of the State and Party, iconized by those around him, and, with his every public utterance, creating and popularizing the mythology of nation, party and trade union.[2]

Early Bird[3]

The outlines of Vere Cornwall Bird's career are straightforward. Born in 1910 of humble origins, he grew up in the impoverished New Street area of St John's, Antigua's small capital town. Following primary schooling, the extent of his formal education, he left Antigua, joining the Salvation Army as a teenager with ambitions to become an officer, and at the age of sixteen he travelled to Trinidad to train at the Salvation Army Training School. During this four-year sojourn he had an assignment in Grenada and attained the rank of captain in the army, an experience that he regarded, along with his New Street background, as important in the formation of his later career. Recognizing that there were secular and political issues in his home island that needed resolution, he returned to Antigua in the early 1930s. Back home, he became involved in the genesis of the first trade union movement in the island, following a visit of members of the Moyne Commission and an address in St John's in 1938 by Sir Walter (later Lord) Citrine, then general secretary of the British Trades Union Congress.

Antigua had largely escaped the labour disturbances that many of its neighbours experienced in the 1930s, but the conditions that generated those risings were abundantly present in the island's countryside and towns. Thus, when the spark of unionization was struck, giving birth to the Antigua Trades and Labour Union (AT&LU), inevitable confrontations with management in the sugar industry were set in motion. Many of energy and ability were found ready to take up the challenge, Bird foremost among them.[4]

Bird's ascent within the union was rapid. By 1943 he had assumed leadership, supplanting the first president, Reginald Stevens, a St John's jeweller. In 1945 Bird was elected to the island's Legislative Council after Stevens's death left a vacant seat. Uniquely in the Eastern Caribbean, the AT&LU was able in 1946 to elect a full slate of five candidates to the Legislative Council, five years *before* the advent of universal adult suffrage: Bird, as union president, had become the leader of the island's popular element, despite the fact that most of the adult population would not be able to vote until the 1951 elections.

Although the AT&LU grew in membership under Bird's presidency, the Second World War resulted in colonial restrictions on industrial action, and union activity waned. After the war, however, the union took up the cause of working conditions in Antigua, particularly within the sugar industry, and the battle between labour and management was joined. Labour disputes over problems in agrarian production led to Commissions of Inquiry in 1948 and 1951, and the union played a critical role in the drive to transform the Antiguan economy. Again, Bird was a central figure in these struggles.

We can consult the record to capture the tone of the workers' struggle in its early days after the imposed cessation of industrial agitation during the Second World War. Much of this is in the words of V.C. Bird, or is at least attributed to him. It is worth quoting at length, first from Bird's foreword to the union's *Twelfth Anniversary Souvenir Magazine:*

> It is common knowledge that in all communities there has been developing a consciousness on the part of the labouring classes, of the need to organise themselves in order to be better able to secure their rightful share in the control of the Government of their country, and to seek their protection in industries and in the general living conditions of the masses. This effort has constituted a social crisis of unparalleled proportions which has not evaded our shores and accounts for much of the stirrings in our community that we so often hear dismissed as signs of lawlessness and irresponsibility.
>
> While it is true that appreciable advancement has been achieved, we must be aware, however, that the changes effected have been earned amidst sharp differences of opinion, carping criticisms of our organisation, and, at times, Machiavellian devices by those determined to have the *status quo* preserved. It must constantly be borne in mind that if the ground is to be firmly laid, if the community is ever able to offer to all equality of opportunity and security in the various phases of the social, economical, and political life of the community, there must be no resting on our laurels nor sleeping on the watch. There must be determined and undeviating perseverance from us all. (AT&LU 1951, i–ii)

In case there are doubts as to why this vigilance must be maintained, Bird says,

> But for some time now the World in which we live has been beclouded by propaganda aimed at the hiding of the real fundamental issues. It has been troubled by the clash of rival aims between those determined to continue appropriating the rights and resources of others, by those who want to put national institutions before the freedom of the citizenry and by those who are even calling for the supreme sacrifice in order to preserve the privilege of

man exploiting man. Among these can also be found those endeavouring to make justice and freedom the common lot among all peoples and every land. (AT&LU 1951, ii)

In a document speaking more specifically to issues that concerned Antigua and the Antiguan working classes, especially agrarian workers, Bird issued a lengthy minority view to the report of the Soulbury Commission, on which he served and which studied the situation of the troubled Antiguan sugar industry in 1948. In his statement he addressed the organization of production, access to land and the ownership of the means of production. Commenting on the concentration of land in the hands of the few, specifically the ownership of most estate lands by the Antigua Syndicate Estates (ASE), Bird wrote,

> A growing political consciousness among the people has given rise to an articulate recognition of the irreconcilable viewpoints of the handful of landlords and their sugar factory associates on the one hand, and the impoverished majority population on the other. It is apparent from the facts that the attitude of the plantation owners is deeply rooted in slavery and that they are interested, not in seeing the land reorganised for production which will accrue to the benefit of the community of the whole, but actually in opposing and obstructing any rearrangement of land ownership which will assist in building up an independent peasantry likely to deprive them of using a large standing body of unemployed, serflike, landless workers to keep down wages with the object of keeping sugar profits up. (Antigua 1949, 110)

Representing the position of the AT&LU, he calls for the ASE to "be prevented from acquiring any further properties" and states that a "Land Authority" needs to be initiated to acquire lands for farming by peasants (Antigua 1949, 110). Bird further proposes the nationalization of the sugar industry, offering two alternative paths to this end:

> *(a)* That Government acquire the major shares in the Sugar Factory, *i.e.*, at least 51 per cent, and the right to a controlling voice in the industry by having the right to appoint a majority of the directors. The shares not owned by the Government could be left in the hands of, or be subscribed for by, local or overseas investors.
> *(b)* The conversion of the Factory into a co-operative organisation, in which ownership will be shared by all parties actively connected with the operations of the Factory, and who will elect representatives to the Board of Management. (Antigua 1949, 117)

After summarizing events that led to the industrial disputes of 1948 in the sugar industry, Bird's report discusses the conflation of race, class and historic circumstance in the island's economic history and the implications for just resolution of labour disputes:

> The tradition of slavery still hangs heavy over Antigua and imbues the attitude of the European employers towards coloured workers. Hence the employers are unfavourably disposed to meeting on common ground as equals the leaders of the Union, who are men from among the ranks of the workers. Their state of mind is that the workers should unquestionably accept any kind of work which is made available to them at wages which the employers feel disposed to pay, and be glad to get it at that. . . . With the racial line so sharply drawn when it comes to coloured people of ability, it can easily be imagined what sort of relationship existed between the workers and their masters. Some aver that things were peaceful before the Union came to the island. This it is possible to concede, for circumstances did not permit otherwise. After all, there is peace in a graveyard. The people were cowed by the fact that the owners of the sugar factory and the plantations were as a rule from the same country as the Governors and Administrators, and from their vantage point, saw little to distinguish the one from the other. The workers thus have always regarded the employers as rulers to be obeyed. But in these conditions suspicion and prejudice take deep roots, and the possibility of friction is ever present. The European employers have not taken kindly to meeting labour leaders on equal terms. On the other hand, signs of condescension are quickly resented by Labour. It is against this background that the starting off of the 1948 strike must be viewed. (Antigua 1949, 118)

And finally, lest there be any doubt that these proposals constituted anything less than a concerted programme on behalf of the union and its political wing in the island's Legislative Council, the following resolution was forwarded by AT&LU members during a 1946 Legislative Council session:

> Be it resolved that this Council strongly recommends that the Government take all steps necessary and calculate to obtain the consent of, and secure permission from, the proper responsible authorities in the United Kingdom, to use part of the Colonial Development Welfare ten year grant for the colony (Antigua) for the acquisition of the Antigua Sugar Factory, and its operation as a public concern, under the direction of a statutory factory

management board, constituted on the lines of the coal mines [in England]. (Hector, 11 December 1981, 8–9)

It was a call that would be repeated five years later during a period of the most intense labour dispute the colony had yet endured. The *Workers Voice,* the organ of the AT&LU, editorialized that

> the Control of the only Factory in the Island should be taken out of the hands of the inhuman sets who now enjoy the privilege, and turned over to the Government [and that] decisions in the Managing of the Factory is [*sic*] taken either by Government or by a Committee consisting of Workers both in the Factory and the Field, cane suppliers and one member of the Factory Staff. (6 May 1951)

I have cited copiously here because these expressions of the resolute, class-conscious positions of the AT&LU, particularly as articulated by its president, are examples of what Paget Henry (1985) refers to in his discussion of the second phase of the Antiguan working-class movement, a phase characterized by its anti-imperialist, class orientation. These statements called for a restructuring of the economy, including radical land reform and worker control of the sugar industry, the creation and expansion of an independent peasantry and recognition and redress of the racial oppression that had been a fundamental feature of the Antiguan social formation since its creation as a plantation-dominated structure.

They also contain, inescapably, the elements for a charter and national mythology within which a greater sense of national identity and realistic appraisal of the historical specificity of the Antiguan experience is feasible. Within this framework it is possible to critically understand the historical forces that produced the condition that is the Antiguan legacy. In its first decade of existence, the trade union movement appears to have been on the path of constructing a historically valid and self-aware national myth.

V.C. Bird and the Political Directorate

To use the local phrase, "All so don't go so." The radical imagination suggested in the above-quoted documents was not sustained. Henry (1985) has insightfully probed the process by which the labour movement, exemplified in the course pursued by the AT&LU, moved to a phase in which "labourist" goals – improved wages, conditions of employment and so forth – came to dominate the activity of the union. Any transformative restructuring of the economy and society was seldom mentioned or specifically denied. As the AT&LU political section, later to become the Antigua Labour Party (ALP), attained political domination within the dependent colonial state and became more attuned to working an accommodation with the representatives of the Colonial Office, the union cast itself in a more accommodationist stance, seldom engaging in industrial action, content to negotiate conditions at the workplace. Concern for the establishment of a viable peasantry stagnated, and during a period when establishment of the West Indies Federation became the dominant regional political preoccupation, advocacy for nationalizing the sugar industry disappeared.[5]

As the political section of the union gained unchallenged ascendance in the political arena, V.C. Bird and his colleagues became a political directorate, focused on the process of transforming a sugar-based agrarian economy to one reliant on tourism, commercial property and financial services. The old antagonisms between labour and planters diminished after 1951 and the political directorate, although still prominent among the AT&LU executive, became increasingly distanced from the concerns of the rank and file. However, an electoral strategy of rhetorical opposition to planters, "elites" and "capitalists" continued, and the ALP continued to self-identify as "socialist" as late as 1965.

These shifts in political orientation are exemplified by the following examples. An editorial appearing in the *Workers Voice* as contract negotiations began for the 1958 crop indicates the changed approach to structuring the sugar contract:

> Negotiations today are not merely based on what the workers want, or on what the employers do not want to give, but on the economies of the industry. It is a question now of what the industry can pay after taking all factors including economical and efficient production into account. (30 January 1958)

The first revisionist accounts of the earlier period also appear. Writing of the late 1940s twenty years after the fact, Novelle Richards suggests that "although the question has been raised several times the

Union never seriously considered that the [Antigua] Syndicate lands and the sugar factory should be nationalized" (1965, 40). Of course, by the time of Richards's writing the accommodationist approach and the willingness of the ALP government to disregard worker considerations were well established. In an agreement with the West Indies Oil Company in 1961, the incentive package to induce the company to set up a refinery included government assurances that there would be swift resolution of any trade disputes (Henry 1985).

Ironically, as the AT&LU–ALP government reached an expanded level of devolved powers, it precipitated Antigua's most serious political crisis. In 1967 Antigua, like her neighbours in the Eastern Caribbean, was granted a new constitution, establishing Antigua and Barbuda as an associated state within the British Commonwealth. Virtual local autonomy, including control over financial matters and the police, accrued to the state, substantially enhancing the influence of the locally elected government and, by extension, since they held all of the Legislative Council seats, the AT&LU–ALP directorate.

At that point a split in the AT&LU precipitated a crisis giving rise to a rival union, the Antigua Workers Union (AWU), and nearly bringing down the Bird government. A vigorous opposition party, the Progressive Labour Movement (PLM), emerged when the burgeoning AWU combined with other interests on the right and left of the political spectrum. Forced to accommodate to this challenge in order to salvage its hold on government, the ALP acceded to by-elections held in four specially created seats in 1968, elections in which they put up token candidacies and which resulted in the first viable parliamentary opposition since 1946.

During the next three years the AT&LU was reduced to a skeleton of its former support as the AWU siphoned off some 70 per cent of its membership. The AWU–PLM conducted a continuous oppositional referendum in the streets and at workplaces, and the besieged ALP government stumbled, paralysed, through the last three years of its long run (see Henry 1985; Midgett 1984). The loss of support of the labouring population is exemplified in the manifestos the ALP published for the 1965 and 1971 elections, in which there is no mention of labour and in which emphasis is given to the role of government as director of the economy and provider of social services (ALP 1965, 1970).

The outcome of the 1971 elections was a foregone conclusion. In a contest in which the number of constituencies had been expanded from ten to seventeen, the ALP put up a slate of candidates that included eight of the old union/party stalwarts, most of whom had been in office since the early 1950s. Six were soundly defeated, including V.C. Bird, then sixty-one years old, who lost his seat after twenty-six years in parliament. The death knell had apparently sounded for Bird and the AT&LU–ALP axis, but the obituaries proved premature.

V.C. Bird as Political Icon

During the tenure of the 1971–76 government led by George Walter and the PLM, V.C. Bird's voice was absent from the Legislative Council. However, his relegation to Antigua's political wilderness was not an exile without renewal. With the assistance of his two sons and other young recruits to the ALP, the party was reconstructed during its five-year term in opposition. The PLM, by contrast, served a term fraught with economic problems, punctuated by allegations of corrupt practice and finally beset by the passage of an extremely unpopular Public Order Act, a measure that drew fire from all sides, including the PLM-affiliated AWU.[6]

The consequence was that the ALP faced elections in 1976 with a much younger slate of candidates and with renewed hopes of capturing control of government. The election was the most closely fought in the two-island state's history. With a voter turnout near 95 per cent, the ALP, despite polling a minority vote, won eleven seats to the PLM's five, with an independent candidate elected in Barbuda (Antigua 1976). When the new government took their seats, the man in the premier's chair was once again V.C. Bird, elected to a safe seat when the ALP incumbent stepped aside.

The 1976 election marks the emergence of V.C. Bird as a political and national icon in Antiguan public life. It is an achievement unique to the political history of the Commonwealth Caribbean. Although other heads of state have seen political castles crumble and have returned to once again head governments, no one has returned from the ignominy of losing his own seat to regain the pre-eminent position.[7] Such a loss – indeed, even a defeat of a party in power – has usually relegated the party head to retirement and the relative impotence of elder statesmanship.

After 1976, Bird's iconization took numerous tangible forms, most notably in 1985 in the christening of the airport that bears his name. The ceremony attending this event occasioned the publication of a pamphlet extolling Bird's career and reciting his contributions to Antigua. It also reproduced some of the mythology created by Bird and intoned by him and others during the previous fifteen years (Bird 1985). Other local publications likewise have contributed to the elevation of Bird to iconic status. In a magazine celebrating the constitutional independence of Antigua and Barbuda, a prominent article is entitled "V.C. Bird – Father of the Nation" (Sanders 1981). In 1989 the AT&LU's fiftieth anniversary magazine was "dedicated to the union's founding fathers, including Prime Minister the Rt Hon. Dr Vere Cornwall Bird", and filled throughout with tributes and references to the man, even to the point where most of the advertisements contained copy such as the following:

> Congratulations to the Rt. Honourable Dr. V.C. Bird, Prime Minister of Antigua & Barbuda for His Outstanding Contribution to the Trade Union Movement, and Political Development of Antigua During the Past 50 Years. (AT&LU 1989, 73)[8]

An irony of all of the adulation manifest after 1976 was the reduction of Bird's real political influence to domestic matters, such as the police, and the assignment of important ministries to the party's young arrivals – Bird's sons Lester and V.C., Jr, as well as John St Luce and Adolphus Freeland. It was also a period punctuated with scandals – arms trans-shipping, financial malfeasance, public works and land deals – all of which V.C. Bird stayed above.[9]

In the 1950s and 1960s Bird represented Antigua at nearly every international gathering to discuss political federation. His personal fortitude and strength of will in dealing with the British Colonial Office are the stuff of legend – some of which he enjoyed telling. But in the last years of his long tenure he rarely left the island on official business; the 1979 meeting of the West Indian States in Association (WISA) to discuss the Grenada revolution was his first since 1976. Even on these rare occasions local critics noted his impotence at international or regional gatherings. An exemplary case occurred in 1986 at a special meeting in Grenada of heads of the Organisation of Eastern Caribbean States occasioned by the public relations visit by then US president Ronald

Reagan. In a scene reminiscent of an old-style colonial school inspection the various prime ministers were assigned topics on which to give five-minute addresses. Bird was given no topic; instead he delivered the vote of thanks. This kind of humiliating nonsense is in striking contrast to the near deification of the man in Antigua.

Creating Myths: The Cases

Having discussed the iconization of V.C Bird in the Antiguan political and national arena, I will now focus on a consideration of his role as mythmaker and purveyor in light of two significant events in the history of the Antiguan working class, events that were definitive of a working-class identity and that set important precedents for the trade union struggle. The first concerns a dispute with a local drugstore in which the union became involved on behalf of a dismissed female employee. The second involves a series of industrial actions during the first months of 1951 that spoke to conditions of employment, recognition of the legitimate rights of workers to engage in collective action and issues of land distribution and small-farmer tenancy. In discussing these, I will review the facts of each case and then give the version as presented in later public renditions by V.C. Bird.

The O'Neal Drugstore Case[10]

The O'Neal Drugstore case is justifiably cited as one of the most significant events in the history of trade union development in Antigua. On its face, the case involved an instance of wrongful dismissal in the firing of a female clerk in 1955. Although she was not a member of the union, the AT&LU made representation on her behalf to her former employer and asked for her reinstatement. The request was denied and the case was taken to the labour commissioner, who, after meeting with the concerned parties, attempted a solution involving either reinstatement or compensation. The employers refused, and the union appealed to the government, asking for an inquiry and contending that the case constituted a trade dispute where, in accordance with the Trade Disputes and Arbitration Act, an inquiry could be convened. The employer, however, withdrew from participation, arguing that the case did not constitute a trade dispute and that, consequently, there was no legal basis for an inquiry.

Despite the O'Neals' refusal to participate, the Board of Inquiry met and made recommendations that determined that the employee had been wrongfully dismissed and that she was due thirteen weeks' pay as compensation. These recommendations were submitted to the employers, who again chose to ignore them. At this point the AT&LU decided to picket the store. During the course of the picketing, prospective customers were allegedly threatened and harassed, and the O'Neals retaliated by charging the union with "conspiracy to do damage" to their business; they sought damages and an injunction to restrain the picketing. The outcome of the case involved two separate but related judgements.

The union again held that their action was legal because a trade dispute had occurred, a position with which the judge concurred in his ruling. However, he cited the union with unlawful acts during the course of the picketing, ordered them to pay costs and £80 in damages and enjoined them from further picketing. This judgement satisfied neither side, and when the AT&LU appealed the case to the West Indian Court of Appeals, both contending parties presented cases. The O'Neals continued to press their claim that no trade dispute had occurred, now arguing that the clerk was not a "workman" and thus not covered by the Trade Union Act and the Trade Disputes and Arbitration Act. The court's decision upheld the O'Neals' position, determining that the definition of "workman" was not met and that there was, therefore, no trade dispute. The court also reaffirmed that the AT&LU had conspired to damage the firm and it increased the fine assessed the union.

In its final appeal to the Privy Council, heard in 1959, the union again represented the dismissed clerk, asking that she be awarded thirteen weeks' wages. The Privy Council judgement was a victory for the union in that the clerk was awarded compensation and the AT&LU was found not culpable in respect to any damages inflicted on the firm. The important aspects of this judgement include three precedents for the union movement. First, in determining that the employee was entitled to compensation, the privy councillors held that she did meet the definition of "workman" and was thus entitled to protection under the acts in question. Moreover, they decided that as the event constituted a trade dispute, the intervention of the union in taking industrial action on behalf of the clerk was legitimate. Finally, they determined that the relationship between the AT&LU or its Executive Committee and the pickets was such that the union was not liable for illegal acts performed individually by some pickets. Thus, as a precedent-setting decision, the Privy Council judgement was of singular importance. Coverage under the law was extended beyond a narrow range of what had hitherto been defined as a "workman", and the legitimate activities of the union in representing workers were similarly extended.

V.C. Bird's Version

The AT&LU fortieth anniversary souvenir magazine contains an article, "The Development of Trade Unionism in Antigua", taken from an address by V.C. Bird at the State College in October 1978. Regarding the O'Neal case, he states,

> We had another big strike after this lasting months. This time it stemmed from wrongful dismissal. It was the habit that whenever workers became what the employers thought "rude", they dismissed one or two of them as an example to the others. The significant case surrounded the dismissal of a clerk at O'Neil's [sic]. The Union was determined that the employers would not be allowed to dismiss the workers without cause. We fought wrongful dismissal of the clerk at O'Neil's in the Courts until it reached the then West Indian Court of Appeal, which ruled that the employer had the right to determine the compensation paid to a dismissed worker and to dismiss without showing cause. The strike was protracted for we did not accept the decision of the West Indian Court of Appeal. We appealed to the Privy Council which upheld our view that a worker could not be dismissed without satisfactory cause. On the day the Privy Council's decision was announced there were huge demonstrations by the workers all over St John's.
>
> After that historic event, whenever anyone was dismissed, the Union wanted to know the reason and if it wasn't satisfactory, action was taken. (AT&LU 1979, 35)

Bird takes a similar direction in an interview recorded in 1986:

> Here what the employer did was to use their jobs as an inducement for you to behave yourself and if you weren't properly disciplined from their point of view, you'd lose your job. Well, we felt that this uncertainty in the job was

against the rights of the people – these various agreements that we had been making [with management]. So there was this girl working for Mr O'Neal, and they put the [empty] buckets outside with the lard that they finished using. And so it seemed that this day this girl working inside must have thought she would scrape around the rims and get some of what had remained in there. And for that she was dismissed. Well, we had a view that she wasn't stealing anything. This was a discarded bucket that you were finished with. And if she went and she got some of the leftovers, we didn't think that it was right that she should have been dismissed. And they wouldn't be swayed. And we had a strike at the place; there was some picketing for some time; and they wouldn't be swayed. And then there was a court case on the matter and we carried the case right up to the Privy Council, and we won – that the people should have a measure of responsibility, a measure of security on the job. So that was a big victory for those who work around the counter, you see – the clerks, the shop hand. This gave them the opportunity, now, because their employers were no longer to dominate them to the extent as they used to, having won this O'Neal case in the Privy Council. So they, too, joined up and we formed what we call a clerical workers' section. That branch of the clerical workers continued to organise to represent that type of worker.[11]

Bird's account of the O'Neal case reduces the issue to the union's defence of an employee who has been victimized by a wrongful dismissal. There are no important elements here that relate to interpretations of labour law and that determine the areas of legitimate trade union activity. His version is simply a little morality fable, a struggle between right and wrong.

The precedents established in the definition of "workman" and legitimate union action are the key features of the case. These are the stories that are worthy of being retold and emphasized, for they are the core issues that deserve inclusion in a history of Antiguan labour struggles.

The 1951 Disputes and the Malone Commission[12]

The year 1951 began with a portent of industrial strife. The previous year had been marked by three major disputes and work stoppages (Great Britain 1951). In April 1950 waterfront workers struck for a week and then, after a temporary settlement, walked out again until

May 4. This action spread to the sugar industry, and field and factory employees shut down operations for two weeks. A lengthier dispute involved union workers and the Clarence Johnson Construction Co., which was building facilities at the exclusive Mill Reef Properties in the east of the island. The company's reluctance to recognize the union led to a three-month strike, which was settled by mutual agreement. This last case was significant in that it was settled with an employer who previously had flatly refused to talk with AT&LU leaders (Lowenthal 1955).

Although the industrial disputes of 1950 were settled amicably, lingering problems are suggested in a speech made in December of that year by the governor, Sir Kenneth Blackburne. He deplored the "general atmosphere of suspicion, even of hate in the community as a result of trade disputes", and also condemned the introduction of "the evil bogey of racial feeling into the Leeward Islands" (*Leeward Island Gazette,* 14 December 1950). Despite an apparent accommodation between the AT&LU, as bargaining agent for labour, and the ASE and the Antigua Employers' Federation (AEF), representing the management of the sugar industry, the employers saw in the union movement and in the personal stance of V.C. Bird an approach to the resolution of sugar-production relations and agrarian practice that they found untenable. From the instances of the Legislative Council's resolution and Bird's statement of the union's position on nationalization and peasant development (quoted above) to the 1951 *Workers Voice* editorial, the plantocracy recognized a determination to transform agrarian productive relations in Antigua. Consequently, in 1951, on the eve of the island's first election under universal adult suffrage, the employers in the sugar industry made their move to crush the union and fragment its growing political voice.

In January a strike of waterfront workers ushered in the new year. This was followed in late February by a stoppage among cotton pickers on one estate. A third dispute, of a substantially more serious nature, resulted in a strike on all sugar estates, centring on problems of tenants with the ASE. These problems had been prefigured in the deliberations and recommendations of the Soulbury Commission, which had advocated in 1948 that more arable lands be made available for peasant cultivation, while rejecting some of the union's suggestions for more fundamental reform. Richards (1965) notes that the ASE agreed to implement such changes, but by 1951 the number of allottees had hardly grown and the amount of arable land in allotments was still minuscule relative to any reasonable subsistence provision for the rural population. Thus, the peasant cultivators, who as tenant farmers typically divided their labour time between estates and their own plots, withheld their labour from the estates from March 6 to April 4 to dramatize their plight.

These disputes were only a prelude, for the union, like management, recognized the significance of 1951 not only with regard to industrial issues, but also as a milestone in the political practice of the society. Consequently, the determination of workers at the central sugar factory at Gunthorpes to celebrate the international workers' holiday on May 1 rather than show up for work was met by an intransigent management that threatened a two-day lockout as reprisal.

The situation quickly escalated; work stopped until May 7; the strike spread; Tomlinson's workshop went out on May 8; and on the same day all sugar estates were struck, followed by the workers at the small muscovado factory at Montpelier. The union recognized the situation for the all-out, make-or-break struggle that management intended. Governor Blackburne saw the situation in its stark terms: "Antigua's economy is more seriously threatened than ever before. Strikes prevail in the sugar industry and the waterfront. Today [15 May] red flags and pickets were standing in front of the *Antigua Star* printery" (*Advocate*, 17 May 1951).

With strikes shutting down the waterfront and the island's principal industry, the colonial administration took a hand. In a radio address Blackburne noted the intransigence of the AEF in the face of continuing industrial action: "Peace can only come when the antagonism between the employers and the Union is broken. The Union says that the employers wish to smash the Union. The employers say that the Union is out to wreck the sugar industry. If both want a show-down, nothing I can say will prevent it and the population will suffer" (*Advocate*, 19 May 1951).

Blackburne had got it partially right: the employers were indeed out to break the union's strength. But, of course, the union was hardly determined to wreck the industry on which its members depended for employment; rather, it sought to transform it. Blackburne's solution – that the workers return as a condition for him to arrange an inquiry –

was initially unacceptable to the union. The stalemate continued for another week with no indication of abating. Then, on Empire Day, May 25, Blackburne made another appeal for both sides to resume work in the face of an economic disaster in the colony. This time the union acceded, and a day later the promised Board of Inquiry was appointed, with Sir Clement Malone, the distinguished West Indian jurist, as chairman.

The board convened on June 11, but three days later the governor, acting under a declared state of emergency, and for reasons unfathomable, called in a detachment of the Welsh Fusiliers from Jamaica, ostensibly to maintain order. Under these conditions the union representation withdrew from the proceedings of the board. The decision to bring in troops is a puzzle since no apparent threat to public order existed. Frank Walcott, secretary of the Barbados Workers' Union and a member of the Board of Inquiry, reported that "there were no signs of unrest" (*Advocate*, 21 June 1951). With no disturbance present or threatened, the governor sent the troops back to Jamaica and, after a month's hiatus, the inquiry resumed on July 21 and completed its work on August 2.

The outcome is instructive. The board saw the major problems as arising from disputes in the agricultural sector. Of these, tenancy problems between peasants and the ASE and labour issues in field and factory were paramount. The board's favourable responses to most of the suggestions advanced by the union are in marked contrast to their treatment of those forwarded by the AEF (Antigua 1952). From the union came suggested approaches to dispute regulation and procedures for representation, along with the setting aside of Labour Day (May 1) as a workers' holiday. The employers, however, continued to evidence their disdain for labour, suggesting among other things that people be educated "to think for themselves" and that measures be adopted to enforce law and order. Of the list put forward by the AEF, the board responded favourably to only one suggestion, a proposal to establish means for professional training of trade union officials. In its conclusions the board stressed the need for mutual good faith and respect in the industry, while pointing out problems inherent in the monopoly position of the ASE. It recommended that a statutory body be established to regulate the industry in the public interest and again insisted on the need for government to acquire lands from the ASE for peasant development (Antigua 1952).

Two areas require further comment: the underlying economic (as opposed to political) issues and their resolution, and the duration of the strike and response of the labouring population. The first of these has been buried in rhetoric and in an account contrived to present the strike purely in its political terms – as a power struggle between the union and management, personalized in the contending figures of V.C. Bird and Alexander Moody-Stuart, managing director of ASE and chairman of the Employers' Federation (Richards 1965). Indeed, even the proposals forwarded by the union during the inquiry, apposite as they were, focused on conditions of work, representation and dispute regulation – "labourist" issues. But these were not the causes that the board identified (correctly) as those underlying much of the 1951 unrest. The fundamental issues of 1951 go back to the situation addressed in the Soulbury Commission report. The monopoly situation of the ASE and its failure to create the conditions in Antigua for the formation of a viable peasantry were at root. The ASE had not acted in good faith after the 1948 Commission investigation in that the ASE had failed to abide by recommendations that it release arable lands for peasant cultivation. Nor had it attempted to deal with peasant grievances in marketing, the peasant share of the sugar cess fund, weight checking of peasant canes delivered to the factory and conditions of tenancy. These were again addressed by the Malone Commission in its recommendations, some of which were subsequently instituted. Thus, the most salient issues underlying the labour unrest of 1951 related to the peasantry, concerns that focused on ensuring its growth and viability in a society historically dominated by the plantation.

The second issue is of lesser significance in the labour history of the island, but it has received the most attention in subsequent accounts of the events of 1951. These accounts, in particular a bowdlerized version of aspects of the 1951 strikes, are examined below. The solidarity demonstrated by the labouring classes during 1951 was, without doubt, heroic. The intention of the ASE and AEF forces to crush the trade union movement was manifest. The workers' forbearance has been commented upon by observers of the strikes and in subsequent accounts. Richards speaks of "numerous stoppages of work on the estates" in early 1951 (1965, 51), apparently in reference to the March-April disturbances. He details the event of the May Day dispute and the ensuing general strike up to the period of the inquiry. Although he adds nothing further about the strike, the impression remains that the conclusion of the inquiry and its issuing of recommendations generally favourable to the union's position created the climate for uninterrupted work for the remainder of the year.

In a more cursory treatment, Henry mentions "the struggle for land for peasants in 1951", contending that "workers struck for six months and left 40,000 tons of cane standing in the fields", an indication that much of the crop was reaped (1985, 91). Elsewhere he gives a production figure of over 170,000 tons of reaped cane (p. 106), substantially lower than either 1950 or 1952. From this it appears that some considerable labour time was withheld from the industry during 1951.

A reasonably complete sequence of events is found in the pages of the Barbados *Advocate* in 1951. The newspaper chronicled with particular care the events of this pivotal year in the Eastern Caribbean, and its accounts of the Antiguan struggles are unusually full. With regard to the period from the May Day protest to Governor Blackburne's call for an inquiry, there was apparently no work done on the estates or the docks. After both sides accepted Blackburne's terms for the board's appointment, work was resumed and evidently continued even during the visit of the Welsh Fusiliers. A report quotes Walcott to that effect: "he was told that the production of cane to the factory had reached its highest peak for the year" (*Advocate*, 21 June 1951).

A week later, following the troops' departure, the situation was reported as calm with no labour disturbances (*Advocate*, 27 June 1951). A month later an item related that the sugar factory expected to extend grinding operations until the end of September because of the cutting interruptions, and that half of the canes had been ground at that point. The story detailed how the strike not only had disrupted operations for 1951 but would have some serious consequences for planting and rationing in subsequent years (*Advocate*, 24 July 1951).

In early September an *Advocate* story relates the experience of Grantley Adams, the Barbadian political and labour leader, who was representing the AT&LU in a case in Antigua: "Mr Adams said that Mr Bird . . . was out in the country with Mr Moody-Stuart . . . exhorting the labourers to go on with the reaping of the sugar crop" (4 September 1951). Finally, in late September the *Advocate* reported that the crop had ended with 18,000 tons of sugar produced and that "about 50,000 tons of cane remain standing, 25% of which are owned by the peasants, the rest is owned by the ASE" (23 September 1951). The story also notes that the factory had been idled for ten weeks during the season. It is likely that this account does not fully sum up the 1951 crop, for I was told by a veteran union official that much of the standing cane was eventually reaped and ground with surprisingly good yields (Ishmael Roberts, personal interview, 27 October 1985).

The lengthy description of events, particularly the disposition of the cane crop, is necessary in light of the account of these events cited below and the consequent reconfiguration of their significance for political practice and the history of the workers' struggle in Antigua.

V.C. Bird's Version

In the sources noted above, V.C. Bird discusses the 1951 episode in terms that have been often repeated during the past fifteen years. In the AT&LU fortieth anniversary publication Bird notes the visit of the Welsh Fusiliers and the resolve of the workers in the face of this show of force. His account continues,

> The following year was 1951 [in fact, the same year], and the President of the Employers' Association, Mr Moody-Stuart, in January made his pronouncement – "No more negotiations, no more signing of contracts, no knowing of rates."
>
> The Union recognised a last-ditch effort by the employers. This was the final confrontation. Union leaders advised the workers not to go to work, and after a few days the Governor called the Union and Employers and he asked, "What is this all about?" The President of the Employers' Association, Mr Moody-Stuart, said that he had been given the undertaking that when the Union started it wouldn't last nine months but despite that, it had continued for years. He stated categorically that he was determined to break it once and for all. The Governor told him to be careful, warning that he was making a mistake. Mr Moody-Stuart became angry, saying all he needed was police protection and in three months he could starve the workers into submission. The Governor agreed to police protection but again he warned Mr Moody-Stuart that he was making a mistake.
>
> The Union leaders reported to the workers that it was Mr Moody-Stuart's intention to starve them into submission, and this statement increased the workers' resolve not to surrender. The workers remained on strike for the three-month period. By this time, the sugar-syndicate was losing money

and Moody-Stuart telephoned me saying that he would like a joint meeting with the workers. A number of these meetings were organised, the first being at the tamarind tree at the entrance to Bethesda. Great crowds of people had gathered and Mr Moody-Stuart insisted on speaking first. He told the workers, "I know you are losing a lot of money, you are losing wages, and may I admit I am losing money myself. I think you should stop this thing and that you should go to work." The answer from the workers was unanimous, "You said you are going to starve us into submission. Nobody shall ever use that remark to us again. We are not going to work for the balance of the year." (AT&LU 1979, 38)

Here is the genesis of the myth of the full-year strike. Bird further describes this phenomenon:

For the balance of the year people didn't work at all. For the whole of 1951 no crop was reaped. How they ate? They went into the pasture and they picked the widdy-widdy bush and cooked that every day. Sometimes on Sundays some went to the beach and they got some cockle with it. Widdy-widdy bush and cockles – that is what they ate for the whole year. I think it was one of the greatest accomplishments by the people of Antigua. At the great centres of Trade Unionism in the world this year-long strike in Antigua is remembered. As far away as Australia they quote it, showing the determination of a people to rid themselves of injustice and tyranny. The Union leaders could not tell the people to make such a sacrifice because we didn't have anything to give them to eat. But, the people themselves were determined. (AT&LU 1979, 39)

The full-year strike story is coupled with the fable of widdy-widdy bush subsistence. It has been related on numerous public occasions, including a televised speech I witnessed in 1985. What follows, of course, is the capitulation of the planters in the face of this heroic intransigence of the workers:

On January 2nd, 1952, Mr Moody-Stuart rang me saying, "Bird, I think I would like us to have an early negotiation." Those words were his end. The big master was being forced to surrender. He had issued his pronouncement the year before, "no more negotiation, no contracts, no knowing the rates before you go in to work". But after a whole year's strike, he was asking for an early negotiation. The strength, determination and sacrifice of the workers fighting against tyranny and injustice, had brought the sugar-barons to their knees. (AT&LU 1979, 38–39)

Thus, the issue focused on a power play between the union and management, a situation settled when management, faced with the incredible resolve of the workers, blinked and submissively agreed to terms set by Bird on behalf of the union. But what about the issue of the establishment of a peasantry? In Bird's version this is given scant attention:

> One of the first things we did was to point out that the people had no lands to work. The Government was scared to give the people their own plots for this would make them too independent. Half of the island was bush and uncultivated. When the Government would not distribute lands to the people we called a 2-month strike [also in 1951]. The message went out, "Don't reap any crops. Don't work for anybody, for if they have half of the island in bush and they won't give you land to cultivate because they feel you will become too independent, that is an injustice."
>
> After a two-month strike the British government stepped in and listened to our request for the provision of money to purchase unused lands for distribution to the workers. So it was that the British government gave the money. They bought the lands and we set up PDO – the Peasant Development Office. (AT&LU 1979, 38–39)

After its early iterations, this depiction of the events of 1951 underwent little significant change in subsequent retellings. It has now been concretized into a fable of the time, incapable of revision and utterly resistant to question. Consider the following excerpt from a 1986 interview with V.C. Bird:

> Q: Were the employers dealing with you, were they recognizing you?
> VCB: They were discussing with us, but in 1951 Mr Moody-Stuart, the general manager of the Syndicate Estates – and he was over the factory too – announced there would be no negotiations from 1951. The people must go in and work, and if they didn't go in and work that he would starve them. And so the governor called up Mr Moody-Stuart and I went representing the workers, and Mr Moody-Stuart said that all he wanted was police protection. In three months' time, he told the governor, he would starve them into submission. The governor told him, "Alright, you will get your police protection, but take my advice, mind you do not butt your head against the wall". And for that, he became very angry with the governor. And he got his police protection. And the people did not go out to work. Three months – January pass, February pass, March pass. When he saw the end of March, he came and he asked to let us go out and hold some meetings among the

people. So we held the first one at the tamarind tree at the entrance to Bethesda Village. A great crowd gathered there. And he spoke first; he told the people he knew they were suffering, they were losing a lot of money; he admitted he, too, was losing quite a lot, and he came to advise them to go in and do their work and stop their sufferings. Well, the people told him, "No, you said you will starve us into submission in three months, but we are not going to work again for the balance of the year". So we left there and we went to Betty's Hope Estate. And we met another large crowd there. And he spoke to them about going back to work, and the sufferings was great for them, he realized it. And they told him, "No, you realize that? Well, we are not going back to work". And it seemed there was a general understanding what they too told him. They were not going to work for the balance of the year because nobody else shall ever use those remarks to them again. And so he said we better leave them and go back to town and we came back to town. And the people never worked again for the balance of the year. Of a days they would go to the pasture and they would pick what you call the widdy-widdy bush. And that they cooked for themselves and their children until the end of 1951.

Q: What else did they eat besides the widdy-widdy bush; what did they do? Fish?

VCB: Some days they would go to the sea and they would get some cockles to put with the bush.

Q: There were also people who were union members who were small growers [peasants] and also some fishermen in the south. Did those people supply other folks who were on strike?

VCB: They would help as they were able to. But this lasted for the whole year. You see? This lasted for the whole year. That is what they depended upon, most of the poor – the widdy-widdy bush.

Q: Let me ask you, that was the year that the Malone Commission was formed to inquire into the strike. . . .

VCB: Well, what happened is that . . . As I told you, it would have to be '52 because in '51 there was no work and there were no negotiations, and the people were determined. We weren't talking at all. But the day after New Year's Day [1952], he [Moody-Stuart] went to the phone and he asked me to let us have an early negotiation. And so a meeting was arranged for the 5th of January, and when we went he asked, "What will satisfy the people to let them go back to work?" And we told him they want 25 per cent increase in their wages. And he said, "Let them have it". And they got their 25 per cent increase; they went back to work; and they worked very well.

Q: That was as a result of the Malone Commission?
VCB: We didn't get the increase as a result of the Malone Commission. At the negotiation on the 5th of January 1952, Mr Moody-Stuart asked, "What will satisfy the people to let them go back to work?" And we told him they wanted 25 per cent increase in their wages and he said, "Let them have it". And that settled that and they went back to work. (V.C. Bird, personal interview, 10 May 1986)

In consideration of Antigua's turbulent 1951 year, historic fact had become captive to the myth of the "whole year" strike. Close questioning could not shake the notion of worker heroism, and the 1986 version, like a rote exercise, is a virtual replication of the 1978 address. The intervention of the Malone Commission and its role in resolving the disputes of 1951 cannot have happened in that year because *nothing* eased the heroic stand taken by the people of Antigua with the leadership of their union. The universal consumption of widdy-widdy bush precludes any alternative outcome of the 1951 confrontation.[13] As with the O'Neal case, the salient features of the 1951 strikes are lost to any thoughtful examination of Antiguan labour history.

Conclusion: Alternative Myths

The consideration of national myths in Antigua must begin with recognition that the fundamental proposition in these reformulations of history is that the historic workers' struggles have concluded and have been won. There is no notion of continuing examination of Antiguan society in light of the past. Indeed, Richards presaged this determination in 1965 when he titled his account of the AT&LU *The Struggle and the Conquest*. At that time the "conquest" seemed assured; the struggle of working-class Antiguans against the plantocracy had been won through the efforts of their union. When the union disintegrated in 1967–68 and the ALP was displaced, a new kind of struggle had to be waged, this time in the party political arena, and it took the form of a profound division of the society and electorate along partisan lines. Hence, Richards's second volume by the same title appeared in 1982 and chronicled not class struggle but the fight of the party to resurrect itself and regain the political kingdom. After 1976 and with subsequent decline of opposition political elements, this struggle, too, had apparently been won (Richards 1982).

V.C. Bird contributed to this image of Antiguan society as well. In a 1989 interview he stated that he wanted young Antiguans to study their history so they would be aware of the conditions that had existed a half-century before. He supplied the reason for his advocacy of historical understanding: "I want them to know that it was the common man of Antigua who formed himself into a trades union and then into a political party that had to fight all these evils and bring Antigua to its present position where there's equality of opportunity for all. A man is a man here" (AT&LU 1989, 23). In the same publication the message is amplified by Bird's son Lester: "We should . . . put aside parties, politics and personalities and understand that we are a part of history and that we should ensure that as such we pay enough respect to it so that others from outside will respect what we have achieved" (p. 63).

What kind of history is this endeavour to which father and son pay homage? V.C. Bird mentioned the trade union, by which he meant the AT&LU, but in the years following the return of the ALP to power the influence of the trade union movement was seriously eroded, mostly as a result of punitive and restrictive legislation enacted by V.C. Bird's own government. It may follow from the argument presented here that if the battles the union engaged in have been substantially won, the vitality of unions is now of less consequence. However, there is another reason for neutralizing their influence. It is quite evident that the legislative assault on the union movement was initially directed against the rival AWU. It mattered little that as the AT&LU regained some of its membership and strength the restrictive measures weighed equally heavily on it. The ALP had determined that the events of 1967–68 would not be repeated – that never again would the party be held ransom by the union (Midgett 1991).

There is likewise no need for close attention to the meaning of actual events for the labour movement if the message is that the task has been accomplished. There is no continuing struggle, no revolution in progress, no persisting social contradictions; the victory for labour – read, Antiguans – is a historic fact and belongs to history.

A more recent addition to this line of thought is found in parts of the 1989 interview with V.C. Bird and in other revisionist accounts. Here the emphasis shifts to a struggle in which the antagonist is the British government and Colonial Office. Instances are provided: Britain's maintaining Antigua as a sugar-producing colony, preventing a more diversified development; British intransigence in the face of Antiguan desires for independence.[14] To other aspects of the myth is added the element of a nationalist struggle, and it follows that once the autonomy issue is won, that struggle is likewise history. Thus, this latter confrontation is relegated to a purely political issue, now settled with the attainment of constitutional independence.

A final aspect of this enterprise is the appearance of articles written by quite evidently worshipful scribes, articles that have both contributed to the adulation of V.C. Bird and repeated the historic revisions noted above (see also Richards n.d.; Sanders 1984). These have served two functions. The first is the further iconization of the man. The tone of these is captured here: "The Right Honourable Dr Vere Cornwall Bird, the undisputed Father of the Nation, provides a feeling of protection, confidence and assuredness while at the helm. This confidence, assurance and protective feeling pervade both the nation and the whole region" (Ford 1989, 59). In advancing the historical interpretations originally given voice by V.C. Bird, the scribes have contributed to legitimizing these renditions. Written by someone other than Bird himself, claiming to be the result of "meticulous research" and with some published locally by the Government Archives Committee, they bear a resemblance to scholarship. With their housing in Antigua's new, modern archive building, the appearance of scholarly authority is enhanced.

Finally, in Antigua today the prevailing view is that there is no need for continual historical re-examination; there are no lessons to be learned; there are no continuing contradictions in the society productive of class conflict. The actual content of the dominant myth, its attention to an accurate portrayal of events, are irrelevant. The purpose is to give a snapshot of the triumph, a sense that it was heroic and that Antiguans were all participants. It has become utterly divorced from issues of the relations of production and control of the means of production, issues addressed with such precision and resoluteness in the 1949 Soulbury minority report. It has no more significance than the final score of an athletic contest – how the score came about, the events of the game, make no difference. The people, the players, need no longer be amazed by the revelations of history. They have their archive and the texts, the accounts of themselves, parts of the illusion that defines the political culture of this small place.

Notes

1. Prior to the 1994 election V.C. Bird retired from active political life. He was succeeded as party leader by his son, Lester, who became prime minister upon the victory of the ALP. V.C. Bird died on 28 June 1999.
2. The lionizing of V.C. Bird continued after his retirement. In June 1998 he was honoured by receiving the Order of the Caribbean Community at the nineteenth meeting of the CARICOM heads of state in St Lucia, and tributes poured in from the Caribbean region and abroad following his death in 1999.
3. Sources for Bird's early career include Hector (1981–82), Sanders (1981) and a personal interview with V.C. Bird (10 May 1986).
4. Sources for the early development of the union include Richards (1965) and personal interviews with V.C. Bird (10 May 1986), J.O. Davis (23 May 1979, 22 October 1985) and Joe Stevens (31 October 1985).
5. This was also a period of intense anti-communist activity in the Caribbean. The co-opting of the Caribbean trade union movement by the AFL-CIO–affiliated International Congress of Free Trade Unions (ICFTU) was one element in this campaign, and it had the effect of blunting union efforts at internationalism and addressing class-based issues; see Hart (1982).
6. Although the ALP campaign in 1976 repeatedly hit at the Public Order Act, the party did not repeal it after its election, preferring to make use of some of its provisions to stifle opposition. In 1986 sections of the act were declared unconstitutional in a case involving the *Outlet* newspaper and its editor, Tim Hector.
7. Other prominent area politicians, including Eric Gairy in Grenada, James Mitchell in St Vincent and John Compton in St Lucia, have seen their parties defeated under their leadership, but they were not personally defeated and – except for Gairy, who lost his franchise between 1958 and 1961 – they retained their seats in Parliament.
8. This magazine offers a striking illustration of the changed orientation of the party and its relationship to the union. In contrast to the fortieth anniversary magazine, which is completely given over to tributes to AT&LU stalwarts at all levels, the fiftieth anniversary publication devotes much space to a "who's who" section of business leaders and high-ranking civil servants, giving little space to historic union figures. An irony is that the Mill Reef Club, the site of early labour acrimony, sponsored this advertisement.
9. Tony Thorndike characterizes Antigua as having "acquired the regrettable image of being the most corrupt society in the Commonwealth

Caribbean, hosting a notorious amorality from top to bottom" (1992, 147).
10. Sources for the O'Neal case include *Leeward Islands Gazette,* supplement (12 January 1956), and Richards (1965).
11. V.C. Bird, personal interview (10 May 1986). In fact, the clerical section of the union had been in existence for some time prior to 1955; it is noted in the 1951 anniversary magazine.
12. Sources for the events of 1951 include Richards (1965), Henry (1985) and Antigua (1952).
13. By the time of a 1989 interview, the specific year is not mentioned, only the "whole year's strike", an indication of its now legendary image; see Arif Ali's interview with V.C. Bird in the fiftieth anniversary brochure (AT&LU 1989, 16–25).
14. More than any of their Eastern Caribbean neighbours, there appeared to be an urgency on the part of the ALP government to move towards independence. In 1964, after the demise of the "Little Eight" Eastern Caribbean federal attempt, Bird announced that his government would seek independence (*Antigua Star* 24 October 1964), and the ALP manifesto for the 1965 election reiterated this goal. When, in 1967, Antigua advanced to statehood in association, it was celebrated as "independence" (Antigua and Barbuda 1967).

References

Antigua. 1976. *Report on the General Elections during 1976 of Members to Serve in the House of Representatives.* St John's, Antigua: Government Printing Office.

Antigua. Commission Appointed to Enquire into the Organisation of the Sugar Industry of Antigua. 1949. *Report of the Commission Appointed to Enquire into the Organisation of the Sugar Industry of Antigua.* London: Crown Agents for the Colonies.

Antigua. Board of Inquiry Appointed to Inquire into Disputes Disrupting Industrial Relations in Antigua in the Year 1951. 1952. *Report of the Board of Inquiry Appointed to Inquire into Disputes Disrupting Industrial Relations in Antigua in the Year 1951.* St John's, Antigua: Government Printing Office.

Antigua and Barbuda. 1967. Untitled commemorative magazine for Antiguan "Independence". St John's, Antigua.

Antigua Labour Party (ALP). 1965. *The New Horizon Political Platform, 1965–1970.* St John's, Antigua: Antigua Labour Party.

──────. 1970. *Save Our Country . . . For a Better Future*. St John's, Antigua: Antigua Labour Party.

Antigua Trades and Labour Union (AT&LU). 1951. *Twelfth Anniversary Souvenir Magazine*. St John's, Antigua: Workers' Voice Printery.

──────. 1979. *Fortieth Anniversary Magazine*. St John's, Antigua: Antigua Printing and Publishing.

──────. 1989. *Fiftieth Anniversary Commemorative Brochure*. St John's, Antigua: Antigua Trades and Labour Union.

Bird, Vere Cornwall. 1985. Untitled pamphlet to accompany naming of the V.C. Bird Airport. St John's, Antigua.

Ford, Ivor. 1989. "Father of the Nation". In Antigua Trades and Labour Union, *Fiftieth Anniversary Commemorative Brochure*, 49–59. St John's, Antigua: Antigua Trades and Labour Union.

Great Britain. 1951. *Leeward Islands 1949 and 1950*. Colonial Reports. London: HMSO.

Hart, Richard. 1982. "Trade Unionism in the English-Speaking Caribbean: The Formative Years and the Caribbean Labour Congress". In *Contemporary Caribbean: A Sociological Reader*, vol. 2, edited by Susan Craig, 59–96. Port of Spain, Trinidad: S. Craig.

Hector, Tim. 1981–82. "The Making of a Prime Minister." *Outlet*, various issues.

Henry, Paget. 1985. *Peripheral Capitalism and Underdevelopment in Antigua*. New Brunswick, NJ: Transaction.

Kincaid, Jamaica. 1988. *A Small Place*. New York: Plume.

Lowenthal, David. 1955. "Economic Tribulations in the Caribbean: A Case Study in the British West Indies". *Inter-American Economic Affairs* 9: 67–81.

Midgett, Douglas. 1984. "Distorted Development: The Resuscitation of the Antiguan Sugar Industry". *Studies in Comparative International Development* 19, no. 2: 33–58.

──────. 1991. "Assaults on Labour in Changing West Indian Economies: Antigua and St Kitts-Nevis". *Labour, Economy and Society/Travail, Economie et Societé* 22: 140–64.

Richards, Novelle. 1965. *The Struggle and the Conquest*. St John's, Antigua: Workers' Voice Printery.

──────. 1982. *The Struggle and the Conquest (II)*. St John's, Antigua: Benjies.

──────. n.d. *Trade Unionism and Its Effects upon the Antigua and Barbuda Society*. St John's, Antigua: Archives Committee.

Sanders, Ron. 1981. "V.C. Bird – Father of the Nation". In *Antigua and Barbuda Independence Official Magazine*, 27–31. St John's, Antigua: Antigua and Barbuda.

———. 1984. *Antigua and Barbuda, 1966–1981: Transition, Trial, Triumph.* St John's, Antigua: Archives Committee.

Thorndike, Tony. 1992. "Revolution, Democracy, and Regional Integration in the Eastern Caribbean". In *Modern Caribbean Politics,* edited by Anthony Payne and Paul Sutton, 147–75. Baltimore: Johns Hopkins University Press.

to
[8]

Imagined Communities
Articulating a Return to Mythical Homelands in the African and Indian Diasporas

Simboonath Singh

Introduction

The cultural and political dispositions of diasporic groups in the colonial and postcolonial Caribbean have engendered specific types of separatist movements geared towards a return to original or ancestral homelands. But, in comparison with past and contemporary separatist movements that have resulted in ethnic nationalism and ethno-political instability (Basque separatism in Spain, Kashmiri nationalism in India, Arab-Israeli conflict in the Middle East, Hutu and Tutsi tribalism in Rwanda, and Québécois nationalism in Canada, to name a few), the particular nature and character of ethno-nationalist movements in the Caribbean have been fundamentally different. For one thing, Caribbean nationalist movements have not been characterized by such things as genocide, wars and "ethnic cleansing".

This chapter seeks to clarify the different ways in which Africa and India were constructed, or "imagined", as it were, in the attempts at African and Indian nationalism in the Caribbean.[1] To demonstrate their differences, I will draw upon the research and events that were associated with the Garvey movement, specifically the back-to-Africa movement of the 1930s, to illustrate the attempts at black nationalism in the Caribbean. For Indian nationalism in the Caribbean, I will use the sparse body of research – there have been no systematic studies to date looking at Indian nationalism in the Caribbean – to highlight the particular character of Indian nationalism in Trinidad and Tobago during the 1940s.

Finally, this paper will attempt to shed some light on how both the African and Indian attempts at ethno-racial and political self-determination were grounded in essentialist as well as primordialist conceptions of race and culture. I will show how in both movements an approach idealizing Africa and India was used to inform racial and cultural consciousness. I argue that a "raced" Caribbean political culture, with its origins in imperialism, colonization, dependent capitalism, slavery and indentureship, and the attendant problems associated with these various forms of social inequalities such as racism, classism and sexism, continues to this day to create political instability in the Caribbean.[2]

Diaspora Studies: Theoretical Considerations

Diaspora studies has at its core two dimensions. First, it pertains to migration and the dispersion of people from their original homelands to other locales. Second, it has been associated with sentimental and ideological characteristics that have the tendency to essentialize and homogenize ethnicity and/or race and which, for all intents and purposes, create hostility towards the Other. Both of these characteristics will be dealt with in the discussions to follow. Thus, it is no surprise that what constitutes a "diaspora" has created some confusion in the social scientific literature. One of the earliest definitions of *diaspora*, for some time considered the most acceptable, constituted it "minorities lacking a homeland", as in the case of the Jewish and Armenian diasporas, in which collective persecution (for example, the Jewish Holocaust and the Armenian genocide) resulted in claims to and a longing for an "original" homeland. Implicit in this notion of the dispersal of a religious or ethnic group from its original homeland is the idea of a "collective memory" that transmits not only a set of historical facts that precipitated the dispersion in the first place, but a cultural heritage as well. Gérard

Chaliand and Jean-Pierre Rageau (1997) argue that what characterizes a diaspora is the will to survive as a minority by transmitting a heritage. This is why both the Jewish and the Armenian diasporas have traditionally been viewed as the ideal or archetypal diasporas (see Armstrong 1982). However, this definition of diaspora has been increasingly criticized for being narrowly applied to the Jewish experience (see Hall 1994; Helmreich 1992).

For the past decade or so, the term *diaspora* has been theorized in a way that distinguishes it from more general notions of immigration and other forms of transnational dispersions. James Clifford, for example, argues that the term *diaspora* "is a signifier not only of transnationality and movement, but of political struggles to define the local, as distinctive community, in historical contexts of displacement" (1994, 308). However, conceptualizations of diaspora vary, from static and fixed notions that distinguish it from other immigrant groups (Safran 1991) to less static, more fluid notions including any ethnic collectivity living outside of a homeland (Conner 1986). Milton Esman (1986) argues that the concept of diaspora has been generalized to refer to any population that has migrated from its country of origin and settled in a foreign land while at the same time maintaining its continuity as a community.

More recently, Alan Anderson (1998) has provided a more comprehensive theoretical framework for understanding comparative diasporic situations, which he defines broadly as "diaspora minorities". Anderson offers a typology of diaspora minorities ranging from minorities lacking a homeland to minorities with a concept of a re-created or imagined homeland to diaspora minorities created through colonialism, and "forced" diasporas which may have been exiled, redistributed, enslaved or indentured. In adopting a relativistic view, I argue that notwithstanding the complexities associated with the term *diaspora*, some use may be found in all of the various diaspora models. However, the application of a specific conceptualization of diaspora will depend on the particular diasporic context that ethnic groups find themselves in. In other words, the determination of a specific type of diaspora will depend on the "nature" of the diaspora, such as how and in what historical context it emerged. This situational approach to diaspora will help explain integral aspects of many diaspora movements, such as the experience of exile and how the rhetoric of return is articulated and forged. Therefore, the most useful and relevant conceptualizations of diaspora for understanding Caribbean diaspora situations would require two different diaspora models: forced diasporas that have been exiled or enslaved, as in the case of the African diaspora, and diaspora minorities created through colonialism, such as the Indian diaspora in the Caribbean.

Black Identity Politics in the African Diaspora

To fully understand the African diaspora in the Caribbean it is necessary to differentiate it from the "archetypal diaspora" and other widely scattered ethnic collectivities or diaspora minorities. As discussed earlier, the historical origin of the term *diaspora* was in application to the Jewish exile and dispersion, and some scholars, such as Chaliand and Rageau (1997), have argued that the term becomes ambiguous when applied to other ethnic collectivities, thereby distinguishing it from other diaspora minorities. However, it is not impossible to unravel some of the complexities involved in the term *diaspora*. For example, an entire ethnic group could be subjected to genocide, exile or both (as in the case of the Armenian genocide perpetrated by the Turks during the 1920s), while another ethnic group could be subjected to exile through slavery. In the cases of the Caribbean and the United States, millions of people of African descent can trace their origins to continental Africa. The Atlantic slave trade and the crossing of the notorious Middle Passage conjure up images not only of extreme dehumanization, demoralization and cruelty, but also of the forced dispersion or removal of Africans from their homeland.

It seems appropriate, then, to attribute the emergence of the African diaspora in the Caribbean to a particular strand of the larger concept of diaspora. Thus, various types of ethnic collectivities such as Afro-Caribbeans were created through colonialism and imperialism – a process involving a forced or involuntary dispersion of people. Alan Anderson states, "These minorities recognize both their original historical country of emigration and a receiving imperial metropole as a 'mother country' " (Anderson 1998, 26). Ethnic groups who have experienced exile and dispersion through a forced diaspora may lay claim to an "original" homeland – a homeland that Anderson argues may be "real and immediate, or historically and geographically distant or recreated" (p. 26). This is a particularly important insight insofar as it allows for an understanding of the specific character of the African diaspora in the Caribbean. I will show how a "lost" Africa was constructed and re-created by its diasporic children in the Caribbean.

To locate my analysis of the Afro-Caribbean diasporic experience in some of kind of theoretical and historical context, the following question ought to be asked: Why did Afro-Caribbean peoples have a focus, specifically a re-emphasis on an "original" African homeland? In constructing a definition of *diaspora,* Safran (1991) isolates some essential features of a diaspora community, two of which are these: there is a general tendency among diasporic groups to retain a collective vision, memory or myth about the original homeland – its history, achievements and physical location; and because of their alienated experience in the host context, they tend to regard the ancestral homeland as the true, real and ideal place to which they belong and to which they should return when conditions permit. I find these two postulates very useful in analysing the Afro-Caribbean diasporic experience.

Esman (1986) argues that depending on historical experience, the "homeland" may be a less specific point of reference. That is to say, the tendency of the vast majority of Afro-Caribbean peoples to identify with all of Africa rather than a particular tribe, territory or cultural community from which they originated may be related to the fact that the experience of enslavement in the Caribbean homogenized all slaves to the extent that they were deprived of any notion of tribal solidarity and of specific historical memories. As such, Africa from the perspective of Afro-Caribbeans is, to use Benedict Anderson's (1983) definition of *nation,* an "imagined community" because they will never know or meet most of their fellow Africans, yet in their minds they see all Africans as a homogeneous group of people, which, for all intents and purposes, consciously or unconsciously denies or discredits notions of Otherness.

Time and again, African diaspora scholars have emphasized the dangers associated with this type of essentialism, arguing that it is particularly difficult to ascertain what is truly African and what is not. Herein, then, lies the problematic scenario around which the African imagination in the Caribbean diaspora has been constructed. Benedict Anderson's (1983) idea of "imagined communities" is akin to Esman's (1986) analysis of the "homeland" concept, which he calls an ideological construct or myth, or to what Eric Hobsbawm (Hobsbawm and Ranger 1983) refers to as "invented traditions". Even Ernest Gellner's view that nationalism "invents nations where they do not exist" (1964, 169) finds useful applications when examining the imagining of Africa in the Caribbean.

Following Esman, Anthony Smith (1992) adds further to the analysis of the "homeland" concept by arguing that historical myths based on common ancestry and a collective romanticization of a past play a significant role in sustaining and maintaining the survival of an ethnic community in a diaspora situation. The experiences and conditions of oppressive plantation social structures in the New World inevitably led to the shedding of tribal or parochial "African" identities in favour of a more collective and shared black identity (see, for example, Brathwaite 1974; Mintz and Price 1992; Robotham 1988). Whereas the construction and eventual emergence of a shared black ethnicity translate into an effective political force, at the same time, this construction promotes a certain degree of ethno-racial consciousness and insularity. The problematical nature of this type of racial and ethnic construction has been critically addressed in black diaspora discourse.

Black Diaspora Criticisms

Edward Kamau Brathwaite (1974) has described an anthropologically grounded black cultural nationalism, in which he posits an originary "merry Africa" – the idea that the history and culture of Africans in the New World has left them with an identifiable authentic past, and one that continues to persist into the present. David Scott (1991, 1999) takes issue with this conceptualization by questioning the black cultural nationalist dream of a full and homogeneous "blackness". For Scott, "Africa" operates as an ongoing mytho-historical force in which " 'Africa' and 'Slavery' " constitute a discursive tradition . . . community and tradition are discursively constituted principally in and through the mobilization of a common possession" (Scott 1999, 124). He goes on to say that whereas "tradition seeks to secure community, it does not presuppose consensus or uniformity. . . . It is a space of dispute as much as consensus, of discord as much as accord" (p. 124). Scott's basically anti-essentialist perspective breaks away from the cultural nationalist and rationalist historiography that have informed black diaspora criticism.

Similarly, Paul Gilroy, in *The Black Atlantic* (1993), attempts to rethink and remap black diaspora criticism by focusing on the concept of tradition. Like Scott, Gilroy sees as problematic the Afrocentric deployments of the concept of "tradition" by the adherents of black nationalism. The strongly essentialist dimensions associated with this conception of tradition smack of racial assurance – a situation involving the privileging of an essential racial or ethnic self, or what Gilroy calls "ethnic insiderism" (1993, 119).[3]

Notwithstanding the validity of the anti-essentialist critiques of black diaspora criticisms, and despite the lack of an understanding of the workings of a real Africa, there is something to be gained by embracing a mythical Africa as "home". "Black nationalism" is an umbrella term for a variety of different perspectives, some of which are emancipatory and others essentialist and, therefore, potentially dangerous. However, it is difficult to imagine how a particular historical experience of marked proportion would be easily forgotten, or "imagined away" by a group of people and their ancestors who were victimized by such an experience. The experience of racism and other forms of brutal exploitative social relations would result in resistance, be it physical, psychological, cultural or political. Resisting oppressive systems would necessarily take the form of a validation and reassertion of the denigrated and despised. As such, black nationalism has, as one of its central tenets, the reclamation of one's sense of self, worth, dignity and pride. Blacks' assertions of their own humanity against centuries of degradation, dehumanization and repression are, therefore, expected, and would entail the mixing of the political and cultural to forge renewed positive ethno-racial self-conceptions at both the individual and group levels. To this extent, then, Africa becomes essentially a place of psychological escape rather than a spatial and cultural reality.

Africa Romanticized

The emergence and development of an African imagination and the cultural embrace of all things African in the Caribbean was one of the hallmarks of the back-to-Africa movement. Marcus Mosiah Garvey probably had more worldwide impact than any other person from the

Caribbean, and was one of the first and greatest pan-Africanists. Garvey's activism led to the formation of the Universal Negro Improvement Association (UNIA), an organization that advocated equal rights and economic independence for black people. One of its main aims was to create a united Africa to which all black people, whether from the Caribbean or from North America, could one day return and which they could lay claim to as their real and original homeland. Garvey's statement that "every race must find a home ... and blacks are raising the cry of 'Africa for Africans', those at home and those abroad ... because we realize it will be our only hope of permanent existence" (cited in Tafari 1985, 9–10) revealed unequivocally the UNIA's pan-Africanist orientation. A fundamental tenet of Garvey's philosophy, therefore, was the idea of African repatriation. Garvey's belief in repatriation was based on the idea of the physical return of all black people to their ancestral African homeland. Having experienced for centuries European racist, colonialist and imperialist oppression, subjugation and exploitation, black people's only hope of escape from such oppressive structures, according to Garvey, was to return to a supposedly united Africa. Garvey's slogan, "Up! Up! you mighty people, you can accomplish what you will" (cited in Thompson 1999, 30), reflected this sentiment.

The focus on Africa, therefore, found its most profound expression in the Garvey movement. Garvey's attempt to reconstruct a world view in response to European cultural and economic dominance in the Caribbean has led to the "idealization of Africa" perspective. Barry Chevannes (1995) argues that the idealization of Africa is a broader concept in which Africa or Ethiopia becomes a symbolic point of reference, whether as an ideal "home" denoting repatriation or as a source of identity, and hence ethnic and cultural identification. The ideologically constructed character of black nationalism within the Garvey movement helped to develop and transform African diaspora culture and consciousness in the New World. Notions of "Africa", "Africanness" and "blackness" point to the deep cultural resonance that typified the Garvey movement and upon which Garvey himself drew so effectively (Carnegie 1999).

Africa and African consciousness undoubtedly played a crucial role in black consciousness movements in the Caribbean and globally. Indeed, it was the fundamental organizing element in the ideological framework of the "transatlantic black imagination", to use C.V. Carnegie's (1999) term, which included not only Garvey's back-to-Africa movement, but also the Black Power movements in both the United States and the Caribbean, the Rastafari movement and all of the other African nationalist movements worldwide. It helped, in no small measure, to sustain and create a black diasporic identity and consciousness.

Garvey's mobilization of "racial consciousness" was expressed not only in political and ideological terms, but also in religious beliefs. Garvey asserted that blacks were the chosen people created in the image of God, and that Africa was the promised land to which all blacks had to return. Thus, Garvey's passionate demand for social justice in a "worldly" context – Africa as a national home where blacks could achieve economic self-sufficiency and political power – was enhanced by a strongly spiritual orientation. Garvey's religious and political beliefs, for example, were particularly influential in the early Rastafari movement in Jamaica. This influence may have had to do with Garvey's prophecy of the coming of a black king in Africa – a prediction which proved to be a very important element in the Rastafaris' religious beliefs. The crowning of Ras Tafari as Emperor Haile Selassie I of Ethiopia shortly after Garvey's prediction led the Rastafaris to view Garvey's prophecy as a fulfilment of scripture. Following Garvey's view that all blacks were the chosen people, the Rastafaris, too, saw themselves as the chosen people and believed that the only escape from oppressive Babylonian structures was to return to Africa. Just as blackness epitomized cultural resistance and racial pride in the Garveyite movement, so too was it in the Rastafari movement. Both movements propagated a transnational consciousness that was produced in cultural and symbolic terms (Carnegie 1999) and, therefore, represented global forms of resistance.

What was particularly distinctive about the Garvey movement in its attempts to reconstruct blackness and re-create Africa was the specific type of racial mobilization strategy that was employed. For example, an organized intelligentsia within the back-to-Africa movement in the Caribbean made it possible to effectively disseminate and propagate a specific type of ideology and rhetoric based on pan-Africanism and Afrocentricity. The African-centred nature of the Garvey movement was reflected in its main theme, namely, Africa and "Africanness". This "race-nationalist" perspective, according to historian David Cronon, was reflected in Garvey's insistence that "a black skin was not a badge of shame but rather a glorious symbol of national greatness" (Cronon

1955, 4). Garvey's unflinching and consistent commitment to his idea of a return to Africa as the source of black peoples' culture and identity is testimony to the indelible "race pride" legacy that continues to endure till this day.

The ideology behind pan-Africanism was premised on the historical and cultural resistance by people whose present-day reality is the direct consequence of a history of slavery. Institutionally, through the UNIA, Garvey was able to create transnational racial consciousness in the United States, the Caribbean and Africa by inculcating in the minds of the oppressed black masses that their bitter "historical memory" based on discrimination and violence could, in effect, be transformed into something more positive if they turned their gaze to Africa as their true homeland, and as a place to which they truly belonged. Salvation for Afro-Caribbean people therefore lay in Africa. This, then, is what constitutes the transatlantic black imagination: advancing the aspirations among black people around the world – the idea that peace, freedom, equality, dignity, pride, unity and solidarity among all Africans could in fact be achieved. Thus, Garvey's pan-Africanist ideological stance was unmistakably Afrocentric: Africa and all things African was the starting point for all of his ideas and beliefs.

This preoccupation with Africa and Africanness could also be seen in the types of cultural and symbolic devices that were employed in the Garvey movement. The movement effectively dramatized cultural resistance by employing a variety of Afrocentric symbolic devices. For example, the UNIA promoted African nationalist consciousness by adopting the distinctive red, green and black colours as the flag of the African race; it also adopted the Ethiopian anthem as the universal anthem for all blacks. It is believed that the use of the red, green and black colours in the Garvey movement was Garvey's own idea since he believed that those were the colours of the Ethiopian flag (Savishinsky 1998). According to Carnegie (1999), the UNIA used the colour red, which signified blood and implied the shedding of sacrificial blood, as a way of nurturing the relationship between people and the imagined land. The deployment of other cultural and symbolic devices such as the lush vegetation of Africa, Negritude or "Black Is Beautiful", black nationhood and the envisioning of an imperial African state under black rule,[4] and transnational consciousness were all contextualized and articulated in an explicitly Afrocentric framework. Within this race-centred framework it is clear that Garvey marshalled his forces by activating primordial sentiments and memory expressed through "race": "blood was made to serve as a mythological mark of shared corporeality, and of difference"(Carnegie 1999, 58).

A significant organizing symbol that served to nurture transnational consciousness and Garvey's black nation was the Black Star Line – that glorious ship that would take black people back to their true homeland. As a symbol, the Black Star Line reverses the historical bitter memory associated with the pain and suffering of the earlier Middle Passage crossing: "while the ships of earlier memory carried people away from Africa . . . into exile, this new fleet would take people back to a bounteous Africa" (Carnegie 1999, 61–63). Seen in this light, the Black Star Line symbolically represented a reconnection with one's original roots, that is, the reunification and reconstitution of community. However, the Black Star Line goes well beyond its symbolic dimensions by taking on a more instrumentalist character.

In looking at ethno-nationalist movements, the role of the elites and their interests cannot be ignored. The idea that leaders of nationalist movements – a great many of them ethnic entrepreneurs themselves – invariably appeal to ethnic sentiments and rhetoric to advance their own political and economic interests has profound implications not only for the realization of the aims and goals of the movement, but also for the grassroots members themselves. The Black Star Line, in terms of its elitist agenda, was not spared criticism. For example, Theodore Vincent (1971), in discussing the Garvey's movement and its impact on black nationalism in the United States, fleshes out its elitist characteristics by arguing that the Black Star Line would have enabled black Americans to deal with Wall Street, which in turn would have connected them with international financial corporations. The key question then is this: To what extent did the Black Star Line enable the UNIA's elite to solidify their own class interests? The answer is simple. Even if this was the intention of the UNIA's elite, it was not realized, primarily because as a business venture it failed miserably.

Notwithstanding the instrumentalist dimensions associated with the Black Star Line,[5] I concur with Carnegie (1999) that what ought to be appreciated is the transnational political implications of the Garvey movement with its rich array of symbolism, such as its emancipatory and empowering features. Garvey's transnationalism not only crystallized the socially constructed aspects of culture and ethnicity with all their transformative trappings, it also demonstrated the uncanny ability to put in place a creative and imaginative world view and ideology that offered hope and promise to marginalized millions. At the same time, however, the deployment of a distinctively Afrocentric and black race-pride rhetoric took on some strong primordialist overtones. Garvey's passionate claims for "race and space" were couched in essentialized notions of "race" in which physical and cultural factors, the former typified by a rhetoric based on assumed blood ties, that is, race and common origins, and the latter by region or country of the ancestors, were disseminated to create an emotional, albeit irrational "oneness" among blacks, while at the same time fostering an overpowering and ineffable primordial feeling of being not only black but African.[6]

Generally, ethno-cultural nationalist movements have, as their main aim, the liberation of marginalized groups from their oppressive conditions. Thus, there is nothing fundamentally wrong with confronting not only racist subjugation but also all other forms of oppression, including sexist, classist, religious and homophobic structures. So we should fight against all of these repressive structures to advance the emancipation of all subaltern voices – but also in doing so we should be cognizant of the ever-present essentialist political forces that promote the naturalization of ethnic and racial allegiances and categories.

While the "naturalness" of racial and ethnic identification, as an obvious indicator of primordialism, was present in the Garvey movement in sometimes subtle and sometimes not-so-subtle ways, it is safe to conclude that its effects did not take on the violent or genocidal characteristics so common in other ethno-nationalist and ethnic self-determination movements in history. Nazism in Germany, expressed through Aryanism, premised on notions of racialized "superiority" and "inferiority", is a good case in point. Indeed, modern examples of "ethnic cleansing" and other forms of genocidal activities abound. Recall, for example, the recent ethnic Albanian refugee crisis in Kosovo that resulted from Serbian ethnic-cleansing policies, the bloodshed between the Tutsi and the Hutu in modern-day Rwanda and the continuing violence in Northern Ireland between Catholics and Protestants.

Following Clifford Geertz (1963), scholars have also stressed a primordialist dimension to ethnicity, wherein assumed blood ties reflected in common descent, religion, race, language or nationality have been strategically used in ethno-political movements around the world (see Hutchinson and Smith 1996; Ignatieff 1993; Isaacs 1975; van den Berghe 1995).

Identity Politics in the Indian Diaspora

One of the more obvious similarities between the African and Indian diasporas in the Caribbean is that they can both be subsumed under the category "diasporas created through colonial or imperial policies" (see Anderson 1998). However, the fundamental difference between the African and Indian diasporas in the Caribbean is that whereas the former was based on the "forced" dispersion of people from their original homelands, the latter was based on voluntary migration. The establishment of the system of indentured labour in the British colonies in the mid-nineteenth century culminated in the large-scale migration of Indians across the globe, to Mauritius, Fiji, Guyana, Suriname, and Trinidad and Tobago, to name a few.

The Indian diaspora is by no means homogeneous in terms of its characteristics. The fact that Indians were dispersed to different locations under very different circumstances led to the conceptualization of two types of Indian diaspora situations: the "old" and "new/border" Indian diasporas. According to Vijay Mishra (1996), the "old" Indian diaspora is characterized by a degree of exclusivity – a resistance to assimilation to the host culture that inevitably leads to isolation from the homeland and marginalization within the host country, and the inability to maintain active discourse with India – resulting in the active re-creation and maintenance of memories of Indian culture in the new homelands (see also Ghosh 1989). In contrast, the "new" Indian diaspora mediates between the homeland and the host country, and, as such, maintains active participation in the homeland. An example of the "new" Indian diaspora is South Asian immigrants to the United States, Canada and the United Kingdom, who are largely derived from the middle class and are seeking professional or educational opportunities. Members of the "new" Indian diaspora have been referred to as PIOs (people of Indian origins) or NRIs (non-resident Indians).

Mythical India

Unlike the back-to-Africa movement with its strong intelligentsia, consistent organizational framework and solid Africanist ideological and philosophical underpinnings, the so-called back-to-India movement – or, more appropriately, the attempts to return to India in terms of its world view, ideology and intent – were fundamentally different from the back-to-Africa movement. First, there was no organized and defined intelligentsia that organized for the repatriation of Indians to India, compared with the pan-Africanists with their systematic and organized efforts to repatriate Afro-Caribbeans to Africa. H.P. Singh (1993), in his analysis of Indian nationalism in Trinidad, argues that there were no clear political parties that specifically addressed issues of Indian nationalism. According to Singh, "Indian nationalism never expressed itself in the formation of any political party though there was the pronounced fear of the possible political force that the Indian community represented" (1993, xxxi). The formation of the largely Indian party in Trinidad, the Democratic Labour Party (DLP), for example, represented the potential for Indian political domination and was perceived as such by the larger African community; thus it was seen as a threat to African political domination. But the DLP, like the PNM (People's National Movement), was a "national" party.

Even Indian nationalists, such as Adrian Cola Rienzi, Timothy Roodal, George Fitzpatrick and Bhadase Sagan Maraj, never advocated repatriation to India. To be sure, some of them participated in politics as individuals or as members of political organizations led by non-Indo-Trinidadian individuals, such as Uriah Butler and Arthur Andrew Cipriani, and preferred to align themselves with the so-called Creole parties rather than establish their own Indian political party (Singh 1993). Similarly, Indian organizations were formed in Trinidad and Guyana along secular and Indian lines devoted mainly to self-improvement, self-reliance and progress within their respective communities, and organized mainly along religious, cultural and social lines. The experience of leaving India, the harsh conditions experienced in the crossing of the Kala Pani, the brutalities experienced on the plantations and the hostile host environments to which the Indians were subjected bonded all Indians by creating a type of *deshbhai/bahin* (country brothers/sisters), which resulted in the founding of Indian religious and secular organizations throughout the Caribbean. This "ship bonding" may have also led to caste breakdowns among Indians migrating to the Caribbean.

There were a number of Indian organizations and associations that represented the interests of Indo-Caribbeans. In Trinidad, for example, the rise of these organizations had to do with the Indian Centenary Celebrations of 30 May 1945 – an occasion that commemorated the one hundredth anniversary of the Indian presence in Trinidad. The occasion created a sense of "Indianness" among Indo-Trinidadians that had never before been witnessed in the island. India's independence movement also fuelled the strong feelings of Indianness among Indo-Caribbean peoples. The emotions derived from India's independence were expressed in marches, speeches and reverence for Indian nationalists and heroes such as Gandhi, Tagore and Nehru (Singh 1993).

The India Club, for example, was one of the most prominent organizations during the 1940s, and was significant as an expression of Indian nationalism in Trinidad. Singh (1993) argues that the name India Club was itself indicative of an ideological position that highlighted two things: the presence of an Indian identity in Trinidad, and a desire to maintain links with India. It was clear to most Indo-Trinidadians that they had made great progress and contributions to Trinidad and, more generally, to the Caribbean, and they were committed to the future of Trinidad as their homeland. India was looked upon merely as the common ancestral motherland of all overseas Indians (Singh 1993), and the India Club in Port of Spain reflected this idea of Trinidad as home and India as a symbolic cultural reference point among Indo-Trinidadians. The latter point is extremely significant inasmuch as it allows for a clearer understanding of how homelands are imagined among diaspora groups.

Diasporas have a strong interest in maintaining emotional links to their ancestral homelands. In diaspora communities, music, for example, plays a vitally important role in the formation of cultural meanings and identities. It is through music that members of a diaspora are united and that an imagination of a shared homeland is constructed. Music in diasporic contexts reinforces homeland values and traditions and, in turn, both unites and empowers diaspora groups by allowing them to carve out a distinct cultural space and to assert cultural difference in the host environment. Indo-Caribbeans' imagination of India is strongly informed by Hindi films (Bollywood) and Hindi film music. It is a well-known fact that Hindi films are very popular throughout the Indian diaspora, representing perhaps the most important aspect of the Indian diasporic imagination. For Indo-Caribbeans, Hindi films and music enable them to idealize a long-lost and far-removed ancestral homeland without having to actually experience the reality of that homeland. In this way they can only imagine and symbolically identify with an ancient heritage and tradition that are no longer "real" to them. This symbolic connection to India by Indo-Caribbeans finds expression in Stuart Hall's view (1994) that tradition, as a significant aspect of cultural identities, is subject to the continuous play of culture and history. In other words, tradition, be it real or imagined, provides diaspora groups with cultural identities and allows for an "imagined return" to unlived pasts.

However, diaspora groups have been able to create new cultural spaces for themselves by borrowing from the motherland traditions and incorporating them into their own home/host repertoire. For example, the emergence of chutney as a distinctly Indo-Caribbean musical genre represents and expresses a local Indo-Caribbean identity and culture. Particular aspects of traditional Indian culture in the areas of religion (Hinduism, for example) and food have been Caribbeanized, undergoing sufficient changes that one can now speak of a distinct Indo-Caribbean culture. Indo-Caribbean traditions such as music, food, religion, marriage and the like are testimony to this reality.

Notwithstanding the celebrations, maintenance and transformations of their ancestral and cultural heritage, there did not exist any systematic efforts by the Indo-Caribbean intelligentsia to launch a cultural movement that advocated repatriation to India. Unlike the pan-Africanist agenda, Indo-Caribbean activism was based on a "local destiny" perspective, that is, the Caribbean not as Babylon but as home. In other words, the "golden ages" of homeland culture to which diasporas often appeal were discernible in Indo-Caribbean nationalism, but the homeland was not idealized as a place of return as it was in African diaspora nationalism, in which the ancient kingdoms of Ethiopia and Egypt were invoked as the only destination or rightful place to which all Africans belonged. In contrast, the way in which the term *repatriation* was used in the Indo-Caribbean imagination was very different from the way it was used in the back-to-Africa movement. For example, the main reason for advocating repatriation for some Indians was economic. In the immediate post-indenture period (1917 and after) and during the Great Depression of the 1930s, political agitation and demands for repatriation coincided with periods of great economic upheavals and hardships.

Although there are no official statistics showing the exact number of Indians who returned to India, it can be surmised that the periods in which Indian repatriation was the highest would be in the immediate post-indenture period, after 1917, when some Indian indentured workers chose to return to India after their contracts had expired, and during the 1930s, when the global effects of the Great Depression were having a major effect on colonial Caribbean economies.

Conclusion

The history of the modern Caribbean, and subsequently its political culture as we know it today, was born of genocide, slavery, indentureship, racism, sexism and classism – all of which were created by colonialism, neocolonialism, dependent capitalism and, today, global capitalism. I have argued in this chapter that the racialized consciousness of Caribbean people was fostered and developed by the various aforementioned social variables that have defined Caribbean society and history. Thus, this racialized consciousness is the point of departure for understanding the Afro-and Indo-Caribbean quests for community, identity and culture. This idea of wanting to reclaim another nation that has been lost elsewhere in time and space by groups who have been oppressed, and who continue to struggle on the margins, is a powerful political formation inasmuch as it is seen as a way of exiting a particular dystopia.

This chapter demonstrated the different ways in which Africa and India were idealized, imagined and constructed in the Caribbean, and the type of identity politics that emerged as these diasporas reacted to the social, economic, political and cultural realities that they were confronted with. I have also demonstrated in this chapter some of the problematic aspects of diaspora studies, which have tended to invoke the idea of "race" and biology as things that are rooted in, for example, common ancestry, fixed blood ties and common geography. This was clearly discernible in the back-to-Africa movement. These findings led me to conclude that, to some degree, diaspora studies tend to border on the ideological. The Indo-Caribbean expression of identity politics may not have exhibited exactly the same kind of essentialism found in the back-to-Africa movement, but the need to reconnect with a lost India and its culture bordered on essentialism, as India itself, from the perspective of Indo-Caribbean peoples, was imagined as a place where regionalism, political structures, caste, cultural differences and even phenotype were irrelevant. While this essentialist aspect of identity construction is problematic and troubling, the real essence of Indian nationalism in the Caribbean was related to a form of symbolic ethnicity whereby Indo-Caribbean peoples, as a significant cultural segment within the larger Caribbean cultural matrix, expressed an interest in reconnecting with an ancient culture and civilization that was not only lost in time and space but that could be excavated and remembered in both psychological and symbolic ways through music, films, religion, language and the like.

How, then, have both attempts at referring to mythical homelands influenced where the Indo-Caribbean and Afro-Caribbean polities in the Caribbean stand ideologically today, and how – if at all – do they influence the way they perceive each other? Multi-ethnic states in many parts of the developing world today were created from former colonial states that deliberately put in place divide-and-rule policies geared towards ethnic, social and political segmentation between the various competing ethno-racial groups. The initial systematic separation of Afro- and Indo-Caribbean peoples into urban and rural spaces, respectively, inevitably led to the development of the negative construction of the Other. This social-distancing strategy created a climate for cultural misunderstandings between Afro- and Indo-Caribbean peoples and, unfortunately, led to the proliferation of unflattering ethnic and racial stereotypes that, by and large, informed the groups' perceptions of each other. To complicate matters further, the imposition of a competitive parliamentary system by the colonial state, such as the Westminster model of political governance, further accentuated communalism as political parties are engaged in zero-sum struggles for power. The colonial and postcolonial state, then, is *the* source of Afro- and Indo-Caribbean mutual distrust and suspicion and is, therefore, key to understanding the early and enduring legacy of communal conflict in postcolonial societies today.

These old divisions were exacerbated in the postcolonial/post-independence period in the Caribbean as mass politics emerged and capitalized on ethnic loyalties for votes (Premdas 1999). *Apanjaat,* a local colloquial term for "vote for your own kind", became the dominant factor in voting patterns and behaviour in countries such as Guyana and Trinidad. In Guyana, the People's Progressive Party (PPP) under the leadership of the late Dr Cheddi Jagan and the People's National Congress (PNC) under the leadership of Forbes Burnham; in Trinidad and Tobago, the People's National Movement headed by the late Dr Eric Williams and recently the United National Congress (UNC) with Basdeo Panday as its leader – all attest to the *apanjaat* dimension of political behaviour in the Caribbean. These sectional leaders have embraced the old system of political rule by exploiting the ethno-racial divisions for electoral success and power. Thus, the ruling political elites have capitalized on, and continue to capitalize on, the "ethnic factor" not only to maintain political power but also to solidify their own class interests. The type of tribalism that is currently plaguing Guyana is a stark reminder of the profound impacts that the colonial and postcolonial political structures, political leaders and ethnic entrepreneurs have had on ethno-political instability in the Caribbean.

One of the fundamental characteristics of the Caribbean diaspora is its fostering of the development of collective memories by both Afro- and Indo-Caribbean communities based on notions of "shared pasts" – shared histories of slavery and indentureship, resistance to racist subordination, cultural survival – and both groups' endurance of a shared history of British and other European colonizations. Safran's (1991) conceptualization of diaspora focuses on a "myth of return" discourse, a conscious desire to return from "exile" to a specific homeland. The back-to-Africa movement, with its emphasis on repatriation coupled with its ideological and philosophical underpinnings, clearly falls under this conception of diaspora. Relegated to the bottom of the stratification system and dominated by white hegemonic structures, Afro-Caribbean peoples were confronted with oppressive structures that inevitably led to resistance. One way of escaping a Babylonian environment was to return to the African ancestral homeland, Ethiopia. With a strong pan-Africanist intelligentsia and the effective utilization and mobilization of Afrocentric symbols and rhetoric, Africa was "imagined" as the ideal homeland for all peoples of African origin.

Africa and everything African were reconstructed – blackness, traditionally and historically constructed as negative, had now undergone an inversion process whereby blackness was constructed as a positive ethno-racial category.

A return to Africa was idealized, a jubilant re-crossing of the Atlantic was imagined and the empowerment of black people would be finally achieved. The fact that Garvey and other pan-Africanists did not achieve their ultimate aim, which was to physically and literally return to the homeland, points to the *imaginary* dimensions involved in the excavation of historical memory. This point underscores the mythical and ideologically constructed character of "homeland" in diaspora discourse. But in spite of the fact that the African intelligentsia did not achieve its main aim, this aim did exert a powerful influence on many people. The idea of Africa as home not only offered hope for the most oppressed within the African diaspora, it also led to the development of positive black ethno-racial self-conceptions and black empowerment.

The conceptualization of diaspora as it pertains to the Indo-Caribbean reality differs from its Afro-Caribbean counterpart. While it is clear from the evidence presented that links with India played a prominent role in Indo-Caribbean nationalism, the level and degree of Indocentrism were not nearly as visible and tangible as Afrocentrism in the back-to-Africa movement. For one thing, there was no systematic effort on the part of the Indo-Caribbean intelligentsia and by the vast majority of Indians themselves to return to India. In other words, there was no indication of a "homing desire", to use Avtar Brah's term (1996). Instead, the Caribbean was *the* home where futures were to be built and sustained. India, on the other hand, was "remembered", in largely symbolic ways, as the place of their great civilization, on behalf of which some degree of respect, pride and joy was expected.

Gabriel Sheffer (1993) argues that while most diasporas do not wish to return to the homeland, at the same time they do not want to embrace complete assimilation into the host society. He goes on to argue that there is a tendency among diaspora groups to exhibit some degree of loyalty and commitment to the homeland culture, traditions and values. The Indo-Caribbean populations in places such as Trinidad, Guyana and Suriname tend towards a cultural emphasis rather than an articulation of a myth of literal return. This is clearly manifested in their retention of particular Indian customs such as

Hindu religious practices, food, music and films. In looking at the South Asian diaspora, Amitav Ghosh (1989) contends that the major emphasis is not necessarily on reconnecting with one's roots in a specific place or on a desire to return as much as it is on re-creating a culture in diverse locations. For Indo-Caribbeans, then, there was no conscious desire to return from exile to a homeland. However, where there are clear parallels in both the African and the Indian diasporas in the Caribbean are in their identification with remote historical memories of lost "Mother Africa" and "Mother India", and in the fact that both lacked immediate contact with these ancestral homelands.

The experience of Indo-Caribbeans in the Caribbean and the Americas under white colonial rule and then under Afro-Caribbean domination, coupled with the "latecomer" syndrome and the internalization of second-class citizenship, undoubtedly created mass "Indian-consciousness" in places like Guyana and Trinidad. The political ramifications of such consciousness heightened ethnic tensions as Afro- and Indo-Caribbeans continued to engage in a power struggle for scarce political and economic resources. However, a minority of Indo-Caribbean ethnic nationalists and militants with some rather extremist views have been advocating for an Indo-Caribbean ethnic homeland in the Caribbean and the Americas – a homeland that has been referred to as Bharatiyadesh/Industan (Singh 1993).

Currently, a potentially dangerous and unsettling development has been occurring in both Guyana and Trinidad where religious essentialism seems to be superseding racial essentialism, though there are some obvious overlaps between the two, that is, religion and ethnicity. I am referring here to Hinduvta, a Hindu fundamentalist, essentialist political force that espouses a communal ideology wherein Hinduism is not just a passive performer in the realm of the sacred, but an active and aggressive political force geared towards the fostering of a particular type of primordialist-based in-group consciousness among its members. As with its Afrocentric counterparts, Hinduvta naturalizes ethnic and racial allegiances and categories by encouraging the notion that identity exists outside of history. This ideological framework has clear political implications inasmuch as it will derail and disrupt any attempts to facilitate or promote inter-group accommodation in Guyana and Trinidad and Tobago.

As this seemingly elusive Indo-Caribbean ethnic homeland in the Caribbean and the Americas is still awaiting realization, one wonders whether such a radical proposition will ever become a reality given that the vast majority of Indo-Caribbeans are of the view that Bharatiyadesh/Industan makes no practical sense (Ryan 1996). It is my contention that the demand for an Indo-Caribbean "ethnic state" – or any other type of ethnic-based homeland, for that matter – is one of the most counterproductive barriers to achieving any meaningful attempts at national integration in segmented societies such as Guyana, Suriname, and Trinidad and Tobago. The process of attaining Caribbean unity and inter-ethnic co-operation is at its crossroads, and it would be wise for politicians, ethnic entrepreneurs and fundamentalists of all sorts, in their various postcolonial Caribbean environments, to take heed of what the late Eric Williams had to say about the destructiveness of ethnic and racial divisiveness: "there can be no Mother Africa and no Mother India" (1962, 281–82).

Notes

1. Throughout this paper the terms *African* and *Indian* will be used to refer to people of African and Indian origins in the contemporary Caribbean. Henceforth, they will be used interchangeably with the terms *Afro-Caribbean* and *Indo-Caribbean*.
2. The historical legacy of colonialism, slavery and indentureship in the Caribbean created multicultural societies in which social, economic and political statuses were directly correlated with the race, class, culture and colour continua that have been traditionally associated with Caribbean societies and their social structures.
3. For a more recent and unabashedly racially essentialist conception of Trinidad and Tobago's Carnival as an "African" tradition, see Smart and Nehusi (2000).
4. Indeed, the Garvey movement endorsed and drew its strength from the "ideological coupling of 'nation' and 'race'. . . . Garvey capitalised on the viscous, liquid quality of blood and 'race' . . . to seep across the artificially constituted membranes of territorial frontiers" (Carnegie 1999, 53).
5. Like other social movements in history, the Garvey movement exhibited some of the classic features associated with charismatic authority, namely, ethnic entrepreneurship. To achieve their ends, cultural brokers have constructed myths of common descent and ancestry that tended to

homogenize the particular ethnic or cultural group that was being mobilized to effect social and political changes in their respective societies. The back-to-Africa movement was no exception to this rule, because Garvey himself consistently articulated a rhetoric that homogenized blackness to such a degree that the category "African" became, in the minds of many, an undifferentiated term. By employing this strategy, ethnic entrepreneurs are able to make invisible any internal divisions within a particular ethno-racial grouping. For example, divisions based on class and gender are creatively "imagined away". Furthermore, by capitalizing on primordialist and essentialists views on race – the idea that race and ethnicity are grounded on emotional and irrational sentiments and are related to blood ties that are presumed to be natural and fixed – ethnic entrepreneurs have been able to attain their political and economic goals as movement leaders and activists.

6. As was mentioned earlier, race and ethnicity permeate all aspects of Caribbean societies – their social, economic, political and cultural institutions. The academy and scholars of many different persuasions now agree that race is neither a biological nor a fixed category, but a socially defined category (or social construct) that emerges in specific historical, political and economic contexts. Although race is not "real", it is very real in sociological terms because of its ability to deny and exclude groups that have been historically racialized.

References

Anderson, Alan B. 1998. "Diaspora and Exile: A Canadian and Comparative Perspective". *International Journal of Canadian Studies*, no. 18: 13–30.

Anderson, Benedict. 1983. *Imagined Communities: Reflections on the Origin and Spread of Nationalism.* London: Verso.

Armstrong, John A. 1982. *Nations before Nationalism.* Chapel Hill: University of North Carolina Press.

Brah, Avtar. 1996. *Cartographies of Diaspora: Contesting Identities.* London: Routledge.

Brathwaite, E. Kamau. 1974. "The African Presence in Caribbean Literature". In *Slavery, Colonialism and Racism,* edited by Sidney Mintz, 73–109. New York: Norton.

Carnegie, Charles V. 1999. "Garvey and the Black Transnation". *Small Axe: A Journal of Criticism*, no. 5: 48–71.

Chaliand, Gérard, and Jean-Pierre Rageau. 1997. *The Penguin Atlas of Diasporas.* Translated by A.M. Berrett. New York: Penguin.

Chevannes, Barry. 1995. *Rastafari: Roots and Ideology.* Syracuse, NY: Syracuse University Press.
Clifford, James. 1994. "Diasporas". *Cultural Anthropology* 9: 302–38.
Conner, W. 1986. "The Impact of Homelands upon Diasporas". In *Modern Diasporas in International Politics,* edited by Gabriel Sheffer, 16–46. London: Croom-Helm.
Cronon, David E. 1955. *Black Moses.* Madison: University of Wisconsin Press.
Esman, Milton J. 1986. "Diasporas and International Relations". In *Modern Diasporas in International Politics,* edited by G. Shaffer, 333–49. London: Croom Helm.
Gellner, Ernest. 1964. *Thought and Change.* London: Weidenfeld and Nicholson.
Geertz, Clifford, ed. 1963. *Old Societies and New States.* New York: Free Press.
Ghosh, Amitav. 1989. "The Diaspora in Indian Culture". *Public Culture* 2, no. 1: 73–78.
Gilroy, Paul. 1993. *The Black Atlantic: Modernity and Double Consciousness.* Cambridge: Harvard University Press.
Hall, Stuart. 1994. "Cultural Identity and Diaspora". In *Colonial Discourse and Post-Colonial Theory: A Reader,* edited by Patrick Williams and Laura Chrisman, 392–408. New York: Columbia University Press.
Helmreich, Stefan. 1992. "Kinship, Nation and Paul Gilroy's Concept of Diaspora". *Diaspora* 2: 243–48.
Hobsbawm, Eric, and Terence Ranger, eds. 1983. *The Invention of Tradition.* Cambridge: University of Cambridge Press.
Hutchinson, John, and Anthony D. Smith, eds. 1996. *Ethnicity.* Oxford: Oxford University Press.
Ignatieff, Michael. 1993. *Blood and Belonging: Journeys into the New Nationalism.* Toronto: Viking/Penguin.
Isaacs, Harold R. 1975. *Idols of the Tribe: Group Identity and Political Change.* Cambridge: Harvard University Press.
Mintz, Sidney W., and Richard Price. 1992. *The Birth of African-American Culture: An Anthropological Perspective.* Boston: Beacon.
Mishra, Vijay. 1996. "The Diasporic Imaginary: Theorizing the Indian Diaspora". *Textual Practice* 10: 421–47.
Premdas, Ralph R. 1999. "Guyana: Patterns of Ethnic Conflict and the Requirements for Reconciliation". In *Identity, Ethnicity and Culture in the Caribbean,* edited by Ralph R. Premdas, 368–408. St Augustine, Trinidad: School of Continuing Studies, University of the West Indies.

Robotham, Don. 1988. "The Development of Black Ethnicity in Jamaica". In *Garvey: His Work and Impact,* edited by Rupert Lewis and Patrick Bryan, 23–38. Mona, Jamaica: Institute of Social and Economic Research and Department of Extra-Mural Studies, University of the West Indies.

Ryan, Selwyn D. 1996. *Pathways to Power: Indians and the Politics of National Unity in Trinidad and Tobago.* St Augustine, Trinidad: Institute of Social and Economic Research.

Safran, William. 1991. "Diasporas in Modern Societies: Myth of Homeland and Return". *Diaspora* 1: 83–99.

Savishinsky, Neil J. 1998. "African Dimensions of the Jamaican Rastafarian Movement". In *Chanting Down Babylon: The Rastafari Reader,* edited by Nathaniel Samuel Murrell, William David Spencer and Adrian Anthony McFarlane, 125–44. Kingston, Jamaica: Ian Randle.

Scott, David. 1991. "That Event, This Memory: Notes on the Anthropology of African Diasporas in the New World". *Diaspora* 1: 261–84.

———. 1999. "An Obscure Miracle of Connection". In David Scott, *Refashioning Futures: Criticism after Postcoloniality,* 106–27. Princeton: Princeton University Press.

Sheffer, Gabriel. 1993. "Ethnic Diasporas: A Threat to Their Hosts?" In *International Migration and Security,* edited by Myron Weiner, 263–85. Boulder, Col.: Westview.

Singh, H.P. 1993. *The Indian Struggle for Justice and Equality against Black Racism in Trinidad and Tobago, 1956–1962.* Couva, Trinidad: Indian Review Press.

Smart, Ian K., and Kimani Nehusi, eds. 2000. *Ah Come Back Home: Perspectives on the Trinidad and Tobago Carnival.* Washington, DC, and Port of Spain, Trinidad: Original World Press.

Smith, Anthony D. 1992. "Chosen Peoples: Why Ethnic Groups Survive". *Racial and Ethnic Studies* 15: 436–56.

Tafari, I. Jabulani. 1985. "The Rastafari: Successors of Marcus Garvey". *Caribbean Quarterly* 26, no. 4: 1–12.

Thompson, Dudley. 1999. *The Pan-Africanists.* Paintings by Barrington Watson. Kingston, Jamaica: Ian Randle.

van den Berghe, Pierre. 1995. "Does Race Matter?" *Nations and Nationalism* 1: 357–68.

Vincent, Theodore G. 1971. *Black Power and the Garvey Movement.* Berkeley, Calif.: Ramparts Press

Williams, Eric. 1962. *History of the People of Trinidad and Tobago.* Port of Spain, Trinidad: PNM.

[Part 3]

Civil Society and Changes in the Political and Economic Sphere

[9]

Global Culture and the Politics of Moral Deregulation in Jamaica

Obika Gray

Global Structures and Cultural Autonomy

The surfeit of theories about globalization and its impact on non-Western societies has been a mixed blessing. On the one hand, theories of globalization that show how world-level processes influence states and societies abroad are a useful reminder of the intensely interactive nature of international society and of the effect structural processes often have on developments everywhere. On the other hand, this recognition of the importance of global processes for economic, political and cultural outcomes abroad has led to simplistic accounts of their impact.

In the field of international economics, for example, unalloyed assertions that less developed economies invariably benefit from open markets, low tariffs and privatization of industries have been effectively challenged.[1] Such critiques of neoliberalism show that the case for economic globalization has typically been overstated and that for the majority of less developed countries, the reality is neither huge inflows of foreign investments nor inexorable growth and prosperity, but rather the persistence of poverty and economic marginalization (see Heredia 1997).

A similar exaggeration of outcomes can be found in commentaries that predict the cultural convergence of Western and non-Western societies and even the cultural colonization of the latter. Such perspectives typically affirm the coming erosion of national cultures before the onslaught of global forces (see Barber 1996). For advocates of this viewpoint – whether world-system structuralists affirming theories of political and cultural domination or globalization theorists championing the homogenization of everything – societies and peoples appear primarily as blank slates, merely to be stamped with the imprimatur of a determinist and near-tyrannical structure. Fortunately, corrections to this simplistic view of non-Western societies and cultures show that mimicry and cultural erasure are not the only options. These other viewpoints have instead emphasized non-Western societies' cultural creativity, their skilful appropriation of modernity and their assertion of cultural autonomy in the face of daunting historical structures.[2]

This chapter acknowledges that a historical capitalist world system is the defining structure and organizing framework for major processes in global society. However, I shall argue that this structure and its imperatives are not so tyrannical as to make drones of national societies. As I shall show in the case of Jamaica, even as its Westernized leaders embraced the political and ideological imperatives of the international system, counter-tendencies among the urban poor challenged the cultural logic of the interstate system. This group's remarkable display of resistance and cultural self-ownership shows that contrary to simplistic globalist and structuralist approaches that would impose an iron law of system structure on national societies, limited options for autonomy do exist. In a defining structure such as the capitalist world system, then, membership is not always destiny.[3]

National Initiative and the Interstate System

Jamaica's experience after 1938 highlights the variability and contingency of outcomes within national societies that are part of the international system. On the one hand, the island's modern history shows that world-level structures – a capitalist economic system, liberal-democratic discourse, the nation-state form and Euro-American identity models – did impose isomorphism along these lines. Such tendencies allowed for a narrow range of deviation from global structures, and

Jamaica's political history after 1938 indeed shows general conformity with this modular and dependent identity.

On the other hand, this timeframe, which brackets axial developments in twentieth-century Jamaica, saw significant challenges to international structures and deviations from their presumably inexorable logic. Jamaica's modern political history demonstrates that not all political currents on the island surrendered to system imperatives between the 1930s and the 1980s.

Four important and contrasting politico-cultural projects during this time show alternation between an integrative and an exilic impulse. These four projects are the liberal-nationalist agenda, which lasted from 1938 to 1968; the Ethiopian-fundamentalist project between 1930 and 1972; the socialist-communist project that lasted from 1940 to 1989; and the radical-nationalist but still liberally inflected interlude in the period 1972 through 1980. I shall discuss only the liberal-nationalist and the Ethiopianist projects in this chapter.

Still, it should be noted that all four projects were influenced and shaped by the global cultural infrastructure of the time, all four produced decisive alterations in the national society and all of them proved abortive, at least with respect to their announced goals. Those goals were either to integrate into this system, the better to advance within it, or to separate from it on the basis of alternative approaches to "development". It is arguable that institutional barriers constrained populist attempts at cultural and political de-linking, on the one hand, and moderates' efforts to advance within the system by means of bandwagoning, on the other. Structures of economic dependence, the machinery of the interstate system and the operations of dominant, legitimized cultural scripts hobbled all projects and seemed to confirm the extremely limited scope for dramatic social change after 1930. Yet despite this frustration, it is equally clear that dissident politics and cultural action in Jamaica broke with the institutional logic of global structures, and these actions, as I shall show, opened avenues for cultural otherness and self-ownership.

Global Culture and the Liberal-Nationalist Project: Bandwagoning

The liberal-nationalist project came to fruition in the context of a Caribbean-wide upheaval in the 1930s. That project employed a national and anti-colonial rhetoric in which a demand for national self-determination became the organizing principle for the opposition. At the world level, political clashes in the colonized countries and then a global war that was fought in the name of European freedom and self-determination helped reshape political and cultural relations.

By 1938 system-level liberal political language associated with an ideological script of "self-determination" was taken up and articulated by native political actors in the European colonies. The geoculture of the world system was extremely dynamic in this period, as social movements and their counter-discourses challenged the tenets of liberalism. This tension inside the geoculture of the world system was particularly evident between 1917 and 1939. In these years counter-discourses associated with global-level black nationalism, Arabism, Soviet communism, as well as German, Japanese and Italian fascism added their counter-scripts to the clashing politics and the medley of ideas.

Under the arduous conditions of world upheaval and challenge to liberal orthodoxy across the globe, a sea change in global culture occurred after 1945. In the aftermath of the defeat of the Axis powers, liberal ideals were extended overseas to restructure the conditions for democracy in the defeated countries. At the same time, under conditions of pressures from below to bring about a greater degree of universality, the applicability of those liberal ideals was extended to some non-white colonies. Their leaders and movements clamoured for sovereignty and self-determination, the better to attain political and cultural isomorphism.

In the English-speaking Caribbean, the demand for self-determination was acceded to with the extension of a universal voting franchise in Jamaica in 1944. A greater degree of political isomorphism with world-level patterns in the West was thus achieved there. The eventual transfer of power to native hands, however, was still governed by a European paternalism that demanded cultural dependence and political gradualism. While concessions were granted in response to colonial insurgencies and to political pressure from native aspirants to power, there is no doubt that elite claimants of a native Jamaican sovereignty had drawn on a universalistic political language. They had borrowed, in whole or in part, the modular political language and the ontological and philosophical presuppositions that set the terms for claims to membership in the interstate system.[4] As commentators such as Frantz Fanon (1967) have observed, the achievement of political isomorphism at the global level (sovereign equality of the colony) was by no means a prelude to the reversal of economic inequalities among national states. Fanon blamed that deficiency on middle-class venality. With the advantage of hindsight, we now know that both class venality and institutional barriers associated with historical capitalism were to blame.

With respect to nationalist appropriation of world-level language and assumptions, it is clear that in the 1930s and 1940s global-level beliefs were thoroughly saturated with anti-black and deeply racist notions. The most odious of these – the belief in the natural inferiority of African peoples – was transmitted through the machinery of the colonial state and by the dynamics of social relations of colonial society. In the Jamaican case, these framing norms of hierarchical cultural difference became embedded in two contrasting colonially inspired icons: the ignorant, culturally backward and black-skinned "Quashee", on the one hand, and the cosmopolitan, "civilized" and brown-skinned Creole nationalist on the other. These nationalist big men, with their self-assured cultural belonging anchored in a European model of identity, assumed the class burden of fashioning a Jamaican moral community rooted in hierarchical difference.

These political big men in Jamaica – and here I have in mind iconic figure such as Alexander Bustamante and Norman Manley – set about inducing the black Quashee into the framing cultural assumptions of hierarchical racial difference long established at the world level. By 1940 this meant the construction of a distinct civilization identity for Jamaicans through the local state machinery. In this cultural construction, African racial belonging would be neutered and the new moral community defined as a multiracial confederation. However, this was a community in which counterclaims to black consciousness were tightly regulated. In this new national community, preference for racial indeterminacy, not African racial belonging, became the dominant cultural tendency.

Against the backdrop of the freshly concluded military and ideological battles between liberalism, fascism, communism and Ethiopianism at the world level (and between liberalism, communism and Ethiopianism at the national level in the colony of Jamaica), Creole nationalists made the destructive choice of repudiating the cultural claims of Ethiopianism. With its ethno-national allegiances and alternative conception of Jamaican personhood, Ethiopianism in Jamaica offered an alternative nationalism and an alternative grounding for membership in the emerging moral community.

That conception, as Erna Brodber (1997) has shown, did not reside in the cultural deficit model and racial neutering employed by the Creole nationalists. Rather, the Ethiopian project offered the Zionist version of empowered black personhood. In this variety of cultural empowerment, African sojourners, self-consciously representing an honourable, ancient civilization, understood themselves to be a people special to God and destined for "moral world leadership" (Brodber 1997, 76). Here was the local-level antithesis to the cultural model transmitted by global-level liberalism's racist and socially atomizing ontology. Both the political and religious varieties of this Ethiopianism therefore offered vital cultural materials for the creation of a national spirit and a culturally grounded sense of nationness that was not alienating to the African majority.

As we now know, for the nationalist big men nation building had to proceed on the basis of contrary principles, namely, deference to world-level cultural scripts of European provenance. These principles valorized European whiteness as the embodiment of a civilized identity. Recognition of this allegiance to world-level racism does much to explain the peculiarity of nationalists' exaggerated emphasis on black Jamaicans' adherence to proper manners, good behaviour and genteel etiquette. Such preoccupations were in sharp contrast to other tropes of nationalist progress that invoked a contrary cultural aesthetic linked to a people's martial struggle against colonial domination.

With these historical realities in mind, I see no need to apologize – as political revisionists now fashionably insist on doing – for the assertion of a heroic counter-myth and radical critique of decolonization by the postwar generation of radical activists. Political independence and the ideological neutering of African subjectivity that Creole nationalism entailed *were* deeply flawed achievements. The architects of Jamaican self-determination not only had accommodated themselves to the machinery of the interstate system, they had also comfortably adopted its crippling cultural prescriptions. The epithet of "flag independence", however harsh, was not undeserved and was not without a real historical basis.

Still, the radical critique had its own problems. Critics made too much of the nationalists' cultural impairment. The nationalists' predicament, we now know, was not just one of impaired cultural consciousness. Their real dilemma was in failing to understand how much the colonizer's "parting gift" of juridical state sovereignty would be wholly subject to structural dependence on the world economy and submission to the institutional compulsions of the interstate system. In consciously hitching their nationalist project to the world economy, to the interstate system and to a correlative geoculture, nationalist leaders accepted and scarcely challenged the ensemble of framing principles that defined global capitalism. Our nationalist leaders therefore accepted the modular prescriptions elaborated by dominant ideologies that were part of the ideological canopy of global capitalism.

These discourses legitimated and rewarded acceptance of a number of scripts: national development and industrialization through economic aid and investment from the central capitalist countries; acceptance of juridical sovereignty in an interstate system of militarily and economically unequal states; and acceptance (with appropriate gestures to a valorized national culture) of an inferior ethnicized and gendered status within the global hierarchy. Inside the Jamaican post-colony, this meant the policing of the black and poor population according to these world-level cultural prescriptions. Such prescriptions were governed by world-level liberalism and by its cultural correlative, white supremacy. In political terms, then, integration in the interstate system meant more than just the importation of the Westminster model of governance – it meant subjection to the dynamics of geopolitics, which in our region meant acceptance of US imperialism and its suzerainty over the Americas.

With respect to political relations inside Jamaica, belonging to the interstate system meant the creation of a national form of political domination. Establishing this domination was essential to the maintenance of a legitimated place in the interstate system. Membership in it demanded that certain obligations be met, and these were enforced through rewards and sanctions. After 1944 a distinct local-level form of postcolonial allegiant membership in the interstate system was established in Jamaica. Because exact political isomorphism with the metropolitan countries was not possible, fashioning the proto-nations of the political parties and sending them off to war in the urban ghetto established our local analogue to modular democratic forms at the world level.[5]

Making war on the urban poor through the mechanism of clientelist "democratic factionalism" was our method of exercising political domination and our way of securing our legitimated position in the interstate system. Exact political and cultural isomorphism was therefore not mandatory. Peripheral capitalism and national cultural forms made that unlikely. However, what was required was the elaboration of a form of political domination that did not disturb the accumulation of capital and did not go beyond the parameters of legitimated membership in the interstate system. Thus, where other colonized peoples sought to secure their relatively autonomous status by rejecting the claims of the interstate system, our political big men made war on the urban poor to maintain legitimated membership in the interstate system. To do otherwise would have meant acceding to the demand of the black majority for economic justice and full democratic rights. This interpretation is one way of grasping the meaning of key developments in Jamaica since 1944.

At the cultural ideological level, then, the liberal-nationalist project encouraged cultural dependence, at least in the early incarnation of this project in the 1930–64 period. It also fashioned a form of domination that secured authorized membership in the interstate system. Thus, inside Jamaica, state agents and civic leaders emphasized to the black population their cultural deficits in a "civilized" and highly ethnicized world. In such a world, "national development" was premised both on the importation of foreign capital and on the cultural acceptance of a world-level cultural etiquette. In this world to become a "civilized" person meant the neutering of racial primordia and the erasure of "national" traits lodged in local language, speech, skin colour and physical appearance.

This model of national development collapsed in 1968. It crumbled because it could neither sustain its own claims for the economic development of Jamaican society nor satisfy mounting demands for economic improvement by a growing and youthful unemployed population. Worse, it collapsed because state adoption of world-level scripts of racial inferiority directed at the local black majority population clashed in the 1960s with counter-ideologies of black nationalism at both the global and domestic levels. Indeed, local-level liberal nationalism found itself embarrassingly defending outworn cultural scripts whose potency had evaporated at the world level. Moral deregulation, it seems, had advanced faster at the global level than at the national level in Jamaica, and the former swept aside national-level attempts to retain an outworn cultural order.

Here again, it is clear that world-level geocultural developments were critical for political outcomes in the island. Consequently, even though exponents of Ethiopianism such as Robert Love and Marcus Garvey had long been champions of black nationalism, it was not until the cultural upheaval in world society around 1968 that long-standing local-level anti-system cultural claims finally found their vigour and broad appeal in the island. In these circumstances it is evident that geoculture, more than being merely contextual, was actually constitutive of real change within a national setting.

Retreat to Exilic Space

Let us examine more fully how geocultural forces – not all of them associated with global-level liberalism – structured consciousness and political cultural orientations in urban Jamaica. First, around 1947 urban political culture was marked by working-class retreat to exilic social spaces. These were primarily autonomous spaces of refuge, yet they remained subject to surveillance and state penetration. Exilic space offered those who "lived" there a place to recover from cultural injuries, such as the lack of effective citizenship and the denial of law. Retreat to exilic space also permitted the fashioning of repertoires of survival, and it gave the black poor the means to exert a social power.

Such means were always under challenge. The urban ghetto was patrolled by the police and invaded by competing politicians. At times, partisan factionalism, political violence and emergency curfews threatened to destroy an already limited autonomy in the slums. Still, the level of state penetration was not so pervasive or draconian that it disabled those wishing to culturally evade the state. Indeed, even when factionalism and intervention were significant, their impact was limited to discrete episodes and particular locales. Disruptive state intervention occurred primarily during electoral cycles and in contexts of episodic partisan competition. Thus, while state penetration in the ghetto was disruptive, and though it conditioned the sensibility of the urban poor, the reach of the state was not so overwhelming that it obliterated everyday forms of autonomous cultural life. Nor did the cultural authority of state agents wholly determine social consciousness in the urban ghetto.

Second, despite room for lower-class autonomy, exilic space was also a place for the morally excluded and the culturally disenfranchised. The rebellious black-skinned ghetto dweller was denied membership in the national moral community and robbed of cultural citizenship in Jamaica. Because their membership in the national community was in doubt, the poor in the ghetto were akin to cultural non-persons in Jamaica. Thus even though the Rastafarians and others champions of black self-respect strove mightily to remind ghetto residents of an honourable cultural past and of their role as a historic "chosen people", a palpable sense of displacement, psychic dislocation and cultural homelessness informed feelings in the slums. Like marginal populations everywhere, the urban Jamaican poor experienced cultural disenfranchisement, and it deepened their alienation even as they strove to uphold an alternative moral authority based on neo-African values.

Third, physical segregation aggravated this cultural homelessness. As a dominated group in a class-divided and racially discriminatory society, the black poor became a tenant of segregated, inferior places. Such places included gullies, street corners, slums, tenement yards and ghetto neighbourhoods. The ecology of these places, with their inferior amenities, lack of infrastructure and cramped and overcrowded conditions, aggravated the historical social confinement of the black poor.

Last, exilic space was characterized by the urban poor's participation in multiple time-spaces with their contradictory impact on consciousness. In the 1960s three confluent forms of consciousness reflected the different time-spaces inhabited by the urban poor. One form of consciousness was expressed in the persistence of residual Africanisms in the society, especially among rural dwellers who had trekked to the major towns and to the city of Kingston. This sensibility and its amplification in the Kingston slums confirmed a widespread assertion of a civilization-consciousness powerfully oriented towards the continent of Africa.

This social outlook was apparent in the unyielding insistence among the more militant sectors of the urban poor during the 1960s that Ethiopia was the font of black civilization and that the role of Ethiopia in African affairs and in global culture could not be diminished. Africanisms were also apparent in the myriad cultural forms among the black poor. Such expressions were apparent in religious practices, patterns of entrepreneurship and forms of leisure and family life. This inclination to an Africanist identity found dramatic expression in the publicly and militantly expounded Rastafarian demand for repatriation to Africa.

Imperial Legacies: Encrustation and Liberation

At the same time, a receding but still influential culture of British imperialism defined the second form of consciousness at large among the urban poor. In the 1960s the centuries-long impact of European imperialism on Jamaican society remained powerful. The cultural residue of empire influenced the entire field of consciousness in Jamaica, shaping political ideology, religious beliefs, social attitudes, marriage customs and personal etiquette, as well as tastes in food, clothing and fashion. This imperial influence on customs, taste, etiquette and fashion conditioned lifestyles, shaped social identities and inclined the poor to habits of imperial provenance. There remained among poor women, for example, a desire for formal marriage and for the respectability of a "church wedding". For these women, this legitimate form was preferable to the myriad unsanctioned and socially disrespectable "common-law" conjugal patterns on the island.

Similarly, broad sections of the Jamaican population preferred a fair skin colour to a "dark" complexion. Poor black communities were not immune to these sentiments. With notable exceptions, many among them accepted norms that regarded the texture of Europeans' hair as superior to the "bad" texture of African hair. The rural and urban poor, like those above them in the class structure, retained a fondness for the British royals and for the pageantry of empire. For example, the homes of poor urban dwellers carried framed pictures of the reigning royals, Queen Elizabeth II and her husband, the duke of Edinburgh. All

Jamaicans keenly followed broadcast accounts of the royals' travels throughout the empire. The largest turnouts for their visits to the island were invariably from poor- and working-class neighbourhoods as residents massed on sidewalks and strained behind barriers to catch a satisfying glimpse of the white-skinned visitors in their official car. A similar summoning of imperial culture was evident in the widespread preference among the urban poor for various styles of British imported goods, including shoes, hats and choice fabrics for trousers and dresses. The inclination was typically against preferences for locally produced products. Finally, popular island sports and games such as cricket and soccer and the rituals that informed them were also defined by their European origin.

The penetration of American power and the authority of its moral culture on the island shaped the third sensibility in the island. The ascent of the United States to global dominance in the postwar world was felt keenly in Jamaica. The impact of US economic power was evident in its investments in tourism, mining and banking. By the 1960s, the United States had replaced Britain as the island's major trading partner, and some of the prodigious output of the postwar US economy found an open, welcoming space in Jamaica as economic policy threw open the door to foreign imports. Indeed, American manufactured goods, its cars, food and luxury items, were the vogue on the island, and Jamaicans of all classes increasingly consumed these US exports.

The dominance of US exports matched the growing global authority of the US world view. In addition to the powerful effect on Jamaican migrants returning from the United States, US cultural and political ascendancy was felt on the island in many ways. One vector for the transmission of this cultural authority was the growing tourist traffic from the United States. The postwar period had seen an expanded tourist trade on the island, and North America – particularly the United States – had become the major source for visitors to the island. Confident in their relative prosperity, visitors from the United States brought with them a seemingly boundless optimism about their own fortunes and about America's place in the world. As beneficiaries of the postwar economic boom and as witnesses to the authority of US commercial, military and political power in the world, American visitors confidently confirmed for islanders – including poor and low-wage workers – the moral virtues and material rewards of the American way of life.

Whether ensconced in hotel properties devoted to their leisure, living in the homes of welcoming Jamaicans or meeting poor islanders on their sojourns, US tourists and the tourist trade itself exercised a not-inconsiderable impact on the social consciousness of Jamaicans. As agents of this cultural transmission, American visitors communicated to their island hosts North American optimism, its easy affluence and its members' confident satisfaction with the virtues of the consumer society.

If North American visitors' national pride, displays of affluence and consumerist optimism failed to morally compel low-wage workers and their unemployed kin, then the latter groups were even more powerfully influenced by another key vector of American power. This was the dissemination of American popular culture by way of print, film, radio and other media. The penetration of American popular culture was felt through the extensive distribution of Hollywood B movies and in the importation of American popular magazines, comic books and pulp fiction. Hollywood films, particularly the so-called Westerns, were extremely popular in working-class neighbourhoods across Kingston. The Ambassador Theatre in west Kingston, as well as the Rialto and the Gaiety in east Kingston, carried a wide-ranging fare of B movies whose images of savage violence, animated gunplay and romantic melodrama proved compelling for the poor who attended the cinema. In all these films, white actors presented an unmistakable melodramatic narrative in which the lawful and the good triumphed over the illegal and the evil.

The cinema in working-class neighbourhoods therefore became more than just a vehicle for conveying social drama. It was also a medium for the communication of ideology and values, in this instance primarily US political ideology and social values. In addition to the social values in these films, the political newsreels of the day that were shown in the theatres affirmed the virtues of American society and the moral struggle of the United States against communism and other evils. The "news ideology" contained in these propagandistic newsreels of world events marked out a clear Manichaean boundary for poor theatregoers.

For these viewers, then, there was hardly any difference between the moral dicta in the apocalyptic newsreels on the politics of the cold war and the normative lessons in the onscreen melodramas. If the insistent sermons of American evangelists like the Reverend Billy Graham (whose apocalyptic programme *Hour of Decision* was transmitted to Jamaicans on the radio on Sunday mornings) are included in this Americanizing cultural ensemble, then the enveloping reach and authority of US ideological power on the island is unquestioned.

Besides news ideology, evangelical summoning and onscreen Hollywood fare, the urban poor were exposed to American lifestyles and social attitudes from other media available to them. They perused imported American glossy magazines ranging from the tabloid *Photoplay*, which focused on the lives of Hollywood stars, to the sober *Time* magazine, which served up extensive pro-American coverage of world events. The urban poor also pored over Disney fare in print; they experienced the passions of British schoolgirl romantic fiction; and they amused themselves in the torrent of American comic books such as *Popeye* and the heroic *Superman*.

Similarly, like other Jamaicans, the urban poor consumed US culture through its popular music. They listened to it on the local radio stations, heard it in city theatres from the mouths of its leading exponents and brought it back from sojourns in the United States. This vogue was particularly true for the idioms of rock and roll, black American soul music and the blues, as well as country-and-western music. Local artists, arrangers and singers from the urban poor embraced these American forms, adapted and imitated them, and filled them with local political and social content. Despite such episodes of adaptive creativity, however, few local artists and Jamaicans who imbibed US popular music could escape the simulacrum of American experience that the music and other media had introduced. Indeed, locals with limited or no direct contact with US society and culture experienced nostalgia for the culture and the ambience of that nearby industrial society as if it were their own.

One consequence of this de-territorializing effect of America's cultural reach was that many among the urban poor experienced a palpable cultural disjuncture – this between the misery and hardships of their lived experience in the island and the imagined experience of participating in the material well-being, consumer tastes and popular culture imported from a highly industrialized society. This contact with distant American Others through travel, film, music, radio broadcasts and pulp fiction therefore transported Jamaicans, including large contingents of the urban poor, into a worldwide US-dominated cultural space. The urban poor, like other Jamaicans, embraced American codes and social tastes inside this space, and many among them experienced these values as familiar and as culturally their own.

Like many imperial systems, American civilization in the postwar years asserted itself as a universal civilization. Jamaicans experienced the global reach and ubiquity of US political, economic and cultural power as a universal world culture appropriate for them. Hence, even as a European civilization with claims to universality went into recession in the region (the British Empire), the newer authority of American power at its apogee now inclined the urban poor and others on the island to experience American ideologies and social values as their own.

This confluence of multiple time-spaces and the cultural disjuncture between a global awareness and a lived Jamaican experience that was miserable and confining defined the existential life of the urban poor. Such an overlapping of time-spaces gave the poor opportunities for shared customs other than the narrow partisanship offered by the political parties. Still, these alternative culture-forming experiences were not unproblematic since they produced contradictory summonings. On the one side, a pattern of moral hailings drew the poor to Africanist obligations; on the other side, a different set of appeals pulled them to the simulacrum of American experience. A third pattern linked them to the residues of British imperial culture, and still a fourth hailed the poor either as members of the proto-nations of the parties or as obedient subjects of the Creole ideology of Jamaican exceptionalism.

Inside this culturally diverse space, unemployed male youth in the ghetto lived a hybrid cultural existence by juggling lived experiences and their simulacra from abroad. Some urban youths adhered to an Africanist sensibility by choosing to "defend" Rastafarian beliefs against anti-black sentiments in the society. Their kin tried to make their world intelligible by invoking Jamaican folk wisdom. Others borrowed a media-informed metropolitan-transmitted male *savoir faire* and fused it to the local "sweet boy" and "face-man" aesthetics in the urban ghetto.[6]

By the late 1960s, many ghetto youths found the simulacrum of the Hollywood badlands genre usable for the production of the violent "rudie", "screwface" and avenging Gorgon identities.[7] Others among the unemployed drew on the shibboleths of a faded empire by employing its racist and abusive terms to pre-emptively settle interpersonal disputes with their black-skinned neighbours. In the most extreme cases, hybridity and de-territorialized experience among the young meant the juggling and combination of all these identities into an inchoate ensemble that revealed a pastiche of time-spaces with their lifestyles and moralities. Which identity or morality prevailed in such cases necessarily depended on the wider global context and on the exigencies of community life in Jamaica.

Regardless of the kinds of moral clothing worn by the poor under these circumstances, what is not in doubt is that competing allegiances and moral dispositions blunted politicians' hope for an unchecked exercise of a party-driven hegemony over the poor. These rival compulsions drew the poor away from the moral sway of law, divorced them from official society and isolated them from the compulsions of state politics. Competing allegiances inclined the urban poor to search for and build social and cultural empowerment zones in which they exercised alternative forms of black mastery. The construction of these zones of empowerment inside an exilic social space, the exercise of forms of black mastery within it and the proliferation of contrary social identities and moral cultures all acted as powerful constraints against state-driven attempts to dominate the lives of the poor.

Poor Neighbourhoods as Moral Incubators

The foregoing has suggested that exilic social space had a dual identity. It was both a site of repression and a place where social autonomy was possible. Ghetto neighbourhoods around Kingston reflected this double feature. Poor and working-class neighbourhoods were therefore simultaneously zones of empowerment and places of marginality and confinement. As with all such exilic spaces, a poor neighbourhood – by reason of its segregation and relative isolation – permitted the flourishing of relatively autonomous subcultures. Such tendencies were much in evidence, for example, in poor and working-class precincts across Kingston.

On the one hand, the ecology of these neighbourhoods, with their narrow lanes, exposed dwellings, overcrowded tenement yards and cheek-by-jowl living, invited conflicts and hostilities between residents.

At the same time, these circumstances generated forms of mutuality and self-help. Neighbourhood life in urban Kingston in the late 1960s was therefore defined both by normal incidences of conflict between neighbours and by acts of communal obligation. While these circumstances are not remarkable in poor neighbourhoods, it is arguable that the ecology of ghetto life aggravated the residents' alienation and increased their discontent. In the context of Jamaica's highly charged sociopolitical relations, with its mobilization of the poor by means of racial, class and social-justice ideologies, the physical circumstances of life in the ghetto intensified residents' latent moral sentiments.

One such sentiment was the concern for dignity and social respect. Most poor individuals affirmed this need, and they often sought to achieve it in the one place where a sense of personhood was at stake and needed to be protected most – in the neighbourhood, on the streets and in the tenements and communal yards where they lived. In these contexts individuals' concerns for social regard were heightened in the 1960s, and respect from neighbours was insisted on.

This insistence assumed dramaturgic form in a public and highly stylized manner that drew attention to the individual's concern that his imperiled, honourable self be publicly and vigorously protected. The ecology of the ghetto made a vigorous public affirmation and defence of this endangered self all the more urgent. Living in poor neighbourhoods imposed more than just material deprivations on residents – the deficit of living space induced its own moral responses. Lack of living space could provoke anger and violence among herded residents. Cramped quarters also meant a loss of individual privacy. This deprivation was particularly worrisome for a lower class that, like the rest of the society, valued the norm of privacy.

The development of an alienated moral culture was one consequence of the crowded, close-quarters life the poor were forced to accept. Living in these circumstances in urban Kingston condemned the poor to a peculiar condition of ghetto residency: the subjection of their person to constant exposure, unyielding spectacle and public display. This intensely public nature of daily life in the ghetto caused slum dwellers to adopt protective poses. These poses allowed the poor to assume militant identities they hoped would ward off shame and protect their dignity.

Ridicule and public shame were constant threats to social respect in the ghetto. Jealousy, spite, traffic in rumour and the flow of personal gossip ensnared residents and caused them to be wary of neighbours. Caution against "bad-minded" people in the ghetto arrested conviviality and led to pre-emptive moral judgement of neighbours. Neighbourhood scorn for individuals on the basis of rumour could scar and ruin reputations. Persons deemed untrustworthy or "licky-licky" in their gluttony and those regarded as "tight-handed" in refusing to share often became community pariahs. Community gossip, with its moral injunctions, put residents on their guard and stimulated in them protective poses to maintain personal respect. In such cases targets of anonymous gossip dealt with threats to their reputation by pre-emptive and strenuous assertions of their righteousness while promising menaces to the gossips. This vigilance in the interest of personal respect encouraged aggressiveness among the poor, independent of provocation or manipulation by political parties.

But threat to personhood in the slums did not come just from destructive talk. The outdoors existence typical of the slum created moral values, as residents battled for space and assumed protective identities. Life in lower-class neighbourhoods typically meant living in makeshift dwellings or in tenement yards. Such yards normally consisted of simple one-room dwellings abutting a common outdoor space. Residents cooked, bathed, ate and washed clothes outdoors in this common space. Ghetto life meant the public sharing of "private" facilities and the inconvenience of waiting one's turn to use scarce amenities. Individual conduct, the intimacies of family life and social interactions in the yard took place mostly in full public view and within earshot of neighbours. All such activities were subject to the constant scrutiny and moral judgement of neighbours. While offering opportunities for mutuality and sharing, tenement-yard life was cramped, and the constant surveillance of personal lives tended to undermine sociability and trust. Open disputes, fights and public quarrels punctured occasions of neighbourliness in the yards.

Tenement-yard space and its relations extended into the streets. This nexus also intensified a sense of alienation. Though streets and lanes in the slums were physically separated from dwellings by fences, gates and other crude delimiters, there was much physical overlap between the street and the yard. Despite residents' tenacious effort to maintain privacy by erecting simple fences, dwellings in the slums abutted the street without any protective intervening space. The overlap between street and yard meant that each contributed to the public spectacle in which all residents participated. Indeed, what transpired in the open yards and dwellings of the tenements was generally visible and audible from the street. Conversely, a vibrant street life intruded into the yards.

This outdoors and a life of public spectacle in the ghetto sharply reduced personal privacy, and with it any individual effort to maintain a life or identity that kept the residents' public and private "faces" separate. To many residents this separation was important to their sense of enjoying a civilized existence. Constancy of exposure "at home" in the yards and "in public" out in the street forced residents into a struggle for personal space and denied them the social and physical context for the norms of civility they very much coveted. Achieving social respect under these circumstances therefore depended on the ability to manage appearances in neighbourhood spaces and to compel others to accept these protective poses. The street and the yard became platforms for the construction of identities, and together they helped foster a moral culture often at odds with the civic culture to which many residents aspired.

In the streets and tenement yards individual identity was closely linked to gestural and oral-kinetic repertoires. Somatic poses, variable "facial utterances" and verbal tonality enabled slum dwellers to compel respect from neighbours by using the body as a vehicle of moral communication. To know someone and to be someone in the ghetto was in part a function of the use of bodies in public space. To acquire a "self" required its public construction in the form of physical gestures before one's neighbours. For young men in the streets and yards, this meant the deploying of a heterosexual, manly etiquette in which voice, gesture and orality confirmed an unassailable masculine aura. This assertive body was generally effective in addressing the everyday encounters that threatened residents' search for a potent self. Depending on the circumstances, threats to an honourable identity could be warded off by means as various as aggressive stances and "cool poses" by males. For women, protective measures might include the wearing of modest clothing or the public affirmation of a devout commitment to religious faith. In deeply influential ways, community social relations and the ecology of the ghetto created the basis for a theatre of identity revolving around corporeal acts and the political uses of bodies.

Social relations in the slums and the ecology of the yard and the street therefore induced in the urban poor a kinetic morality that offered a somatic complement to their ideas of personal autonomy and black freedom. Public gestures often implied ideological needs. Moreover, for many in the ghetto its streets, yards and public squares were not just places to claim public respect for one's identity as human.

Neo-African Moral Intelligence in the Slums

Social and physical spaces in the slums were also domains for the practice of forms of neo-African moral intelligence and neo-African aesthetics as racial consciousness saturated corporeal acts. Both moral intelligence and aesthetic form were bearers of civilizational values and carriers of popular-democratic impulses. They affirmed the value of black personhood and the righteousness of the poor's claim to social honour. This role of the street and the yard as powerful identity-creating platforms was strengthened in a country in which law and society offered few protections and meagre affirmations of the black poor's right to respect. The spectacle of yard and street life therefore encouraged somatic norms and a performance culture in which residents publicly claimed protective identities against possible threats.

In these circumstances both the aggressive "rude boy" and the menacing "screwface" identities adopted by juveniles and grown men during the 1960s become intelligible. These identities of Hollywood origin but adapted to local circumstances were deployed for strategic purposes: to avoid public shame and to deter threats to an imperilled self. Though commentators have correctly identified the adoption of these identities as instances of nihilistic rage against injustice and state abuse, it is worth remembering that they were also deployed to influence neighbours and to hold at bay their intrusive habits. State politics induced anger in the slums and provoked these wary identities. But a life of spectacle, the threat of humiliation before one's neighbours and the battle for space in the neighbourhood induced in the urban poor moralities that were formed well outside the ambit and play of predatory politics.

The spectacular quality of daily life in the slums, with its risk of shame and public ridicule, therefore made already anxious individuals feel even more threatened and concerned for their dignity. Residents' heightened sense of vulnerability to spectacle and public humiliation encouraged in them a powerful need to dramatically affirm their dignity and claim their self-respect from neighbours. The "battle for space" and the avoidance of public shame in yards and tenements therefore became goads to the well-known stylized aggressiveness of the Kingston poor. Quite independent of the pressure of political parties upon their lives, then, the poor were inclined to adopt aggressive and vigilantly defensive postures partly because of the ecology of the slums. Thus, the constancy of this "battle for space" and the search for an honourable identity in both society and the ghetto inclined poor residents to wariness and martial postures of self-defence.

Autonomous Lifestyles: Sources of Social Power and Cultural Capital

Two conclusions can be drawn from the preceding discussion. First, it is apparent that despite the tremendous power of the parties and of predatory politics in the lives of the poor, the reach of US power, the residual culture of European imperialism and pervasive Africanisms among the poor blunted the parties' colonizing effect on ghetto residents. All three sources of alternative cultural existence conspired to hold invasive state politics at bay and to give the urban poor cultural living space. In the 1960s contingents of the urban poor drew on the triple heritage of American, European and African cultural influence to invent new customs. This variable heritage helped them construct hybrid, emancipated selves that eluded the monopolistic reach of politics and the domesticating influence of local institutions and moral agents.

Second, the insecurity of outdoors existence and the vulnerability to spectacle that threatened black esteem in the slums could also be employed to recover it in the ghetto and elsewhere in the society. Among such places were public theatres where popular performers contributed to group moral culture by providing entertainment in song, music and dance. Dramaturgy and role-playing in the slums, as a response to the spectacular quality of everyday life there, could be transferred to this other theatre of identity, where slum dwellers, in their role as public entertainers, affirmed the cause for social autonomy and black esteem.

Myriad cultural practices in the 1960s seemed to confirm this assessment. For example, the phenomenal popularity of ska and reggae music in these years offered a dramatic illustration of the point. The rise to national prominence of popular singers and performing artists from working-class and poor neighbourhoods was achieved partly on the basis of the triple heritage and partly by drawing on the availability of dramaturgic opportunity and experience. Popular musicians, DJs and singers embodied the cultural styles within the triple heritage. Crooners, shouters, balladeers and religious chanters of popular song displayed in public performance the mimetic, distant inspiration for the lyrical content of their songs and musical styles.

Musical and stylistic forms from Africa, Europe and the United States coexisted in contrapuntal unity with local innovations. This simulacrum of worldwide experience captured in song styles and lyrical content was evident, for example, in performers' stage attire. Formal suits, top hats and imperial regalia of British origins were mixed with African-inspired dreadlocks and fashions of local derivation. Both on- and offstage, male performers' gold-capped front teeth of local invention complemented the wearing of impenetrable black sunglasses whose aesthetics reflected the influence of the "hipster" in black American popular culture. Similarly, stage gestures echoed a medley of expressive styles and affective-libidinal norms drawn from elsewhere. Performers' majestic struts and martial stances in the concert halls complemented the stagy soul-group choreography borrowed from North American rock-and-roll culture.

If public exposure and invasive scrutiny in the ghetto induced belligerent poses and self-regarding "performances" among slum dwellers, then entertainment on the public stage was not very different in its mobilizing cultural impact on them. There, too, public spectacle, within the context of social inequality and the triple heritage, became a vehicle for heroic performance and the communication of a dissident moral culture.

The popularity of the Wailers singing group, and later of Bob Marley himself, epitomized the dynamics between spectacle, performance and moral culture. Like other reggae bands, the Wailers' public performances mirrored for poor audiences the corporeal intensities and dramaturgy of ghetto life. Their mimetic in concert of libidinous joy in the slums and representations of cultural injury to the downtrodden won the group a huge following among the poor.

Occurring in exilic spaces beyond the reach of official scrutiny and censorship, the spectacle in concerts and dance halls in working-class neighbourhoods became an occasion of celebratory, collective racial joy. In these places poor audiences revelled in their particularity as black "sufferers" and in their anonymity as opponents of social injustice. The sensational content of these musical performances allowed the black poor to indulge libidinous norms. Concerts found them shouting affirmations to the band and indulging exuberant racial pride in the aesthetic content of the music. Likewise, revellers in the dance halls were capable of falling into near-hypnotic trances in response to the extended, instrumental dub interlude with its insistent, deafening bass line. For revellers in the dance halls, the pulsating sound of reggae music seemed as important to the formation of their social and moral identity as the race-pride–enhancing message in the music's lyrical content.

Like its counterpart in the neighbourhood, then, the spectacle of the public concert and the dance hall created opportunities for identity-making, black mastery and heroic performance. Musical skill and creativity in oral-kinetic dramaturgy enabled performers from the slums to achieve public honour and heroic reputations. Because of his mastery of these repertoires Bob Marley became the iconic reggae artist of the 1960s. He was simultaneously creative exponent, heroic performer and cultural tribune. Musicians and singers in the Wailers' band as well as "producers" and "sound system" engineers won similar notoriety for their creative expertise in synthesizing voice, drums, pianos and guitars to fit the demands of the new music. The public appreciated this musical creativity of singers and sound-system engineers so much that enthusiastic audiences attended concerts and went to the dance halls as much to witness virtuoso performances by individual artists and sound engineers as to experience the aesthetic, public affirmation of their values.

Thus, spectacle and performance in the dance and concert halls were nothing without the moral culture for which they were the vehicles. Public performance in concert permitted the collective assumption of poses and social identities thoroughly infused with racial and class content. As a component of exilic space, the dance hall allowed the ecstatic indulgence of collective black joy and cultural dissidence. There, contingents of the black poor affirmed their equal claim to an honourable identity. Sound-system engineers bearing honorific titles such as "Duke" and "King" vied with each other and with popular singers to bring ecstatic audiences the latest and greatest in popular "sounds".[8] In the specular domain of the concert and dance halls, well beyond the immediate scrutiny of an intrusive state and a racially discriminatory society, the aesthetic experience of the urban poor achieved authentic representation.

In this regard, performers' kinetic prowess, verbal play and instrumental virtuosity onstage could carry little force without related norms of cultural autonomy, personal excellence and black mastery. In the eyes of both artists and audiences, performance was never divorced from black excellence and the search for cultural autonomy. For artists as well as audiences, artistic techniques and their mastery were usually linked to racial group awareness; concern for aesthetic values and technical expertise was never far from sentiments of collective cultural redemption. Consequently, even as the lyrical content of reggae music advanced an explicit moral and political agenda of black redemption and racial pride, the orienting norms of that agenda – black mastery and black freedom – were tacitly reinforced by these ethnic artists' self-conscious concern for mastering their craft. Group moral culture and its larger social concerns therefore informed the quest for superior technique.

This overlapping of public performance, heroic individualism and moral culture can be generalized to other cultural practices in urban space. Positive examples of the twinning of these three values were evident in popular culture in the 1960s and after. Sports and games, as well as entertainment, are well-known domains in which performance values, individual mastery and socio-political values have historically overlapped for the poorer classes. Sports and entertainment verified the ubiquity of shared customs among members of this group; both confirmed the fact of cultural construction beyond the realm of partisanship; and both attested to the striving for black esteem and liberty.

Accomplishment in sports and popular entertainment created new forms of cultural capital for the poor and helped establish a positive basis for their widening social power in Jamaican society. In the postwar years, acclaimed sports figures and entertainers from humble origins came to exercise an unparalleled moral authority based largely on their roles as icons of black excellence. Leadership, technical competence and outstanding achievement in these areas of popular culture did much, therefore, to enhance racial pride, alleviate feelings of inferiority and build community spirit. Indeed, natal community identity became a source of personal pride among poor and working-class youth as flourishing talent and outstanding achievements earned working-class communities public recognition.

For residents in these urban neighbourhoods, community identity and pride came not so much from the claims of partisan politics as from the satisfactions of contributing to the transformation of the nation's cultural identity by fielding talent in the areas of sports and entertainment. Social power from below came from sources other than partisan political engagements. The urban poor therefore found in these other, non-political domains cultural space in which they tried to fashion a relatively autonomous existence free from the debasing effects of factional politics.

This freedom should not be exaggerated, however. Autonomy was strictly limited, as urban politicians were determined to harness this cultural flowering to their partisan agendas. Nevertheless, even when political partisanship encroached on that existence with state funding of community sports and by the fashioning of "community development" projects to suit partisan ambitions, politics could not control the meaning of this cultural flourishing for the poor. The poor did not see individual excellence in sports and entertainment as an achievement won by politics or for the glory of politics. On the contrary, in their eyes, a hardy people had excelled despite the odds and had won laurels for themselves outside politics. Triumph in sports and entertainment thus became a triumph over poverty and politics.

In fact, performing artists, athletes and community folk saw their achievements as their very own. These forms of black mastery from below were therefore something that belonged to the ordinary people and were won by them despite political encroachment. Thus, even as these agents of cultural empowerment would find it necessary to accommodate the intrusion of politics, they also tried to keep politics in its place by recognizing its contingent and episodic role in their lives. Though personal and group ambition might at times require accommodation to predatory politics, such ambitions did not countenance the suppression of black cultural autonomy. Indeed, for the vast majority of the poor, cultural autonomy was sought for its own sake; as a result, involvement in political partisanship was regarded as an encumbrance and as a necessary evil that was typically subordinated to the quest for group cultural respect.

Here again, the quest for cultural space should not be overstated, as it was informed by a covert desire for inclusion in the cultural mainstream. For while cultural affirmation greatly increased the social power of the poor in opposition to a dismissive society, it is worth remembering that conventional morality and shared values also undergirded popular claims for respect. Thus, even as icons of black excellence challenged the cultural inequities of the society by highlighting cultural empowerment and advancing alternative modes of existence, they were demanding inclusion, and they did so by tacitly invoking common Jamaican values and widely shared norms.

Those values were rooted in notions of personal ambition, competitive individualism and achievement norms of merit and reward based on the mastery of a creative domain. By embodying precisely these values, the search for black excellence among the poor echoed shared but neglected values in Jamaican society. In their quest for social acceptance, many icons of black mastery from below sought to win respect and to acquire respectability in ways that were thoroughly consistent with the values of the wider Jamaican society. In displays of ambition and in the harnessing of discipline to positive goals, icons from the poorer classes established a delicate relation between two contrary impulses within lower-class groups. One was the fashioning of a culturally grounded aesthetic that was conscious of differences in social identity between the black poor and their social betters; the other was tutoring a dismissive society in its neglected norms, particularly those that linked social worth to individual and group achievement.

The Quest for Empowerment: Heroic Criminality

Still, by the late 1960s this quest for social empowerment was not merely supportive of prevailing values. It was also infiltrated by sentiments that were increasingly hostile to conventional values. This much was clear from the actions of a rebellious lumpenproletariat that openly rejected the dominant morality and societal norms of civility and upward mobility through lawful achievement and competitive individualism. Paradoxically, the quest for social respect and regard in the slums was expressed in two competing tendencies: the imitation of official norms and the negation of those norms. Together they solidified divergent yet affiliated social identities in the slums.

The ghetto therefore had both its exemplars of positive black achievement and its iconic rebels intent on challenging conventional achievement norms. Sports heroes and popular entertainers won public acclaim for succeeding despite the odds. But such exemplars also had to share notoriety and community recognition with the likes of heroic gunmen, youth gangs, political enforcers and agents of a criminal underground. Poor communities held model figures from sports and popular entertainment in awe. But these communities also feared celebrated outlaws in their midst. They included urban bandits – several of whom held Rastafarian and socialist views – gun-wielding juvenile gangs and lumpen collectivities inclined to predation and street crime. In contrast to the exemplars in sports and entertainment, this latter group had also carved out alternative paths to survival and recognition in the slums by means of outlawry and a convention-disrupting indiscipline.

In the postwar years, the storied reputations of some of these outlaw actors became more than just the stuff of legend; they also offered models of emulation for the unemployed young. These contrary yet kindred forms of heroic individualism – black excellence in sports and entertainment and notoriety in outlawry – illustrate the dialectics of the struggle for cultural space unfolding in the slums against the background of the island's unequal social relations and multiple historical inheritances.

The Ethiopianist Project

This detour into the dynamics of Jamaica's recent cultural formation highlights the intersection between national and global phenomena. It indicates how local-level cultural materials form and re-form in association with world-level cultural processes. Cultural forces at the world level were key to these local developments, but they were not so overwhelming in influence that they negated freedom to culturally innovate. A major effect of this external determination is that the liberal-nationalist model failed because it had lost the ability to control the defining and framing assumptions *inside* Jamaica. This debility was a direct result of transformations in the geoculture and in local responses to it. This conjunction undercut powerfully held notions of black inferiority in the island. Cultural change at the world level and competing cultural allegiances among the poor had subverted obstacles to change in Jamaica. Indeed, the failures of the liberal-nationalist project became all the more apparent by the late 1960s as this liberalism sought to reconcile the claims of its emancipatory agenda with the simultaneous vicious party-inspired civil war it had unleashed on the urban poor. These poor, it should be clear, were the foremost opponents of "modernization" and "civility" and had frontally challenged the liberal-nationalist agenda.

In this encounter, liberal-nationalists faced a mighty contradiction, especially after 1947 when the Jamaican party civil war really took off. On the one hand, the national-liberal project was blocked by the economic and structural impediments of peripheral capitalism. On the other hand, however, achieving the liberal agenda had become more difficult from the inside. Legitimated membership in the interstate system had spawned violent state predation and the prosecution of a war against an important section of the national population. These two determinants thoroughly divorced the alienated poor from the claims of the liberal-nationalist agenda. It is no secret that we are now living through the latest phase of this double process.

The Ethiopianist project is the ideological antithesis to global liberalism's cultural ideology of white supremacy. Ethiopianism in Jamaica between 1930 and 1970 frontally opposed all the legitimating myths and prescriptions of this global liberalism and its local counterpart. Ethiopianism in Jamaica, especially in the 1950s and 1960s, rejected the institutional processes of the capitalist world system. It rejected the logic of the world economy, with its marginalization of peripheral economies; it repudiated the world system's political ideal of a parcelled nation-statehood in a hierarchical and ethnicized system; and it fought the seductive tenets of white supremacy encoded in Jamaican multiracialism as articulated by the nationalist big men and their allies.

As the latter group correctly understood, Jamaican Ethiopianism in its various forms was a fundamental challenge to their liberal-nationalist project. On the one hand, Ethiopianism demonstrated early on an active withdrawal of consent from liberalism as a world-embracing cultural ideology. Jamaican Ethiopianism in its Garveyite and

Rastafarian guises sounded urgent early ontological warnings and threw up cultural and political barriers before liberalism's global onslaught. Complementing this pioneering and defensive role, the Rastafarian form of Ethiopianism in Jamaica offered an alternative cultural etiquette and a contrasting philosophy and social ontology. What at first blush appeared to be an assimilation of the evolving language of liberalism, with its assertions of universal social justice, individual freedom and the right to equal identity, was something rather different and more subversive.

The Rastafarian project of self-determination, rather than being a paean to liberal values, was instead a repudiation of them. The Rastafarian project of 1930–70 was about the de-modernization and the de-Westernization of black persons and of the neocolonial societies in which they lived. It was also about something more dangerous because of what I shall call its anti-Westphalian thrust. That is, Ethiopianism in Jamaica butted against the interstate system and the world-historic political relations inaugurated by the Treaty of Westphalia.[9]

The Ethiopianist project, then as now, is about a rejection of the modern cultural narrative of national development by means of a dependent, parcelled nation-statehood in a capitalist world system. Ethiopianism's redemptive call for a return to Africa to shelter under "our own vine and fig tree" seems to me to be less a claim for inclusion in a parcelled notion of membership in the interstate system than a yearning for a return to a pre-Westphalian condition of decentred political and cultural units. It is in this sense that Rastafarian calls for a return to "anciency" were interpreted as atavistic by Creole nationalists.

In contrast to the inequalities of modernity, the call to anciency carried with it a more encompassing universalism, a clear non-Westphalian doctrine and a radicalizing cosmopolitanism. Ethiopianism in its 1960s guise rejected "bourgeois politics", whether of the proto-national parties of the JLP and the PNP or of their opponents on the Marxist or nationalist Left. Here again, Rastafarianism is instructive. For in its famous rejection of middle-class politics, Rastafarianism was really repudiating the political legacy of Westphalia, and that included a repudiation of the social ontology of both liberalism and its cultural sibling, Marxism (Wallerstein 1995).

Whatever the differences that informed the family civil war between these two rivals, both became signatories to the worldwide political culture associated with the Westphalian nation-state system. No wonder, then, that when confronted by the alternative of Jamaican liberalism and its cultural twin, New Left socialism in Jamaica, the rude boys and the Rastas were united in their demand to "vank" politics.[10] This repudiation was not just rejection of local-level Jamaican politics; it was simultaneously a repudiation of liberalism's ideology of modernity and of the Westphalian thralldom into which Jamaican liberal-nationalists and Marxists had fallen.

In truth, the Rastafarian project, born in the cauldron of a culturally essentializing world system, bore an undeniable anti-modern impulse. This could not have been otherwise, since liberalism and its sibling, Marxism, clothed themselves in the language of progress, both claiming to be the superior embodiment of modernity and development. Because modernity and development meant acquisition of a state with a correlative class and ethnicized structure enforced by the interstate system, the challenge from the victims of these structures inevitably meant a challenge to modernity, to the interstate system and to their political champions, whether of a left or a liberal persuasion.

We can now see how ideologically dissonant such assertions were for Jamaica's political class in the years 1930 to 1968. To oppose modernity was to question foundational tenets of the world system: namely, "subject" membership and genuflection before the altar of capitalist civilization by gendered and ethnicized peoples. Such tenets permitted and justified the unequal distribution of income and honour at the world level. The panoply of system-wide ideas and practices, which were also embedded within national states, therefore tightly regulated ethnic and gender advance within this system. This ensemble of practices insisted on the required demonstration of "competence" and "merit" on the part of women and "minorities" as the precondition of upward mobility.

In this context we can retrospectively appreciate why a Black Power movement occurred in the Caribbean with its majority black populations. For in these precincts of the interstate system, the ideologies of "merit" and "colour-blind" equal opportunity, far from securing mobility for blacks, had actually maintained gendered and ethnicized rewards. Thus, the expulsion of Walter Rodney from Jamaica in 1968 and the quarantine against Black Power across the Caribbean can be seen for what it was – a defence of local class political power, a defence of encrusted ethnicized class and gendered differentials and an attempt to shore up an ideological pillar of the world system, namely anti-black racism. Attacking the Black Power movement in black-majority countries was therefore simultaneously a "home-grown" local event of political contestation and a "world-level" event premised on struggles over the terms of securing legitimated membership in the interstate system. In butting against the systemic logic of Westphalia and the geoculture of liberalism, Ethiopianism appeared to be in near-perfect alignment with the emergent international Weltanschauung of 1968. The spirit of that age was not just about an instinctual-libidinal rebellion against state repression and ossified bureaucracy. On the contrary, Ethiopianism was, at its most profound level, a rebellion against both Westphalian political culture and liberalism's social ontology.

The operative principle for the new Weltanschauung in Jamaica was of course the satisfaction of instinctual needs and the right to self-ownership. It was also about the quest for cultural autonomy, the right to membership outside the compulsion of the patriotic nation-state community and a right to membership in smaller subnational cultural communities. If we compare this ethos with its counterparts at the world level, a high degree of cultural isomorphism between the home-grown version of anti-systemic rebellion and world-level opposition is apparent. In both cases the notion of "lifestyle" assumed new vigour; new moral cultures and communities celebrating instinctual and identitarian needs sprang up; and subnational communities and the identity movements gained new authority at the expense of the nation-state identity.

Yet there were some wrinkles in the cultural isomorphism between world-level processes and local-level developments in Jamaica. Cultural rebellion in North America and Western Europe in the 1960s was anchored largely among the educated sons and daughters of the bourgeoisie; US ghettos revolted, but these revolts had as their tacit agenda inclusion in the system and access to what the majority white youths were rejecting. In the home-grown version of Jamaican counterculture, a rebellion first sprang from the opposite social pole and was launched by disadvantaged youths in the urban ghettos.

Over time, in the metropolitan countries, dissident affluent youth were reabsorbed as adults into the system when they went on to assume normal careers. That option of reintegration into society was unavailable to the unemployed youth in Jamaica. This break in isomorphism had dramatic local consequences for Jamaica. There, the leading force for social change was not affluent youth or jaded intellectuals, but the dispossessed urban poor. Where workers and peasants had rebelled in the 1930s, the lumpenproletariat provoked social change in the 1960s and after. Where workers and peasants had attacked the colonial order, the lumpenproletariat attacked the ideological and foundational principles of the postcolonial order. They did this in their own way, by a mixture of contingent compliance and rejection of state power. And they did it with repertoires at their disposal using the weapons of the weak: violence, theft, predation, indiscipline, non-compliance and the celebration of instinctual needs. That rebellion was congealed in the dramaturgy of "badness-honour", in which outlawry was employed to achieve respect and public honour.

The righteous racial indignation of groups like the Rastafarians and the outlawry of the rude boys are quintessential expressions of badness-honour. It is a cultural style that may be used to intimidate through menaces or histrionic gestures. It may also be employed to bargain and negotiate the terms by which power, social respect, honour, deference or resources are granted or denied to claimants. The norm of badness-honour is therefore a gestural-symbolic system and carrier of moral communication. In the dramaturgy of badness-honour, intersubjective understanding about the meaning of unequal power is conveyed by intensive corporeal acts of speech and gesture.

To return to our discussion of the nested relationship between national developments and world-level forces, it is clear that Jamaican badness-honour from the slums and elsewhere is simultaneously an assault on and an expression of the decay of liberalism in peripheral societies. Badness-honour should therefore be seen as a "national" cultural expression of liberalism's failure to deliver on its promise of progress.

The Exhaustion of Ethiopianism

We now need to ask why the Ethiopianist project proved abortive by the year 1972. Consistent with our earlier claim, Ethiopianism – for all its cultural potency in piercing the ideological canopy of the world economy and its framing beliefs and mentalities – could not advance beyond its decentralizing and de-Westernizing thrusts. By 1970 it had run out of steam, its ideological originality weakened by the success of its cultural appeal and by rival movements' and parties' cannibalization of its themes.

By 1972 Ethiopianism was being overtaken – indeed, swept aside – by two converging political developments. On the one hand, Ethiopianism was swept aside by the rapid growth and ascent of a hardened lumpenproletariat whose harsh material circumstances yielded a moral culture that was not immune to a contingent and calculated acceptance of liberalism's core principles. This lumpenproletariat, which spanned both a criminal and a political underground, was morally uncoupled from the disciplinary effect of Ethiopianist doctrine; it was emancipated from the deferential acceptance of liberal dogmas of both the home-grown and the world-level varieties; and it was impervious to the ideological counterclaims of Marxist activists, who, by the mid-1970s, wanted nothing to do with this contingent.

On the other hand, Ethiopianism fell victim once again to its nemesis, the Westphalian interstate system and the machinery of its home-grown expression in Jamaica. By 1974 Ethiopianism as a project had been surpassed in a manner similar to its supercession in the 1930s: powerful fluctuations in Jamaican and global politics marginalized its claims. In the 1930s Ethiopianism had been swept aside when the dominant interpretive frame of nationalist "self-determination" overwhelmed it. The end of colonial rule based on acceptance of a modular independent state within the interstate system dominated national attention. After 1972, new fluctuations at the global and national levels put forward other interpretive frames, including the demand for sovereignty in an unequal interstate system on the basis of the right to affirm an independent political ideology. In sum, the Ethiopianist project fell victim to its own shortcomings and to its supercession by more powerful ideological claims triggered by geopolitical dynamics.

Conclusion

In reviewing Jamaican politics thus far, I have emphasized how our political and cultural developments since the 1930s were shaped by institutional structures of the world system. Those relations were not only economic, but also cultural-political. I have balanced this attention to exogenous forces by showing that grand structuration of a national society by world-level forces does not preclude the unfolding of unique local-level dynamics.

This nested process and dialectic is still unfolding. The movement away from the cultural and political orders associated with the Westphalian interstate system continues. At both the world level and the local Jamaican level, moral deregulation within national societies persists. This has happened in large part because of the ideological exhaustion of liberalism and the demise of its cultural sibling, Marxism and the communist system. The deregulation of capitalist markets and the weakening of the interstate system have brought with them the correlative deregulation of norms and values. Nihilism, incivility, mercenary activities, warlordism and "donmanship" are consistent with this unravelling.[11] These phenomena express, at the level of social consciousness and action, a loss of faith in liberalism and a rejection of the authority of the nation state.

Against this background, a new geoculture is emerging. Contrary to earlier formative scripts in which the liberal narrative of individual freedom and self-determination were triumphant, the new geoculture is informed by ideological dispersion and by the unrestrained supremacy of market values and a tendency for the commodification of everything. As national states withdraw from their previous legitimating functions, it should come as no surprise that the sense of social nakedness, and the nihilism it entails, has assumed massive proportions. The defensive popular response to these conditions in Jamaica, as elsewhere since the 1960s, is to dig defensive political and cultural trenches.

Here again the isomorphism in cultural structures across the Third World is unmistakable. In Jamaica and abroad this has meant the fissioning of social groups into parcelled, nearly hermetic, subnational units. The spawning of self-helping moral communities in Jamaica reflects a troubling pattern: deepened class division reinforced by spatial segregation; proliferation of criminal gangs and the expansion of the transnational family system; the depoliticization of the professional middle class and their flight from politics; and the decentralization of violence.

The present moment is defined by a stunning dispersion of power and violence. The older and formerly relevant categories of "democracy", "citizenship", "civility" and "self-determination" are not merely exhausted, they are becoming ontologically vacuous, and that's increasingly recognized by defecting populations. The source of this problem has less to do with primordially violent and lawless Jamaicans than with the fact that the norms and manners of Jamaican society have lost their material foundations.

A historical mutation of international society since 1968 has facilitated the transformation of both the interstate system and the geoculture of capitalism. Central to this mutation is the collapse of liberalism, Marxism and the communist system – core pillars that helped shape the edifice of the Westphalian system and its geoculture. At the world level, another species of cultural and moral compulsion is being imposed, particularly on states and peoples on the periphery of the global system. The relevant term for the new compulsion is *neoliberalism*. The search for the accumulation of capital on a world scale now pits neoliberal states of all varieties against deeply restive societies.

If the turn to self-help in the form of theft, smuggling, sexual economics, plunder of state resources and riotous rebellion is any guide, then it is clear that the remaining act in this drama will pertain to the following issues. What are the outer limits of tolerance in the world system for the many species of moral and political deregulation? What ideological justifications will be offered for setting new limits on the flow of capital and on uncivil forms of social action? And finally, how will the bearers of these disruptive social identities respond to the coming, inexorable effort to restore political and cultural order?

Notes

1. For a perceptive critique of the limits of economic globalization as a development strategy, see Rodrik (2001).
2. For perspectives that insist on this point, see Appadurai (1996) and Nettleford (1993). Harvard political scientist Samuel Huntington (1997) has rejected these authors' soft multicultural perspective in favour of hard-bitten, bunker-like claims for the cultural uniqueness of the West.
3. This conclusion seems consistent with Immanuel Wallerstein's pioneering world-systems approach, which leaves room for contingency, agency and national initiative in spite of structural constraints. I have been

influenced by this sophisticated version of world-system theory, and this chapter draws heavily on Wallerstein's critique of liberalism (1995).
4. For a structural perspective on the interstate system that has influenced this study but whose iron law of modular identities I do not accept, see Meyer et al. (1997).
5. *Proto-nations* refers to fanatical supporters of the two Jamaican political parties. These supporters' fervour is often so intense that their political behaviour and associated factionalism resemble the communal violence of ethno-national communities.
6. In Jamaican parlance, these terms refer to stylized charmer and romantic poses adopted by male suitors.
7. In Jamaican street parlance, *rudie* is the shortened version for *rude boy*, or rebellious youth. The *screwface* is typically someone who employs fearsome scowls to intimidate.
8. In Jamaican Rastafarian language, *to make sounds* is to affirm a black nationalist standpoint through music, intense dialogue and intersubjective communication.
9. This treaty, signed in 1648, ended the Thirty Years' War in Europe and established the architecture of international politics and the basis of the modern state system (see Kegley and Raymond 2002).
10. The rebellious young in the ghetto used this locution to warn their kin to avoid all forms of Jamaican party politics, to withdraw from it as a totally useless, bankrupt and corrupt activity.
11. The progressive breakdown of state authority in Jamaica since the 1970s abetted the advent of new patrons in the slums. Residents of poor communities, long inured to Italian gangster movies, appropriately referred to the new patrons as their "dons".

References

Appadurai, Arjun. 1996. *Modernity at Large: Cultural Dimensions of Globalization.* Minneapolis: University of Minnesota Press.

Barber, Benjamin R. 1996. *Jihad vs McWorld.* New York: Random House.

Brodber, Erna. 1997. "Re-engineering Blackspace". *Caribbean Quarterly* 43, nos. 1–2: 70–81.

Fanon, Frantz. 1967. *The Wretched of the Earth.* Translated by Constance Farrington. Harmondsworth, Engl.: Penguin.

Heredia, Blanca. 1997. "Prosper or Perish? Development in the Age of Global Capital". *Current History* 96: 383–88.

Huntington, Samuel. 1997. "The Many Faces of the Future". *Utne Reader*, no. 81 (May/June): 75–77, 102–3.

Kegley, Charles W., Jr, and Gregory A. Raymond. 2002. *Exorcising the Ghost of Westphalia: Building World Order in the New Millennium*. Upper Saddle River, NJ: Prentice Hall.

Meyer, John W., John Boli, George Thomas and Francisco O. Ramirez. 1997. "World Society and the Nation-State". *American Journal of Sociology* 103: 144–81.

Nettleford, Rex. 1993. *Inward Stretch, Outward Reach: A Voice from the Caribbean*. London: Macmillan.

Rodrik, Dani. 2001. "Trading in Illusions". *Foreign Policy*, no. 123 (March/April): 54–62.

Wallerstein, Immanuel. 1995. *After Liberalism*. New York: New Press.

[10]

The Frontline
Valentino, Pablo Moses and Caribbean Organic Philosophy in the 1970s

Brian Meeks

Do you know?
Social Living is the Best
 – Burning Spear

Three Stories

Three events from the early 1980s serve as an introduction to the purposes of this chapter.[1] The first relates to a close colleague and friend, Barrington Chevannes, now dean of the Faculty of Social Sciences at the University of the West Indies, Mona, then a member of the Central Committee of the Workers' Party of Jamaica (WPJ). Barry had delivered a paper at the Caribbean Conference of Intellectual Workers, held with much fanfare in revolutionary Grenada in 1982, on revolutionary music in Jamaica. To the great consternation and dissatisfaction of the audience, he spoke about the contribution of the small and relatively obscure musical trends that were emerging around the Jamaican Marxist Left, including his own compositions, with very little if any reference to the broader field of reggae music, which, even as he spoke, was blazing a trail across the world's stage. For this elision, he received the opprobrium of many in the gathering, who considered his approach to be contemptuous of those forms that were genuinely popular. The irony is that among the leadership of the WPJ, Barry was one of the few who really had a handle on the nature and character of the consolidating popular music, on which, if it had been his intention, he could have elaborated in great detail.

The second and third events are related. The second event was the effect of Bob Marley's funeral on Jamaican politics in 1981. At a time when Edward Seaga's pro-Reagan Jamaica Labour Party (JLP) had just triumphed, when "deliverance" from radicalism had yet to lose its gloss, when consumerism, America and the greenback ruled supreme, when Michael Manley's People's National Party (PNP) and the broader organized Left had been cowed, the massive turnout and enthusiasm for Marley's funeral reminded all that there was another and perhaps a more profound social movement on which the politics of the 1970s had built its foundation.

The third event was my own perceived response of some leaders of the WPJ after the funeral. I had written an article for *Struggle,* the WPJ newspaper, essentially arguing that the size and enthusiasm of the crowd of "mourners" represented an important watershed, a symbolic reassertion of a popular ethos under the banner of Rastafari and an indication that the progressive forces had not simply dissipated after the recent electoral defeat. For this, a top member of the Political Bureau of the party roundly attacked me at the weekly study group meeting for overemphasizing the event. After all, I was told, we had to make a distinction between the struggle of the proletariat, led by the vanguard party, and petit bourgeois manifestations of populism, as this clearly was. Truly humbled by this display of superior ideological prowess, I never wrote for *Struggle* again.

What these three events reflect in the Jamaican context was the half-hidden, intermittent, yet barely recorded struggle for the hegemony of ideas in the radical Caribbean movement of the 1970s. Crudely put, while the resilience of the Caribbean revolutionary movement was largely due to an alliance between middle-strata intellectual tendencies and popular grassroots supporters, this alliance was fraught with contradictions. These contradictions surrounded questions of the appropriate philosophy that would guide these parties, the tactics to be applied to different phases of the popular struggle and, in some instances, which of these social tendencies should lead. Broadly generalizing, the intellectuals were Marxist, more often than not of the Marxist-Leninist variety, and they adopted the strategies and tactics of a certain Marxism-Leninism of the 1970s. Again, broadly generalizing, the popular grassroots supporters were not Marxist, even when on occasion they supported Leninist tactics, but had their own world view of African-centred revolutionism.[2]

It was the failure even to understand that such a world view existed, much less to comprehend its critical components, which contributed in no small measure to the demise of the once vibrant Caribbean Left of the 1970s. It is this failure that led Mervyn Alleyne, referring more specifically to the academic field, to write,

> studies of contemporary Jamaica have failed to come to grips with two fundamental aspects of Jamaican culture: its value system(s) (or ethos) and its worldview or cognitive orientations. But these are the aspects of culture that impinge most on political ideology and clash most with the culture and technology of modernization. (1998, 151)

It is this failure that Paget Henry, in his magisterial study *Caliban's Reason: Introducing Afro-Caribbean Philosophy*, is, in part, trying to correct, particularly when he asserts that "Afro-Caribbean philosophy needs to come to terms with the history of its own historicism" (2000, 59). It is the failure to theorize and to come to terms with the popular perspective that might help to explain the early alienation of the New Jewel Movement (NJM) in Grenada from grassroots Muslim and Rastafarian elements that had given initial critical support to the revolution (see, for instance, Patterson 1992 and Campbell 1988).

This sporadically documented event was, in turn, an early portent of the subsequent alienation of the entire party from the Grenadian people and the collapse of the revolution in 1983. It can help to explain, though there are obviously other causative factors, the failure of the WPJ, despite (or, on closer scrutiny, because of) its almost hegemonic hold over a generation of young intellectuals, to ever seriously accumulate popular support in Jamaica. The December 1978 *Programme: Workers' Party of Jamaica,* for instance, calls for a cultural revolution, including the ending of illiteracy, modernization of the education system and democratization of the media. There is barely a nodding recognition of the specific strengths of the popular culture that precedes the revolution and the potential of this culture as a fountainhead for popular organization and post-revolutionary reconstruction.

And it can, in an ironically contradictory fashion, help to explain the failure of the revolutionary movement in Trinidad after 1970, where the intellectuals around the National Joint Action Committee (NJAC), unlike in Grenada and Jamaica, readily adopted Afro-Trinidadian cultural forms but deprived them of revolutionary content. The result, in a peculiarly convoluted Trinidadian way, was that NJAC lost its sting and evolved into a sort of cultural fraternity (Meeks 1978). The reaction to this cultural turn was that grassroots revolutionaries grouped around the National United Freedom Fighters (NUFF) sought to be Marxist, though with strong Africanist overtones and an uncompromising grassroots militancy, in order to distance themselves from the perceived elitist culturalism of the middle-class revolutionaries in NJAC (Meeks 2000). The resulting guerrilla movement ended in a debacle in the mid-1970s, as Trinidad and Tobago segued into the early phases of its long oil boom.

Two Interventions

Radical Caribbean social and political theorizing, particularly around the upsurge and collapse of the popular movement of the 1970s, has evolved in two distinct waves. The first, operating within the confines of Caribbean historicist traditions, sought to find essentially institutionalist, geopolitical or narrowly ideological explanations. Thus, to take the best-known instance, the extensive work surrounding the collapse of the Grenadian revolution, while necessarily varied in analysis and conclusion, is largely concerned with the role of parties, the CIA, the Cubans or narrowly defined ideological issues.[3] Though it is not altogether absent, there is very little on deeper questions of philosophy, of episteme – in other words, of world view.[4] A second wave, influenced by, or in opposition to, what Henry calls "the linguistic turn",[5] is far more sensitive to these matters.

Two recent and important contributions reflect this new thinking. Henry's *Caliban's Reason* searches for an underlying ethos to Caribbean thinking. Critically scanning a variety of Caribbean theorists – from James to Fanon, Wilson Harris to Sylvia Wynter and others, including Jürgen Habermas, a number of Afro-American philosophers and Caribbean Marxists – he concludes that this ethos is to be found in a veiled Afro-Caribbean philosophy. The fundamental weakness in Caribbean "historicist" thinking – the term Henry uses to refer broadly to historians, social scientists and the like – is that it has failed to include in its focus matters of the self, of "ego-genesis" and ego-maintenance. The Afro-Caribbean self is differently constructed from the European self, he posits. It is deeply influenced by African mythopoetic traditions which advance the immanent and transcendent relationship of the spiritual to the material worlds (Henry 2000, 184–94). This has profound implications for how humanity is perceived in relation to nature and, importantly, for notions of community, which trump the mythical, liberal construction of the unencumbered individual.

By placing psycho-existential matters on the agenda for legitimate Caribbean social theorizing, Henry has opened up an entire field. Future analyses of the Grenada crisis, for instance, can no longer ignore hypothesizing on the character of the Grenadian ego, its autonomous intervention and its role as contributing element in the tragedy. Important, too, is that Henry maintains a space in his ideational framework for Marxist "political economy" and its respective categories, though the exact modalities of how, from the perspective of critical analysis, they operate within and around his notions of ego-genesis are not sufficiently elaborated.

The most serious weakness, however, in an otherwise stimulating presentation is that Henry focuses too much on the ideas of the traditional intellectuals. Despite a promising start, in which he locates African philosophy as arising out of popular traditions, he then, in the Caribbean centre of his study, largely elides discussion of popular philosophic forms. His only sustained discussion in this sphere – around Rastafari – ends up being less nuanced than his textured critiques of the "formal" intellectuals. Thus, for instance, while Henry considers Rastafarianism to be a "powerful and legitimating force for black identities" (2000, 213), he argues unconvincingly that "Rastafarian historicism leaves the social and developmental problems of Jamaican society largely unaddressed" (pp. 212–13). This, as I have argued elsewhere (Meeks 2002), fails to appreciate the extent to which Rastafarian notions of "livity" speak to an alternative relationship of individual to community, of community to environment and of humanity to commodity, countering, in significant respects, Western individualism and materialism. Henry's failure to seriously engage Rastafarian philosophy reveals a critical weakness in an otherwise insightful study with broad theoretical implications.[6]

The other perspective I wish to focus on is that of David Scott. In *Refashioning Futures: Criticism after Postcoloniality* (1999), Scott engages in an equally, if not more, ambitious attempt to redefine the parameters for radical thinking and (presumably) action in the contemporary world. Using his Sri Lankan and Jamaican roots and experiences as points of departure, Scott develops his perspective through a series of elegantly argued theses. First, he argues that the old narrative of revolution, associated with the myth of rapid social upheaval and cataclysmic change, if it ever had any real meaning, is now largely empty of content. This is a result of both geopolitical shifts that have transformed the terms of reference of that narrative and of new criticism that has undermined its philosophical assumptions. In his words, "Many of the epistemological assumptions that held [that narrative] together and guaranteed the salience of its emancipatory hopes – assumptions about history, about culture, politics, resistance, freedom, subjectivity – have been steadily eroded by the labor of antimetaphysical and antiteleological strategies of criticism" (Scott 1999, 198–99).

Second, Scott argues that in the world that is emerging, the old dominant, hegemonic ruling alliances are collapsing and space is opening up for autonomous popular movements and strata to flourish and engage in their own self expression and "self fashioning" (1999, 213). Third, he argues that this New World requires new thinking. Scott codifies and encapsulates his approach in what he sees as a folding together of Frantz Fanon and Michel Foucault.[7] By this, he means a borrowing and incorporation of Foucault's concern with power over the self and autonomy from overarching notions of domination, whether they be statal in origin or incorporated within the framework of societal norms.

Scott, however, is sensitive to the nihilist dangers inherent in a certain interpretation of Foucault, in which there can be no emancipation as all emancipatory projects ultimately end up reasserting dominance through power. The answer, then, is to preserve a space for Fanon, who in *The Wretched of the Earth* epitomized the notion of anti-colonial revolution. It is a Fanon, however, from whom the state and the nation have been expunged. Instead, the notion of liberation is preserved towards the goal of establishing vaguely defined communities of "self fashioned peoples", or, as Scott describes it in his analysis of contemporary Jamaica,

> This will enable me to think of political society in Jamaica not as a domain centered on the state and the competition for its offices, but as a field of interdependent pluralities governed simultaneously by a desire for settled identities and by an unsettling genealogical ethic of pluralization. . . . On the one hand, I want to imagine spheres or constellations of discursive and performative activity which would be semi-autonomous and self governing in relation to each other, and in which embodied subjects – that is, not merely rights-bearing subjects, but subjects embodying lived traditions – would be able so to speak, to stand forth and represent themselves in their own languages, stories, images and so on. On the other hand, I imagine that while these spheres would presuppose something held in common, they would not be presumed to be internally homogenous. (1999, 217)

Scott is not so much concerned with Henry's "self" and its construction as he is with the sort of epistemological and political framework that will allow a variety of "selves" to flourish. I am sympathetic with this central dimension of his argument, particularly out of the experience of the many national liberation movements that have disappointed, by reimposing authoritarian structures on their presumably liberated citizenry. However, I suggest, Scott's analysis has important weaknesses that compromise its utility.

The first of these weaknesses is his opening argument that the world of the immediate past, of Fanon's *Wretched*, is dead and buried. The Soviet Union is gone, US hegemony has been asserted in international institutions in unprecedented ways and the prestige of what Scott describes as "social-democratic energies" (Scott 1999, 199) has faded. Scott uses this fairly self-evident information to argue that the oppositional language of the old Left is no longer effective and we therefore need to look beyond it, in the direction of his notion of refashioned futures. While it is certainly true that the old Left is moribund, I disagree with the perspective that says that its projects and strategies must, therefore, be largely abandoned. The fundamental issues around which the older narratives of resistance were constructed are still very much present. The relentless transformation and domination of the world by capital has not changed. The ideological forms through which that domination is assured have certainly been modified to suit the new situation, but its central features – Euro-American centrism, racism, liberal individualism and uncircumscribed materialism – are still remarkably intact. The recent moves by the US government to penalize Europe for protecting Caribbean banana exports in favour of Chiquita is not some novel postcolonial manoeuvre, but a classic, if prosaic, instance of imperial domination in the interest of maximizing profits (see, for example, Sandiford 2000).

Such a world requires not the abandonment of the old and tested forms of struggle, but appropriate revisions and modifications to suit the complex new situation. By this, I suggest that in a world still composed of (albeit weakened) nation states, the struggle against capital and hegemony will, inevitably, have to take a national struggle as one of its central forms. This is the level on which governments battle with the International Monetary Fund (IMF) and World Trade Organization (WTO) to undermine their domination and push for a new international economic order. Scott, in his analysis, then, seems to mistake conditions unfavourable to such a struggle for the absence of conditions altogether. The unprecedented local and international mobilization around the 1999 WTO conference in Seattle, including Internet mobilization and alliances between trade unions, environmental groups and nation states, is but a first indicator of the new forms of struggle for old objectives (see, for example, Gills 2000; Starr 2000). Scott, by too quickly conceding defeat, theoretically excludes the possibility of a new frontal, more global, yet still very national confrontation with capital, a struggle that is emerging even as I write.

My second worry is with Scott's conclusions, his autonomous, self-fashioned communities. How do we get to this point where we have free-floating, critical, autonomous communities of free subjects? What is the process that takes us out of the contemporary state and into this new context? Who mediates between the communities when there are the inevitable disputes over resources, space and conflicting rights to self-expression? Will any perspective be allowed to flourish in the new situation? Scott gives precedence in his analysis to communities of the poor, captured in his notion of the "ruud bwai"[8] as the epitome of autonomous, rebellious self-expression. But on what basis does he foreground the cultural assertiveness of the "ruud bwai" and the poor? What is it about the poor that makes them intrinsically interesting and worthy of theoretical precedence? Why not give equal weight, for instance, to the increasing tendencies among the upper middle classes to refashion themselves with "Jamerican" identities? And what is the place, if any, of communities with embedded racial hierarchies or gender biases? Will there be a body *über alles* to decide on which communities will be allowed to flourish and which will not? Will this body be called "the state"?

I ask these decidedly leading questions to suggest that while I am sympathetic to Scott's search for modes of liberation beyond the Fanonian "national", there seems to be no shortcut through which to avoid a frontal political confrontation with the old state in order to transform it into a popular institution that will then facilitate popular autonomous development. The question of mediation, of weighing between competing notions of the good, even of ruling certain collectively unacceptable forms of "the good" out of court, appears unavoidable short of the Marxian notion of a post-socialist revolution in human consciousness. The real possibility, then, seems to lie in the democratization of the state in such a way that it becomes a genuinely transparent tribune of the largest possible majority of the people and not the mechanism to ensconce the rule of a minority. This, clearly, is somewhat different from Scott's conclusions.

I want to suggest further that embedded in his foregrounding of the importance of "ruud bwai" is a continuing subterranean adherence to a narrative of resistance that invests the poor with a particular intrinsic importance. This investiture of the poor as subject of historic transformation itself operates within multiple narratives. One version, of course, is Christian, and there are numerous contemporary instances before and beyond liberation theology to support this. The other is Marxist, and I suspect that Scott, even as he distances himself from Marx, is still beholden to him in this regard.

The sum of my argument is that in searching for modes of autonomous self-fashioning beyond Fanonian "liberation", Marxist political economy and its central placement of the struggle against capital cannot be abandoned. What we certainly need to do, however, is rescue the baby from the bathwater. Much of that which is Eurocentric in Marx's narrative needs to be jettisoned. A certain story needs to go, one in which proletarians are forged in occidental factories, learn collectivity gradually, overcome "economism" and overthrow European capital "in the interests of" the poor, helpless, subjected masses in the rest of the world. Instead, we need to begin to write an alternative story, one in which Jamaicans and Sri Lankans, African Americans and Peruvians, through developing their own modes of living, their own cultures of resistance, form themselves and are simultaneously formed in the struggle to survive. These autonomous processes, with their own genealogies, give their own names to that struggle and in the course of this quite different notion of self-fashioning, in the battle against capital and for a better world, open up their own possibilities for a better future.

My own approach, then, is closer to Henry's, with a strong appreciation of his incorporation of the self and of African culture, though it is also sympathetic to Scott's (and Foucault's) assertion that power extends, and in turn must be curbed, beyond the barrel of the gun. It is closest, I would like to think, to Stuart Hall's approach in "The Problem of Ideology: Marxism without Guarantees". Here, and elsewhere in his extensive (and still evolving) oeuvre, Hall makes the case for an approach to historical analysis that appreciates the importance of the economic, not in the sense of absolute "determinacy", but

> in terms of setting of limits, the establishment of parameters, the defining of the space of operations, the concrete conditions of existence, the "givenness" of social practices, rather than in terms of the absolute predictability of particular outcomes. . . . The paradigm of perfectly closed, perfectly predictable systems of thought is religion or astrology, not science. (1996, 45)

Within these broad parameters, human subjects struggle to transform systems of domination with varying degrees of failure and success. The critical object of analysis, then, is to understand how the complex, human construction of egos, of ideas, of cultural forms and of leadership modalities operates within given, if constantly shifting, constraints to open or close the door to various possible futures. Or, as Hall (1996, 41) more succinctly puts it,

> This approach replaces the notion of fixed ideological meanings and class ascribed ideologies with the concept of ideological terrains of struggle and the task of ideological transformation. It is the general movement in this direction, away from an abstract general theory of ideology and towards the more concrete analysis of how, in particular historical situations, "ideas organise human masses, and create the terrain on which men move, acquire consciousness of their position, struggle, etc.".[9]

Following from this, the tasks of critical Caribbean historical analysis would include, first, an attempt to understand the (contingent) boundaries to political and social action set by a particular socio-economic and geopolitical moment and, second, an exploration of the ideological terrain, the contours of thinking that define it and how these help to determine unique social and political outcomes.

Antonio Gramsci's notion of the organic philosopher is, in this regard, particularly useful. In "The Study of Philosophy" (Gramsci 1971, 323–77), he makes the famous argument that all men are philosophers, but that this "spontaneous philosophy", captured in language itself, in "common sense" and in popular religion, is limited, disjointed and episodic. The thrust of Gramsci's argument is to understand the nature of "spontaneous philosophy" in order to push it in the direction of a "philosophy of praxis", that is, one that would understand the world in its "true" nature and act upon it to change it for the better. His innovation here – certainly from a Marxist perspective – is that he conceptualizes his philosophy of praxis as building on spontaneous philosophy and not simply trumping it; thus, the thoughts and activities of "ordinary" people are to be taken seriously. Of a series of four notes, which he uses to elaborate the argument, I choose Note Three to introduce my own addendum. In it, he argues that language is not simply a means of communication, but is philosophic, in that the words themselves contain a conception of the world and of culture. He goes on to say,

> Someone who only speaks dialect, or understands the standard language incompletely, necessarily has an intuition of the world which is more or less limited and provincial, which is fossilized and anachronistic in relation to the major currents of thought that dominate world history. His interests will be limited, more or less corporate or economistic, not universal. (Gramsci 1971, 325)

I both agree and disagree with this assertion. On the one hand, it is quite acceptable that there may be people who, through isolation, obscurity of language and disconnection from the mainstream of modernity, simply do not have a full and proper grasp of the world around them. Parochialism of thought and philosophy is therefore conceivable. On the other hand, all is not necessarily as it appears to be. Thus, "dialect speakers", or persons apparently on the fringes of modernity, may in fact be in its engine room, at its very heart. In this respect, their insights into and intuition of its true nature may transcend that of persons with a formal, even rigorous understanding of its mechanics. Further, the very dialect(ic) through which they grasp and name this modernity gives to the struggle against it a particular quality and character. Finally, this quality and character is never transcended by a moment of truth, a moment when philosophy of praxis merges with spontaneous philosophy; rather, the genealogical imprint of that dialect remains as a feature of that particular process of resistance, through defeat and victory and beyond any hypothetical transcendence of modernity.

If significantly greater weight is then to be placed on the speakers of dialect than Gramsci allows, we need to take seriously the perspectives of the organic philosophers – those who most intimately represent the popular perspectives – and critically locate their ideas in a particular time and place. The concluding part of this chapter seeks to broach some of these issues in relation to two significant Afro-Caribbean organic philosophers of the 1970s.

Two Singers

I use Valentino, the Trinidadian calypsonian, and Pablo Moses, the Jamaican reggae vocalist, two artists who came to prominence in the 1970s, as illustration.

Pablo Moses was born Pablita Henry about 1953 in Plowden, Manchester, in rural Jamaica. Apart from a two-year stint in New York, he spent most of his youth in the countryside before travelling to Kingston. In school in Jamaica's capital, he formed a vocal group, the Canaries, which sought to record in the burgeoning music industry in the 1960s, but they met with little success.[10] Moses gained some popularity in the mid-1970s, with his single "Grasshopper", followed by his classic album *Revolutionary Dream*. This is how the liner notes for Moses's album *Reggae Greats* describe his appearance on the reggae stage:

> In a crowded East London record shack on a steamy August afternoon in 1975, Spy chalked up his current singles chart. High in the Top 20 appeared a parable-like single with the abstruse title of "I Man a Grasshopper", the

singer a mysterious Pablo Moses. The off beat half-spoken, half-sung tale of a rum drinking ex-police officer who had informed on the herb-smoking singer, was delivered over a chugging rhythm, spliced with radical bursts of lead guitar. Produced for a mere hundred dollars, the mix bore all the hallmarks of Lee Perry's Black Ark Studio and the single was destined to elevate Pablo Moses to a near-myth status.

Anthony Emrold Phillip began singing calypsos as "The Lord Valentino" in Port of Spain in the 1960s.[11] His early compositions were in the traditional vein, with some social commentary, but largely in the celebratory mainstream. Under the influence of the Black Power movement and the 1970 revolution, Valentino deleted the traditional "Lord" in his title for the popular "Brother". In the early part of the new decade, he was dubbed "the People's Calypsonian" and became closely associated with the many popular concerts initiated by NJAC. As NJAC, however, became increasingly "culturalist", Valentino began to distance himself from the organization (see Regis 1999). In the late 1970s, he took up the cause of the Grenadian revolution, though, like many other calypsonians, he was deeply disturbed by its fratricidal destruction. Valentino, now a Rastafarian, remains committed in his most recent work to a radical restructuring of Trinidad and the Caribbean.

I choose Moses and Valentino for a number of disparate reasons. The first is my own fascination with the quality of their music and lyrics and the fact (itself worth exploring) that neither of them ever truly broke into the mainstream.[12] Neither Moses nor Valentino was a regular inhabitant of, in the first instance, the top one hundred, or, in the second, the annual Calypso King finals. The second reason, as shall be further elaborated, is the evident and striking similarity in their form and content, even though they operated within distinct Afro-Caribbean genres. The third reason is that they fit neatly into the Trinidad/Jamaica dichotomy, providing rich comparative material from two of the most distinct cultures within the Caribbean continuum. The last reason is my own assessment that in the consistency of their messages is to be found the cutting edge of popular philosophical resistance to neocolonialism in the early phase after independence. I use two broad categories to organize a preliminary look at their work: style and content.

Style

Moses and Valentino, operating independently and a thousand miles apart, possessed a common, almost indefinable style. I was impressed when, as a young student at the University of the West Indies, I first saw Valentino perform in the tent in 1971, some months after the Black Power revolution. How different he was from all the other calypsonians! He stood, laconically, in a corner of the stage as though he was not really there, or certainly was not the centre of attention. He was dressed in a sombre, all-black outfit; his hair was combed in a neat, not massive Afro; and he was wearing "peepers" – the tiny circular glasses then popular on the Port of Spain blocks. This contrasted dramatically with those who came before and those who followed him. They, for the most part, were clad in the traditionally gaudy, sequined garb and performed onstage in a typical physically ebullient manner.

A similar feeling was evoked when I first heard Pablo Moses sing "Blood Money" on a scratchy radio in 1975 and later when I saw him perform it. The cover of his first album, *Revolutionary Dream,* captures this mood, with Moses featured in mirrored dark glasses, obscuring all emotion yet twice reflecting reality. If there is a common phrase to capture both, then "cool and deadly" is as good as any. If, as Dick Hebdige (1997) suggests, style is a critical space in which scripts of resistance are written, then Valentino and Pablo Moses occupied the same style corner. The key elements included a certain quiet dreadness, exemplified in limited motion and an almost epic stillness of being, combined with the delivery of lyrics in a matter-of-fact way, yet possessing great profundity.

I make no attempt to understand the origins of this complex phenomenon. Certainly in the Jamaican case, there is a tradition of dreadness – of philosophical meditation, associated with ganja smoking and Rastafari – itself, perhaps, having a lineage into the African-derived authority of the griot.[13] Undoubtedly, though, there are also other, newer elements. Thus, anyone who ever saw the Valentino of the early 1970s perform would undoubtedly recognize the cool but deadly hero of the Spaghetti Western, arriving in town alone but with a Gatling gun concealed in the ubiquitous box he drags around with him. He seems harmless, if a bit eccentric; but when he is confronted with vicious and seemingly overwhelming force, the Gatling gun appears and the hero (coolly) opens the box, cranks it up and, inevitably, wins the day.[14] There is nothing novel in suggesting the Western as a template for popular cultures of various kinds (including the Jamaican rude boy culture of a decade earlier), but it is important to recognize it as a specific garb for a certain revolutionary discourse.

This question of style also segues into the matter of musical form. While it is true that the reggae music of the mid-1970s had slowed down to a walking beat,[15] Moses carries this to the extreme. It is very difficult to dance to "Blood Money", where the entire song appears to be at the wrong speed, like a 45-r.p.m. record being played at 33-r.p.m. A similar, though less extreme, slowing down is to be found in pieces by Valentino such as "Barking Dogs" (1973) and "Third World" (1972), though this might also be related to Valentino's tent style, where slowing down to listen to serious lyrics can trace its origins back to the early *sans humanite* tradition.[16] Thus, one simple explanation might indeed be that both Moses and Valentino want their lyrics to be heard.

There is also a certain common otherworldliness in the style of both artists. There is a casual offstage quality, quite different from, say, the strident assertiveness of a Peter Tosh or, in a Trinidadian vein, the musical effervescence of a Black Stalin. This quality of being there and at the same time being offstage, in the audience, is characteristic of both men.[17] It is as if to say, "If you're ready to hear what I have to say, here it is, but if you aren't, here it is anyway. Store it up for the time when you are ready."

Content

Moses and Valentino are on the frontline. They voice, perhaps more explicitly than any others of their generation, an autonomous, African-centred notion of revolution that operated around the parameters of the broader anti-imperialist and revolutionary movement of the 1970s, but never completely within it.[18] Thus, Valentino, perhaps more than Superior, Stalin or even Chalkdust, was the "People's Calypsonian", and Moses was the natural musical bridge between the more Rastafarian Marley and Burning Spear, on the one hand, and Mikey Smith, Joe Ruglass and Barry Chevannes, who were clearly identified with left-wing politics, on the other. Among the critical elements in their oeuvre are the assertion of Africa and Africans at the centre of

Caribbean life, a well-developed notion of revolution, and the assertion of an alternative notion of community.

The Assertion of Africa and Africans at the Centre of Caribbean Life

Both artists emphasize key themes surrounding the reclamation of an African identity and the struggle for African liberation. Both of them envisage a unity of the broader African diaspora. Moses carries this further by questioning whether it is feasible to effectively carry out a liberation process in the Caribbean alone, in what he derisively refers to as "this square of land".

Thus, Valentino's "Third World", from *Third World Messenger,* proclaims and reclaims the biblical prophecy that "Ethiopia shall rise again":

> I no longer see the African
> Primitive man with a spear in his hand
> But I see a civilized intelligent man
> Walking that proud land
> And I see like Ethiopia go rise again
> And in the Third World the African shall reign.
> (Constance 1996, 10–11)

The glaring contradiction here is that even as Valentino asserts a pride in being African, he simultaneously falls into the trap of the primitive/civilized dichotomy (see, for example, Henry 2000) by characterizing traditional African society as something backward, to be turned away from. Thus, to be intelligent is coupled with being civilized, with its inevitable baggage of being like a European.

A further problem lies in assertion of an African predominance in a Third World of numerous ethnic and racial groups and, even more so, in Trinidad, with a large Indian population and a history of ethnic contestation. It is appropriate to recall Scott's (1999) expressed concern with avoiding the essentializing of the native subject and allowing differences to flourish freely and equally. Yet the reclamation of an African identity, denied most vehemently in the postcolonial period for a neutral nationalism, is a constant, irrepressible theme that is sustained far beyond these two, through the entire list of leading reggae artistes and calypsonians.

Moses, hailing from Jamaica, with its overwhelmingly African-descended population and its correspondingly strident official denial of Africanness, presents his assertion within the oppositionist Rastafarian tradition, though with his own revolutionary spin. Thus, in "Revolutionary Dream", he is a freedom fighter in Africa, but just when he is about to kill "the head man", he is awakened from his "wonderful vision" (*Revolutionary Dream,* Shanachie 1992). In "We Should Be in Angola", he develops a theme not uncommon to reggae compositions of the era, where unnecessary tribal warfare in tiny, marginalized Jamaica is counterpoised to the need for a just war to free Africa from colonialism and racial hierarchies:

> Fighting here in Jamaica, it's a shame my brother
> Destroying our culture by killing one another
> Away from the gates of Africa
> Giving way to the intruder
>
> We should be in Angola, oh yes, my brothers
> We should be in Angola, oh yes, my sisters
>
> To drive away the intruders I say
> From the land of our forefathers I pray
> Instead of fighting ourselves here
> For the Arawak Indians piece of square.
> (*Revolutionary Dream,* Shanachie 1992)

And in "Give I fe I Name", Moses asserts the fairly well-trodden theme of reclaiming an African identity, but in a typically commonsense and humorous way, worth quoting at length:

> Take back you name and give I fe I name
> I and I don't want dis ya name
> Chinese name Chin and Chong
> Macintosh came from Scotland
> Indian name Rajah and Gavaskar
> I man sure Smith no come from Africa oh no!
> When I reach Ethiopia I feel embarrassed
> After telling I idrens I name is Morris
> Because the name I have is for a European
> Not the name of a black, black African.
> (*Revolutionary Dream,* Shanachie 1992)

Revolution as a Turning of Things Upside Down

A consistent theme from both artists is the well-developed notion of revolution. While there is little elaboration of what will happen post-insurrection, for both the process of revolution is inevitable, necessary and cleansing. Thus, to quote again from Valentino's "Third World", a calypso in the same vein as Moses' "Revolutionary Dream",

> Meditating in my house just the other day
> Is like I charge up myself and I trip away
> I travel whole day, I travel whole night,
> Where I went and what I saw
> To tell you is my delight
> Way over yonder I did behold
> Because in front of my eyes
> Was a brand new world
> But like a wheel the world turn around
> And all the people who was up they come right back down.
>
> (Constance 1996, 10–11)

This clarity on the possibility of a revolutionary outcome is equally demonstrated in Moses's classic "Blood Money". The youth have been held in thrall by the power of money, have taken up the gun and are involved in fratricidal war. But with a supreme will and the guidance of God (Jah), they shall overcome. It should be underlined here that in both instances, revolution is simultaneously secular and associated with the spiritual. One gets to understand its possibility through higher meditation ("charge up myself"), and the act of upheaval itself is both carried out by man and fulfilled by spiritual cataclysm:

> Oh there shall be lightning and thunder
> For the heathens who take advantage of sufferer
> To gain their vanity of power
> They shall reach their final hour
> They will be cut off forever.
>
> (*Revolutionary Dream,* Shanachie 1992)

Finally, in what is for me one of his most complete compositions for its sense of timing, satirical lyrics and plain good music, Valentino, in "Dis Place Nice", chants that Trinidad is nice – but for the rich. The sting in the tail, left for the last line of the chorus, is that out of all of this hypocrisy, revolution is on the way:

> They don't know their worth
> Like they haven't a sense of value
> They don't know their rights
> Even that they cannot argue
> Three quarters of a million people
> Cannot get up and do something 'bout the struggle
> But could plan for the next holiday
> To fete their lives away
> And forgetting that they own the soil
> Of which their fore-parents toil
> For the people who form the constitution laws
> For the oppressors and foreign investors
> Trinidad is nice, Trinidad is a paradise
> Amoco and Shell business did went swell
> On your oil them foreign parasites dwell
> Trinidad is nice, Trinidad is a paradise
> Yet the song I sing like if I hearing
> The chorus singing "God save the King"
> Trinidad is nice Trinidad is a paradise
> But the people getting ready for this revolution day
> Changes on the Way.
>
> (Constance 1996, 16)

In a feature common to both artists, the nature of these earth-shattering changes is never really made clear.

The Naming of an Alternative Community of "Idrens"

The central feature in the work of both Valentino and Moses is the assertion of an alternative notion of community. This is not the Lockean commonwealth of self-seeking individuals bound together by minimal contractual ties, nor is it the socialist unity of shared proletarian class interests, though this inhabits some of Valentino's work. It is, rather, a shared community of African survivors who have, from bitter experience, forged their own notions of freedom, equality and justice. This accords with Alleyne's suggestion of an existent but besieged "collectivist ethos" that is at the heart of Jamaican culture. It is this collectivist approach that is at the fountainhead of the alternative community:

Jamaicans, especially rural Jamaicans, tend toward a collectivist or communalist view of society – here too they follow Africa. For example, in Jamaica the whole community considers itself responsible for children. . . . Adherents of this European world view believe that the unbridled exploitation of nature is the inalienable right of individuals; that individuals can claim as their boundless property and boundlessly profit from however much forest or farmland, or natural wealth they conquer and stake out. . . . To put it at its most abstract, traditional Jamaican collectivism is being confronted by European individualism. (Alleyne 1998, 158, 162)

The implicit purpose in the work of both artists is to excavate, rekindle and, where necessary, reinvent this community for the purpose of a spiritually uplifted and better world.

This is most subtly illustrated in Moses's remarkable piece "Grasshopper". On one level it is a song written in favour of the legalization of ganja. Taken on this plane, it does a better job than, say, Peter Tosh's forthright "Legalize It" because of its subtler, indirect method of attack. Thus Moses presents his argument on the ground of equality of treatment, the cornerstone of Western jurisprudence. Yet in the failure of the law to live up to its promise is revealed its hypocrisy. Beyond it, then, is the implicitly stated need for brotherly respect and for the building of a world in which there is genuine freedom, which demands a community with equality of treatment:

> That man saw I man eating I man Collie weed
> That man should never call Babylon to spoil I man irie feed
> I man don't want to cause any wrong
> I man only eating weed and thinking of love song
> To I man that man a fish da man deh love water
> I man I love collie weed I man a grasshopper
> That man love seed and fish bone
> I man love to keep high right in my soul.
> (*Revolutionary Dream*, Shanachie 1992)

This sense of brotherhood and community is even more explicit in Valentino's "Every Brother Is Not a Brother", where again the question of hypocrisy is used to argue for a greater community of brothers and sisters that must find its true self and come together:

> Don't call me your brother
> If you know you come out to gesture

> This case is a serious matter
> But it's not so with your behaviour
> The brotherhood to some doesn't mean a thing
> Daily this is what I'm experiencing
> If you don't check up on your foolish ways
> You will just dream about the better days
> You still backbiting, you not uniting
> And then you wishing one another the worst thing
> Your mental attitude towards each other
> Like you forget that we came from the same mother
> Vice-versa like a sister
> Every brother is not a brother.
> (Constance 1996, 18)

And in "Blood Money", Moses calls for the bredrens to end their days of wrath and to unite for the greater cause of the joint community of blood and spirit:

> So bredrens, Bredrens, wrath no more
> Let's inite in these troublous times
> Vank the moneymen vank the oppressor
> Let jah spirit give guidance iternally
> Let the moneymen be the sufferer
> Then man I grow with like a brother
> Will never shoot I for them nor them
> Blood Money, Blood Donesa
> I and I don't want them Blood money
> Blood donesa.[19]
> (*Revolutionary Dream*, Shanachie 1992)

This notion of community is a common, yet strangely underemphasized theme in analyses of mid-late 1970s reggae. Burning Spear's "Social Living" (*Reggae Greats: Burning Spear*, Mango Records 1994), for example, used in the epigraph of this chapter, cleverly counterpoises "Social Living" as a third option to capitalism and socialism, as he chants that it is the "best". This sense of a collective task of survival is also present in the Congos' equally iconic 1977 release "Row Fisherman Row" (*Congos*, Blood and Fire 1996). Myton, the lead, calls on the mythical fisherman (fishers of men?) to bring in his catch, for there are many hungry children to feed:

Row Fisherman row, keep on rowing your boat.
Row fisherman row
Lots of hungry belly pickney deh a shore.

One Conclusion?

The preliminary conclusion here is, somewhat disingenuously, that this is still very much a work in progress. Beyond this, however, its most important innovation is possibly the attempt to place in the foreground this notion of community. David Scott (1999), Tony Bogues (forthcoming) and others have sought to explore the concept of "dreadness" as a metaphor for the recognition of alternative cultural forms and communities. In some respects, however, the concept of dreadness can be seen as one-sided. It is more a stance of resistance to dominant narratives than a construction of alternatives. The notion of community, of "social living" as "the best", provides a somewhat different space for exploration. Having asserted this, it should be noted that the title of the section above refers to a "community of Idrens" (brethrens), and purposively so. For while both Moses and Valentino reach for a revolutionary reconstruction of society, they operate within a certain paradigm of the revolutionary movement of the 1970s in which women were largely relegated to the margins. Thus, there are numerous references to "Idrens" and "bredrens", "I-man" and "brothers", and while "sisters" and "sistren" are occasionally tacked on, it is more often as as afterword, if not an afterthought. The movement of the 1970s, whether defined from the intellectual middle or from below, was led by men and reflected, in great measure, their interests. Any critical reappraisal of a popular philosophy from below must, therefore, also critique its glaring lacunae and weaknesses.

It must also be underlined that while Valentino, with his sense of African-Indian unity, inspired by the slogan of the 1970 Black Power revolution, was certainly not the most guilty, the assertion of Africanness in the peculiar topology of Trinidad was always fraught with the possibility of the exclusion or relegation to the margins of Indo-Trinidadians and required a subtlety of exposition often missing in the popular discourse. Finally, it should be restated in parting that while organic philosophers sharply identified the need for substantial change, little was elaborated beyond the broadest parameters of community, providing only the barest blueprints for disenchanted multitudes to imagine their visions of utopia.

Much more needs to be done in this project of exploration. Thus, I have mentioned but not elaborated on the underlying commonality of the spiritual that is, as Chevannes, Henry and others have argued, central to any understanding of world view. Other differences need to be further considered. For instance, the differences between the more overtly political Valentino, in his scathing attack against US President Reagan's Caribbean Basin Initiative, "The Basin Spring a Leak in the Caribbean", and the more metaphoric Moses of "Grasshopper" and "Where Am I" suggest real distinctions in the way organic philosophers address matters of politics in Trinidad and Jamaica, requiring further thought and analysis.

Yet as Valentino's and Moses's common construct of community suggests, the process of teasing out the peculiarities of the popular world view is never an abstract act of excavation. For it is on the real foundation of lived histories and traditions of resistance and not on a blank slate that future projects of social and political transformation will have to be constructed.

Notes

1. I use *frontline* in three senses: as the central field of engagement in a battle, as the lead group of singers in a chorus, and as a gathering place on Red Hills Road in Kingston, where cutting-edge reggae artists displayed their talents in the early 1990s.
2. I accept Barry Chevannes's (1994) notion of world view as a "substrate" of underlying ideas that influence and guide other more immediate practices and actions.
3. See, for instance, Gordon Lewis's otherwise excellent study *Grenada: The Jewel Despoiled* (1987).
4. Horace Campbell's study on Rastafari (1988) is a notable exception.
5. See Henry (2000). Henry is referring to the extent to which postmodernist and postcolonial notions of deconstruction and signification have become influential among Caribbean intellectuals in recent times. Among other important interventions are Holger Henke's attempt to understand the "nature" of the Caribbean (1997), Antonio Benítez Rojo's *The*

Repeating Island (1996) and Tony Bogues's new work on "dread history" (forthcoming).
6. For a sustained argument in support of this perspective, see Clinton Hutton and Nathaniel Samuel Murrell (1998).
7. This approach is further elaborated in response to a more recent phase of Jamaican politics; see David Scott (2000).
8. Rude boys were the 1960s predecessors to the contemporary heavily armed urban gangs with loose affiliations to the two major political parties (see also Scott 1999).
9. Hall is quoting Gramsci (1971).
10. See the liner notes for *Reggae Greats: Pablo Moses* (Mango Records, 162-539 790-2, 1984).
11. For the only attempt to gather his calypsos together, with some biographical treatment, see Constance (1996).
12. How we wish to describe "mainstream", though, might alter this conclusion. Moses's liner notes, for instance, suggest his iconic status if not his broad popularity, and at least one Web site has listed Valentino's "Life Is a Stage" as among the one hundred best calypsos of the twentieth century (see www.djtonytempo.com, accessed 23 October 2002).
13. Both David Scott (2000) and Tony Bogues (forthcoming) explore the nature and politics of dreadness.
14. This exact scene is utilized effectively in the cult movie classic *The Harder They Come*, when the hero attends the cinema for the first time in the city.
15. Gordon Rohlehr described an earlier slowing down, the transition from ska to "rock steady", as an "almost conscious attempt to cool the country down" (1992, 89). This is as good as any, though Rohlehr enigmatically leaves out the "by whom" and "for what".
16. Literally "without mercy", it refers to the early calypso tradition of singing against one's opponent in a verbal duel, the intention being to defeat the adversary by sheer superiority of rhetoric and allusion (see Rohlehr 1990).
17. Interestingly, biographies of the jazz giant Miles Davis and comments on the life of the Jamaican trombonist Don Drummond point to an almost identical relationship between artist and audience.
18. For earlier references to the respective references to Africa and black consciousness in calypso and reggae, see Boyce Davies (1985) and Brodber (1985).
19. *Donesa* is a typical mid-1970s Rastafarian play with words. Money is never enough; it is always finishing. Thus, it becomes "doney" and then evolves, through a more obscure process, into *donesa*.

References

Alleyne, Mervyn. 1998. *Africa: Roots of Jamaican Culture*. Chicago: Research Associates School Times Publications.

Benítez Rojo, Antonio. 1996. *The Repeating Island: The Caribbean and the Postmodern Perspective*. Durham, NC: Duke University Press.

Bogues, Tony. forthcoming. "Dread History". *Africana Heretics and Prophets: Radical Political Intellectuals*. London: Routledge.

Boyce Davies, Carole, 1985. "The Africa Theme in Trinidad Calypso". *Caribbean Quarterly* 31, no. 2: 67–86.

Brodber, Erna. 1985. "Black Consciousness and Popular Music in Jamaica in the 1960s and 1970s". *Caribbean Quarterly* 31, no. 2: 53–66.

Campbell, Horace. 1988. *Rasta and Resistance: From Marcus Garvey to Walter Rodney*. Lawrenceville, NJ: Africa World Press.

Chevannes, Barrington. 1994. "The Jamaican Worldview and Africa: Spirit as Power". Paper presented to the Monthly Graduate Seminar, Dept of Sociology and Social Work, University of the West Indies, Mona, Jamaica, April.

The Congos. 1996. *Congos*. Blood and Fire BAFCD 009.

Constance, Zeno Obi, ed. 1996. *Life Is a Stage: The Complete Calypsoes of Brother Valentino, Anthony Emrold Phillip, 1971–1996*. Port of Spain, Trinidad and Tobago: Pro Print.

Gills, Barry, ed. 2000. *Globalization and the Politics of Resistance*. London: Macmillan.

Gramsci, Antonio. 1971. *Selections from the Prison Notebooks of Antonio Gramsci*. Edited and translated by Quintin Hoare and Geoffrey Nowell Smith. London: Lawrence and Wishart.

Hall, Stuart. 1996. "The Problem of Ideology: Marxism without Guarantees". In *Stuart Hall: Critical Dialogues in Cultural Studies*, edited by David Morley and Kuan-Hsing Chen, 25–49. London: Routledge.

Hebdige, Dick. 1997. "Subculture: The Meaning of Style". In *The Subcultures Reader*, edited by Ken Gelder and Sarah Thornton, 130–48. London: Routledge.

Henke, Holger. 1997. "Towards an Ontology of Caribbean Existence". *Social Epistemology* 11, no. 1: 39–58.

Henry, Paget. 2000. *Caliban's Reason: Introducing Afro-Caribbean Philosophy*. London: Routledge.

Hutton, Clinton, and Nathaniel Samuel Murrell. 1998. "Rastas' Psychology of Blackness, Resistance and Somebodiness". In *Chanting Down Babylon: The Rastafari Reader*, edited by Nathaniel Murrell, William Spencer and Adrian McFarlane, 36–54. Kingston, Jamaica: Ian Randle.

Lewis, Gordon. 1987. *Grenada: The Jewel Despoiled*. Baltimore: Johns Hopkins University Press.
Meeks, Brian. 1978. "The Development of the 1970 Revolution in Trinidad and Tobago". MSc thesis, University of the West Indies, Mona.

———. 2000. "NUFF at the Cusp of an Idea: Grassroots Guerrillas and the Politics of the 1970s in Trinidad and Tobago". In Brian Meeks, *Narratives of Resistance: Jamaica, Trinidad, the Caribbean*, 48–74. Mona, Jamaica: University of the West Indies Press.

———. 2002. "Reasoning with Caliban's Reason". *Small Axe*, no. 11: 158–68.
Moses, Pablo. 1992. *Revolutionary Dream*. Shanachie 44016.
Patterson, Maurice. 1992. *Big Sky, Little Bullet: A Docu-Novel*. St George's, Grenada: Maurice Patterson.
Reggae Greats: Burning Spear. 1984. Mango Records 422-806 204-2.
Regis, Louis. 1999. *The Political Calypso: True Opposition in Trinidad and Tobago, 1962–1987*. Mona, Jamaica: University of the West Indies Press.
Rohlehr, Gordon. 1990. *Calypso and Society in Pre-Independence Trinidad*. Port of Spain, Trinidad: Gordon Rohlehr.

———. 1992. "Sounds and Pressure". In *My Strangled City and Other Essays*, edited by Gordon Rohlehr, 86–94. Port of Spain, Trinidad: Longman.
Sandiford, Wayne. 2000. *On the Brink of Decline: Bananas in the Windward Islands*. St George's, Grenada: Fedon.
Scott, David. 1999. *Refashioning Futures: Criticism after Postcoloniality*. Princeton: Princeton University Press.

———. 2000. "The Permanence of Pluralism". In *Without Guarantees: In Honour of Stuart Hall*, edited by Paul Gilroy, Lawrence Grossberg and Angela McRobbie, 282–301. London: Verso.
Starr, Amory. 2000. *Naming the Enemy: Anti-Corporate Social Movements Confront Globalization*. London: Zed Books.
Workers' Party of Jamaica (WPJ). 1978. *Programme: Workers' Party of Jamaica*. Kingston, Jamaica: WPJ.

[11]

Cuba
Civil Society within Socialism – And Its Limits

Bert Hoffmann

Introduction

In the 1990s Cuba experienced a unique debate about the role of civil society within the country's socialist system. While the dynamics after the revolution of 1959 led to a strong politicization of social relations and institutions in Cuba, the economic crisis and the far-reaching social transformations of the 1990s gave rise to an intensive discussion on the island about the necessity of finding more plurality in the expressions for an increasingly less homogeneous society. Leading Cuban scholars who introduced the concept of civil society into the debate argued that the concept should not only be used as an instrument for analysis but should be thought of as a socio-political project to renew Cuba's socialism, aiming at "the strengthening of Cuban civil society and its necessary autonomy within the framework of the revolutionary project of which it understands itself to be a part" (Azcuy 1995, 105).

This understanding contrasts sharply with the vision of some liberal authors who interpret the notion "civil society" almost by definition as an antithesis to Cuba's current political system. In a similar sense, the

US government has openly adopted the fostering of Cuba's civil society as a second track in its strategy to bring down the Castro government (see the Cuban Democracy Act of 1992, also known as the Torricelli Act). Against the backdrop of this political polarization, the intellectual civil society debate in Cuba remained "the reform that did not happen", receiving a devastating refusal by the Communist Party and state leadership.

The following chapter will sketch and analyse these conflicting views of the role of civil society in Cuba and their political implications. As a first step, however, it will focus on a factor central to this debate: the outright boom of so-called NGOs (non-governmental organizations) that Cuba experienced in the course of the 1990s and that led observers to ask whether these NGOs are "government puppets or seeds of civil society" (Gunn 1995). Using concrete examples, this chapter will attempt to characterize these organizations, thereby demonstrating the scope and ambivalence with which the term NGO is used in Cuba. By focusing on the question of the relative autonomy of these organizations, we can arrive at a schema that distinguishes four different types of NGOs in Cuba.

Non-Governmental Organizations in Cuba

Traditional NGOs

Following the triumph of the revolution in 1959 many social organizations that had existed before disappeared or evolved into organizations that identified with the process of the revolution and that accepted subordination under its political leadership. The exceptions to this development shall be termed here *traditional NGOs*.

Although many times not counted as non-governmental, probably the most prominent case is the Catholic Church. The socialist government was in open conflict with the church without actually reaching the point of outlawing it. The church lost its economic and political power, as well as much of its social position and influence; strict control by the state set narrow limits on its public activities. Nevertheless, the Catholic Church always kept a solid and legal organizational structure with a clear non-governmental character.

In the mid-1980s a gradual process of rapprochement in the relations between the church and the Cuban state commenced.[1] The Catholic hierarchy and the socialist government found a modus vivendi which in many ways resembled the concept of the "church within socialism" in the former East Germany. The church presents itself as an apolitical institution and assures the state that it will not use its structure and potential to mobilize political opposition; the state for its part guarantees the "normalization" of relations and spaces, albeit limited, for the religious and social concerns of the church.

Nevertheless, until today the relations are characterized by a constant contest over the degree of autonomy and the limits for free action of the church. Where the state has the monopoly of the media, such a minor public forum as a pastoral letter read out in the churches of the country can become an important means of mass communication. Only this can explain why a critical pastoral letter from the Cuban bishops in 1993 was able to trigger a high-level reaction by the state, which contested the letter in front-page editorials of the party organ *Granma*.

In recent times the relations between church and state have experienced a marked improvement. For the first time since the revolution an open-air mass was allowed in 1997, and the spectacular climax of this politics of peaceful "cohabitation" could be seen in the Pope's visit to Havana in 1998.

Besides the Catholic Church, there are other Christian confessions which, however, have less social influence, although some Protestant churches have experienced strong growth in recent years. Still, the real popular Cuban religion is the Afro-Cuban religion, commonly known as *santeria*.[2]

Some non-religious social organizations of the time before 1959 are also resurfacing, in particular the Masonic lodges, which in Cuba have a long tradition (which is connected positively to the liberation struggle) but after 1959 had gone practically underground.[3] Today the Masonic lodges are legally registered with the Ministry of Justice and officially count no fewer than 22,530 members organized in 324 lodges throughout the country (Gunn 1995, 8).[4]

New NGOs

The crisis of the 1990s not only revived old organizations, it also saw the evolution of a series of new organizations operating within a broad spectrum of cultural and ecological activities, or as academic associations or women's support organizations. These differed strongly in their structure and the extent of their formal organization. Because of the drastically reduced financial capacity of the state, the establishment of NGOs was also a mechanism to better secure international financial solidarity and aid. The term *NGO* was increasingly found in the official Cuban political discourse.

The operations of these "new NGOs" are torn between their striving for autonomy and the state's attempts to control them.[5] Thus, almost all of the NGOs that received official registration are led by people who are integrated into the intellectual or political establishment in Cuba and who have proven their loyalty to the political system (despite the discontent they may express with particular aspects). This personal loyalty in the leadership of these organizations is closely connected to an institutional loyalty to the respective political authorities to which the NGOs are officially assigned (for example, for groups in the cultural sphere, the Ministry of Culture).

As much as – given the term *non-governmental organizations* – it may sound like a paradox, these officially legalized and formalized "new NGOs" usually had a para-statal character. For example, the ecological NGO ProNaturaleza was founded primarily by leading bureaucrats and scientists in the Ministry of Science, Technology and Environment; it is primarily directed by them, and even has its offices in the building of the ministry itself. Given such closeness to the official state authorities, critical voices in Cuba have expanded anew the abbreviation *NGO* (in Spanish, *ONG*): not as "Organización no-gubernamental", but as "Organización *neo*-gubernamental".[6]

New organizations from the grassroots developed as well. However, to some extent these remained much less integrated into the political establishment, and at the same time much more informal and limited in their size. One example is the gay association GALEES (in English, the Action Network for the Free Choice of Sexual Orientation). This organization attracted attention by its unconventional public actions – for example, when in 1995 it participated in the May 1 parade unfolding a huge rainbow flag, the symbol of the gay movement, in front of the podium occupied by the state leadership. GALEES was never officially prohibited, but it was also never officially recognized; in the meantime it has de facto dissolved.

Thus, a part of the "new NGOs" started from the grassroots, while another, larger part was initiated from the top. However, in almost all the cases the approaches coexisted. Many of the state bureaucrats hoped to find greater freedom of action in the NGOs than they could in strictly public institutions. On the other hand, the grassroots interests are to some extent also led by material interests. With the devaluation of peso salaries and the withering of privileges which hitherto had come with employment in the public sector, internationally funded NGOs appeared to be very attractive job opportunities.

Probably the most prominent of these "new NGOs" was the Foundation Pablo Milanés, founded in 1993 by the famous Cuban singer of the same name. This NGO was born of the initiative of the musician himself, not that of the state authorities. Even long before its establishment, Milanés had used part of his foreign exchange income for the support of young Cuban artists and had thus become an individual who is colloquially termed "an institution". In a sense, therefore, the establishment of this foundation was initially a kind of formalization of an already existing praxis. However, it quickly outgrew these origins. Due to Milanés's international reputation and a growing number of different cultural projects, his foundation had impressive success in the acquisition of international development aid – probably more so than any other Cuban NGO.

At this point it has to be noted that Milanés is closely connected to the Cuban political establishment, including as a delegate to the National Assembly, the Cuban parliament. Therefore, Milanés was the guarantor for the "personal loyalty" of his NGO. Nevertheless, in 1995 the foundation and its institutional body of control, the Ministry of Culture, came to openly disagree. In an unusually sharp public protest, Milanés criticized the ministry in no uncertain terms, lamenting the constant violation and curtailment of the foundation's autonomy, which at no time had been able to work as it had been assured it could. Milanés himself then decided to close the foundation.

Although in this situation Milanés broke with the cultural authorities, he affirmed at the same time his unwavering support for the revolution and its political leadership. He also kept his seat in the National Assembly. Although this conflict obviously pointed to a structural problem of autonomy versus control, Milanés repeatedly characterized it as a purely personal problem with the then minister of culture Armando

Hart, whom he called "incompetent" and "ignorant". However, although the minister has in the meantime been dismissed, the Foundation Pablo Milanés has hitherto not been revived.

Relabelled NGOs

Not only were new organizations created as NGOs, but institutions and organizations the socialist state had created in the past decades were also repackaged as NGOs in the 1990s. This happened, for example, with professional associations such as the writers' association UNEAC, which posed as an NGO even though its president, Abel Prieto, was a member of the Politburo. Similarly, scientific centres that had been founded in the 1970s by decisions of the Communist Party's Central Committee increasingly operated as NGOs at the international level. Not least, the official "mass organizations"[7] in which nearly the entire Cuban people are organized began to call themselves NGOs. In the international sphere the presence of Cuban mass organizations as NGOs probably reached its climax with the participation of the women's organization FMC, led by Raúl Castro's wife, Vilma Espín, as an NGO at the United Nations Women's Summit in Beijing in 1995.

Obviously, these "relabelled NGOs" are affected more than the "new NGOs" described earlier by the critical characterization "*neo-governmental.*" Remarkably, though, it was precisely this sector which evoked the harshest reaction from the state and party leadership. We will take a closer look at this conflict later in this chapter. Before that, however, the fourth type of Cuban NGOs, which may be termed "dissident NGOs", shall be examined.

Dissident NGOs

In many analyses of Cuban civil society, dissident NGOs are not even mentioned; in others, their importance is hopelessly exaggerated. An unbiased analysis will first of all have to state that the number of people in Cuba who openly come forward as dissidents is very, very small; their organizations often consist of only a few members, and many are short-lived; the majority of the population is hardly aware of them. Nevertheless, there are dissident organizations, and under the conditions of a one-party state their political importance is without doubt higher than their social effect or embeddedness. The often harsh repression by the state is an indirect acknowledgement of this. (Cuba's general population often only learns about the existence of these groups or persons only in the course of Cuban state campaigns against them.)

Historically the anti-Castro opposition was primarily organized in "fronts", "parties" or "movements". In other words, they postured as the legitimate, albeit outlawed, political society, rather than as an expression of independent civil society. There were also groups who understood themselves as single-issue organizations, pursuing a specific goal, in particular human rights. In practice, however, this distinction remained mostly theoretical because the human rights groups were usually seen as an extension of the political opposition.[8]

In the 1990s, however, a number of dissident organizations were founded as spin-offs from professional organizations and other specific interests claiming to be authentic expressions of Cuban civil society. None of them has received legal status, although many of them have applied for it. Even though their membership is relatively small, their organizational existence is in direct competition with the respective official socialist unity organizations. The term "non-governmental organization" is not used by these dissident organizations because, paradoxically, its meaning has been tainted by the new and relabelled NGOs, now connoting undesirable closeness to the government. Instead, these groups identify as *independiente;* they are not seeking merely more autonomy within the system, but rather an independent existence outside of the system.

An example of such dissident professional organizations is the Unión Agramontista, which comprises lawyers and barristers (more precisely, persons who have an education or former employment as lawyers and barristers, because most individuals admitting membership in the Unión Agramontista are not allowed to practise any more).[9] Members of this organization are united by their dissatisfaction with their respective official organizations and the representation of the professional interests. In practice, however, these concerns are also related to a larger, particular agenda: Unión Agramontista is clearly advocating the establishment of the liberal democratic rule of law in Cuba, to replace the socialist legal system (personal interview, Leonel Morejón Almagro, 27 October 1995). Therefore it comes as no surprise that Unión Agramontista – like many other dissident professional organizations – became part of the Concilio Cubano, an attempt to establish an umbrella organization of all dissident groups. The Concilio Cubano was dissolved by the authorities in February 1996, and several of its leading members received prison sentences – among them Unión Agramontista's Leonel Morejón Almagro, who was sentenced to ten years in prison.

In recent times the independent journalists, in particular, have had a public effect in Cuba. Most of them are trained journalists who had worked with the official state media and who are now practising a clearly oppositional journalism. These independent journalists operate various press bureaus or agencies of varying quality and level of international presence. They transmit their articles and commentaries abroad by telephone (usually to the Cuban community in Miami), where they are published by the local media or on Web sites (see, for example, http://www.cubanet.org). Their readership is therefore almost completely limited to foreign nations because in Cuba private access to the Internet is highly restricted.

Civil Society in Cuba: Notes on Different Concepts and Their Consequences

Civil Society as Oppositional Political Society

Given this panorama of – depending on the observer's point of view – distinct types of NGOs in Cuba, not only does the question of whether the NGOs in Cuba are seeds of civil society arise, as Gillian Gunn (1995) puts it, but also this question: Which type of NGO is meant in each instance, and what concept of civil society is implied?

In the widely used liberal concept, *civil society* comprises the autonomous intermediary groups and organizations between the family, on the one hand, and the state and political society (parties, parliaments and so on), on the other hand, who articulate and organize specific group interests (see, for example, Fernández 1993). According to this definition, civil society in post-revolutionary socialist Cuba has been extraordinarily weak. At almost all levels of society, organizations were established which in the final instance were subordinated to the Communist Party. This is in line with the 1976 Constitution, which formalized the Communist Party's "leading role in state and society". In the logic of socialist law, any and all autonomy finds its limits at this point.

In the view of some observers, this means that only the dissident NGOs, which openly reject the "leading role of the party" (and, perhaps, traditional organizations of the time before the revolution, such as the Catholic Church or the Masonic lodges), can be subsumed under the term *civil society*. From this perspective, civil society is the antithesis of the socialist state. A variant of this conceptualization was formulated by Espinosa (1996, 25–28), when he contrasted the "official" or "patronized civil society" with the "real civil society" of the independent associations. With quite a similar intention, Puerta (1996) opposes authoritarian civil society to democratizing civil society.

The problem with this view is not particularly its criticism of official tutelage of the legal NGOs. Even if this is often argued in a strong ideological fashion, it really points to the central conflict within which these NGOs operate. A more important problem is the emphatic and uncritical superelevation of the dissident organizations, which stands in an odd contrast to these organizations' lack of social embeddedness. The reasons for this can be discussed – and, without doubt, state repression and a lack of means of communication play a critical role – but, nevertheless, for an analysis it has to be acknowledged that the openly active members of dissident groups in Cuba are to be estimated at probably less than five thousand within a total population of eleven million, and this simply does not go well with a concept that is supposed to speak of "the society".

Apart from openly expressed bias, a fundamental problem with this concept of civil society is its silence about the fact that even today the dissident NGOs continue to be – albeit in somewhat modified form – an oppositional political society, rather than an organic civic articulation of certain social interests within the wider society, even where they have constituted themselves as professional organizations. Instead of being sectoral interest groups, they have transfigured themselves into different forms of *Dasein* of the political opposition.

Given this situation, they fall victim – like almost everything in Cuban politics – to the old and persisting confrontation between the Cuban Revolution and the United States. Just as the hardliners in Washington and in the Cuban exile community are able to see all legal NGOs in Cuba only as "government puppets", so the hardliners in the

Cuban state apparatus seem to automatically regard all unofficial NGOs as "government puppets" of Washington. It is precisely the lack of possibility of independent interest representation in Cuba itself that turns this charge into a self-fulfilling prophecy. The situation of dissident journalists who are able to publish only through Miami is a case in point.

Against this background, Washington's Torricelli Act of 1992 has gained particular significance.[10] Besides tightening the embargo (which, in 1996, was tightened again by the Helms-Burton Act),[11] it established a new approach to US policy on Cuba: Track Two. With Track Two, the selective strengthening of "civil society" in Cuba became an official US policy designed to achieve a transition to liberal democracy and a market economy. Quite remarkably, the Torricelli Act demanded not only support for dissident groups in the island, but also a strengthening of contacts with the academic, media and cultural establishment within the system, that is, precisely those institutions which have here been characterized as new or relabelled NGOs. Subsequently, Track Two of the Torricelli Act became the main focus of criticism by the Cuban government of these NGOs, whose call for autonomy tended to be seen as collaboration with the enemy.

A concept of civil society which a priori defines it as political opposition to the system remains analytically unconvincing. Politically, it hardly promotes the domestic pluralization of Cuban society. On the contrary, it promotes a hardening of the existing political polarities, which has proven to be an efficient instrument for preventing a process of gradual socio-political reform.

Civil Society as a Project of Pluralist Renewal of Socialism

Despite the strong instrumentalization of the concepts "NGO" and "civil society" in the political and academic discourse in the United States, the term "civil society" also became a focus – albeit with quite different emphases – of academic debate in Cuba during the 1990s. In a first step, "civil society" was rehabilitated as a useful analytic term for the description of Cuban reality; in a second step, "civil society" became a conceptual frame for the project of a pluralist renewal of socialist society from inside. The protagonists of this debate were trying, as Azcuy writes, to "re-invent" Cuban socialism, not to abolish it (1996, 108). The development and discussion of such a "Project Civil Society" in the framework of the "real existing socialism" was not only a new discussion for Cuba, but also an international first.

An article by Rafael Hernández, a researcher at the Center for American Studies (CEA) in Havana, initiated this debate in 1994. In this article, he argued for "the necessity and usefulness [of applying] the concept (i.e., civil society) to the analysis of current problems in Cuba" (1994, 30; my translation). Even at this early point, the resistance to such an approach became evident. The article was published in a journal of the writers' association, prefaced by a letter to the editor in which a member of the association reprimanded Hernández for his "imprecise" use of the term "civil society", despite the term's identification with the anti-communist and counter-revolutionary strategy of the US governmen (Pérez 1994, 28). By way of reply, Hernández quotes in his article Hegel, Marx and Gramsci as authorities against all interpretations claiming an insoluble contradiction between civil society and the socialist state. Rather, both civil society and the socialist state are "organic segments of the socialist system", which are interconnected and mutually reinforcing (Hernández 1994, 31; my translation). Moreover, as Hernández argues, the distinction between civil society and the state is of great practical importance for Cuba because "the dynamics of civil society have been overshadowed by a strong politicization of social relations and institutions in Cuba" (p. 30; my translation). Thus, Hernández provides the guidepost for the ensuing debate: the reclamation of the social sphere indicates an always relative autonomy from the state.

The background of this argument is the deep economic crisis in Cuba since the demise of its socialist allies overseas in 1989–90 – and its concomitant structural consequences for Cuban society, from massive underemployment to dollarization or the introduction of markets. While the official discourse had hitherto admitted only an economic crisis, which it bracketed as "special period during peace time" while denying a social or even political crisis, Hernández argues that

> the problems the Cuban society is facing cannot be contained within the limits of an economic analysis. Both the causes and the consequences of the crisis transcend this dimension. However, even within this narrow framework

it is obvious that "the realm of economic relations" in Cuba has changed. ... It now comprises phenomena such as the informal economy, which is characterized by the growth of independent work and the black market, as well as the rise of new forms of labour in the mixed sector of the new, markedly differentiated, economy. (1994, 30; my translation)[12]

The concept of civil society suggested by Hernández is not only (or even just primarily) a response to the above-described growth of NGOs, but rather a response to the increasing differentiation of Cuban society following the economic crisis. For example, with regard to the revival of religious communities Hernández emphasizes that "the most important religions of African origin ... comprise at the level of civil society a net of social relations and mobilization that is of greater importance than the Catholic Church" (1996, 92; my translation), even if it is usually not institutionalized in formal organizations.[13]

Such a conceptualization of civil society bears remarkable similarities to some international studies about Cuba's rethinking of this notion. Thus Damián J. Fernández writes,

> The notion of civil society, with its liberal democratic roots, presents conceptual difficulties when applied to one party socialist states. Can one talk of civil society at all in such a context? The answer is a qualified yes, if we expand the definition of civil society in two ways. The first way to expand the definition of civil society is to include civil social groups *within* the state. ... Second, the value of civil society as a concept would be greater in the context of communist states if one includes grassroots informal resistance to state authority. (1993, 99)

One would have to add that for an analytically more open approach, "informal resistance" would certainly have to be replaced by "informal behaviour", because not only resistance but also mechanisms of supportive or indifferent behaviour have explanatory value.

A number of analyses focus on the first expansion of the concept mentioned by Fernández and elaborate on the ambivalent character of official organizations and institutions. The second expansion has probably been argued for most convincingly by Susan Eva Eckstein in her plea for dedicating more attention to the role of ordinary people in the social research about socialist societies (1994, xii).[14] Thus, Eckstein, explicitly using the term "civil society", analyses the everyday activities and social nets of "ordinary people" who indirectly, but persistently, have influenced official policy. From this perspective, the NGOs are not the civil society but only its formalized elements.

Regarding the discussion in Cuba itself, several contributions elaborating Hernández's argument followed his 1994 article. Hugo Azcuy, one of Hernández's colleagues the Center for American Studies, wrote about the "necessity of more plural *expressions* in Cuban society", for which the concept of civil society "should not be used only as an instrument for analysis, but also as the *project*" (1995, 105; my translation). This "Project Civil Society" became, explicitly or implicitly, a sort of common denominator of the reform discourse in the Cuban social sciences of the 1990s. As its basis, Azcuy posits the "the strengthening of Cuban civil society and its necessary autonomy within the framework of the revolutionary project of which it understands itself to be a part" (1995, 108; my translation).

In the past, as Azcuy puts it, "paternalism and the – direct or indirect – vertical control by the state dominated Cuban civil society – a consequence of the overextension of the political" (1995; my translation). Now the demands not only were for more freedom of action for civil society, but constituted virtually the reversal of its relation to the state. As Hernández puts it,

> As the sphere in which the tensions and conflicts facing the state are enacted, it is in the interest of and the responsibility of the state to search within civil society for new forms of legitimacy and arenas of consensus. . . . Without the consensus of civil society, not only will the legitimacy of the government suffer damage, but also the stability of the system itself. (1996, 88; my translation)

Some critics have noted correctly that these ideas and demands did not arise from a broad debate within Cuban society itself, but, in this form, have been confined to a relatively small group of intellectuals. Nevertheless, the sum total of this discursive process has to be regarded as a publicly voiced project of socio-political reform towards a more pluralist form of socialism, which can find only very few comparisons in the history of socialist states.[15]

Civil Society as an Instrument of the Enemy

However, this "Project Civil Society" is a reform that never happened. A so-called Report by the Politburo ("Informe del Burú Político"), which Raúl Castro, Fidel's brother and the head of the Cuban army, read at the Fifth Plenum of the CP Central Committee (Castro 1996), put an end to the debate. This "Report by the Politburo" put the topic and notion of "civil society" at the centre of its rebuttal against the "ideological subversion" to which the academic centres of study in Cuba had presumably fallen victim. The charges were put into the harshest possible words: "diversionism", "lowered the flag of socialism", "annexationist orientation", "the fifth column of the enemy" (Castro 1996, 6 ff.; my translations). No names were mentioned, but "the bitter experience with the Center for American Studies" was explicitly referred to as a particularly severe case – and with the articles by Azcuy, Hernández, Dilla and Juan Valdés Paz, as well as by the economists Carranza and Monreal, the CEA had been the centre of the Cuban debate about reforms.[16] Consequently, the "Report by the Politburo", in its stern tone, marked the unequivocal rejection of such an opening of the political system or of the climate for intellectual debate (see Hoffmann 1997).

It is interesting to see what twists the notion "civil society" took in this debate. Before Raúl Castro's speech, a devastating opinion article had been published in *Granma*, the official newspaper of the Cuban Communist Party. In this article, Raúl Valdés Vivó, the director of the party's academy, frontally attacked the term "civil society" as an instrument of US policy's Track Two and as a "new tactic of the enemy". Already at this point the Cuban scientists using the term are condemned as a "fifth column in their own country". In support of his argument, the director of the party's academy contrasted the notion "civil society" with another, new term: Cuba could accommodate only a "cohesive society" ("la Sociedad Cohesionada") (Valdés, 1996, 3; my translations).

However, while Raúl Castro's "Report by the Politburo" cites entire passages of this opinion article, it does not use the newly created term "cohesive society". Instead it contrasts the critiqued notion "civil society" with the concept of "socialist civil society" ("sociedad civil socialista"), which "consists of our powerful mass organizations" supported by the official professional associations and "other NGOs working within the legal framework" (Castro 1996, 7; my translations).

These remarkable semantic stretches throw light on the ideological constructions which have – even in the official discourse of the socialist government – become diffuse. This confusion reached its (inadvertently) comic climax with an article by the former minister of culture Armando Hart entitled "Civil Society and Non-Governmental Organizations" ("Sociedad civil y Organizaciones No Gubernamentales"), published in the party's newspaper, *Granma*. Following the "Report by the Politburo", it argues, "Thus, in the medium and long term we can strive to replace civil society by the socialist society, but this is a distant objective" (Hart 1996, 3; my translation). Here, the veteran minister declared in passing that what had for three and a half decades been called the socialist society now obviously no longer was to be regarded as such.[17] The term *NGO*, although used at times in the official discourse (and even, as we have seen, in the "Report by the Politburo"), is still disliked. A *Granma* article of 13 April 2001 explains, "Cuba's juridical norm does not use the term Non-Governmental Organization because it is a characterization by exclusion, and, in addition, it is ambivalent and reminiscent of political content. Instead, the term 'associations' is used, because it is conceptually wider and, thus, includes the NGOs" (Luis 2001, 3; my translation).

Conclusion

The semantic conflict over the notion of "civil society" is symptomatic of the persisting limits imposed on the autonomy of NGOs or the project of a pluralist reform of Cuban socialism. However, within the academic discourse the concept "civil society" still is being discussed, albeit in somewhat more cautious ways (see, for example, Hernández 1997). Nevertheless, the emphatic rejection by the state prevents this concept from assuming the character of a possible project of socio-political renewal. The situation of the Cuban NGOs also remains ambivalent. On the one hand, the "Report by the Politburo" has levelled a broad indictment against them because, supposedly, "this Trojan Horse intends to promote the division and subversion of the country" (Castro 1996, 7; my translation); on the other hand, it is precisely this report which also confirmed the legitimacy of Cuban NGOs, provided they "work within the legal framework" (p. 7).

Today, many of the "new NGOs" are working in their respective fields within the limits outlined by the authorities and without greater political conflicts. Many "relabelled NGOs" have switched into reverse: the "mass organizations" are once again expected to carry that name and no other, and it has been made clear that they hold a higher position in the socialist value hierarchy than the "non-governmental organizations". In other cases, such as the academic centres, it has been publicly emphasized that they are not NGOs but institutions founded by directives of the Communist Party's Central Committee, and that they continue to be subordinated to it.

The ideological rollback begun by the "Report by the Politburo" ignores (or at least pretends to ignore) Cuba's social crisis rather than offering an alternative or answer to it. The documents prepared for the October 1997 Congress of the Communist Party confirm this attitude. Many pages simply give a narrative of Cuban history in order to deduce from this the legitimacy of the revolution and of the current political system is then deduced. In contrast, there are only a few words about the economic, social and political challenges of the present or about future prospects.

As the Cuban economic and social model of socialism continues to be exposed to massive transformations, it is precisely the non-transformation of the political superstructure which will contribute to the growing chasm between the political system and Cuban society. This is a crucial point, because one of the strengths of the Cuban socialist system (distinguishing it from "real existing socialism" in the East European countries) was the relatively high level of authentic popular support it enjoyed for a long time.

The project of "Civil Society within Socialism" that was pursued by reform-minded intellectuals on the island was an attempt to find an answer for the social changes of the 1990s. The need for an opening of social spaces with greater autonomy has not diminished since the debate was initiated. If Cuba's state leadership insists on allowing such valves for an expression of the social crisis only within very narrow limits, it may succeed in leaving the political structures unchanged for a considerable period. The price, however, would be the growing erosion of its own social legitimacy – a high price for the Cuban Revolution and with uncertain consequences in the long run.

Notes

1. See Malone (1996). For a compilation of key church documents from 1914 to 1994, see Obra Nacional de la Buena Prensa (1995).
2. For a more comprehensive discussion of the different Afro-Cuban religions and their contemporary social resonance, see the focus on religion in issue 4 of the Cuban social science journal *Temas*.
3. The Masonic lodges were abandoned in 1895 by colonial Spain because many of their members participated in the struggle for Cuban independence. After 1959 the lodges were not entirely prohibited, but they continued to exist on a low-intensity basis and almost completely unnoticed by the public; for example, they operated a retirement home in Havana (even partially supported with money from the Cuban state).
4. As a matter of principle the lodges do not admit women, except to a separate lodge, Las Hijas de la Acacia, which currently has one thousand members.
5. How fluid the limits within this typology can be can be seen in the Asociación Cultural Yoruba de Cuba, which, organized as a "new NGO", remains an institutional expression of the traditional cultural and religious community associated with *santeria*.
6. In all fairness, this is not an invention of Cuban socialism alone but can be found in different forms in many countries of the "Third World". In the jargon of the international development community, the ironic term GONGO (government-organized non-governmental organization) has been coined for this phenomenon (see Koschützke 1994, 39).
7. This includes the Unity Trade Union (CTC), the Committees for the Defence of the Revolution (CDR), the small farmers' association ANAP, the women's organization FMC, the students' organization FEU, the pupils' organization FEEM and, for the youngest, the Young Pioneers.
8. The example of the internationally best-known Cuban dissident, Elizardo Sanchéz, is instructive. He is at the same time the highest representative of the Cuban Commission for Human Rights and National Reconciliation and of the political organization the Cuban Democratic Socialist Movement.
9. Another example is the so-called Cuban Institute of Independent Economists (Instituto Cubano de Economistas Independientes, ICEI); for

publications by ICEI members, see, for example, Herrero (1996) and Lauzurique (1996).
10. Named after its author in the US Congress, Robert Torricelli; the law is officially the Cuban Democracy Act.
11. Named after its authors, Senator Jesse Helms and Representative Dan Burton; the law's official name is the Cuban Liberty and Democratic Solidarity (LIBERTAD) Act of 1996.
12. Following this, Hernández drafts a perhaps somewhat surprising agenda for the study of the contemporary social development of Cuba. However, in a country in which the faculties of sociology and political science at the universities were closed in the 1970s because they were no longer needed in a socialist system based on social equality and the unity of politics, economics and society, this agenda appears sensational. Officially, the Faculty of Sociology was replaced by "Scientific Communism", Political Science by the Communist Party's academy. At the end of the 1980s sociology was reintroduced as a course of study at the university. However, suspicions of it have obviously not yet been surmounted: although the establishment of an official sociological association has been applied for, its approval has not yet been granted (López Vigil 1997, 38).
13. Other central elements in this discussion can be found in the collection edited by Haroldo Dilla (1996), whose leitmotif is the plea for greater autonomy in the social sphere, elaborated in articles on such diverse topics as agrarian co-operatives, the participation of women and the generation gap in Cuba.
14. Eckstein writes,
    > Underestimated in Communist studies in general, including of Cuba, has been the role of ordinary people. Even though citizens were never entirely free to organize on their own or to express their points of view in any Communist Party-run regime, in none did they simply march to state orders. They have influenced policy implementation, if not policy formation, informally and indirectly: through, for example, foot-dragging, pilferage, desertion, black-market and sideline activity, absenteeism and hoarding. They have done so in patterned ways shaped by their traditions and everyday experiences. (1994, xii)
15. There has also been an intensive debate about economic reform: see Carranza, Gutiérrez and Monreal (1995); for an overview, see also Hoffmann (1995, 1997).
16. The centre's director was immediately relieved of his duties, and a commission under the leadership of José Ramón Balaguer, a member of the Politburo, was put in charge of investigating the CEA in the light of the

guidelines set by the report. Following this, all leading scientists of the centre were transferred to other institutions.
17. Since Hart was regarded as an exponent of the "old guard" and nobody suspected him of being a reformer, his article was also not interpreted as a decided criticism but rather as an expression of considerable confusion. The minister of culture was replaced by a younger colleague shortly thereafter.

References

Azcuy Henríquez, Hugo. 1995. "Estado y sociedad civil en Cuba". *Temas*, no. 4 (October–December.): 105–10.
Carranza, Julio, Luis Gutiérrez and Pedro Monreal. 1995. *Cuba: la Restructuración de la Economía: Una Propuesta para el Debate*. Havana: Ed. de Ciencias Sociales.
Castro, Raúl. 1996. "Informe del Buró Político (en el V. Pleno del Comité Central del Partido, 23 marzo 1996)". *Granma Internacional*, 10 April, 4–8.
Dilla, Haroldo, ed. 1996. *La participación en Cuba y los retos del futuro*. Havana: Ediciones CEA.
Eckstein, Susan Eva. 1994. *Back from the Future: Cuba under Castro*. Princeton: Princeton University Press.
Espinosa, Juan Carlos. 1996. "The 'Emergence' of Civil Society in Cuba". *Journal of Latin American Affairs* 4, no.1 (Spring/Summer): 24–33.
Fernández, Damián J. 1993. "Civil Society in Transition". In *Transition in Cuba: New Challenges for U.S. Policy*, edited by Lisandro Perez, 97–152. Miami: Florida International University.
Gunn, Gillian. 1995. *Cuba's NGOs: Government Puppets or Seeds of Civil Society?* (Cuba Briefing Paper 7). Washington, DC: Center for Latin American Studies, Georgetown University.
Hart Dávalos, Armando. 1996. "Sociedad civil y Organizaciones No Gubernamentales". *Granma Internacional*, 13 September, 3.
Hernández, Rafael. 1994. "La sociedad civil y sus alrededores". *La Gaceta de Cuba* 31, no. 1: 28–31.
———. 1996. "Sobre la sociedad civil en Cuba". In *La participación en Cuba y los retos del futuro*, edited by Haroldo Dilla, 82–97. Havana, Cuba: Ediciones CEA.
———. 1997. "Y sin embargo se mueve. Reordenamiento y Transición en Cuba Socialista". Paper presented at the conference Seguridad,

Transiciones Post-Autoritarias y Cambio Social en El Caribe de la Post-Guerra Fría: Los casos de Cuba, Haití y República Dominicana, Santo Domingo, Dominican Republic, 14–15 March.

Herrero, Sánchez. 1996. "El 'Igualitarismo' en Cuba". *Journal of Latin American Affairs* 4, no. 1: 11–15.

Hoffmann, Bert. 1997. "Cuba – la reforma desde adentro que no fue". *Notas* (Frankfurt), no. 9: 48–66.

———, ed. 1995. *Cuba: Apertura y reforma económica: Perfil de un debate.* Caracas, Venezuela: Editorial Nueva Sociedad.

Koschützke, Albrecht. 1994. "Die Lösung auf der Suche nach dem Problem: NGOs diesseits und jenseits des Staates". In *Lateinamerika Analysen und Berichte 18: Jenseits des Staates,* edited by Dietmar Dirmoser et al., 39–64. Bad Honnef: Horlemann.

Lauzurique, Ramos. 1996. "La Crisis Económica Cubana: Causas, Paliativos y Expectativas." *Journal of Latin American Affairs* 4, no. 1: 16–23.

López Vigil, María. 1997. "Sociedad Civil en Cuba. Diccionario urgente". *Envío,* no. 184: 17–40.

Luis, Roger Ricardo. 2001. "Laboratorio social. Más de 2,300 Organizaciones No Gubernamentales laboran en Cuba amparadas por la Ley de Asociaciones". *Granma,* 13 April, 3.

Malone, Shawn. 1996. *Conflict, Coexistence and Cooperation: Church-State Relations in Cuba.* (Cuba Briefing Paper 10). Washington, DC: Center for Latin American Studies, Georgetown University.

Obra Nacional de la Buena Prensa. 1995. *La voz de la Iglesia en Cuba.* México, DF: Obra Nacional de la Buena Prensa.

Pérez, Armando Cristóbal. 1994. Letter to the editor. *La Gaceta de Cuba* 31, no. 1: 28.

Puerta, Ricardo. 1996. "Sociedad Civil en Cuba". In *Ensayos Políticos,* edited by Ricardo Puerta and Maida Donate Armada, 1–57. Miami: Ed. Coordinadora Social Demócrata de Cuba.

Valdés Vivó, Raúl. 1996. "¿Sociedad civil o gato por liebre?" *Granma Internacional,* 24 January, 3.

[12]

Fidel Castro's Heirs
Obstacles to and Perspectives on a New Political Culture in Cuba

Hans-Jürgen Burchardt

Introduction

When the fall of the Berlin Wall in 1989 inaugurated the collapse of socialist regimes, analysts predicted the Cuban regime would not have scope for survival either (Wiarda 1991). The island suffered from the same structural deficits which had led to the demise of other socialist states: on the one hand, a monolithic and centralized public sector, that is, a fusion of power between state, government and the Communist Party (PCC) maintaining its authoritarian hegemony over all socio-economic and political spheres; on the other hand, the dominance of purely extensive forms of production which since the early 1980s had rendered Cuba's economy more and more inefficient (Burchardt 1996).

In addition, Cuba's external determinants deteriorated. As is well known, since its integration into the Council for Mutual Economic Assistance (COMECON), the country had enjoyed massive economic support from the Soviet Union. After this well of support dried up, Cuba lost, within three short years, three-quarters of its export markets and of its imports – its economic basis. This foreign-trade crisis was, and continues to be, amplified by the US economic blockade (Gunn 1993; Mesa-Lago 1993).

The Return to Inequality and National Unity as Rallying Point of Political Culture

While economic policies are stagnating, incoherent reforms and the segmentation of the economy have spurred on social change. The most obvious phenomenon is the increasing heterogenization of the social structure. Today not only is Cuba's economy growing, so is social inequality. The primary catalysts for the new mobility are, respectively, economic privileges and discrimination caused by the reforms.[1]

The new social inequality is created by the informal sector. Though its most excessive consequences have been curbed in the last few years, the informal sector has not lost its importance. Shopping-basket research has shown that an average family requires twice its regular income to satisfy its most basic needs. Such additional income is usually available only by means of black market activities. As a result of this widespread use of the black market, many incomes no longer rely on social or meritocratic criteria. Incomes and state transfers therefore tend to lose their function as social recompense. Instead, the standard of living increasingly depends on informal nets, illegal activities and so forth, with a clandestine income redistribution as consequence.

Another source of redistribution is the legalization of the US dollar. There is an entirely new infrastructure for foreign exchange–based consumption promising a comprehensive gratification. Profits, income opportunities and consumption preferences are concentrated in this sector. This embrace of the "enemy's currency", known as *dolarización*, dominates all socio-economic circuits of the island: wealth and status are often based no longer on work and social functions, but on access to dollars. According to official sources, more than half of the population enjoys this privilege, although a significantly smaller percentage commands a regular foreign exchange income.

On the one hand, the benefits of the inflow of dollars depend on foreign contacts (*remesas*), which are mostly family bonds. This implies a critical selection discriminating against two particularly loyal groups: revolutionary cadres (for example, party, military, security apparatus) that terminated all contacts abroad for political reasons, and the formerly lower stratum of black Cubans who did not tend to migrate because the revolution improved their social condition (Izquierdo 2002).

On the other hand, earning a foreign exchange income is also possible by working in the "emerging sector". Since Cuba's global competitiveness is often confined to low-skilled jobs, overvalued dollar incomes tend to upset the correlation between qualification and standard of living. Thus, a waiter may earn the monthly salary of a university professor in a single day just by getting tips. As a result, there is a transfer of highly skilled labour to low-skilled jobs, which dramatically devalues qualifications and specializations. This shift has devastating consequences for the entire social structure: the increasing share of highly qualified labour in, for example, the 1994 exodus is only the tip of the iceberg.

A looming marginalization is occurring, especially at the social dividing lines of pre-revolutionary Cuba. It affects in particular the black Cuban population (about 50 per cent of the total population). The revolution eliminated institutionalized racism, but without initiating a broad-based anti-racism learning process. Cuban analyses document that "racist stereotypes and prejudices are still present in Cuba society" (Alvarado 1996, 43) and that they continue to reproduce. A clear sign of this subjective discrimination is the low presence of black Cubans within the political structure, in positions with high social prestige and in the dollar sector. As mentioned before, most black Cubans have no access to the *remesas* (money sent from family or friends living outside of Cuba) because of their low level of migration (about 5 per cent of total migration). In addition, they are disadvantaged by the system that grants permission for smaller private business, because this liberalization is restricted to private residences and consequently requires sufficient property. This, however, is a condition more often fulfilled by the descendants of the old – white – middle and upper classes, whereas the black population more often is living in precarious living conditions. This persistent discrimination holds the danger of an ethnic restructuring of the social pyramid.

Even once harmonious urban-rural relations are giving way to an increasing disparity. Internal migration to the capital rose after 1990 in ups and downs, and in 1995 reached for the first time a dimension greater than the pre-revolutionary rural exodus. Because of stagnating agrarian policies, which are aggravating the working and living conditions in the country, the cities – offering profitable and mostly informal income activities – are becoming more and more attractive. The most deplorable of these new fortune hunters of Cuban socialism are the so-called *jineteras*. These casual prostitutes offer themselves for quick money to tourists.

The increasing disparity in the development of town and country is an additional indicator for a social regression in Cuba. Some other phenomena, to be mentioned here only in passing, are the decline in female employment, the increase in crime, public begging and increasing corruption.

How can the stability of Cuban society be accounted for in face of these centrifugal developments? Two factors might explain it. First, the former social cohesion of the island continues to be significant. This cohesion is based on five aspects: the principle of social equality, a comprehensive social net tending to prevent marginalization, modest material wealth, the integrity of the state and the claim of undivided leadership by the party and by Fidel Castro. Even if single elements of this cohesion have broken off and others are in a process of dissolution, the government still has avoided the emergence of social decay – until 2001, social transfers amounted to over 30 per cent of the budget (CEEC 2002; Mesa-Lago 2000).

Without doubt, these are the bright sides of Cuba's socialism. These transfers include the health system, which, substantially, has not lost its efficiency despite growing material bottlenecks; the education system, which continues to guarantee free access to all its institutions; the social security system and unemployment insurance.

The stabilization potential of this social cohesion – albeit with a connotation of material inequality – can be conceptualized with the help of political sociology. Political sociology considers knowledge and social integration as a resource, equal to material wealth, for the realization of individual and collective opportunities (Kreckel 1992; Wilson 1992). Following this definition, there is neither structural inequality in Cuba nor its more severe form of social exclusion. Access to the realm of knowledge is distributed on an egalitarian basis and is broadly socialized. General compulsory education, the health system, fragmentary public social services and the promotion of sport and culture prevent social isolation. These public goods tend to equalize asymmetrical income distribution and to prevent the reproduction of social and ethnic selection by means of the social structure; together with state repression, they have prevented the new material inequality from expressing itself politically. So social differentiation in Cuba is accommodated, but differently from such processes in other transformation countries. Though there is a commercialization of social relations, so far it has not provoked comprehensive dissolution of solidarity and increasing individualization. As a symptom of the crisis we can observe a concentration on exclusive reference groups that inwardly continue to adhere to principles of solidarity but that increasingly function externally as economic actors (Fernández, Perera and Díaz 1996).

The second stabilizing factor in Cuba is the collective will to preserve national independence: the double colonization by Spain and by the United States has left traumatic marks of oppression on the historical memory of the Cuban population. The revolution is, however – because of the successful defeat of the Batista dictatorship and the revolution's persistent, adamant position with regard to US aggression – the emblem of self-determination. Hitherto, only the Castro government has succeeded in integrating this collective historical consciousness into its policies.

Thus, the Cuban brand of socialism basically merges doctrine with an extensive social security system in a Leninist state, legitimated by the imperative of defence of national sovereignty. Consequently, Cuba could be understood less in terms of an orthodox socialist doctrine than as a radical nationalist regime.

Social cohesion and national independence can be summarized under the rubric of national unity. This national unity can be described as identity of a single social group, contained by territorial borders, whose growth has benefited from the following factors:

- social homogenization
- collective upward mobility
- extensive social security components within the system
- high levels of organization and networking
- the possibility of geographical exclusion of any opposition or individual dissatisfaction (so far, about 10 per cent of the population has left the island)
- the authoritarian-to-repressive policies of the state
- the ubiquity of the state's doctrine
- the spatial containment of information because of deficient freedom of the press and lack of pluralistic discourse

This group identity, which political sociology (Bourdieu 1983) conceptualizes as social and cultural capital (that is, incorporated forms of capital that can become productive), is in a permanent interdependence with politics, economy and the nation. Even after the loss of material stability, the legitimacy of the system could be guaranteed on the basis of incorporated forms of capital and social reproduction. It seems to be one of the central stabilizing factors of the Cuban regime, as well as the first element of political culture in Cuba.

The government is fully aware of the critical importance of this national unity. Since the 1990s it has consequently promoted nationalism and has turned it into a programme: at the Fifth Party Congress in 1997, the formerly socialist positions of the PCC mutated more clearly than ever before in the direction of a radical nationalist doctrine. Party, state and nation became identical. In addition, Cuban domestic politics in the last few years has been dominated by the invocation of a threat scenario: its external enemy, the United States, is held responsible for all difficulties – successes can therefore be sold as revolutionary nationalist acts presupposing internal unity.

The most vehement expression of the new doctrine was in the events surrounding the fate of the Cuban boy Elián González, which for months preoccupied more than the international media. In a massive populist mobilization campaign in Cuba, all political and honorary leaders within the system were required to publicly prove their loyalty to the government. With this *Eliánismo,* as some critics ironically termed the political event, it became possible, by subtle appeals to the Cuban sense of family (a traditional enclave of solidarity) and to national pride, to push aside all other topics and demonstrate the persistent threat of the United States to Cuban national sovereignty. This self-styled state of emergency, which became a permanent excuse for pleadings for national unity, put all symptoms of crisis on the back burner and silenced the debates about conceivable solutions. The child's return to Cuba proved the unquestionable role of the revolution as guardian of its own traditions and its independence, which further legitimated its other policies.

Nevertheless, in the medium term material inequality will assume a structure and articulate itself within the social structures of Cuba's socialism. Most likely, one day this dynamic no longer will be able to be contained with a single political maxim such as "the nation", and the social crisis will become a political crisis. In the long run, political unity will be possible only through social equalization and participation. Thus, the question of Cuba's future becomes primarily a political question.

Fidel Castro's Political Heirs

Political culture does not end with institutional and formal politics; rather, it begins there (Alvarez, Dagnino and Escobar 1998). Political actors, moulding the political structures with specific interests and turning them with their individual styles into real politics, are just as important as the structures themselves. In this section, therefore, I will focus on some of these specific styles that are giving shape to Cuba's political culture.

However, below the gigantic fusion of state, government and the party, it is extremely difficult to identify political actors since hitherto they have had little chance to articulate themselves freely. After the revolution, civil structures clearly lost their importance. To the extent that they had supported the last dictatorship, they were discredited and became channels of the new administration of public affairs. Social topics such as racism or feminism were occupied by the state itself, and their civil representation was regarded as unnecessary. Thus, until the late 1980s Cuba knew only a very rudimentary civil society – be it in Gramsci's sense of the space of the *società civile* or in the sense of a nongovernmental space (Gramsci 1992). The development of the island was directly and unequivocally determined by the state, which absorbed all important civil spaces. The borders between state and civil society became blurred and were made to disappear. A "civil public" existed only rudimentarily:

> No policy in Cuba is entirely visible. . . . Rather, there are little clandestine politics which are separated from each other and do not flow into a open public sphere where the citizens can relate to them and where they can become part of a dialogue and contestation. . . . It is almost possible to say that in Cuba politics is everywhere except in politics. (Rojas 1997, 24; my translation)

Since the crisis of the 1990s, the situation in civil society has slowly changed; civil society has clearly grown. Its largest network can be found in the informal sector, which is tolerated by the government because it fulfils important tasks. By definition this shadow economy has a non-governmental character; a great variety of groups operate in it, and new private initiatives are emerging. Even if the informal sector has no political character yet, it has become the space of a new economic potential, which one day is likely to express itself politically.

Other examples are the clearly growing spaces of religious activities. Quantitatively speaking, the popular Cuban religion *santeria,* whose practices have become enormously popular in recent years, has to be mentioned first. Of even greater importance is the Catholic Church, which because of its high level of organization and international support has become one of the most important civil actors on the island.

Furthermore, there always have been limited forms of a counterpublic, in particular in the sciences and in the cultural sphere. The best-known of these is the Cuban film industry. It is also an expression of civil society that the term *civil society* itself – formerly known as an ideological instrument of the arch-enemy the United States – has won some influence.[2]

In contrast to these new forms of civil discourse, almost all organized activities in the realm of political opposition are suppressed. The formation of or participation in political opposition movements is persecuted by the Cuban coercive apparatus, and initiatives attempting to create alternative public forums are rigorously suppressed by the Cuban state. However, despite the *raison d'état* with regard to any opposition, it should be noted that the primary reason for the absence of a political opposition is not repression in Cuba, but the lack of alternative political activities that would guarantee the maintenance of national unity. Any opposition would have to take account of stability in its programme.

It is not likely that the opposition will succeed with this balancing act as long as it remains stuck between state repression and North American aggression: not only is Cuba's opposition being harassed by the state, it is being instrumentalized by organizations in the United States too. In particular, the US-based Cuban exile groups are trying to build dissident groups which discredit and try to destabilize the Cuban regime. Because opposition groups in Cuba have no access to the public sphere, their voices can be heard only through Miami – and they are immediately branded as traitors.

Further, the economic crisis has contributed to a weakening of possible opposition. A creeping depoliticization is taking hold of the island; it appears to exist side by side with the daily fight for survival. Frustration, individualization and retreat into family and survival networks, as well as increasing crime, are the most obvious signs of a future political crisis.

In order to identify political actors, the underdeveloped civil structures in Cuba make it necessary to take the state apparatus into consideration. Closest to non-governmental politics are the political cadres at the bottom of the state and party apparatus. Their upward social mobility is often related directly to their political functions. Because it is not unusual that their functions were completely devaluated by the crisis, many of them are frustrated. According to their life experience and expertise, they blame the government's structural conservatism for their own situation. This view is often confirmed when their informal but flexible survival strategies are successful – at the point at which this occurs the margins of the state are eroding and merging into the wider society. These groups often demand an acceleration of the domestic reforms to increase their own status. However, they have little political influence.

The next higher group of politicos comprises the public servants of the middle level. Significant parts of these cadres lost their influence during the crisis because their fields of activity shrank or became completely obsolete. Of course, the natural interests of these reform losers are the preservation of power, that is, privileges they can no longer justify by their social functions. If, for example, such cadres are prevented from having access to foreign exchange, they compensate with different strategies. One such strategy is to become susceptible to corruption, hitherto a relatively unknown phenomenon in Cuba. The black market, which relies to a large extent on the theft of public goods, could hardly exist without administrative assistance. Another reaction to the crisis is attempts by public servants to expand their positions; for example, leadership personnel grew by 20 per cent between 1988 and 1994 (Espina 1997). While some sectors of the administration are dynamic enough to adjust to the new situation, others – probably the larger part – resist the further decline of their status quo by openly or passively rejecting the reforms.

Above this group we find the leading administrative levels of the system. Following the trajectory of the reform during the last few years, the cadres working in the foreign exchange sector have won influence. Presumably, their private and political motives are personal enrichment, occupation of a particular position that is neutral to the system (that is, resistant to the crisis) and, to attain these objectives as fast as possible, acceleration of economic liberalization.

Finally, there is the power elite at the very top, which basically relates to its own interests and those of its clientele. From the post-socialist transition, this elite should have learned that in the best case a collapse of the system would set an end to their privileges, and in the worst case it would mean a politically and personally highly problematic situation. Depending on their analysis of the political situation, the elite have the options of securing their personal positions and material benefits, of promoting a reformist policy of gradual transition or of preparing for exile or political retirement.

The Cuban military, whose influence within the power structure has increased significantly over the past years, is connected to different actors at all levels within the system. The army, which also administers the Ministry of the Interior and the secret service, has so far remained loyal to the political system which it continues to serve. There are no signs of further political ambitions within the army. But it is not only for this reason that the army enjoys great respect from and prestige within the population. Cuba's Fuerzas Armadas Revolucionarias also enjoys the aura of an invincible army – they are the guarantor of national sovereignty and are regarded as the respected guardian of the revolution.

However, the army's frontline has changed and migrated into the economy. Today it is mainly preoccupied with the preservation of its economic position and, in this effort, has proven to be extraordinarily open to reform: since the beginning of the crisis in 1989, the military budget has been slashed by half, and a significant reorganization process has begun in Cuba. A military-industrial sector was built, and it emerged as a significant and innovative economic sector. Because of its economic consolidation and political legitimacy, Cuba's armed forces can be regarded as a political force likely to play a critical role in the near future of the country.

The most important actor in Cuban politics, towering over the state apparatus, is, of course, Fidel Castro. Within the Cuban political leadership, he occupies a multiplicity of central positions, and during all phases of the revolution he has played a fundamental role. At the turn of the century his power is greater than ever: in 1997 he was elected first secretary of the Cuban Communist Party's Politburo, in 1998 he was elected secretary of the State Council and he is the old and new chair of the ministerial council; thus he is the most important person in the three most important political organs in the country. Besides this, he is president and commander-in-chief of the army. However, Castro's power is not institutionally bound but relates to several networks that are exclusively answerable to him:

> In reality, Fidel Castro is the only person in Cuba having full political rights. He has the freedom to relate to the public directly via the mass media as long as he considers it necessary; he has the liberty to receive foreign politicians and economic representatives and to negotiate with them; he has the right to think and to say in public what he thinks of the future of the nation; he even has the freedom to have bourgeois whims, to live in the world of jet-setters, to be frivolous, revisionist and heterodox, and he may criticize the Revolution. Basically, Fidel Castro is the only person in Cuba who is permitted to be counterrevolutionary and anti-communist because in his case this will be understood as personal ideology, as a fundamental human right. (Rojas 1997, 26; my translation)

The importance of Fidel Castro for the political culture in Cuba rests not only in the power concentrated in his person, but equally in his integrative and consensus-creating authority with regard to the growing sectarian interests within civil society and the state. He has always managed to balance the different directions within the leadership elite. Because of this balancing act, no side has managed to win superiority and become independent of him. At the same time he continues to enjoy high regard within the population as the patron of national unity.

This combination of non-institutionalized power and integrative authority can be described best with Max Weber's term *charismatic domination*. *Charisma* in Weber's definition is understood as an extraordinary quality of a person, for the sake of which the person is considered exemplary and a leader. Weber emphasizes two aspects of charismatic domination, which he describes as a "great revolutionary force": its extraordinary quality (*das Ausseralltägliche*) and its distance to the economic (*das Wirtschaftsfremde*), that is, its lack of economic interests (1972; my translation).

Both are valid components to describe Fidel Castro's domination. Even today he embodies an extraordinary quality in his role as initiator of the revolution. A myth has been created around him and Ernesto "Che" Guevara, and he was styled as – and elevated to – a leader giving hope and a vision to the masses. The lack of economic interests is also hard to overlook in his leadership: even if critics list innumerable possessions, compared to his power this assumed enrichment appears rather modest. Although he is interested in power, he does not have an interest in money. His leadership style is based on a rigid moral philosophy which – with his Jesuit-trained messianism – he is able to transmit to the masses convincingly.

Some attempts to define the Cuban regime by taking into account the role of Fidel Castro speak of *caudillismo,* or more specifically *Castrismo*.[3] Although this concept recognizes sufficiently the patrimonial structures of the system, its low degree of institutionalization, the autocratic character of its political culture and Castro's charismatic domination, from a historical perspective it can be shown that *caudillismo* has blocked the development of a modern state, whereas Cuba has a very efficient and dynamic state apparatus.

A more useful approach to an understanding of Cuba's political culture is provided by Weber's definition of charismatic domination: "With its routinization, the charismatic domination complex flows into other forms of everyday domination: patrimonial and, particularly, in class-related domination, or bureaucratic domination" (1972, 146; my translation). In Cuba, where charismatic domination had more than four decades to consolidate, precisely these routinized and rationalized mechanisms evolved. Functionally, it created a state apparatus that can be identified as bureaucratic-authoritarian. When asking about agency, Weber's hint of patrimonial domination will help to advance the analysis.

Patrimonial domination is based on a (protective) domination according to the social position of a patron; in addition, it requires a particular legitimacy which it draws primarily from local-traditional and patrimonial-charismatic motifs. It tends to command legitimacy rather than legality or institutionalization. Its holders are patrimonial personalities by virtue of their ability to legitimate – both to themselves and to their followers – their domination by protectionism. Thus, patrimonial domination *sui generis* possesses a basic interpersonal relationship with its clientele. In other words, the holder of power is not a superior but rather a personal patron.

In neo-patrimonial societies, the claim to patronage is no longer founded on traditional grounds, but rather on the basis of common political interests and economic spoils. There are two central conditions for neo-patrimony. The first is a lack of solidarity within the power elite, creating a general insecurity that leaves the patrimonial relations unpredictable. It promotes an autocratic leadership style and increases loyalty towards the leadership. The second is a monopolization of basic resources, which is necessary to provide an economic basis to the clientele system. Extended hierarchical networks of clientele relationships organize the whole system by means of a huge number of dependencies legitimating the regime and held together by the top leadership. In an autocratic system, patrimonial relationships structured in this way can hold together the state apparatus and also arrange its relations with society (Eisenstadt 1973).

The Cuban regime has both conditions for neo-patrimony. First, it has a power elite with heterogeneous interests and without any "wing" that is able to articulate its positions publicly. Though there is some speculation about a reformist wing faced with "orthodox" forces, the public learns very little about such internal debates and power struggles. Since Cuba's realpolitik cannot be identified with any particular interest group, the legitimacy of domination depends to a large extent on Fidel Castro's charisma. Castro has always known how to maintain the balance of power between different political groups and how to neutralize particular interests.

Second, Cuban socialism's economic mode of production has greatly facilitated patrimonial relations: the economy is almost completely monopolized by the state, and, not less important, its administration is organized in a strictly vertical-hierarchical way and thus has the necessary differentiation for patrimonial relationships. In addition, in a socialist state, money does not have the function of an instantly available exchange value. This function is still fulfilled by the products themselves. In other words, a socialist state has a barter economy based on small business cycles (*Naturalwirtschaft*) rather than a commodity economy based on the exchange of goods (*Warenwirtschaft*). In the former, the human factor (social position, contacts and so forth) remains more important in the exchange process than the product or commodity (value). In these ideal conditions for patrimonial relationships, neo-patrimony was able to thrive.

Weber's observation that the routinization of charismatic domination often leads to bureaucratic patronage offers the key to a deeper understanding of Cuba's political culture: with the revolution Fidel Castro began a charismatic domination which eventually turned into neo-patrimony. Due to the specific conditions under socialism, neo-patrimony permeated the entire political system and Cuban society, and it continues to tie them together. To the extent that patrimonial relations became more important, the system of charismatic domination was legitimated. The more charismatic domination became entrenched, the better clientele relations were able to hold their ground against all attempts to institutionalize the revolution. While in Soviet and East European socialism the depersonalized apparatus was soon able to exert (and ultimately lose) control, in Cuba the charismatic figure of Fidel Castro supplies legitimacy. Castro's political unpredictability and partly ignorant autonomy with regard to the institutionalized apparatus becomes an important stabilizing factor of the regime – charisma and patronage affect and complement each other. This arrangement guarantees Castro (almost) unlimited power and also the loyalty of the elite, the apparatus and the masses. Consequently, I will define this mode of domination as *charisma-based neo-patrimony*. It is the second element characterizing Cuba's political culture.

This analysis allows us to understand a central source of Cuba's socialist dynamic and its continuing impressive political stability: its charisma-based neo-patrimony stands in a tense relationship to and depends on the bureaucratic-authoritarian state. In order to consolidate, Fidel Castro's charisma requires a well-functioning apparatus, and the apparatus requires Castro's charisma to legitimate his domination. However, the more functions and competence the apparatus gains, the more legitimacy the bearer of charisma is likely to lose. Fidel Castro's unconventional political style, often ignoring the proper institutionalized channels, is the best expression for this growing ambivalence.

On the other hand, this tense relation energizes the political culture. Two examples may demonstrate this. When Castro in 1993 called the legalization of the dollar "unintended", he was in search of legitimacy for this measure. The apparatus instantly translated the political decision into a broad-based legitimacy that supplied the system with an extended chain of foreign exchange shops that increased the supply to certain parts of the population. And when in 1994 Fidel Castro turned political unrest in Havana into a foreign-policy issue, he also defended the legitimacy of the regime. The bureaucratic-authoritarian apparatus secured this stabilization by the legalization and swift development of the farmers' markets, which complemented Fidel's charisma with improved food supply. The characterization of Cuba's system in terms of charisma-based neo-patrimony and a bureaucratic-authoritarian state therefore allows insights into the functions, sources of legitimacy and dynamics of Cuba's policy (Burchardt 1999).

Obstacles to and Perspectives on a New Political Culture in Cuba

Castro's charisma still is the greatest guarantee for stability in Cuba because it prevents the formation of political groups within the power apparatus. However, one day a high price will probably have to be paid for this guarantee. Charismatic domination usually remains authentic only until the death of the charismatic person. The pronouncements and attitudes of Fidel Castro point to the fact that he also intends to remain in control until his death. Thus, he carefully monitors that nobody is challenging his claim to leadership and he promotes a political conservatism that tolerates structural reforms only as a last resort and only in most the minimal terms. Following the maxim "conservation of power at any price" creates a problem which Weber, with regard to charismatic domination, has defined as the question of succession (*Nachfolgefrage*), and its complexity may lead to a breakdown: "The actual political regime depends so strongly on the person of Fidel Castro that its future is now more than ever to be identified with his biological longevity. This loss of perspective destroys the ideological basis of the old regime" (Domínguez 1997, 10; my translation).

Since the Cuban state apparatus publicly presents itself as a monolith, there is a lack of additional charismatic figures; and because there is no established opposition, it becomes extremely difficult to answer the question of succession. Basically, Cuba's political future will depend on which involved persons, with what potential, will be able to persist.

A large role in this scenario will be played by the United States and the Cuban exiles living there. However, I will de-emphasize this aspect here and focus on the domestic processes.

Most attempts to decipher the actual political constellations on the island are taking the "emerging sector" as a starting point. A political coalition of the technocrats in the dollar sector and parts of the traditional bureaucracy is often believed to guarantee economic stability, societal control and elite privileges. Other analyses even fear that this technocratic-entrepreneurial group and the influential private entrepreneurs in the informal sector could merge into a new power elite, which, as a Cuban bourgeoisie, would become the avant-garde for a capitalist transformation (Dilla 1999).

Such social constellations are, however, not yet consolidated realities. The specific character of Cuban neo-patrimony makes functionally defined alliances – subsystems within the system – too risky.[4] It must be assumed that the agents who benefit from an expansion of foreign exchange sector and the existence of a dual economy are those who are best organized and have the greatest potential for assertion. The nepotist political arena, already having had the experience of a personalized political culture, would be able to articulate itself quickly, to impose its interests by means of inner circles and to form alliances with wealthy foreign and domestic investors.

Other actors would first have to learn political culture – that is, learn to constitute themselves, to define themselves and then ally themselves with others. In a process of rapid and radical change, their ability to act is not likely to develop very fast. This would be particularly true for social groups which are currently economically discriminated against by the reforms but because of the state's omnipotence have no interest groups to represent them and therefore would first have to establish such emancipative organizations.

Such a scenario for the future – which appears relatively likely – would cement economic heterogenization; accelerate social inequality, leading to the marginalization and possible stigmatization of certain groups; impede the growth of a participatory political culture in Cuba; and, consequently, reduce the chances for a civil and socially sustainable transformation.

In order to reduce such risks, it would be necessary to form a new political culture, even under the leadership of the current charismatic figure: Cuba's greatest challenge is an *incremental* democratization of state and society, that is, an autochthonous change of the political system and a gradual building up of the system.

The state's authoritarian character, however, is rooted less in the formal absence of democratic structures than in its political culture, which promotes a de facto paralysis of most institutions. A change in these processes would initiate a huge democratization and modernization. Some Cuban analysts suggest the following focuses for a reform: de-ideologization of the state, decentralization of its administration and horizontalization of its structures, depersonalization of the system, liberalization of the economy and of civil rights, expansion of the rule of law, democratization of the state's search for legitimacy and partial diversification of the media. The Cuban Communist Party should be asked to allow different political groups in order to heighten its internal democracy, to take decisions only collectively and to disallow the occupation of multiple positions in order to curb the prevalent overlap of offices (Valdés 1994).

A central issue for the implementation of such a strategy is the strengthening and differentiation of the Cuban parliament. For example, the question arises whether Cuba's problems should not be a reason for the highest legislative organ in the country, the National Assembly, to meet more than twice a year. Continuous sessions would tend to create a public forum in which current problems could be explained and discussed in front of the public.

Effective democratization through the liberalization of the party and through the strengthening of institutional parliamentarism and of the subordinated levels of public administration would gradually reduce the authoritarian character of the Cuban state and would support political participation. However, a reformed state would have to secure not only its own autonomy, but also the independence of other societal subsystems. It would release religion back into the social sphere and depoliticize it at the same time. It would guarantee the independence of the rule of law and also depoliticize it, in order to create the conditions for the rule of law; it would no longer draw its legitimacy from external threat scenarios, but from a domestic policy of integrative and consensual negotiations. The call for a new political culture in Cuba is not necessarily a call for less state, it is a call for a strong yet different state. A new political culture does not necessarily mean a dismantling of the centralized state, but rather a functional adaptation to decentralized, participatory and indirect mechanisms of rule.

The increasingly heterogeneous social structure also demonstrates that the Cuban state is no longer able to supply the entire population with its traditional strategies of integration. Instead of leaving the social sphere unoccupied, as it has done hitherto, the government must consciously and publicly endorse and integrate other political actors. Besides a reform of the state, civil society has to be granted a broader space, and, free of public tutelage, it has to be re-politicized.

This argument does not necessarily imply an antagonism between civil society and the state. In principle, it is quite possible for civil society and the state to merge synergetically and provide new legitimacy for the system; studies have shown that institutionalized hierarchies and subordinated selective networks of co-operation are able to synergetically promote the self-coordination skills of the involved actors (for example, Scharpf 1993).

Several intermediary institutions may help to demonstrate the self-coordination of skills of the actors: private economic initiatives do not necessarily have to be based on private property. They also can spring from the latest creation of agricultural co-operatives in Cuba, from which about one-fifth of the population benefits. This model could lead to a broad-based and publicly supported co-operative culture forming an economically and politically stable social sector that in the further development of the island would become a factor any future government would have to reckon with (Burchardt 2000, 2001). However, in order to achieve this, the co-operatives would have to be granted pluralistic interest groups and forms of articulation the state has hitherto refused them.

Moreover, there is a need for greater autonomy on the part of Cuban trade unions. The way in which the privatization of industries is handled and the influence labour representatives exert in this process will determine the future political economy of Cuba: it will decide the employment question and, therefore, questions of distribution. However, Cuban trade unions still consider themselves to be the transmission belt of the state, and they act rather more like collaborators with the employers than like representatives of labour. It is no surprise, then, that in a representative poll in several state-run companies, 61 per cent of the workers said that the trade unions "do not play an important role" (Dilla 1996). In order to change this, the functions of the trade unions have to be redrawn completely. The trade unions have to divorce themselves from their traditional understanding of politics, recognize different social interests and transform themselves into advocates of employees' interests instead of supporting public policy.

Besides the trade unions, other political mass organizations – often representing large groups such as women or youth – have to assume a more civil character. Usually their functions are confined to the task of political instruction, rather than seeking practical solutions for the everyday demands and problems of their members. According to one Cuban study, the most important wish of nearly 50 per cent of the young people in Cuba is for an improvement in their material conditions; 10 per cent would prefer founding a family, 10 per cent their work and 10 per cent their pastime; political activities were one of the lowest priorities (Domínguez 1994). It is obvious that a youth organization focusing on political mobilization and ignoring the interests of its members is not very attractive. Opening up the mass organizations, therefore, would mean a diversification of their programmes and an improved service to their members. It would not depoliticize them, but rather would start a re-politicization of their base, which, through their social self-organization, would allow them to find new possibilities for involvement and articulation.

Relating to the possibilities of articulation, a final example of Cuba's political culture shall be introduced here. Civil structures always require a space for communication in order to initiate the increased participation of the political public. Sadly, the Cuban situation in this regard is a wasteland. Print media, radio and television have been reduced to almost exclusive dissemination of official perspectives of the government, which in both style and content are heavily ideological. There is no pluralistic debate. However, the increasing international flow of information can no longer be kept from entering the island; increasingly, the state's media monopoly is undermined and, with it, the legitimacy of the government. Legitimacy can be recaptured only if the media become a mirror of the country's reality. However, in Cuba's increasingly complex society this will be possible only if the media have a more pluralistic structure.

The above examples demonstrate not only that Cuba needs a new political culture, but also that it actually has the basis to build and expand it. A broader political participation by means of the civic structure could help this increasingly heterogeneous society secure its capabilities of self-regulation. Frequently, such networks and initiatives, often with overlapping memberships, are able to bridge social lines of conflict. They can assist in defusing political crises, in mitigating societal conflicts and, not least, in stabilizing the state's ability to act in a case of crisis.

However, at the same time, civil society will have to be embedded in strong political institutions. Civil society is not necessarily a civic society. Civil societies are not inevitably egalitarian, democratic or tolerant, nor do they necessarily act in the interest of the common good. They can also be aggressive, intolerant, reactionary, anti-democratic and highly egoistic. Thus, if civil society confines itself to a defence of the autonomous and rational individual without institutional intervention, the (in principle desirable) reclamation of the *citoyen* often turns out to be merely an apology for an unbridled market society. For this reason, the civil society in Cuba's new political culture should not be constructed without having in mind a strong state.

Local Society and Local Economy: A New Political Space in Cuba?

An analysis of local spaces in Cuba shows that these could potentially be a prime field in which democratization and decentralization of both state and civil society could meet because they are in very close relations. Local spaces as fields of coordination for a local economy, a local political system, local culture and local environmental conditions increasingly capture attention in debates about political development. In the Caribbean, the topic of local spaces has also come to the fore because it is closely connected with neoliberal projects of decentralization. But from another perspective, local spaces can be conceptualized as areas where development projects may be implemented that are economically viable, socially just and ecologically sustainable and that support a democratic political order.

Little attention has been paid to local government and communal politics in Cuba, and until today they are perceived only as executive organs of national objectives. Consequently, communal organs of representation have a weak institutionalization and a low ability to implement their concerns. At the lowest level of communal representation, the so-called *Consejos Populares,* representing the interests of communities, have no constitutional or normative basis. They have neither a legal basis, which would clearly define their rights and obligations, nor juridical instruments for sanctions that would protect vital interests of the community (pollution, communal planning and so forth). With regard to national decisions that directly affect communities, they have only an advisory or executive function; planning and implementation of communal policies is permitted only after consultation with and according to instructions from superior administrative sources. This, however, leads to a political culture that concentrates its administrative and representative efforts only on the organization of focused local interests, and cannot even deal with basic issues such as electricity and water supply or housing.

Thus, Cuban local politics are faced with several problem clusters. Cuba's communal districts have not grown historically, but were constituted in the 1970s. In many communities, this led to a heterogenization of their economic and social structures, creating a deficiency in their ability to integrate and, because of numerous conflicts of interests, complicating the implementation of coherent communal policies. Another serious drawback is the low potential of political initiatives, the lack of decision making and the lack of capability for implementation. Moreover, to a large extent, the communities are economically dependent on the state: they get their budget from it without having substantial influence over its size and without the possibility of attuning it to local economic development. They do not usually receive any money to invest in new infrastructure, and they are not allowed to have their own revenue. The consequences of this economic dependence are exacerbated by the fact that quite often agricultural or industrial public enterprises with greater budgets and financial autonomy than the communities themselves are sitting on their lands and are able to exert significant influence. There are insufficient channels of information and communication between the councils, and these potent local actors are often directly answerable to the national ministries.

On the other hand, the political culture on the communal level has strong participatory characteristics: the grassroots democratic procedures mentioned before. Observations of community parliament and council sessions have shown that in Cuban local politics, democratic traditions and procedures (the broad flow of information, transparent decision making, free speech and so forth) are adhered to. Despite low salaries and disastrous technical equipment, most communities have efficient administrations. A high fluctuation of candidates for elections, a remarkable level of participation in the public sessions of the local parliaments, a very frequent submission of direct concerns by citizens and numerous initiatives by citizens and town districts aimed at self-organized improvements of their living conditions point to the great local potential for participation (Roman 1999).

A new evaluation of communal structures in Cuba would therefore appear to be desirable. An important step in this direction could be taken by giving these structures higher autonomy and legal security. Also, the communities need more authority within their own territory. This authority would include a greater ability to sanction infractions (such as pollution) and to establish a higher correlation between local economic results and the communal budget (such as through local business taxes). In turn, this would motivate local administrations to provide an infrastructure conducive to economic activity, would increase interest in the promotion of local production (small business, food production, private services) and open up possibilities, through greater investment volume, for implementing integrated social and environmental policies. Such policies could lead to a wide net of local economies, which would not only counter administrative red tape, but would also give decentralizing impulses for the overcentralized economy and improve the supply situation of the population.

Another requirement is the adaptation of local political culture to the new divergence of interests which, since the early 1990s, can be observed in local societies. Such an adaptation would entail the inclusion of social groups which are economically marginalized by the reform process. It would also mean the creation of new public spaces and the permission of different political forms of organization, which would strengthen the civil elements in communities and allow a more intensive dialogue between local administrations as representatives of the state and citizens. The direct contact guaranteed in local spaces would make such a dialogue easier and would make the implementation of partial interests more difficult. Strong, competent communities could thus become an important guarantor of public integrity and efficient policy, and thereby evolve into an important point of reference for the imminent political reforms in Cuba (Burchardt and Dilla 2001).

The thrust of all these proposals is clear: there is a need to find a new form of governance in Cuba, that is, to reassess the levels of autonomy and interdependence of various actors in the state, market and society. This is possible only with a strong state and a strong civil society, which basically would have to negotiate a new social contract. This social contract would not have to attempt to restore the already brittle old consensus, but rather would seek a renewal which would define the nation in terms of agreement and not in terms of unity. A participatory politics would have to be set up in which the reconfiguration and reconstruction of national unity as a stability factor became a social project. Weber, in his definition of charismatic rule, termed this metamorphosis a transfer of genuine charisma into a "charisma of office" (*Amtscharisma*) (1972, 44). This challenge cannot be achieved by the retention of state socialism but only by its gradual, yet fundamental reorganization (which, in turn, requires the conception and implementation of a consistent reform strategy). As a central objective, the state's basis of legitimacy would have to be maintained for the process of a gradual transition and subsequent change through bargaining processes.

In Cuba, reforms would not necessarily lead to the same collapse of the system as occurred in Eastern Europe. But if the resurrection of political culture is not successful, it is likely to follow the example of these countries in many details. We would likely become witnesses of how history would be repeated in slow motion.

Notes

1. Cuban economists confirm a significant income stratification: while the savings of the poorest declined by about 50 per cent in the last years of the twentieth century, the assets of the richest nearly doubled. About one-tenth of the population owns over 80 per cent of all savings and most liquidities (Beruff 1997). Upward mobility is prevalent among private entrepreneurs and in the foreign exchange sector. In sharp contrast to this minority, the majority of the population are losers: the underpaid public-sector and state employees, industrial and agrarian workers, the

unemployed (the official size of which oscillates at around 5 per cent of the population), women, youth and retirees. However, it is difficult to construct on this basis a new model of the stratification of contemporary Cuban society. On the one hand, income opportunities may overlap: a retiree, seemingly impoverished by a moderate pension, may, as the recipient of weekly US-dollar remittances, become privileged. On the other hand, there are no legal ways in which Cuba's new rich can invest their money productively: capital accumulation remains solely within the domain of the state, which obstructs the emergence and reproduction of a social group.

2. There are currently three interpretations of the notion of "civil society". One is a theological interpretation which goes back to Christian concepts of salvation, with units such as the family as its basis, and which is engaged in an intensive dialogue in its own ranks and with the state. The church has been given a key role in this discourse. The second approach has been developed by academic reformers, who intend to change the system incrementally and who argue for a revaluation of "the civil" in order to achieve a more dynamic communication between state and society and in order to secure a greater dimension of political pluralism. The third interpretation is offered by the state apparatus itself, which does not separate the state from civil society, but rather demands a complete loyalty of "the civil" to the state. In their view, the political state is basically the official expression of the civil society and therefore does not require or hardly requires any civil society beyond the realm of the state (see also chapter 11 in this volume).

3. The emphasis on personality which is so characteristic of Latin American political culture tends to promote a leader-follower relation used by the leader(s) as a means to domination and legitimacy. This is usually a patrimonial and personalistic domination of local, regional or national potentates who are prepared to defend their presumed rights by force. However, this preparedness to use force is not rooted solely in brute force. It also requires a voluntary recognition of the *caudillist* leader by his or her followers.

4. With Karl Marx, one could provocatively term the contemporary division of power in Cuba a *reverse bonapartism*. Marx described *bonapartism* as a form of government "in which the bourgeoisie has already lost the ability to control the nation but the working class has not yet gained it" (Marx and Engels 1968, 338; my translation).

References

Alvarado, Juan Antonio. 1996. "Relaciones raciales en Cuba: Notas de investigación". *Temas,* no. 7: 37–43.

Alvarez, Sonia E., Evelina Dagnino and Arturo Escobar, eds. 1998. *Cultures of Politics/Politics of Culture: Revisioning Latin American Social Movements.* Boulder, Colo.: Westview.

Beruff, Alejandro. 1997. "Las finanzas internas en Cuba". In *La economía cubana en 1996: Resultados, problemas y perspectivas, informe anual del CEEC,* 10–24. Havana: Centro de Estudios de la Economía Cubana.

Bourdieu, Pierre. 1983. "Ökonomisches Kapital, kulturelles Kapital, soziales Kapital". In *Soziale Ungleichheiten,* edited by Reinhard Kreckel, 183–98. Göttingen: Reinhard Campus-Verlag.

Burchardt, Hans-Jürgen. 1996. *Kuba: Der lange Abschied von einem Mythos.* Stuttgart: Schmetterling.

———. 1999. *Kuba: Im Herbst des Partiarchen.* Stuttgart: Schmetterling.

———. 2000. *La última reforma agraria del siglo.* Caracas: Nueva Sociedad.

———. 2001. "Cuba's Agriculture after the New Reform: Between Stagnation and Sustainable 'Development' ". *Socialism and Democracy,* no. 28: 141–54.

Burchardt, Hans-Jürgen, and Haroldo Dilla. 2001. *Mercados globales y gobernabilidad local: Retos para la descentralización.* Caracas: Nueva Sociedad.

Centro de Estudios de la Economía Cubana (CEEC). 2002. *La economía cubana en el 2001.* Havana: Universidad de La Habana.

Dilla, Haroldo. 1996. "Pensando la alternativa desde la participación". *Temas,* no. 8: 102–9.

———. 1999. "Comrades and Investors: The Uncertain Transition in Cuba". In *The Socialist Register 1999: Global Capitalism versus Democracy,* edited by Leo Panitch and Colin Leys, 227–47. London: Merlin.

Domínguez, Jorge I. 1997. "¿Comienza una transición hacia el autoritarismo en Cuba?" *Encuentro de la Cultura Cubana,* no. 6–7: 7–23.

Domínguez Garcia, Maria I. 1994. "La cultura politica de los jovenes cubanos". Unpublished paper, CIPS, Havana.

Eisenstadt, Samuel Noah. 1973. *Traditional Patrimonialism and Modern Neopatrimonialism.* Beverly Hills, Calif.: Sage.

Espina, Mayra. 1997. "El espacio para la igualdad". Paper presented to 20th Congress of the Latin American Studies Association, Guadalajara, Mexico, 17–19 April.

Fernández, Consuelo, Maricela Perera and Maiky Díaz. 1996. "La vida cotidiana en Cuba: una mirada psicosocial". *Temas,* no. 7: 92–98.

Gunn, Gillian. 1993. *Cuba in Transition: Options for U.S. Policy.* New York: Twentieth Century Fund.
Gramsci, Antonio. 1992. *The Prison Notebooks.* Translated by Joseph A. Buttigieg and Antonio Callari; edited by Joseph A. Buttigieg. New York: Columbia University Press.
Izquierdo Pedroso, Lázara. 2002. *Zwei Seiten Kubas: Identität und Exil.* Stuttgart: Schmetterling.
Kreckel, Reinhard. 1992. *Politische Soziologie der sozialen Ungleichheit.* Frankfurt: Reinhard Campus-Verlag.
Marx, Karl, and Friedrich Engels. 1968. *Gesammelte Werke,* vol. 17. Berlin: Dietz.
Mesa-Lago, Carmelo. 1993. "The Economic Effects on Cuba of the Downfall of Socialism in the USSR and Eastern Europe". In *Cuba after the Cold War,* edited by Carmelo Mesa-Lago, 133–96. Pittsburgh: University of Pittsburgh Press.
———. 2000. *Market, Socialist, and Mixed Economies: Comparative Policy and Performance: Chile, Cuba, and Costa Rica.* Baltimore: Johns Hopkins University Press.
Rojas, Rafael. 1997. "Póliticas invisibles". *Encuentro de la Cultura Cubana,* no. 6/7: 24–35.
Roman, Peter. 1999. *People's Power: Cuba's Experience with Representative Government.* Boulder, Colo.: Westview.
Scharpf, Fritz W., ed. 1993. *Games in Hierarchies and Networks.* Frankfurt: Campus Verlag.
Valdés Paz, Juan. 1994. "La transición socialista en Cuba: continuidad y cambio en los 90". In *La transición socialista en Cuba,* edited by Juan Valdés Paz and Mayra Espina, 33–72. Havana: Pinos Nuevos.
Weber, Max. 1972. *Wirtschaft und Gesellschaft.* Tübingen: Mohr.
Wiarda, Howard, J. 1991. "Is Cuba Next? Crisis of the Castro Regime". *Problems of Communism* 1–2: 84–93.
Wilson, William Julius. 1992. "Public Policy Research and the Truly Disadvantaged". In *The Urban Underclass,* edited by Christopher Jencks and Paul E. Peterson, 460–81. Washington, DC: Brookings Institution.

[Part 4]

The Politics of Confrontation and Fragmentation

[13]

Guyana's Dominant Political Culture
An Overview

David Hinds

Introduction

In his work on Third World political culture, Mehran Kamrava (1999) found that the political culture in most postcolonial societies reflects two major distinguishing features. First, he argues that despite attempts by the elites to create "national" political cultures, Third World political culture is fragmented; thus, there is no single political culture. He observes a "dichotomy between the political cultures of the elites and that of the masses and fragmentation along cultural, religious, ethnic, and racial lines" (Kamrava 1999, 123–24). He also contends that there is no single elite political culture because the economic, political and intellectual elites sometimes have different orientations, leading to "a growing nucleus of elite intellectuals who, if not openly oppositional, do not actively support the political establishment" (p. 124).

His second observation is that Third World political culture is elite-driven and is generally classified as a "subject" political culture, whereby the masses are directed by the elites, both with and without their consent. According to Kamrava, this subject political culture obtains mostly in authoritarian settings where "conformity and blind obedience to administrative directives reign supreme" and "there is a one way flow of information between the political establishment and the larger society" (Kamrava 1999, 125).

Kamrava's findings have particular resonance in the anglophone Caribbean, in particular Guyana, whose dominant political culture is the subject of this chapter. This dominant culture is one of the two prevailing cultures that have evolved in the country's postcolonial history, the other being a counterculture whose roots lie in the resistance to the dominant culture. Guyana's political culture, therefore, is not a cohesive and coherent phenomenon; rather, it is a reflection of the country's tortuous politics in both its colonial and its postcolonial experiences. These experiences have left the country with a fragile sense of nationalism and national identity, two key components of a national political culture. Since independence in 1966, the country's political attitudes and values have been heavily influenced by a combination of racial competition between the African and East Indian elites for control of the government and state, the colonial legacy of authoritarianism and class domination and, to a lesser extent, the separate and joint resistance of the lower classes and sections of the intellectual elite against centralized authoritarian rule.

One of the features of postcolonial anglophone Caribbean politics has been an attempt to instil a political culture that reflects the expressed desire of the new political elites to chart a new course that is ostensibly radically different from the old colonial order. In this regard the elites initially found common ground with the masses, who saw independence as an opportunity to create new and different political, economic and social spaces in which their collective material and spiritual condition could be improved. With this popular mandate, the political elites, who assumed the reins of governmental power, proceeded to unilaterally dictate the form and content of the postcolonial political order. Any understanding of the evolution of postcolonial political culture, therefore, cannot be divorced from an understanding of the nature, motivation and political monopoly of the elites.

The fact that these elites were favoured and placed in positions of authority by the departing colonial rulers, coupled with their general endorsement by the masses, ensured that their hold on the postcolonial state was almost complete by the time of formal independence. This elite control in the postcolonial dispensation is at the core of any analysis of postcolonial political behaviour in the region. As Kwayana correctly posits, the departing colonizers' "manipulation and maneuvers in selecting a congenial group of ruling cadres for the independent nations" have had a direct impact on the quality of post-independence politics (1987, 3). In the case of Guyana, Kwayana observes, "Since 1955 all class forces – whatever their ideology – came under the leadership of the petty bourgeoisie. The class struggle was then harnessed by the petty bourgeoisie to its own needs for good or for ill" (p. 4).

Kwayana's thesis is supported by C.L.R. James (1984), Paget Henry (1983) and Clive Thomas (1984), who also contend that this elite control of state power has had serious implications for almost every aspect of postcolonial politics, including the evolution of political culture. Henry and Thomas argue that the postcolonial state, despite some significant modifications or reforms, assumed many of the features of the colonial state, including its authoritarian orientation. According to Thomas, the elite that negotiated the independence arrangements with the departing colonizers found much of the colonial form of governance "very much to its liking, since like the colonial power before it, it was in the petty bourgeoisie's objective interest to use the state machinery to preserve existing relations of alienation and domination intact" (1984, 50). Speaking to the inadequacies of the Caribbean political elites and their implications for the nurturing of a new political order, James writes bluntly, "They have no trace of tradition. Until twenty years ago they have had no experience of political parties or government. . . . Knowledge of production, of political struggles, of the democratic tradition, they have none" (1984, 122–23).

The evolution of political behaviour in the anglophone Caribbean, therefore, has been strongly influenced by a convergence of elite control or middle-class domination, the class alliance between the elites and the masses, authoritarian governance and state institutions, and the resistance by the masses in conjunction with the progressive sections of the middle classes. Another important factor in this regard has been race and ethnicity. Because most of the descendants of African slaves, East Indian indentured labourers and native peoples constituted the poorer classes while those of European stock, including mulattos, belonged to the upper classes, race and class have been inextricably linked. The common class position of East Indians and Africans has not, however, led to a permanent class alliance; more often than not, racial identity has determined political behaviour.

Guyana's Dominant Political Culture

Reflecting Kamrava's finding of fragmentation in Third World political culture, two competing political cultures have emerged in postcolonial Guyana: a dominant state-sponsored culture and a radical non-state culture or counterculture. The political elites have used the state as a means of creating a "new" political culture but have in the process suppressed or manipulated the mass political culture that had begun to take root during the struggle for independence. Insofar as a mass political culture is manifested, it faces manipulation by the elites or incorporation into the elite culture. This has resulted, on the one hand, in a subject political culture in which the masses tend to respond primarily to directives from the elites, and on the other hand, in a counterculture whereby the masses, in alliance with the progressive section of the middle class, in particular the intelligentsia, resist middle-class domination.

Guyana's dominant political culture is characterized by authoritarianism, embrace of racial domination at the political level, one-man rule or "leaderism", confrontation, doublespeak and deference to foreign mediation. As I have observed elsewhere (2001), these characteristics have been cultivated within the context of an adherence to what Anthony Payne (1993) refers to as an adopted Westminster model of governance. This dominant culture is manifested largely by the attitudes of the two factions of the political elite that have wielded state power since independence: the leaderships of the two major political parties, the Indian-based People's Progressive Party (PPP) and the African-based People's National Congress (PNC).

Although these leaderships represent groups with different historical and cultural backgrounds, they nevertheless generally share the same political attitudes and values. This unity of purpose is driven by a common need to secure domination of the state within the context of racial hegemony while keeping the masses, in whose name this dominance is practised, out of the governance of the country. The PPP and the PNC, therefore, individually and together sought, under the guise of nation building, to create a political culture whereby the masses of people and their struggles are directed and co-opted by the elites and their organizations. In this regard, the state-sponsored culture has employed charismatic appeal, racial solidarity, appeal to racial insecurities among the masses and the power of the state to perpetuate itself. Central to this process have been the suppression and manipulation of any autonomous mass culture of resistance, and a simultaneous emphasis on centralized rule and oppression. Given the country's sharp racial polarization, popular validation of regime excesses by the individual segments has been the rule rather that the exception.

However, despite this state-sponsored suppression, there has existed throughout the post-independence period a renegade culture that has sought to sustain an independent mass political culture premised on the need for a more democratic, participatory, racially united and revolutionary political order. In this regard the masses have found an ally in a third faction of the political elite, which Perry Mars (1998) refers to as the Radical Left. This group, which includes radical academics, professionals and progressive labour leaders, is largely associated with the Working People's Alliance (WPA), a party that has eschewed race-based politics as a vehicle of political expression. Instead, the WPA has sought to encourage a parallel political culture that stresses the encouragement of mass resistance to oppression, multiracial solidarity, coalition building, anti-leaderism and independent self-organization by the people, or what Walter Rodney called "the People's Power" (1979, 27). This counterculture, however, has been the subject of state-sponsored intimidation and violence and has been characterized as irrelevant, anti-national and destructive of peace and stability. The result has been a marginalization of this culture both by the state and by the logic of the prevailing racial polarization, thus forcing it to the periphery of the political landscape.

Racial Domination and Party Politics

Race is the most influential factor in the evolution of Guyana's political culture. Almost every political action by both the elite and the masses is motivated by racial considerations, or what Kwayana (1987) refers to as "racial insecurity". These insecurities are rooted in the country's historical development, in particular in the post-emancipation period, when Indian indentured servants were taken to Guyana as replacements for slave labour. This development led to tensions between the ex-slaves and the indentured servants, as the latter were seen as undercutting the ability of the newly freed Africans to bargain with the plantation owners over wages.

Ever quick to exploit divisions, the plantation owners devised a divide-and-rule strategy that exacerbated the already tenuous relations between the two races. Despite instances of united action against colonial excesses, Africans and Indians continued to view each other with suspicion. It was, therefore, not surprising that with the imminence of political independence, both races, led by their respective parties, became engaged in a bitter struggle for control of the post-independence state. So intense was the power struggle that the situation degenerated into a virtual civil war in the early 1960s, an experience that has left the country as one of the most racially segmented polities.

This racial segmentation has had serious implications for political mobilization and organization, political co-operation and democratic governance. Fear of domination by the other group has informed political decision making among both the elites and the masses, leading to the promotion of racial solidarity as the first line of offence and defence. In such a situation, political co-operation has been very difficult, as each group tries to upstage the other. As I have written elsewhere,

> In effect, there has developed a culture where domination is seen as the best defense against bullying and then it becomes an end in itself. This is a critical aspect of the intra-group convergences of expectations. It is shared and promoted by the respective leaderships of the two parties, thus cementing a political culture that is resentful of co-operation, consensus, and notions of equivalence and of united governance. (2001, 1)

This aspect of the political culture is best reflected by the stubborn adherence of the political elites to the Westminster principle of "winner take all", a system of governance that serves as the democratic basis for racial domination in segmented societies (Lijphart 1999). Despite overwhelming evidence of the inadequacy of this system in promoting racial unity and equality, both major political parties when in power, or in anticipation of taking power, have resisted calls to introduce a new system aimed at ensuring a shared governance of the country. As I have argued,

An important reality of Guyanese politics is the reluctance, shared by both sides, to radically reform the arrangements of governance that concentrate power in the hands of one party, even when such reform is crucial to a lasting peace and economic progress. It is this shared reluctance to escape group expectations that has robbed Guyana of the opportunity to engage in new and innovative strategies aimed at confronting the country's deep-seated challenges. Political dynamism, accordingly, is not part of Guyana's political culture. (2001, 1)

While both parties have supported the need for changes when in opposition, this has been a tactic rather than a clear commitment to change. One manifestation of this attitude was the 1998 exercise in constitutional reform that resulted from an accord between the two parties following fierce violence in the wake of the 1997 election. The accord, brokered by the regional grouping of Caribbean countries, CARICOM, mandated constitutional reform as part of a menu of measures aimed at arresting the racial and political antagonisms and laying the groundwork for political trust and stability. However, although they advocated "inclusive governance", both parties ultimately rejected the numerous proposals for a change from the Westminster winner-take-all model to one of executive power sharing.

The PPP, assured of the majority Indian vote, has been a staunch foe of power sharing. This position is a direct contradiction to the party's stance while in opposition, when it tirelessly argued that shared governance was a prerequisite to political peace and economic development. Its 1977 proposal for a National Patriotic Front government was a central plank of its manifestos until the return of electoral democracy in 1992. In fact, in 1985 the PPP was engaged in discussions with the PNC towards the formation of a joint government, a position that was reiterated by party leader Dr Cheddi Jagan:

> We in the PPP in Guyana are calling for a revolutionary democratic, National Patriotic Government. For many years, for economic, ethnic/cultural/and security considerations, we have advocated "winner-does-not-take-all" politics; namely, that even though we consider that we alone could win a free and fair election, we would form not just a PPP, but a broad-based government including other parties, groups and social organizations. Only through such a government, with the people's fullest involvement, can a nation of one people and one destiny be built. (1993, 31)

However, upon winning the 1992 election, the PPP abandoned this position and formed the government on its own. It isolated its allies in the anti-dictatorial front in favour of some handpicked individuals sympathetic to the PPP. The party has labelled calls for power sharing undemocratic, and charges that such calls are aimed at denying the party its legitimate right to control the government. It current leader, Bharrat Jagdeo, has also argued that the system has not worked in other countries (2002).

For its part, the PNC, given its minority African base, relied on electoral rigging to maintain itself in office for twenty-eight years. While in power it repeatedly rejected offers by the PPP to share governance of the country. With the return of electoral democracy and the party's loss of power, it pinned its hopes of victory on the combination of a possible crossover Indian vote and other Indian-based parties' splitting the Indian vote. However, after three elections these expectations have not been fulfilled.

While a majority of the PNC leadership has opposed or has been at best lukewarm towards power sharing, the party has nevertheless challenged the one-party governance of the country on the grounds of discrimination and racial dominance. One may conclude, then, that the PNC finds itself in the dilemma of embracing the winner-take-all principle but rejecting its consequences when the party loses an election. But as the prospects of winning a fair poll have progressively diminished, and faced with pressures from within its ranks, the party has moved closer to power sharing. According to party leader Desmond Hoyte,

> An adjusted system of governance for our country – whether we call it "power-sharing," "shared governance," "inclusive governance" or any other name – appears to be an idea whose time has come. It could hardly be claimed that our present arrangements are working in the best interests of the country and its citizens. The imperfections obtrude everywhere and are a serious obstacle to national cohesion and development. In the circumstances, the imperative of constitutional adjustment appears to be unavoidable. I suggest, therefore, that we as a party give careful and anxious consideration to the insistent voices that are calling for constitutional and political reform. ("Hoyte Plugs Adjusted Governance", *Stabroek News*, 17 August 2002, 1)

Many observers have viewed this changed position with scepticism. According to Clarence Ellis,

Mr Hoyte says that an adjusted system of governance "appears" to be an idea whose time has come. The operative word is "appears". . . . We are, therefore, forced to believe that Mr Hoyte has some concept of shared governance in mind when it is obvious that he is prepared to walk the walk by laying down some markers on shared governance. (2002, 5)

Ellis's observation about the vagueness of the PNC's stance points to the key question of sincerity on the part of the political elites. Furthermore, while the PPP contends that it has been democratically elected, it has ignored the fact that this instance of formal democracy has not led to a democratization of governance and political relations. Adherence to the Westminster model by the elite, therefore, springs not from a commitment to liberal democracy, but from the model's potential for elite political domination and racial hegemony.

Despite their racial bases and leaderships, both major parties have historically refuted claims that they are race-based and have used two devices to prove this. First, they have tried to attract individuals from the opposite race at the leadership level. Thus it was not uncommon to find Indian government ministers and parliamentarians in successive PNC governments, most of them either ex-PPP members or professionals. When the PPP assumed office in 1992, it entered into a partnership with a loose group of Indian PPP supporters and African professionals called CIVIC.

The leader of CIVIC, Samuel Hinds, an African, was named prime minister but functioned as a mere figurehead as some of the traditional functions of the office were given to an Indian Cabinet member. After assuming the presidency in 1997 when President Cheddi Jagan died in office, he was forced to cede the presidential candidacy to Dr Jagan's wife at the next general election, returning as prime minister when the party won the election.

Similarly, the PNC entered into an alliance on the eve of the 2001 election with a group of PNC supporters and Indian professionals called REFORM, renaming the party PNC/REFORM. However, contrary to popular expectations, the leader of REFORM was not named as the party's prime ministerial candidate and the group has operated on the periphery of the party's decision-making councils.

Because of these alliances, both parties have claimed that they are broad-based and see no need for a power-sharing government including both parties. However, neither CIVIC nor REFORM has been able to garner any crossover support for the parties. Upon winning the 2001 election, the PPP broached the idea of a more inclusive government, but rather than embrace the intensified calls for a power-sharing government, it has sought to attract opposition party members into the government not as representatives of their party but in their individual capacities.

The Role of the Masses

This need for racial domination on the part of the elites is shared by the masses. The African and Indian masses, despite generally cordial day-to-day relations, crave the feeling that their leaders are in control of the country's governance. In a country where the masses of people have never had a chance to meaningfully take part in their governance and where the other race is seen as the cause of the country's ills, they settle for a form of governance that appears to protect them from domination by the other side. Thus, the masses have condoned authoritarianism and racial discrimination by their respective parties when they are in government but protest against these same things when the opposite party occupies the seat of government.

Since the split of the national movement in 1955, voting along racial lines has been the norm, as Indians and Africans have voted overwhelmingly for the PPP and PNC respectively. In what can be described as racial censuses, the results of the last three elections, for example, correspond with the racial breakdown of the population, which according to the last census put Indians at 51 per cent and Africans and mixed-race people at 42 per cent. The results of the last three elections were as follows: 1992, PPP 53 per cent and PNC 44 per cent; 1997, PPP 53 per cent and PNC 40 per cent; 2001, PPP 52 per cent and PNC 42 per cent (Election Affairs Bureau of Guyana 2001). The electoral support for the two major parties is, therefore, a vote simultaneously for racial security and against the threat of domination by the other party and race.

The poor showing of other race-based parties and the country's only non-racial party, the WPA, also reflects this phenomenon even when these parties enjoy some degree of popularity between elections. The WPA, which was the most vibrant and popular opposition party during the anti-dictatorial era, has seen its influence greatly diminish with the return of electoral democracy. To the surprise of most observers, the party managed just 1.7 per cent, 1.4 per cent and 2.5 per cent of the vote in the 1992, 1997 and 2001 elections respectively.

A vivid example of this tendency is the African village of Buxton, where the WPA has traditionally enjoyed much support. In a village that the party considers its stronghold, it has been able to garner no more than 15 per cent of the vote. Although this is the hometown of two prominent WPA leaders who enjoy overwhelming respect and popularity in the village, the WPA managed less than 15 per cent of the votes in the 1992 and 1997 elections and less than 5 per cent in 2001. Interviews with residents revealed continued support and admiration for the WPA, but a recognition that a vote for the PNC is the most potent means of achieving power for Africans, which they saw as the most urgent task. Some responses from the villagers include the following: "This is a racial war that only the PNC can win"; "We have to keep the Indians out"; "The WPA cannot win, so we will vote for the next best party" (personal interviews, December 2000).

Similarly, the tendency to vote against the other party and race is manifested by the Indian attitude to the newly formed Indian rights party Rise, Organise and Rebuild (ROAR). In a poll taken before the 2001 elections, 6 per cent of Indian respondents said they would vote for ROAR, but when asked how they would vote if there were a threat of a PNC victory, ROAR's support dropped to below 1 per cent (NACTA 1999). ROAR was accused by the PPP of wanting to split the Indian vote, and along with another party, the Guyana Democratic Party (GDP), led by a former PPP Cabinet minister, it was the object of a PPP smear campaign. ROAR and GDP subsequently received 0.4 per cent and 1 per cent of the vote respectively.

Omnipotence of the Party and the Leader

Allied to the culture of racial domination is the dominance of the political party and its leader. The culture of racial domination engenders an almost religious faith in the power of the political party as the mechanism through which this domination is secured and maintained. The party is the symbol of racial power and domination. While many Guyanese do not actually join parties, they nevertheless defer to their authority and look to them for their political cues. And while criticism of and resistance to the omnipotence of the party by its supporters is sometimes demonstrated between elections, it is often muted or confined to a small section of the population. Even this minor opposition disappears at election time, when everyone closes ranks.

In a country where state institutions are relatively weak, the political party assumes the role of official and unofficial mobilizer and enforcer. In fact the PNC, in 1974, introduced the concept of "paramountcy of the party", whereby the ruling party was deemed to be paramount to all organs of the state. Although the current PPP government has disavowed this idea in theory, it has governed in much the same manner in practice (Ellis 2001).

The parties therefore have taken their racial support for granted. For example, although the PNC has provided weak representation for African Guyanese since it became the opposition in 1992, this population has remained loyal to the party. One PNC official revealed that the PNC has refused to press the government to improve services to and the condition of Afro-Guyanese because it fears the government will take the credit and the party will be robbed of an electoral issue. When asked if the PNC does not fear losing the support of Africans, he said, "They have nowhere else to go" (personal interview, December 2000). A glaring example of this phenomenon is the issue of the relocation of the mainly Afro-Guyanese street vendors from a popular shopping centre to a less accessible location, a move which the PNC city councillors supported. However, the vendors concentrated their venom on the PPP-controlled central government while ignoring the PNC's complicity in their removal.

If the political party enjoys pride of place, the leader is larger than life. He or she is the "Messiah", "Liberator", "the Greatest" and "Comrade Leader". The convergence of the people's expectations of the leader and of the leader's perception of the meaning of those expectations has resulted in the institutionalization of an authoritarian form of leadership that begins at the level of the party and that is transferred to the state when the party assumes office.

This authoritarian attitude to leadership is endemic in Guyana's elite political culture. Both the PPP and the PNC founder-leaders, Dr Cheddi Jagan and Mr Forbes Burnham respectively, ruled the parties with iron fists. Both were unchallenged and consequently dictated who gained ascendancy or fell out of favour within the party. Despite rhetoric of collective leadership by both parties, the concept of "one-man" leadership or "leaderism" is entrenched. The WPA's concept of collective leadership, in the form of rotating leaders or co-leaders, has been ridiculed by both major parties, which refer to the WPA as a "headless party".

The leaders of the PPP and the PNC function less as firsts among equals and more as generals and commanders-in-chief. This unlimited authority is both formal and informal. The PNC's constitution, for example, gives the leader power over all organs of the party. He has the power to appoint and fire senior officers and to dissolve organs if he so desires. Although the PPP's constitution is less explicit about the unlimited power of the leader, its historical adherence to the Stalinist form of party organization ensures that actual power is concentrated at the top.

The current PNC leader, Desmond Hoyte, captured the awesome power of the leader when he explained his summary dismissal of a rebellious general secretary in the following terms: "The General Secretary is the creature of the leader" ("Hoyte: General Secretary Is Creature of the Leader", *Stabroek News*, 15 October 1999, 3). In another highly published episode, Mr Hoyte single-handedly engineered the expulsion from the party of his deputy and rival for the top spot despite the latter's popularity both in the party and among its supporters. Although many executives and rank-and-file members questioned Hoyte's actions in both instances, very little could be done as the leader had acted well within the powers granted him by the party's constitution.

The same culture exists in the PPP. In 1997 Janet Jagan, Dr Jagan's widow and successor, summarily demoted a popular Cabinet member when the latter rebuked the president's son in the media. Janet Jagan was also instrumental in catapulting the present holder of the presidency, Bharrat Jagdeo, over more senior party members. According to party insiders, Jagdeo was preferred to the more popular and senior Moses Nagamootoo because of the leader's dislike of Nagamootoo and because Jagdeo was her protégé. Janet Jagan's power within the party has been the subject of much scrutiny as she is known to be one of those leaders who prefer to wield power behind the scenes. In assessing her leadership role in the party Frederick Kissoon argues,

> She doesn't seek the leadership of her party, but the party knows she owns it, and she is in control, so they know she must have her decisions

implemented. . . . Once you play up to her, you will inherit her kingdom. Everyone who rose through the PPP leadership thinks that she lacks humanism and that she has a motto that either you are for me or you are against me. (2001, 6)

The leaders' authoritarianism is buttressed by the sycophantic attitude of the senior party members, who routinely defer to the leader even when they disagree with him or her. A case in point was a June 2000 move by ten senior PNC members to get the current leader, Hoyte, to step down. Hoyte, however, refused to step aside, and contrary to popular expectation the matter was promptly dropped. The masses have the same attitude to the leader, whose word is all that is needed for the followers to take action against opponents, including violent action.

Confrontational Politics

Another important aspect of Guyanese political culture is confrontation. Consensus is at best a last resort and in most cases is not an option. Even in instances when violence is obviously likely to follow, confrontation is zealously pursued. Political discourse among the political elites takes the form of threats and counter-threats, and meetings among leaders and parties are a rarity.

This culture was aptly demonstrated in the periods after the1997 and 2001 elections. After the 1997 election, the PNC refused to recognize the PPP government, thus robbing it of legitimacy. PNC leader Hoyte vowed to make the country "ungovernable" and led his supporters onto the streets. The PPP in turn insisted on its right to govern and instructed the police to crack down on demonstrators. Street violence, including violence against Indians, ensued. A full-scale civil war was averted only when CARICOM mediated a truce in the form of two agreements: the Herdmanston Accord and the St Lucia Declaration. Part of the truce called for ongoing dialogue between the PNC and the PPP under the supervision of a CARICOM-appointed facilitator. However, after a year the facilitator departed in frustration as the two parties used the dialogue not to address concerns but as a medium for confrontation. Subsequently, when a PPP delegate insisted that the two parties were not meeting as equals, the dialogue broke down without achieving anything. When it became obvious that the deadline set by the Herdmanston Accord for constitutional reform and new elections could not be met, a meeting of the PNC and PPP leaders, along with other parliamentary leaders, mandated an all-party committee to work out arrangements for governance between the Herdmanston deadline and the new date set for the elections. But after five weeks these talks too broke down without any agreement. Subsequent attempts by the WPA leader to broker an agreement also failed.

Similarly, after the 2001 election, which the PPP again won, the PNC rejected calls to negotiate a power-sharing arrangement with the PPP as a means of appeasing its supporters, who had begun street protests on their own. The party urged the supporters instead to escalate the pre-election slogan of "slow fire" to "more fire". The PPP then responded by ordering the police to crack down on a peaceful PNC protest, leading to several persons' being injured or arrested, including two leading members of the PNC. This action precipitated instances of arson that destroyed several (mainly Indian) businesses in the capital city, the erection by PNC supporters of roadblocks in several African villages and physical violence against Indians. Although the two leaders agreed to meet, they both stressed that they would negotiate only from a position of strength. When they eventually did meet, they agreed to a permanent dialogue between them and proceeded to set up several joint task forces to deal with some of the contentious issues. But after just over a year of this exercise, the PNC suspended the dialogue, claiming that the PPP had acted in bad faith. This action led to a resumption of hostilities as the PNC withdrew from Parliament and vowed to engage in what it calls "extra-parliamentary action", which has pushed the country to the brink of anarchy.

Allied to this culture of confrontation is a disdain for mediation emanating from within the country. Given the sharp racial division in Guyana, there is no mediating force in the society. Civil society is weak precisely because the civic organizations – religious organizations, trade unions and other non-governmental groups – are in one way or the other tied to the political parties. Consequently, the role of mediation has fallen on the shoulders of regional and international interests. A characteristic of the elite political behaviour is the ease with which they concede in the face of foreign mediation.

During the independence negotiations both the PNC and the PPP jockeyed for the inside track to the British government. The socialist PPP leader expressed faith in what he termed "British justice", a view that led him to leave the decision on the electoral system solely in the hands of the colonial secretary, Duncan Sandys. Much later, after almost three decades of resistance to pressure for free and fair elections by the opposition, the PNC leader dramatically agreed to almost all of the opposition demands in an agreement brokered by former US president Jimmy Carter. Similarly, in the aftermath of the 1997 elections when the PNC and PPP took the country to the brink of violent eruption, both parties readily signed an agreement brokered by a team of CARICOM mediators. This exercise was repeated six months later in St Lucia in the wake of a fresh wave of disturbances.

Doublespeak

Another strong pillar of the elite culture in Guyana is doublespeak, whereby leaders have two separate messages, one for the nation and another for the supporters. The PPP, for example, insists that it is a national party and projects a multiracial outlook. However, among its purely Indian constituency it resorts to a message aimed at racial solidarity. Similarly, the PNC denies on the national stage that it is a black party, but it refers to its purely African Guyanese audience as "kith and kin". In normal political discourse, the PPP and PNC describe other parties attempting to break into their respective bases as "fringe parties" and "small parties", but when they are speaking to the faithful, these other parties are accused of "splitting the vote" and being agents of the opposite race.

The WPA, for example, though multiracial in membership and ideology, has been projected by the two major parties as a race-based party. According to the PNC, the WPA wanted to seize power for Indians, while the PPP told Indians that the WPA was an African party concerned solely with African people. Such characterizations have largely led to the electoral marginalization of the WPA. Another example of this phenomenon is the Indian rights party ROAR. After ROAR's initial appeal to some sections of the Indian community, the PPP labelled ROAR as extremists bent on creating racial division in the society. However, when speaking directly to its Indian constituency, the PPP accuses ROAR of "splitting the vote" and waiting to join the African PNC. This mode of mobilization has had the effect of consolidating racial solidarity along party lines and stifling the emergence of a viable third party.

Conclusion

One of the peculiarities of Guyana's political culture is that while it generally reflects features of Third World culture, it goes against the general grain in some respects. First, contrary to Mehran Kamrava's finding (1999) that the political culture in racially and culturally diverse countries generally reflects this fragmentation, Guyana's two competing racial segments, with dissimilar histories and heritages, share similar political attitudes and values. However, given the intense political and economic competition between the two, this convergence of attitudes does not translate into a cohesive national culture.

Second, the fragmentation along class lines that is a feature of most Third World cultures does not manifest itself in Guyana. Although there are sharp class differences, these are not reflected at the level of political culture, primarily as a result of the racial cleavages. Racial considerations, therefore, supersede class considerations at the political level.

In these circumstances, the evolution and survival of an independent political culture is at best an exercise in frustration. Such attempts are denied political space, then portrayed as weak or co-opted as appendages of the larger parties. The same applies to the evolution of civil society, the emergence of independent yardsticks of social and economic performance, the functioning of the bureaucracy and the institutional framework – all of which become victims of the sharp racial-political divide. In such a situation, persons, groups and institutions are either for or against one or the other bloc. Even those who brave the frustrations and take pains to chart courses that do not originate in the expectations of domination are labelled as belonging to one camp or the other.

Finally, there has developed a well-demonstrated hostility to intellectuals in the political sphere. This has had the effect of driving academics and professionals to the periphery of political discourse and activity, thus leaving the political arena devoid of broadmindedness, imagination, purposeful conversation and the necessary skills to navigate the national ship in this knowledge-based global setting. In the last analysis, national ideals and vision do not figure heavily in Guyanese politics. Maintenance of the party in power, keeping the other out of power, ensuring the failure of the party in power and mollifying the party's base with the potential of racial security form the building blocks of the party's vision, which is then foisted on the nation as a national political culture.

References

Electoral Affairs Bureau of Guyana. 2001. *Reports on Elections*. Georgetown, Guyana: Electoral Affairs Bureau of Guyana.

Ellis, Clarence. 2001. "Notes on Power Sharing". *Guyana Commentary* 1, no. 4: 1.

———. 2002. "Mr Hoyte's Congress Statement Though Well Expressed Is Too Vague". *Stabroek News*, 21 August, 5.

Henry, Paget. 1983. "Desalinization and the Authoritarian Context of Democracy in Antigua". In *The Newer Caribbean: Desalinization, Democracy, and Development,* edited by Paget Henry and Carl Stone, 281–312. Philadelphia: Institute for the Study of Human Issues.

Hinds, David. 2001. "The Realities of Guyana's Politics". *Guyana Commentary* 1, no. 3: 3.

Jagan, Cheddi. 1993. "Keynote Address". In *The East Indian Diaspora: 150 Years of Survival, Contributions, and Achievements,* edited by Tilokie Depoo, Prem Misir and Basdeo Mangru, 13–33. New York: Asian American Center.

Jagdeo, Bharrat. 2002. "The President's Congress Speech". *Guyana Chronicle,* 21 July.

James, C.L.R. 1984. *Party Politics in the West Indies*. San Juan: Inprint Caribbean.

Kamrava, Mehran. 1999. *Cultural Politics in the Third World*. London: University Press of London.

Kissoon, Frederick. 2001. "The Window Opens Again". *Kaieteur News,* 6–13 April, 6.

Kwayana, Eusi. 1987. "Post-Independent Experiences in the Caribbean: The Guyana Case in Particular". Unpublished paper, Working People's Alliance.

Lijphart, Arend. 1999. *Patterns of Democracy: Government Forms and Performance in Thirty-Six Countries*. New Haven: Yale University Press.

Mars, Perry. 1998. *Ideology and Change: The Transformation of the Caribbean Left*. Detroit: Wayne State University Press.

North American Caribbean Teachers' Association (NACTA). 1999. "Poll Puts PPP/CIVIC out Front". 15 August.

Payne, Anthony. 1993. "Westminster Adapted: The Political Order of the Commonwealth Caribbean". In *Democracy in the Caribbean: Political, Economic, and Social Perspectives*, edited by Jorge I. Domínguez, Robert A. Pastor and R. DeLisle Worrell, 57–73. Baltimore: Johns Hopkins University Press.

Rodney, Walter. 1979. *People's Power: No Dictator*. Georgetown, Guyana: Working People's Alliance.

Thomas, Clive. 1984. *The Rise of the Authoritarian State in Peripheral Societies*. New York: Monthly Review.

[14]

The Dutch Caribbean
Studies in the Fragmentation of a Political Culture

Edward Dew

Introduction

In terms of ethnicity, we can identify three general types of Caribbean society. First, *Creole* societies are composed of two ranked cultural traditions: a dominant one from the colonial power and a subordinate one from Africa, surviving as an eclectic and modified system among the lower classes. These societies are marked by large-scale racial mixing that has produced intermediate socio-political sectors and a search for a national identity to emerge from the reconciliation and especially the modification of these two traditions. Second, unranked or bipolar societies are segmented in two parallel sections, one Creole and the other East Indian; although the Creole sector has generally held the political power, the East Indian has managed to acquire some economic and political resources as well, sufficient to put it into competition with the Creoles for power. In this model there is little intimate contact between groups, and an intermediate group, representing racial mixture or the search for cultural synthesis, is virtually non-existent. Finally, there are the multipolar societies of Belize in the English-speaking Caribbean and of Suriname and the Netherlands Antilles in the Dutch-speaking

Caribbean. Among these so-called plural societies, we find one or more Creole sectors and/or one or more sizable sectors representing still other distinct cultural traditions. In the Belize model, political and economic power is shared and contested by a number of groups divided as much by ethnic as by class characteristics. The process of governing under conditions of ethnic multipolarity would seem to demand prior multi-ethnic understandings and, once in operation, an ongoing spirit of compromise. Like the second type, the absence of cultural synthesis and a limited sense of national identity are stumbling blocks in the mounting of major developmental efforts.

In the Dutch Caribbean we find two more examples of this third type of society. In the case of Suriname, a country located on the South American continent, multi-ethnic complexity derives from the variety of groups imported as contract labourers during the nineteenth and early twentieth centuries. The Netherlands Antilles offers a different example of multipolarity. Here the critical fact is a sense of regionalism induced by the geographic separation of the six component islands, aggravated by highly variable population distributions. With strong feelings of regionalism cross-cutting the culture-class cleavages among a basically Creole population, politics has become seriously fragmented and disorganized.

Before examining these cases in detail, a few general historical observations about the Dutch Caribbean are in order. Commenting on the role of culture in the treatment of slaves, Harry Hoetink (1961) notes that slavery was practised with much greater severity in Suriname than in Curaçao (the most populous of the Netherlands Antilles islands) and that the latter's economy was based on commerce rather than agriculture. In Suriname, "the number of Whites [was never more than] seven percent of the number of slaves", while in Curaçao "Whites outnumbered slaves six to one" (p. 505). Hoetink adds that "in Curacao, the relation of the master to his slaves was based on individual contact [that is, with domestic servants], and nothing drove the insecurity of the owners to the point of sadism" (p. 505).

In both countries there was a considerable number of manumissions, especially of the mulatto sons of the masters. But here, too, there were differences. In Curaçao, the manumissions were frequently caused by economic difficulties that forced an owner to cut back his expenses by letting slaves go. In other words, slaves often functioned as a demonstration of conspicuous consumption. But in Suriname, their greater economic importance reduced this phenomenon considerably. The paradox in the subsequent development of race relations and the condition of freedmen, in general, was the emergence in Suriname, but not in Curaçao, of a strong coloured middle class. Hoetink attributes this to "the absence in Suriname of a European population group" which could perform the intermediate services and occupations that the society needed (1961, 509–13). But perhaps the significance of this variation between the two societies is not so important. Regardless of whether it was whites or mulattos who exercised power in the society, they used it to impede the mobility or participation of the other groups.

Suriname

In 1960, V.S. Naipaul wrote that

> Surinam has come out of Dutch rule as the only truly cosmopolitan territory in the West Indian region. The cosmopolitanism of Trinidad is now fundamentally no more than a matter of race; in Surinam diverse cultures, modified but still distinct, exist side by side. The Indians speak Hindi still; the Javanese live, a little bemused, in their own world, longing in this flat unlovely land for the mountains of Java; the Dutch exist in their self-sufficient Dutchness, the Creoles in the urban Surinam-Dutchness; in the forest, along the rivers, the bush-Negroes have re-created Africa. (Naipaul 1962, 170)

Naipaul adds that the Dutch legacies of religious tolerance and a language of limited utility have stimulated a multicultural and multilingual education: "Having access to so many worlds, the Surinamer is not as colonial-provincial as the British West Indian and is able to have a more objective view of his own situation" (1962, 180).

No one could deny that Suriname has an unusual mixture of races and cultures – "the world in miniature", according to the tourist folders. Table 14.1 shows that no group had a demographic majority at the time of the last complete census: in 1971, East Indians constituted 37 per cent of the population, Creoles 31 per cent, Javanese 15 per cent, Bush Negroes 10 per cent, and Amerindians, Chinese and Europeans 3, 2, and 1 per cent, respectively. The 1964 census offers still further data regarding the extent of cultural mixing that existed then (see Tables

Table 14.1: Suriname, Population by Ethnic Group, Censuses of 1964 and 1971 (in thousands)

	1964	1971
Creole[a]	115.0	118.5
East Indian	112.6	142.3
Javanese	48.5	58.9
Bush Negro	27.7	39.5
Amerindian	7.3	10.2
Chinese	5.3	6.4
White	4.3	4.0
Other[b]	3.5	5.1
Total	324.2	384.9

[a] Black, mulatto, and other individuals with some African parentage, such as black-Chinese and black-East Indian.

[b] Includes Syrio-Lebanese, Portuguese, Jews and unknown.

Source: Edward Dew, *The Difficult Flowering of Surinam: Ethnicity and Politics in a Plural Society* (Paramaribo, Suriname: VACO, 1995), 5.

14.2 and 14.3). For example, although the vast majority of East Indians, Javanese and Bush Negroes maintain their traditional beliefs, Catholic and Protestant missionaries have won many converts among them. Again, although Dutch is the official language, more widespread are Sranantongo, a Creole language with African, Iberian, Dutch and English elements; Sarnami Hindustans, a Surinamized mixture of the Indian languages Hindi and Urdu with borrowings from Dutch and Sranantongo; and Javanese, the traditional language of the Indonesian island of Java. A survey in 1969 that sought to find out the languages spoken by Surinamese heads of households revealed that 68 per cent spoke Dutch, 78 per cent Sranantongo, 36 per cent Sarnami Hindustans, and 21 per cent Javanese – that is, a little over two languages per person (Kruijer 1973, 120–21). The significance of the data rests in the fact that Sranantongo has a utility and range that is greater than Dutch and much greater than that indicated in Table 14.3. Nevertheless, despite the potential of Sranantongo and Dutch as unifying languages, Suriname's ethnic groups have preserved their individual

Table 14.2: Suriname, Population by Religion and Ethnic Origin, Census of 1964

	Protestant	Catholic	Hindu	Muslim	"Heathen"	Other[a]
Creole	59,630	47,658	272	443	–	6,958
East Indian	1,136	4,021	86,911	19,157	–	1,408
Javanese	1,319	1,668	162	43,933	–	1,381
Chinese	804	3,456	4	28	–	1,047
European	1,544	1,666	2	11	–	1,099
Bush Negro	5,548	5,275	–	–	16,875	–
Amerindian	284	5,889	8	16	960	130
Other[b]	802	1,533	216	221	–	736
Total	71,067	71,166	87,575	63,809	17,835	12,759
Percent	21.9	22.0	27.0	19.7	5.5	3.9

[a]Other, "nothing" and unknown.
[b]Other and unknown.
Source: Edward Dew, *The Difficult Flowering of Surinam: Ethnicity and Politics in a Plural Society* (Paramaribo, Suriname: VACO, 1995), 9.

Table 14.3: Suriname, Population over Six Years of Age by Best Spoken Language and Ethnic Origin, Census of 1964

	Dutch	Sranantongo	Sarnami Hindustani	Javanese	Other[a]
Creole[b]	61,389	27,939	195	90	1,318
East Indian	11,250	1,496	71,505	23	443
Javanese	2,724	561	22	34,766	35
Chinese	2,581	237	1	5	1,663
European	3,455	15	1	4	144
Other[c]	2,538	1,100	3	37	975
Total	83,937	31,348	71,727	34,925	4,578
Percent	37.1	13.8	31.7	15.4	2.0

[a]Chinese, African and Amerindian languages, and so on.
[b]Including Bush Negroes living outside their tribes.
[c]Syrio-Lebanese, Portuguese, and Amerindians living outside their tribe, and so on.
Source: Edward Dew, *The Difficult Flowering of Surinam: Ethnicity and Politics in a Plural Society* (Paramaribo, Suriname: VACO, 1995), 11.

cultural riches better than any other West Indian society with the possible exception of Belize.

There are subdivisions, as well, within each group – for example, the caste divisions among Hindus or the divergent cultural orientations among group members arising from the degree of their assimilation to the European culture and retention of native patterns. Conflicts emerging from these subdivisions have triggered the alternating fission and fusion of ethnic parties in the years since the Second World War (see also Dew 1995).

In the years of the Great Depression, conflicts between the Creole masses and the Dutch and mulatto elite culminated in violent disturbances between 1931 and 1933, but later a colonial policy that tried to benefit the Asian groups ironically repaired the breach in Creole ranks (Kom 1934; van Lier 1971). During the Second World War, members of the Staten (legislative council) demanded that the "pro-Asian" governor be removed. Unie Suriname was organized around this issue and the demand for local self-government. Some of its members later took part in organizing what became the country's largest Creole party, the Nationale Partij Suriname (NPS), in 1946. Rejecting the NPS's call for self-government, the East Indians and Javanese, together with a group of Creole Catholics, insisted first on the introduction of universal suffrage. The Catholic Creoles formed the Progressieve Surinaamse Volkspartij (Progressive Suriname People's Party, PSV), and after a number of similar attempts by the East Indians and Javanese to form parties along religious lines, two major Asian parties finally emerged along more secular ethnic lines: the Verenigde Hindostaanse Partij (United Hindustani Party, VHP) and the Kaum Tani Persatuan Indonesia (Indonesian Peasants' Party, KTPI). The power of the last three of these parties, like the case of the *mestizos,* Mayas and Catholic Creoles in Belize, served to convince the Dutch government to concede universal suffrage while submitting the question of autonomy to closer examination by a Roundtable Conference between the Netherlands, Suriname and the Netherlands Antilles.

The electoral system that the Dutch authorities introduced was, however, very much to the liking of the Creole elite. The country was organized into a series of districts, many of them with two representatives and the capital, Paramaribo, with ten. With no restriction on the number of candidates that parties could offer in this last district, the party that had the most votes could win all ten seats and thus a near majority of the seats in the Staten. In the first national elections under universal suffrage in 1949, the NPS won this ten-seat district as well as three other seats with a little over 17,000 votes nationwide compared with 19,000 for the VHP, 7,000 for the PSV and 5,000 for the KTPI. The VHP and the KTPI won six and two seats, respectively, in rural districts, but the PSV was shut out altogether – one man, one vote, ten seats.

Snatching defeat from the jaws of victory, the Creole Protestants almost immediately fell to fighting among themselves for control of the NPS. This struggle was won by representatives of the Creole lower and middle classes, but with the result that the government lost its majority in the Staten. In the new elections that followed, the NPS repeated its 1949 feat thanks to an electoral boycott by the Catholic opposition and the members purged from the NPS.

In these first two elections, ethnic stereotypes were in use, just as they would be a few years later in Guyana. Nevertheless, as politics began to burn all inter-ethnic bridges in the latter country, it was building them in Suriname. In 1953, after a new split in the NPS cost it its control over the legislature once more, the VHP offered to form a "brotherhood alliance" with the populist leader of the NPS, Johan Adolph Pengel. But the mostly Hindu VHP itself suffered a schism when two Muslim representatives joined with the two Muslims in the KTPI to ally with the expelled NPS legislators. It was a moment of great confusion but at the same time one of great significance, because in 1953 and 1954 the last Roundtable Meetings took place dealing with the future autonomy of the colonies. In December 1954, Queen Juliana ratified the Charter of the Kingdom of the Netherlands, giving complete autonomy to Suriname and the Netherlands Antilles. In 1955, the United Nations took Suriname off the list of dependencies for which trusteeship reporting was required.

Resurgence of the elite bloc cost Pengel his ten seats in Paramaribo in the election of 1955. Among the reasons cited to explain the defeat was the "uncivilized style" of Pengel and the fear among Creoles that his alliance with the East Indians could put the control of the country into their hands. The dependence of Pengel on the East Indians was made even more vivid in 1956 when the VHP leader, Jaggernath Lachmon, forced the resignation of one of his own representatives in the Staten so that Pengel could return to that body (as representative of an East Indian district). You could not find a more dramatic demonstration of *verbroedering* (brotherliness).

From 1958 to 1967, a new government dominated by the NPS and VHP worked to bury their ethnic differences, and, together with the smaller PSV and KTPI, produced an almost classical form of consociational (or multi-ethnic) power sharing. Ministries were divided among the participating parties, appointments and public investments were equitably distributed among the ethnic communities, and mutual concessions were made in the name of "brotherhood" and social harmony.

This co-operation was the more extraordinary for the negative stereotypes and attitudes Creoles and East Indians held about one another. Survey research between 1959 and 1961 revealed that 83 per cent of the Creoles disliked East Indians and 63 per cent of East Indians reciprocated the feeling (see Table 14.4). Enlightened leadership and a political willpower hardened by the challenge from Suriname's old elite made this gamble work – at least for a time.

In 1963 the electoral system was changed with the addition of two districts in the interior for the Bush Negroes, one district in the East Indian suburbs and a national district of twelve seats which would be divided according to proportional representation (that is, with seats divided in proportion to the votes parties received). This latter district, it was hoped, could exercise a corrective function in a system in which district representation signified the "waste" (that is, lack of representation) of many votes.[1] The adoption of this reform meant that after five years, without much legislative opposition, the "brotherhood alliance" was almost defeated by an alliance representing the Eenheidsfront and a new party of young East Indian nationalists. Now both the government and the opposition were multi-ethnic. Yet the existence of these consociational alliances did not signal a weakening or disappearance of ethnic politics since each opposition party tried to promise more than its rival in the government and alleged that the other party, through its political compromises, was betraying the interests of its ethnic group for personal gain.

The struggle for governmental benefits among the "brotherhood" partners was naturally aggravated by these opposition challenges. Ironically, the Dutch government chose this moment to disapprove the practice of patronage politics in the Surinamese bureaucracy, sharply

Table 14.4: Suriname, Attitudes of Creoles and East Indians towards Other Groups, 1959–1961 (percentages)[a]

	Positive	Negative	Neutral	No Opinion or No Answer
East Indian attitudes towards				
Creoles	9.5	63.0	9.5	18.0
Javanese	76.0	3.0	1.0	20.0
Chinese	46.0	16.0	12.0	26.0
Dutch	60.0	2.0	4.0	34.0
Creole attitudes towards				
East Indians	2.8	83.3	13.9	0.0
Javanese	76.3	3.5	18.8	1.4
Chinese	15.9	33.3	5.5	45.1
Dutch	39.6	35.4	21.5	3.5

[a]Percentages may not add up to 100 because of rounding.
Sources: J.D. Speckmann, "De Houding van de Hindostaanse Bevolkingsgroep in Suriname ten Opzichte van de Creolen", *Bijdragen tot de Taal-, Land-, en Volkenkunde,* no. 119 (1963): 88; H.C. van Renselaar, "De Houding van de Creoolse Bevolkingsgroep in Suriname ten Opzichte van de Andere Bevolkingsgroepen", *Bijdragen tot de Taal-, Land-, en Volkenkunde,* no. 119 (1963): 103. (The author rounded his data to 0.5 or the nearest whole number.)

reducing its subsidies and leaving the government unable to satisfy its parties' demands. After new elections in 1967, the NPS broke its alliance with the VHP, choosing instead to ally with the smaller opposition East Indian party. A truncated consociationalism emerged in both the government and the opposition,[2] but now the largest two parties in the country were divided, the NPS controlling a majority alliance and the VHP dominating the opposition (see Dew 1972). "Dealing everybody in" at the price of giving everybody something makes consociationalism an expensive political system. But where ethnicity is a strong political fact, "dealing a major player out" can be extremely risky, as Suriname was to find out.

After a prolonged teachers' strike in 1969, the Pengel government resigned, and the opposition, led by the VHP, won new elections, this time with a small Creole alliance partner. In the period from 1967 to

1973, the small parties that opted to go in with the NPS and VHP suffered popular repudiation by the ethnic group from which they sprang. New strikes by civil servants in 1971 and 1973 paralysed the VHP government without toppling it, and the Black Power ideology made its entrance into alienated sections of the Creole population.

Ethnic polarization reached its maximum point in the elections of November 1973. The majority of Creoles supported a new alliance of the NPS, PSV and KTPI, joined by the small Partij van de Nationalistische Republiek (PNR), which defended Creole popular culture and campaigned for independence. More than ever before, East Indians rallied around the VHP, which had small party allies among Javanese and Bush Negroes.[3] All the other independent parties – radical, Communist, moderate and conservative, including those Creole and East Indian parties considered likely post-electoral coalition partners for one of the big blocs – were overwhelmingly defeated. The surprising result was that the winners, the NPS, did not have a single East Indian in their parliamentary (or Cabinet) ranks, while the VHP opposition found themselves without a Creole ally (Dew 1974a, 1974b).

In this polarized setting, the government of Prime Minister Henck Arron[4] horrified his East Indian opposition with the announcement that he would seek independence as soon as possible. Despite large East Indian demonstrations against this move, Arron achieved his objective in November 1975. It should be pointed out that the Dutch government, affected by a rising wave of racism against the large number of Surinamese immigrants arriving in the Netherlands and wishing to put an end to its image as a colonial power, offered Arron its full co-operation (Dew 1973, 1976).

One might expect that Suriname's political development from here on would have been more positive. The conditions seemed propitious: a high level of education; many natural resources, some as yet untapped; a per capita national income of US$1,946 in 1980, much higher than the Caribbean average; the biggest per capita foreign aid programme in the world, with $1.6 billion dollars committed by the Dutch government over a period of fifteen years (Dew 1995); and a democratic system that had survived a number of crises, supported by a vigorous free press, a strong labour movement and a multi-ethnic infrastructure of responsible civic and religious organizations. Nevertheless, there was a great deal of poverty (in certain districts of

Paramaribo one could find shanty-type housing without water or sanitation dating from the days of slavery), and in the countryside living conditions were often crowded and inadequate. Unable to effect improvements in these conditions or to produce new economic growth, the Arron government presided helplessly over a massive migration to Holland, while the combative behaviour of the two great party blocs added to the demoralizing effect. In 1960, Naipaul wrote that "the Surinamers have avoided racial collision not by ignoring group differences but by openly acknowledging them" (1962, 164). In 1980, however, the reality was much more jaded and bitter. Racial incidents were not as frequent as in the immediate pre-independence period, but a flowering of national identity seemed further away than ever.

Thus, when in February 1980 a strike of non-commissioned officers in Suriname's tiny army escalated into a coup d'état, many Surinamers felt a new sense of hope that their political system might be overhauled and freed from the worst excesses of ethnic politics. Despite a flurry of radical reforms, the new leader of the military, Desi Bouterse, set up one civilian government after another, falling out with each of them over military spending, constitutional reform and the military's return to the barracks (Brana-Shute 1981; Dew 1983). After the killing of fifteen prominent opposition leaders in December 1982, the Netherlands cut off its aid programme and hundreds of officials, professionals and technicians fled the country, leaving a critical vacuum (Dew 1983). Having purged the military of officers critical of the killings, Bouterse now found himself increasingly dependent upon two small Marxist-Leninist parties for their expertise. However, warnings by the Netherlands, the United States and Brazil against the new radicalization of his government created a dilemma for both Bouterse and the members of the old parties (see also Dew 1985).

In 1987, faced with growing public restiveness and an unexpected guerrilla action by Bush Negroes in the country's interior, Bouterse permitted a referendum on a new constitution. Once it was overwhelmingly accepted, it was followed by elections for a democratic government (although the military managed to retain considerable power). A chastened consociationalism now re-emerged as the old parties buried the hatchet and ran a common ticket called the Front, made up of the NPS, the VHP and the KTPI.

Standing to the side, the military constituted an ominous force, maintaining its leadership cadre, defending the criminal behaviour of its troops and allegedly using the vast interior of Suriname and its control over the coastline for the trans-shipment of drugs to Europe from the interior of South America. The Front government found threats at every turn: "If you accept [the IMF's] structural adjustment policies, we will not defend you from the people's wrath"; "If you change the leadership in the military, you are asking for trouble"; "If you insist on peace with the rebels . . ."; "If you bring corruption charges on our members . . ." and so on.

In 1990, the military ordered the Front to step down. A military-backed regime held forth, spending sums of money that it had to print. New elections in 1991 brought the multi-ethnic coalition (now called the New Front) back to power, but with a smaller majority. Its leader was Ronald Venetiaan (NPS). Once again the military blustered, but this time the government managed to force Bouterse's resignation. Unfazed, Bouterse moved over to the political party he had earlier set up, the National Democratic Party (NDP), and led the parliamentary and extra-parliamentary attack on the government. Venetiaan brought the guerrilla war to an end and straightened up the government's budget.

In 1996 elections, Venetiaan's coalition slipped further (partly due to the pain induced by its acceptance of structural adjustment, imposed on Suriname by the IMF and the Dutch government). One seat short of a working majority but with small, anti-military alliance partners available, it nevertheless felt secure. To its great surprise, then, Bouterse managed to lure a dozen members of Venetiaan's New Front into crossing the aisle – enough to form an NDP government. Like the 1990–91 interim government, the new government, led by Jules Wijdenbosch (with Bouterse ever in the wings), has overseen a collapsing economy, a continuing drug trade and countless judicial and administrative irregularities. Strikes and street demonstrations led to a vote of no confidence in 1999 (as some New Front defectors switched back to the opposition). Wijdenbosch refused to step down; a two-thirds majority was necessary to install a new president, and the legislature had only enough votes to censure. Intimidation failed to still the local press.

President Wijdenbosch at least followed the timetable, scheduling new elections in June 2000. As usual, a large number of parties competed. The winning coalition, the New Front, once again brought together the NPS, the VHP, the Javanese (with a new name, Pertjajah Luhur) and the small Surinamese Labour Party. This time the coalition held, and Ronald Venetiaan was returned to the presidency. As before, the New Front government was faced with daunting problems, including how to restore a productive economy and re-establish collaboration with the Dutch (who still held hundreds of thousands of dollars in reserved development aid, frozen at the time of the murders in 1982). And what could Venetiaan do about the many human rights violations that had been committed by the military (Dew 1994)?

Suriname's ethnically fragmented society poses a severe political challenge to its aspiring leaders. As no ethnic group comes anywhere near majority status, democratic government must be supported by multi-ethnic alliances. Each group can look back less than fifty years to see its socio-economic origins as an oppressed minority (under Dutch and/or Westernized Creole elite rule), so each is still in the process of asserting its culture, its social place and its right to a share of power.

The Surinamese people may distrust one another, but they are knowledgeable about each other's culture and tolerant of all that goes with it. Children attend ethnically mixed schools, and neighbourhoods are also largely mixed. People attend each other's parties and ceremonies. Even in the workplace, where a more intimate level of co-operation is required, one sees the same mix of peoples. Much of the credit for this can go to the schools and the media, but tolerance and co-operation are also preached at the heart of each culture – in the churches, temples and mosques, whose leaders meet frequently to address common problems.

Political parties have traditionally been ethnically based. This means that election campaigns involve two levels of discourse: the idealistic message of harmony and issue generalities, and the more defensive emphasis on voting for "your own kind" to guarantee your share in the system's outputs. Working out the distribution of power (seats, ministries, policies) is an enormous challenge for parties, whether they form pre-election or post-election alliances. Some parties have entered the field with a claim to being internally multi-ethnic (or non-ethnic). But whatever they say or do, their top leadership affixes their ethnic identity. In this hyperethnic atmosphere, they have usually been marginalized. The NDP is an example. It disdains the ethnic basis of Suriname's politics, yet it has difficulty drawing non-Creoles to its ranks. Bouterse and

Wijdenbosch are both Creoles, as are many of the party's military and non-military members. It was able to come to power by raiding the New Front and taking Hindustani and Javanese members into its government.

Fiscal constraints (even when disregarded) make for a tight decision-making environment. If proportionality is insisted upon by government members, at the risk of pulling out and toppling the government, leaders are confronted with the prospect of stasis as the safest route. If a balance of dissatisfaction is a shaky path to governmental stability, a culturally plural society such as Suriname is fated to see few development breakthroughs. Its best days (under the Dutch in the 1960s) may be behind it.

The Netherlands Antilles

After the collapse of the West Indies Federation in 1962, Prime Minister Erroll Barrow of Barbados said that "we live together very well, but we don't like to live together together" (cited in Lowenthal 1972, 9). This might seem to be a general sentiment throughout the Caribbean. There have been manifestations of "small-islandism" in the behaviour of Anguilla in separating from St Kitts in 1967, in Nevis's strained relations with St Kitts and in Tobago's autonomy movement. But the most extreme case of this phenomenon is that of the Netherlands Antilles. This entity consists of two groups of islands separated by roughly 600 miles: one is found among the Leeward Islands to the east of Puerto Rico and includes the islands of Sint Eustatius (11 square miles with 1,900 inhabitants), Saba (5 square miles with 1,200 inhabitants) and Sint Maarten (13 square miles with 40,000 inhabitants); the other is about 40 miles off the coast of Venezuela and includes Curaçao (171 square miles with 164,000 inhabitants), Aruba (75 square miles with 88,000 inhabitants) and Bonaire (111 square miles with 15,000 inhabitants).

Differences between the islands are significant. In terms of inhabitants, the northern islands possess less than 14 per cent of the total population of 310,100, while the southern islands are sharply unequal among themselves. Linguistically, although the official language of the Netherlands Antilles is Dutch, the popular language on the northern islands is English, while that in the south is Papiamento, a Creole language combining Iberian, Dutch, African and English influences.[5] The

1972 census indicated that almost 90 per cent of the southern population was Catholic, while the northern islands were, for the most part, Protestant (Streefkerk 1977, 53–54). Racial structure also varied among the islands, with important intra- and inter-island consequences. Albert Gastmann summarizes the situation as follows:

> A majority of the people in Curaçao are wholly or in part of African descent. There are, however, small groups of Dutch Protestants, Sephardic Jews, and other Europeans. Blacks and mulattoes constitute the majority on Bonaire, Saint Martin, and Saint Eustatius. Whites are a prominent segment of the population on Saba, while Arubans are mostly mestizos (in part descendants of Amerindians and whites) and whites. (1979, 229)[6]

Demographically, the situation is complicated further by the presence of thousands of resident alien workers in both Curaçao and Aruba. In 1971, for example, Aruba could count 1,250 labourers from the other Dutch Antilles and the Netherlands, 650 from Suriname, 2,000 from the English-speaking Caribbean, 826 from Venezuela and over 2,000 from still other places of origin (Hartog 1980, 68). Among these were many blacks and mulattos, providing a sharp contrast with their very light-skinned hosts.

Slavery did not figure importantly in the history of Aruba. But it did in Curaçao. As pointed out at the outset of this chapter, slaves were not treated as badly in Curaçao as in Suriname or elsewhere in the Caribbean, but at the same time, the opportunities for manumitted freedmen were extremely limited. Hoetink (1960) writes that the poverty of freedmen was so great that they organized gangs to victimize one another and society in general. He adds that "the conversion of the Blacks to Protestantism not only would have damaged a metropolitan symbol of social status, but would also have signified acceptance of the other [that is, lower] segments as potentially equal; . . . 'the others' had to remain 'different', as much as possible" (p. 188). As a consequence, the elites allowed the slaves to be Catholicized, which explains the striking religious contrast between the two historically dominant groups, the white Protestants and the Jews, and the black and mulatto Catholic majority. Sidney Mintz (1971) describes the evolution of Papiamento as a similar product of conscious social differentiation, safeguarding the languages of the two elite groups, Dutch-speaking Protestants and Portuguese-speaking Jews.

Papiamento has accordingly been viewed as a curse, by some, to the future development of this society.[7] In particular, the delay in establishing a public education system meant that the language of instruction, Dutch, was virtually unknown to the majority of students.[8] Yet all efforts to introduce Papiamento into school curricula have been impeded by the political rivalry between Curaçao and Aruba with respect to the proper orthography and use of the language (Muller, n.d.), and public debates have taken place on both islands about the wisdom of using such a language in the schools.[9]

As a consequence of the late development of public education, there was a sharp demand for educated workers when the Shell and Lago oil companies established their huge refineries for Venezuelan crude on Curaçao in 1915 and on Aruba in 1924, respectively. As the islands themselves could not satisfy this need, immigration of foreign workers from other parts of the Caribbean virtually swamped the two islands; in Aruba in 1951, just 50 per cent of the population had been born there (Green 1974, 34), while in Curaçao, although the process of automation had begun to reduce the labour force by 1959, some 29 per cent of the population in that year had been born elsewhere (Hartog 1968, 375). In Aruba, where the native population was light-skinned and, according to Peter Verton (1977b), not as sharply stratified as in Curaçao, the entry of an alien, and mostly black, labour force caused the local population to close ranks and introduce discriminatory practices to preserve their identity and control. In Curaçao, the arrival of these workers complicated a situation that was already fairly conflicted, with blacks and mulattos languishing in poverty and systematic neglect.

Hoetink (1960) says that only in the second decade of the twentieth century was the term *landskind*, or "son of the land", used to differentiate between natives and immigrants. The tell-tale sign that separated Curaçaoans or Arubans from their non-native counterparts was the use of Papiamento. Rene Romer (n.d.) points out that the Protestant and Jewish elites extended the concept *yu di Korsow* ("son of Curaçao" in Papiamento) to the entire native population of the island, but that black and mulatto Curaçaoans spoke of *nos bon yu di Korsow* ("we the true sons of Curaçao") in a more exclusive sense, so as to exclude even the elites. This reflected their sense of grievance against the *makambas* (whites), but it also, according to Romer, derived from their widespread, and incorrect, belief "that the Blacks had arrived [in Curaçao] before the Whites" (n.d., 53).

Political development in Curaçao and Aruba was promoted by a combination of foreign workers, who brought the organizational skills and motivation to develop unions, and elites, who organized political parties to pursue autonomy from the Netherlands. The unionizing activity was continually impeded by the petroleum industry, which, with the help of the colonial authorities, expelled many of the leaders. Ironically, Curaçao and Aruba were considered "schools of Unionism" for the Caribbean, producing leaders such as T. Albert Marryshow and Eric Gairy in Grenada, as well as the first union organizers in Suriname (Lewis 1968, 157; see also Dew 1995; Soest 1977). But for Curaçao and Aruba themselves, this policy of "expel and rule" left the union movement in the hands of poorly educated leaders who, instead of seeking positive benefits, had to fight for the preservation of jobs in an industry that began increasingly to streamline and automate its production (Romer 1979; Verton 1977a). Romer indicates that the number of Dutch Antilleans in the workforce of Shell fell from 4,896 in 1957 to 2,934 in 1970 but that the percentage of "locals" rose over the same period from 48 per cent to 85 per cent (1979, 105).

With regard to the organization of political parties, the Catholics began the process in the 1930s with the Katholieke Volkspartij (KVP), inspired by a young lawyer, Moises Frumencio da Costa Gomez. Da Costa Gomez's doctoral thesis had issued a powerful call for local self-government and universal suffrage.[10] As in Suriname, the former was accepted by many as desirable but the second was rejected by the elites. When universal suffrage was imposed by the Dutch in 1948, the Antillean elites, like those in Suriname, bowed to the inevitable and reoriented their own Demokratische Partij (DP) towards socio-economic reform, autonomy and the replacement of Dutch *makambas* in the civil service with native residents (Verton n.d.).

Although the Catholic parties (the KVP was now named the Nationale Volkspartij, NVP) took power in 1951, the DP and its Aruban counterpart, the Partido Patriotico Arubano (PPA), gave them vigorous opposition. After negotiating full autonomy in the Roundtable Conference with the Netherlands and Suriname in 1954, the NVP–AVP (Arubaanse Volkspartij) government was defeated by the DP–PPA coalition, and this combination remained in power until 1969. It appears that a principal source of this coalition's strength came from non-indigenous voters with Kingdom citizenship (Verton n.d.). However, there were no programmatic differences between the two coalitions, according to Romer (1979), and both had white and mulatto middle- and upper-class leadership. Romer and Verton are explicit on this point: the leaders of all the parties set themselves up as brokers between industry and government, on the one hand, and the masses, on the other. The latter found themselves effectively without power, divided in small groups and dependent upon the patronage of their leaders.

A violent explosion of social and economic resentments occurred in Curaçao on 30 May 1969, when a strike against a Shell subcontractor escalated into a general strike (Romer 1979).[11] A march to the governor's office in downtown Willemstad, the capital, attracted thousands of unemployed Curaçaoans and ended in widespread looting and fires, mostly directed at the stores of non-natives.[12] The escalation of violence surprised the union members participating in the march, and some blame was directed to Black Power organizers. But even if the ideas of the Black Power movement may have been alien to the society, they found a broad and receptive audience among the masses (See Kikkert and Bekman 1977; Romer 1979; Verton 1976).

The consequences of these events were varied. Both the DP–PPA government and the governor of the Netherlands Antilles resigned, and a commission was installed to investigate the disturbances.[13] In the elections of September 1969, the Frente Obrero y Liberacion 30 di Mei (Worker and Liberation Front, May 30; FOL), led by a number of strike veterans, won almost one-quarter of the votes. But their post-electoral alliance with the DP caused great consternation among their followers. Verton (1976) notes that the new government produced legislation that was favourable to the unions but failed to do anything to improve the lot of the unemployed. The nomination of Efrain Jonckheer, former prime minister and leader of the DP, as governor was rejected by the FOL and other groups emboldened by what they called the "uprising". Their pressure against Jonckheer, a white Curaçaoan, succeeded when the Dutch withdrew his name and selected B.M. Leito, a black, in his place. This in turn infuriated the Arubans, who launched a movement to separate from the federation (Verton 1976).

After the promise of self-government enunciated during the Second World War by Queen Wilhelmina, the Arubans had already sought autonomy from Curaçao as well as from the Netherlands. Under the Charter of the Kingdom, international affairs, nationality questions and the protection of civil rights were reserved by the central Kingdom government, with all others matters delegated to the component units (in The Hague, Paramaribo and Willemstad). The constitution of the Netherlands Antilles divided powers between island councils and the federal government, reserving to itself the organization of the justice system, education, money and finances, public administration and immigration.[14] For the Arubans, this division did not signify sufficient autonomy, and the events of May 1969 revived their resentments, in particular regarding the costs they expected to have to bear for solving the unemployment and repairing the damage in Curaçao. Another new party, the Aruban Movimiento Electoral de Pueblo (MEP), led by Betico Croes, grew rapidly in the 1970s, advocating the reduction of the central powers of the government in Curaçao and a *status aparte* for Aruba (Gastmann 1979).[15]

The emergence of the MEP, the FOL and several other parties representing the increased political consciousness of the lower classes complicated national political life more than ever before. Although Curaçao possessed over half of the federal population, the federal constitution had overrepresented Aruba in the national legislature (with eight seats to Curaçao's twelve, and one each to Bonaire and to the northern islands collectively; Kikkert and Bekman 1977). Theoretically, Curaçao could manage a majority government without inter-island co-operation. And nevertheless, party divisions within each of the two principal islands required such coalitions to govern. But the demands of the new parties now produced a national paralysis as bad as that which had produced the 1969 turbulence. Perhaps the only thing that saved the system was a dramatic increase in financial subsidies from the Netherlands (which had apparently learned from its mistake earlier in the 1960s in Suriname). These subsidies, however, have produced popular expectations of a level and style of life that, according to Romer and other critics, are unrealistic and inappropriate (Romer, n.d.; Kikkert and Bekman 1977).

In March 1983, island delegations met in a new Roundtable Conference in the Netherlands. After a week of heated talks, it was announced that the Charter of the Kingdom would be changed in 1986, conceding *status aparte* to Aruba. For ten years, they would participate in a union of the Netherlands Antilles and Aruba, before receiving their independence (Timmer 1983, 11–13). After 1996, the Union could continue, if all the members agreed. Terms for the Union included creation of a new parliament on top of the present one; Aruba and "the five" shared power with twelve seats apiece. This parliament's powers would involve co-ordination of fiscal and monetary policy, and approval of laws would require an absolute majority in each delegation. Moreoever, the Aruban legislature would receive all the powers that now resided in the Staten in Willemstad, while the latter would continue to house the government of the remaining five.[16]

In the Antilles-of-the-Five, divisions initially somewhat reduced Curaçao's representational position in the Staten: Curaçao received 21 seats, St Maarten 11, Bonaire 9, and Saba and St Eustatius 5 each. (After constitutional revision in 1992, the Staten was reduced in size to 22, and seat distribution was 14, 3, 3, 1 and 1.) In societies in which over 90 per cent of basic consumer goods are imported and where the petroleum, shipping and hotel industries have encountered mounting economic difficulties, the consensus required among "the five" may be very elusive (Timmer 1983). Unfortunately, the economy of Curaçao was hard hit in the late 1980s by the Venezuelan takeover of the Shell refinery, as well as by a sharp decline in the use of Curaçao's excellent dry-dock facilities and of its financial services (which were cut in a revised tax treaty with the United States). The Dutch at first offered grants and loans to tide people over, but when the debt level reached US$1.5 billion, they and the International Monetary Fund demanded increased austerity – privatization of some government operations, lay-offs of upwards of a thousand public servants and an end to costly party patronage and corruption (*NRC-Handelsblad*, 12 September 2000). A sharp cut in the government's travel budget is expected only to fray the strands of national community all the more (*NRC-Handelsblad*, 13 September 2000). In 2000 as many as 10,000 of Curaçao's 150,000 residents were expected to emigrate, mostly to the Netherlands (*NRC-Handelsblad*, 13 September 2000). Hard times aggravated the task of keeping this unusual society together.

Conclusions

The ethnic divisions in the Netherlands Antilles and Suriname are so great that socio-political development has been, and continues to be, very difficult in them both. In the one, geographic divisions between the six islands are reinforced by linguistic, religious and racial differences. In the other, the differences are cultural for the most part, although geography and racism play minor roles – the East Indians and Javanese are concentrated more in rural areas and the former exhibit a certain racial prejudice on top of their cultural disdain for the Creoles. In each one of the southern islands, Papiamento might be expected to serve as a unifying force, especially with the decline in the non-indigenous workforce. In Suriname, Sranantongo performs a function similar to Papiamento, but with deeper roots here than in the Antilles, Dutch hangs on as a second, more formal lingua franca. Spanish and English are probably more important than Dutch in the Antilles, with Venezuelan tourism, radio and television exercising especially important influences. One result of this is that the pattern of emigration by Antilleans to the Netherlands has been much more limited than by Surinamers, at least until recently.

It is not surprising that the campaign for independence was much stronger in Suriname. Suriname was more favourably endowed with natural resources and a promising economic future – facts that even under an unpopular dictatorship may not be denied. One factor of importance in the Antillean vacillation regarding independence – in addition to their many internal problems – is their geopolitical position with regards to Venezuela and their consequent fear of annexation. An agreement was reached between the Netherlands and Venezuela in 1977 recognizing the maritime frontier between Venezuela and the islands, but fear of Venezuela may remain a retardant factor in the de-colonization process in the Antilles (see Gastmann 1983). Another factor, as mentioned earlier, is the example of Suriname itself. The unexpected coup of 1980 and the new military Government received a great deal of attention in the Antilles, but after the murders of December 1982, public opinion crystallized negatively towards Bouterse's regime, and the preparatory meetings for the 1983 Roundtable Conference were filled with caution and warning references to the Surinamese experience. At the same time, the restructuring of the federation into a Union of the Netherlands Antilles and Aruba, by its adjustment to an internal geopolitical reality, may be able to liberate the Government of Curaçao from some of its structural impediments and lead to a more direct and adequate translation of the popular will into policy.

In Suriname, the failure of parliamentary democracy has contributed to a higher awareness of the value of democratic institutions and the problems of protecting them and making them work. It might be questioned whether or not the source of the problem is in the society rather than in the institutions or the leaders. The Surinamese people gave no support in the past to multi-ethnic political parties, consequently forcing Suriname's democratic development along increasingly divisive lines. But when the army tried to construct an alternative model of democracy in the radical, populist style of Grenada and Cuba, this suffered an even more profound popular repudiation than the fully ethnicized one. This costly learning process may produce a new general will among Surinamers to restore their democratic institutions and to make them function with greater dedication to the public interest.

Notes

1. In 1967, both the district of Paramaribo, with its ten representatives, and a new district of its suburbs, now consolidated and increased to six representatives, were converted to proportional representation.
2. A new Javanese party had emerged in these years as well, providing strong opposition to the KTPI.
3. The cultural differences between Creole blacks and the Bush Negroes of the interior are immense; see Price (1973) and Herskovits and Herskovits (1934).
4. Pengel died in 1970, and Arron was chosen as his replacement.
5. Sidney M. Joubert (n.d.) indicates that 66 per cent of the principal words are of an Iberian or Hispanic-American origin, 28 per cent from Dutch and 6 per cent from other sources.
6. For more information on the Aruba population, see Green (1974). For an analysis of the northern islands, see Keur (1957).
7. For a different perspective, see, among others, Broek (1999).
8. An investigation by Nelly Winkel in the 1970s indicated that 66 per cent of the Papiamento-speaking students in the sixth grade had had to repeat one or more years in school, while the figure among those speaking Dutch was only 19 per cent (cited in Joubert, n.d., 24).
9. Muller (n.d.) expresses the fear that the introduction of Papiamento in the schools might serve to promote the creation of private schools for the elites, deepening the class divisions in the society. Nevertheless, he asks,

    what does one say to his child when he finds the majority of other children speaking Papiamento everywhere, while his parents speak Papiamento with everyone but Dutch with him (presumably to aid him in his studies and social mobility)? I fear that this generation of children is going to grow up with a certain disdain towards their "native" language and perhaps even towards their country. (Muller n.d., 29–30)

See also *Amigoe de Curaçao,* 11 February 1983 and 8 April 1983, for examples of the debate on the introduction of Papiamento in the schools.

10. M.F. da Costa Gomez, *Het Wetgevend Orgaan van Curaçao: Samenstelling en Bevoegdheid bezien in het kader van de Nederlandse Koloniale Politiek* (Amsterdam: n.p., 1935), cited in Verton (n.d., 13).
11. See also Verton (n.d.; 1977a); Kikkert and Bekman (1977) describe the Curaçaoan political parties and unions as little more than social clubs whose members were united by personal rather than ideological relations.
12. Gastmann writes that the workers were protesting against "the practice of Shell utilizing subcontractors who paid lower salaries while demanding more hours of work" (1979, 227).
13. See *Facts on File* 29, no. 1492 (1969): 340; Verton (1976).
14. There are four councils – one for each southern island, and one for the three northern ones.
15. In an Aruban referendum in 1977, 59 per cent of the electorate actually supported a move towards independence (Gastmann 1979, 233).
16. For all the terms of the accord, see "The Resolutions", *Antillen Review* 3, no. 3 (1983): 7–9.

References

Brana-Shute, Gary. 1981. "Politicians in Uniform: Suriname's Bedeviled Revolution". *Caribbean Review* 10, no. 2: 24–27, 49–50.
Broek, Aart G. 1999. "Literary Historiography: Premises and Consequences: The Case of a History of Literary Writing in Papiamentu". *Wadabagei: A Journal of the Caribbean and Its Diaspora* 2, no. 2: 35–54.
Dew, Edward. 1972. "Surinam: The Test of Consociationalism". *Plural Societies* 3, no. 4: 35–56.
———. 1973. "The Draining of Surinam". *Caribbean Review* 5, no. 4: 8–15.
———. 1974a. "Elections Surinam Style". *Caribbean Review* 6, no. 2: 20–26.
———. 1974b. "Surinam – The Struggle for Ethnic Balance and Identity". *Plural Societies* 5, no. 3: 3–17.
———. 1976. "Anticonsociationalism and Independence in Surinam". *Boletin de Estudios Latinoamericanos y del Caribe* 21 (December): 3–15.
———. 1983. "Surinam Tar Baby: The Signature of Terror". *Caribbean Review* 12, no. 1: 4–7, 34.

———. 1985. "Suriname 1983". In *Latin America and Caribbean Contemporary Record*, Vol. 3, *1983–1984*, edited by Jack W. Hopkins, 445–53. New York: Homes and Meier.

———. 1994. *The Trouble in Suriname, 1975–1993*. Westport, Conn.: Praeger.

———. 1995. *The Difficult Flowering of Surinam: Ethnicity and Politics in a Plural Society*. Paramaribo, Suriname: VACO.

Gastmann, Albert L. 1979. "Continental Europe and the Caribbean: The French and Dutch Experience". In *The Restless Caribbean: Changing Patterns of International Relations*, edited by Richard Millett and W. Marvin Will. New York: Praeger.

———. 1983. "The Netherlands Antilles". In Latin America and Caribbean Contemporary Record, Vol. 1, 1981–1982, edited by Jack W. Hopkins, 598–606. New York: Holmes and Meier.

Green, Vera. 1974. *Migrants in Aruba: Interethnic Integration*. Assen, Netherlands: Van Gorcum.

Hartog, Johannes. 1968. *Curaçao: From Colonial Dependency to Autonomy*. Aruba: De Wit.

———. 1980. *Aruba: Short History*. Aruba: Van Dorp.

Herskovits, Melville J., and Frances S. Herskovits. 1934. *Rebel Destiny: Among the Bush Negroes of Dutch Guiana*. New York: McGraw-Hill.

Hoetink, Harry. 1960. "Curazao como Sociedad Segmentada". *Revista de Ciencias Sociales* 4: 179–92.

———. 1961. "Diferencias en Relaciones Raciales entre Curazao y Surinam". *Revista de Ciencias Sociales* 5: 499–514.

Joubert, Sidney M. n.d. "El Papiamento: Lengua Criolla de Curazao, Aruba y Bonaire". *Kristof* 3: 1.

Keur, Dorothy L. 1957. "Metropolitan Influence in the Caribbean: The Netherlands". In *Caribbean Studies: A Symposium*, edited by Vera Rubin, 796–801. Mona, Jamaica: Institute of Social and Economic Research.

Kikkert, O.H., and A.A.M. Bekman. 1977. *Drempelvrees: Een Book over Curaçao aan de Vooravond van de Onafhankelijkheid*. Assen, Netherlands: Van Gorcum.

Kom, Anton de. 1934. *Wij Slaven van Suriname*. Amsterdam: Contact.

Kruijer, G.J. 1973. *Suriname, Neokolonie in Rijksverband*. Meppel, Netherlands: Boom.

Lewis, Gordon. 1968. *The Growth of the Modern West Indies*. New York: Monthly Review.

Lier, R.A.J. van. 1971. *Frontier Society: A Social Analysis of the History of Surinam*. Translated by M.J.L. van Yperen. The Hague: Martinus Nijhoff.

Lowenthal, David. 1972. *West Indian Societies*. New York: Oxford University Press.

Mintz, Sidney. 1971. "The Socio-Historical Background to Pidginization and Creolization". In *Pidginization and Creolization of Languages,* edited by Dell Hymes, 481–98. Cambridge: Cambridge University Press.

Muller, Enrique. n.d. "Papiamentu and the Search for a Better Community". *Krisitoff* 6, no. 1: 28.

Naipaul, V.S. 1962. *The Middle Passage*. New York: Vintage.

Price, Richard, ed. 1973. *Maroon Societies: Rebel Slave Communities in the Americas*. New York: Doubleday.

Romer, R.A. 1979. *Een Volk op Weg-Un Pueblo na Kaminda: Een Sociologisch Historische Studie van de Curaçaose Samenleving.* Zutphen, Netherlands: De Walburg Pers.

———. n.d. "Het 'Wij' van de Curaçaoenaar". *Kristof* 1: 2.

Soest, Jaap van. 1977. *Olie als Water: De Curaçaose economie in the eerste helft van de twintigste eeuw.* Zutphen, Netherlands: De Walburg Pers.

Speckmann, J.D. 1963. "De Houding van de Hindostaanse Bevolkingsgroep in Suriname ten Opzichte van de Creolen". *Bijdragen tot de Taal-, Land-, en Volkenkunde,* no. 119: 76–92

Streefkerk, C. 1977. "Godsdienstige Gebruiken en Opvattingen". Cultureel Mozaiek van de Nederlandse Antillen, edited by Rene A. Romer, 43–55. Zutphen, Netherlands: De Walburg Pers.

Timmer, H. 1983. "Status Aparte: Freedom with Commitments." *Antillen Review* 3, no. 3.

van Renselaar, H.C. 1963. "De Houding van de Creoolse Bevolkingsgroep in Suriname ten Opzichte van de Andere Bevolkingsgroepen". *Bijdragen tot de Taal-, Land-, en Volkenkunde,* no. 119: 93–105.

Verton, Peter. 1976. "Emancipation and Decolonization: The May Revolt and Its Aftermath in Curaçao". *Revista/Review Interamericana* 6, no. 1.

———. 1997a. "Modernization in Twentieth-Century Curaçao". *Revista/Review Interamericana* 7, no. 2.

———. 1997b. *Politieke Dynamiek en Dekolonisatie*. Alphen aan den Rijn, Netherlands: Samson.

———. n.d. *Kiezers en Politieke Partijen in de Nederlandse Antillen*. Aruba: De Wit.

[15]

Rethinking Democracy in the Post-Nationalist State
The Case of Trinidad and Tobago

Percy C. Hintzen

Introduction

In Africa and throughout the African diaspora, a black elite has employed notions of black diasporic intimacy as a basis of political mobilization. It has done so in pursuit of aspirations for inclusion in national and international arenas of power. Since the advent of colonialism, these arenas were the exclusive preserves of a white elite organized internationally in support of racialized forms of national domination. The black elite exploited popular sentiments of diasporic intimacy to organize racial challenges to white supremacy within and across national borders. In the process, it rendered invisible its own aspirations to whiteness. Its challenge to the racial exclusivity of white power was based on its own claims, as an elite, to white status and privilege. The argument implicit in such claims was that its acquisition of the cultural capital of Europe justified a status of equality with the European colonizer and the white colonizing elite.

In making their claims to white elite status, the elite of colonial Africa and its colonized diaspora have managed to reproduce, in post-colonial political economy, the very forms of domination that existed under colonialism. These forms are rooted in racial exclusivity and racial privilege. In their quest for power, its political leaders employ identical divide-and-rule tactics across subjectivities rooted in notions of belonging to make exclusive claims to governance. Race, tribe, religion, region, and ethnicity have become tools in the competition for power by this Europeanized elite.

Trinidad and Tobago is presented here as a case study in the organization of black communal intimacy, which has resulted in the institutionalization of a system of racialized politics organized for elite domination. Popular understandings of blackness and a collective sense of black intimacy were exploited in the fashioning of a nationalist agenda to serve the exclusive interests of an Europeanized elite. Racial politics, in turn, have jeopardized and undermined the collective interests of the black population in whose name nationalism was represented. By the end of the twentieth century, this very population found itself and its interests excluded in the power dynamics of elite control of governance. The social and economic conditions of a new, globalized political economy rendered its support less important in a new constitution of elite interests.

Background

The Republic of Trinidad and Tobago is a twin-island former West Indian colony of Britain, the second largest of the English-speaking territories of the West Indies. It came under British colonial rule after capture from Spain in 1797. At the time, its history of slavery was less than fifty years old. The British colonizers joined a white Spanish colonizing elite and a French elite of merchants and planters, many of whom had fled the Haitian slave revolt in the organization and support of a system of racial capital. As Britain solidified its political and economic domination, the Spanish and French "Creoles" became quickly differentiated from the white colonizing class in colonial reproduction.

Trinidad's unique history differentiates it from the rest of the English-speaking Caribbean in many respects. The country's Spanish colonial heritage has had a significant influence on national cultural expression. Its French planters' class came to be historically reproduced into a "local white" elite that dominated the private economic sector. Continued importation of Africans as indentured labourers after the abolition of slavery in 1833 has left the country with much more of an "African" heritage than is evident in most other English-speaking countries of the region. And the largest segment of its population comprises Hindu and Muslim descendants of indentured labourers shipped from South Asia (India and Pakistan) after slavery's abolition. These indentured labourers were brought to the island in the nineteenth and early twentieth centuries along with indentured labourers from Portugal and China. They replaced African plantation labour.

The colonial project sustained and supported a group of domestic businesses, almost exclusively from the population of "local" whites that was joined later by a small but influential number of Lebanese and Syrian immigrants. In the face of a colonial strategy of exclusion from the public sector, aimed at sustaining agricultural labour, successful middle-strata East Indians sought out opportunities that were opening up in manufacturing and commerce. By the latter half of the twentieth century, rich and powerful East Indian businessmen had managed to break the stranglehold of whites at the apex of domestic capital. By 1996, East Indians owned and controlled 54.2 per cent of all businesses employing five or more persons, 60 per cent of businesses in the distribution sector and 51 per cent of manufacturing establishments (Ryan 1996, 254). Close to two-thirds of large businesses as well as 78 per cent of small businesses owned by East Indians in 1993 were established after 1980 (Stewart 1994, 15).

In the middle strata, the colour/class hierarchy of colonial construction gave the mixed "coloured" and "near-white" (light-complexioned coloured) populations privileged access to professional training and professional occupations and to small- and mid-scale private sector business. In the wake of postwar upward mobility, members of the black population soon began to carve out a significant presence in the professions. Blacks and coloureds also predominated as teachers, civil servants and, later on, managers in the country's state-owned business ventures. These occupations became the mainstays of their middle-class status.

The majority of the population is dependent upon earnings from urban and rural working-class occupations and from the cultivation and sale of cash crops. For most of this century, this majority has been bifurcated along racial lines. Traditionally, members of the East Indian lower and working classes have made their living in agricultural or agriculture-related occupations. Some have used these earnings to branch out into small service-type businesses. Their black counterparts depend upon non-agricultural labour, with a few engaged in subsistence agriculture. Increasingly, however, the East Indian population has become much more urbanized. Many are joining blacks in public and private sector non-agricultural occupations.

In 1996 the estimated population of Trinidad and Tobago was 1,272,000. Census figures show the Afro-Trinidadians to be 39.6 per cent of the population. Combined, the descendants of interracial unions of blacks and whites (coloureds) and blacks and East Indian (*dooglas*) make up 18.4 per cent of the population. East Indians are 40.3 per cent of the population. Whites, including "Portuguese", "French Creole", "Spanish Creole" and the descendants of the English colonizers, make up 0.6 per cent. A distinctive identity of "local white" has emerged in the racial lexicon of Trinidad. It has allowed the accommodation and inclusion within the white social category of many with mixed "racial" backgrounds. There is also a small number of persons collectively classified as Chinese (0.4 per cent).[1]

The Racial Organization of Trinidad's Political Economy

There has been a historical development of contingent differences, related to religion, in the organization of social relations among East Indians. Hindus (who are exclusively East Indian) constitute 23.8 per cent of the country's population. Muslims (predominantly East Indian with a very small number of blacks) constitute 5.8 per cent. East Indians make up 9.7 per cent of the grouping of Christians, who are 43.7 per cent of the total population of the country. Whites are almost exclusively Christian (Central Statistical Office 1993).

Racial and ethnic categories occupy centre stage in almost all aspects of Trinidadian society, and this is no less true for its political organization. Historically, the social system of colonial organization and regulation has produced and sustained contingent social groupings, defined, perceived and identified idiomatically in racial terms. The particular circumstances of a group's introduction to the ex-colony, the history of its collective participation in Trinidadian society and the nature and type of resources and interests to be protected and enhanced have placed racial groups in competition with each other. At the root of such competition are the acquisition and protection of political power and economic resources.

The colonial political economy was organized around the exercise of centralized control by a powerful colonial bureaucracy. With the granting of independence, the governing institutions were inherited by an educated grouping of black and coloured bureaucrats and professionals who assumed functional control of the governing institutions of the state. The politicization of black identity created the conditions for their assumption of power.

There was a developing relationship between the process of elite reconstruction, the politicization of black identity and the practice of parliamentary democracy. The Westminster model of parliamentary democracy, inherited from Britain, and the institutionalization of racial voting combined into an instrument of regulation for the country's elite. At the time independence was granted, it provided the political representatives of the black and mixed elite with a guaranteed electoral majority employed to secure control of the governing institutions of the state. Racial regulation was particularly well suited to the black elite contenders for power. Despite its large numbers, the East Indian population was placed at an electoral disadvantage because of its concentration in the sugar-growing areas of the country. The political regulation of the population along racial lines left the East Indian political elite with victories in fewer constituencies than their black and coloured counterparts. The numbers of the whites and Chinese were too small to support the power contentions of their leadership in the developing racialized politics.

Nationalism and Anti-Colonialism

Nationalism was the instrument of black regulation. The anti-colonial nationalist movement was born and nurtured in a twentieth-century tide of rising expectations among urban wage labourers frustrated by the structure of organization of the colonial political economy. In the second decade of the century, these frustrations fuelled sporadic episodes of labour unrest. They led to the formation of a unified labour movement demanding better wages, improved conditions of work and the establishment of formal collective bargaining procedures (see Oxaal 1968; Ryan 1972).

Quickly, educated and professional members of the colonized population assumed positions as leaders in the new trade union movement. They formalized union organization and changed its demands to reflect their own interest in political reform. By the 1930s they were using labour mobilization to back demands for more representative government, for the sharing of political power between colonial and local leaders and for a shift of political control from the British Colonial Office and its colonial functionaries to "representative" institutions. In other words, the educated and professional elite used its leadership position to transform labour mobilization into a proto-nationalist political movement aimed at inserting its members into the colonial domains of power (Oxaal 1968; Ryan 1972).

Widespread labour riots in the late 1930s forced Britain to concede to demands for a more "representative" government. By 1946 the British Colonial Office began to initiate a process of gradual devolution of power. For the first time, universal adult suffrage was introduced and elected local officials were allowed significant participation in the political affairs of the colony (Hintzen 1989). This paved the way for the development of political parties in the 1950s under the leadership of a black and coloured intellectual and professional elite and that of East Indian and white businessmen and professionals. In their appeals for political support, the emergent political leaders exploited the racial affinities and sentiments of the voting population. As the appeal to race took root, the role of labour, with its class implications for political organization, began to diminish. This became immediately evident with introduction of adult suffrage in 1946. The People's Democratic Party (PDP) was formed in the early 1950s by a group of East Indian businessmen who controlled a predominantly East Indian sugar workers' union and the major Hindu religious organizations. Their appeal for votes was pitched exclusively to East Indian workers and agricultural peasants. In the process, East Indian identity – and, more purposefully, "Hindu" identity – became politically salient.

The politicization of black identity was much more profound. Black and coloured intellectuals and professionals began to fashion an ideology of Creole nationalism that was directly linked to Afro-Trinidadian culture (see Yelvington 1992). In 1956 they formed the People's National Movement (PNM). From the party's inception, the PNM leadership reflected the multi-ethnic composition of the country's elite. East

Indians were included among the party's leaders. But the appeal of the party was organized around the regulating idiom of race, and this was highlighted in the Creole nationalism preached by its black and coloured intellectual and professional leaders. The cultural symbols of the black population were appropriated and used in mobilization campaigns directed at the black lower strata. Rejection of "white" domination of the economy was accompanied by references to East Indians as "a recalcitrant and hostile minority" (cf. Yelvington 1992, 13, citing Ryan 1972; see also Oxaal 1968).

The nationalist movement was neither "nationalist" nor "black". Rather, it was the embodiment of a strategic reorganization of the non-capitalist and non-farming educated, bureaucratic and professional elite. This elite constituted itself into a single aggregated interest group. Its goal was to capture control of the executive, legislative and bureaucratic branches of the postcolonial state. Its agenda had little to do with the social, cultural and economic interests of its black lower-strata supporters except through the delivery of politically strategic patronage.

Whites and "near-whites" had seen their own opportunity for political power dashed in the throes of majoritarian politics. With the introduction of representative government, white Creole politicians, representing the interests of the business and planter elite, saw their chances for control of a postcolonial state rapidly diminishing (Hintzen 1989; Ryan 1972). They organized around the newly formed Political Progress Group (PPG), which also received support from the near-white social grouping of fair-complexioned coloureds. Many members of this near-white grouping soon became incorporated into the population of Creole whites in a reformulated category of "Trinidad white" (see Segal 1992). By 1950, the relationship between this all-inclusive Creole white population and the colonizers had become quite strong. Its members benefited from the discretionary power of the governor, who assured their representatives almost exclusive access to that portion of executive authority reserved for locals.

The elite interests being served by the newly formed racialized political parties became immediately obvious. The PPG and the PDP initially opposed independence, fearing that the interests of the business and planter classes would be jeopardized if the PNM came to power. The PDP also mounted a campaign of opposition to a proposed federation with the rest of the British West Indies, which was overwhelmingly black.

The issue of federation was critical in the racialization of politics. The Butler Party had become, by 1950, the single largest political organization in the country. It did so through reliance on the vote of black and East Indian wage labourers and small cultivators. Despite its multi-racial composition, the party was influenced somewhat by the philosophy of Marcus Garvey. Its lower-class leadership successfully employed an anti-white and anti-colonial agenda in a campaign of mobilization. But in the developing racial terrain of nationalist politics, the issue of federation proved the death knell for the party. It was deserted by most of its East Indian supporters, propelled by fears of black domination in a federation with the rest of the British West Indies. The theme of black domination was pivotal in the opposition to federation mounted by the PDP. And this is the party to which the erstwhile East Indian Butlerites turned (see Albert Gomes, cited in Ryan 1972, 100).

The PNM won general elections held in 1956 by winning in thirteen of twenty-four electoral constituencies. The PDP managed to capture only five seats, all in rural constituencies with overwhelming East Indian voting majorities. In the wake of this defeat, the PDP merged with the political representatives of the white business and planter elite to form the Democratic Labour Party (DLP). This was a strategic reorganization aimed at ousting the PNM from power. The conjoining of the two parties was quite natural given the rooting of their political interests in a common socio-economic base. As businessmen, professionals and planters, the East Indian and white leaders of the new party were opposed to any form of statist expansion. This placed them on a collision course with the black and coloured educated salaried and professional elite. The interests of the latter, concentrated in the public sector, were best served by the very statist agenda that the former perceived as anathema.

An almost universal feature of the post–Second World War era in underdeveloped countries is the historical emergence of an ascendant grouping of white-collar clerical, bureaucratic, professional and intellectual elite. Its members own neither capital nor land. This elite is distinguished by its Western education, upward mobility and ascending social status, all derived from colonial privilege.[2] Political leaders coming from and representing this social grouping have managed to erect and institutionalize systems of organization that serve its members' vested interests in economic accumulation and control of the state. They have done so by regulating the relations of politically strategic social groupings. In Trinidad, this was accomplished through the development of the ideology of nationalism.

Nationalism as Neocolonial Construction

The complex of ideas that has had the most significant and profound impact upon twentieth-century West Indian political economy are those contained in the ideology of anti-colonial nationalism. This form of nationalism became the basis for the rejection of colonialism and for the development of a political strategy for overthrowing colonial domination. It has served, also, as the basis for legitimizing the transformation of the political economy in the postcolonial era. The blueprint for such transformation was fashioned and formulated by an ascendant anti-colonial elite. It was justified on the grounds of self-determination, racial equality and developmental transformation.

Embedded in nationalist discourse were two distinctive sets of constructs. One was directed at the intensification, clarification and crystallization of identity. These are what I term *identity constructs*. The other was directed at the legitimization of forms and structures of postcolonial political authority. These I choose to call *legitimacy constructs*. Idioms of identity encoded in nationalist constructs were integrally linked to notions of self-determination. They became bases for organizing and channelling the participatory experiences of those engaged in contesting the colonial order and for the "invention" of the "imagined political communities" (Anderson 1983, 15; see also chapter 8 in this volume) that were to be the independent nations of the British West Indies.

Political parties in the Caribbean have become the organizational (power) instruments through which the "images" of the new nations are hegemonically imposed. Democratic participation and developmental transformation were organized as legitimizing constructs authenticating the authorial power of an educated elite. This elite managed to secure the legitimate right to organize and fashion postcolonial society. Its right to do so was justified by what French philosopher Michel

Foucault calls a regime of "political rationality" (1979; see also Dryfus and Rabinow 1983) exercised in the postcolonial state as the "proper subject matter of new technical and administrative knowledge" (1979, 137). In other words, the technical and administrative knowledge possessed by this new elite was employed, through the mechanisms of the state, in the exercise of "disciplinary power" (Foucault 1979). This power to discipline the masses through political organization characterizes the exercise of postcolonial democratic practice and its nationalist precursor. The argument of this chapter is that it is exercised in the service of the different and changing constellations of interests of the most strategic segments of the elite populations. The interests of this strategic elite are rendered invisible by the formal practice of democracy.

The language of liberation is central to the ideology of anti-colonial nationalism. Explicit in its formulation is liberation from colonial domination. Colonialism becomes translated into *the* universal metaphor for all forms of domination (both external and internal) and into a symbolic allegory for poverty and want. Domestically, it came to signify the repressive and exploitative conditions of domination of the colonized by the colonizer. Internationally, it came to signify the imperialist exploitation of the peripheral economies by the European metropole. Anti-colonialism signifies the quest for liberation from domination, poverty and want. But in its formulation, nationalist discourse is devoid of any possibilities for liberation. Historically, postcolonial political economies have failed to reflect the ideological promise of self-determination, development and de facto democratic participation. Its promise of liberation has failed to materialize in postcolonial social constructions. Instead, colonialism has been replaced by even more egregious forms of domination, superexploitation and dependency.

Embedded in notions of self-determination were the ideas of sovereignty and autonomy of the state. These were central to efforts by the nationalist elite to capture control of its governing institution. Once state authority was transferred, however, self-determination was used as justification for an intensification, deepening and widening of elite access to economic, social and cultural capital. It supported the accumulation of wealth, income, status and prestige by this elite.

Nationalism as an ideology has shown itself to be quite amenable to those whose interests rest in the ownership and control of economic capital. As a construct, it has accommodated the changing technical and social conditions of economic capital without losing its symbolic power. These changes occurred at the same time that colonialism was giving way to the new nationalist movements. They are central elements in newly emergent post-independence neocolonial formations. And they have been responsible for a reconstitution of the power elite whereby businessmen, professionals and managers have displaced salaried bureaucratic functionaries at the apex of domestic power.

Nationalism has supported the maintenance and expansion of relations of affinity with dominant class actors internationally, particularly those in the northern industrial countries. It has supported an intensification of relations with the elite in the very colonial metropole against which it was directed. The focus of new relations of affinity among the ex-colonies of Britain in the West Indies has been the United States. The anti-colonial agenda of the West Indian nationalists demanded the establishment of closer relations with the United States for pragmatic as well as symbolic reasons. As economies that were dependent upon commodity exports, the West Indies had to seek alternatives to economic relationships with the British colonial metropole. There was an inherent contradiction between the quest for sovereignty and continuation of the exclusive pattern of economic relations with Britain: absolute dependence upon the former colonial power was inconsistent with ideas of national self-determination as a critical component of sovereignty. The emergence of the United States as the dominant global economic power led the way out of this dilemma. A symbolic shift in the focus of economic and political relations from Britain to the United States became one of the central elements in nationalist assertions of sovereignty, allowing the newly independent countries to retain relations of economic dependency in the global capitalist economy while freeing such relations from the taint of colonial domination. The establishment and intensification of economic and political ties with North America were justified, also, in terms of developmental transformation. As the dominant, richest and most technologically advanced economic power, the United States offered ideal opportunities for such transformation.

There is a contradiction inherent in an anti-colonial agenda that advocates the intensification of economic and political relations with the uncontested hegemon of international capitalism. But this did not deter the leadership of the Trinidadian ruling party, like their West Indian nationalist counterparts, from doing so. Eric Williams, the leader of the PNM, was among the most strident of these anti-colonial leaders. His quest for the intensification of ties with the United States was also the most vigorous. Williams saw domestic industrialization as the means of escaping the economic strictures of the colonial political economy, and he expressed strong interest in the "Puerto Rican model" of industrialization by invitation (Fraser 1994, 139). The contradiction inherent in neocolonial insertion as a strategy for self-determination quickly erupted into confrontation with the United States. It forced Williams into making a choice that set the stage for US-imposed limits on nationalist self-assertion for the entire region. The conflict erupted in 1957 during negotiations over the location of a site for the capital of the West Indian Federation, which was to be the organizational framework for the region's postcolonial political structure. West Indian nationalist leaders had voted in favour of locating the capital in Trinidad on land leased to the United States during the Second World War, land that was the home of a functioning US naval base. The US administration rejected the proposal on the grounds of the base's strategic military importance. Williams, insisting on his country's sovereign right, demanded release from the agreement made between Britain and the United States in 1940 for the base's establishment. The United States refused to concede to the demand.

The confrontation served to highlight the ambiguities and contradictions of West Indian nationalist representation and practice. It exposed the limits inherent in a nationalist discourse shaped and fashioned by a colonial legacy of racial and ethnic division. In effect, the impossibility of sovereignty was conceded by the nationalist leadership in the fashioning of a new dependency centred upon the United States. Rather than as an assertion of the right of self-determination, sovereignty was employed symbolically to establish the racial boundaries of nationalist construction. The organized East Indian and white opposition strongly supported the United States in an effort to undermine the bid by the black and coloured leadership for control of the postcolonial state. This allowed the black political leaders of the PNM to question East Indian and white allegiance to the "nation" and to impugn the nationalist credentials of their political leaders. They were able to shore up their own support base in the black and coloured segments of the population by exposing the "anti-nationalist" predispositions of the racial opposition. In the process, sovereignty fell victim to the racial strategies of elite contenders for power. In defence of the nationalist agenda and of Trinidadian sovereignty, members of the black and coloured population threw the full weight of their support behind the PNM (Ryan 1972). In the process, the boundaries of the nation state became firmly identified with the country's black and coloured population, and the PNM's role as the sole promoter and defender of nationalist interests was concretized and legitimized in the popular consciousness.

The power of the PNM leadership was undergirded by the political solidarity of its racial supporters cemented through the party's nationalist credentials. In popular imagination, the national will came to be firmly associated with the interests of the party's natural constituency of middle-strata possessors of cultural capital. This "nascent" elite, objectively constrained by colonialism particularly during the period before the Second World War, came to "hegemonize" mass support under the discipline of its political representatives (see Chatterjee 1986) as the technical and social conditions of racial capitalism began to shift in favour of the twentieth-century anti-colonial movements that they organized and fashioned. The racial idiom, deployed as a means of discipline, was sustained through an intensification of the association between the DLP opposition and its exclusive Hindu support base.

In the final analysis, nationalism and sovereignty were deployed in the confrontation over the naval base as instruments in service of the ideological and power interests of the middle-strata elite. The constellation of middle-class power was reflected in developing political alliances established around the ideological agenda of the political leadership of the ruling party. This middle-class elite developed strong ties with the local business elite and the multiracial groups of professionals, managers and skilled and technical labour. It recruited white businessmen to advisory positions in the government, giving them considerable influence over economic policy. All these became linked to the party's middle strata of black and coloured workers in the public sector in a new constellation of elite interests.

PNM leaders used the new alliances to isolate the Hindu-dominated East Indian DLP, highlighting its racial exclusivity. This assured the party's hold on political power by sustaining solidary support from the black masses. The use of the racial idiom freed the political executive to pursue a policy of mixed-economy capitalism that catered to the diverse interests of the country's elite, now organized around the PNM. The policy allowed for growth in the public sector, for the development and expansion of state enterprises and for state-generated and state-supported private sector expansion. To succeed, the policy demanded an intensification of ties with international capital, and especially with the United States as the world's leading capitalist power. In the cold war environment of the time, this required unquestioned allegiance to the superpower. The party expelled its radical leaders, among whom were included the leading ideologues of its successful anti-colonial campaign. In justification, Eric Williams, the party's leader, denounced communism as one of the five "dangers" facing his party. He compromised with the United States over the issue of the naval base, allowing a continuation of the US presence for a negotiated period. And he declared the country unequivocally pro-capitalist and allied with the West in the cold war geopolitical divide (*Trinidad Guardian*, 1 October 1961).

The exclusive identification of the nation with its Afro-Creole population produced anticipations among the PNM's black and coloured supporters that their interests alone would be represented and protected at the apex of state power. Excluded from the national space, the East Indian rural population rallied around its Hindu political leadership, who began to challenge the legitimacy of the claims by the Afro-Creole population upon the nation state. The racialization of national discourse camouflaged the use, by a multiracial elite alliance of moderates and conservatives, of racial support from a progressive working class in service of the elite alliance's interests in the accumulation of social and economic capital. The black urban and rural working-class supporters of the PNM were organized politically under the disciplinary power of a governing and state-controlling elite who pursued policies anathema to these supporters' own objective interests.

The contradiction erupted during an economic crisis in 1965, just three years after the country received its independence. An economic downturn during that year produced significant increases in black unemployment and underemployment, particularly in the oil industry, with its predominance of black workers. The crisis came at a time when PNM antipathy towards the agricultural sector was contributing to an intensification of the downward spiral of economic marginalization of its overwhelmingly East Indian rural workers and peasantry. As the crisis intensified, black and East Indian workers joined together in a campaign of strikes and violence against the government that threatened the racial appeal of the ruling party. In the face of an erosion of its racial support base, the party responded with coercive legislation directed against worker mobilization (the Industrialization Stabilization Act 1965). It was the first of a number of challenges by the black lower class to its racial representatives in government, sometimes in alliance with East Indian rural labour and peasants. It also set the stage for the state's use of coercive mechanisms in retaliation.

The PNM's response to the crisis served to define the limits of democratic practice in the political economy of Trinidad and Tobago. It exposed the true grounding of elite power in coercion and executive fiat. The formalities of democratic practice are tolerated and maintained only when mass mobilization coincides with the interests of the country's middle and upper classes; they serve to give legitimacy to elite power. When this power is threatened, the coercive authoritarian base of governance is exposed. The PNM's response to lower-class mobilization established the organized practice of governance that came to typify Trinidadian political economy.

In sum, anti-colonial nationalism was constructed as the embodiment of Afro-Creole interests. While East Indians contested the legitimacy of this formulation, blacks and coloureds became intent on imposing this understanding upon state organization; it became the basis for making legitimate claims of preferential access to state resources. The middle-strata interests of the PNM conflicted sharply with black working- and lower-class expectations, and this contradiction came to be exposed under conditions of economic downturn. In the immediate post-independence period, it produced a cross-racial working-class alliance between blacks and East Indians, forcing the regime to rely on its arsenal of coercion to stay in power.

The use of coercion and control against black mass mobilization has made visible the role of the state as an instrument of oppression. The strategic use of violence and executive fiat has become a central pillar in the maintenance of political power by Trinidad's governing elite. It emerges, directly, from the construction of nationalist discourse around notions of racial exclusivity in the service of elite interests. This has placed severe limits on democratic practice. The reliance on violence and executive fiat underscores the class basis of power in Trinidadian postcolonial statist construction, a construction that is rooted in the systematic oppression of the working and lower classes by an international and national capitalist elite, its functionaries and allies. The majoritarian demands of a fictive claim to democracy were supported and sustained at independence by the mobilization of the ruling party's black support base. In power, the party maintained support by resorting to racial patronage, but in times of economic crisis, such patronage cannot be maintained.

In 1970 the PNM was again the target of a campaign of mass revolt by the country's urban black workers and students, as well as of a rebellion by the predominantly black army. Borrowing from the struggle for civil rights in the United States, workers, students and soldiers began to rally in support of a demand for "Black Power". The legitimacy of the claim by the ruling party to be the protector of Afro-Creole interests was being challenged. The rebellion was crushed and the ruling party maintained its hold on executive power through a campaign of coercive retaliation. This forced many of the dissident activists to go underground in a prolonged campaign organized by a black guerrilla movement which enjoyed considerable sympathy from within the black lower-class population until economic good fortunes returned to the country. The campaign ended only when an unanticipated tripling of oil prices in 1973 swelled state coffers and restored racial patronage to unprecedented highs.

Notwithstanding the restoration of racial patronage, the legitimacy of the PNM as the political arm of the black lower class was severely undermined by the events of the early 1970s. The 1970 Black Power rebellion and the guerrilla campaign that followed succeeded in inserting the language of class oppression into political discourse. This produced sustained and enduring black lower-class ambivalence, and oftentimes rejection, of the PNM. It opened the door to an acceptance by the country's black and coloured population of an alternative to the ruling party, whatever its racial designation. It also resuscitated a willingness to enter into cross-racial coalitions.

In 1975 black radical challenge to state legitimacy combined with East Indian contestation of the Afro-Creole nationalism to produce a mobilization campaign against PNM rule. Radical black intellectuals and union leaders established formal ties with Hindu socio-political organizations. Many of these leaders had participated in the anti-PNM campaigns of the early 1970s, and they were buoyed by the weakness exhibited by the PNM during those disturbances. The United Labour Front (ULF) was formed in 1976 as an alliance between black labour and East Indian rural agriculture. This was to signal a new chapter in political-party organization and to presage a shift in the dynamics of power. The strategic significance of the East Indian population was increasing rapidly, both from the growth in relative numbers and from a pattern of rural to urban migration that was changing the population dynamics of constituency politics. The mobilization of the East Indian population in a multiracial alliance presented an opportunity for representatives of middle-strata elite to challenge the domination of the PNM. They opposed what they considered to be policy excesses in the development of a system of racial patronage targeted at the black urban population. The lessons of the early 1970s forced the PNM into the dilemma of maintaining its mass support base while continuing to cater to its natural constituency of elite interests. Faced with the experience of a mass rebellion that had left the party barely clinging to power, it chose a programme of progressive redistribution that taxed the economic surpluses of the middle and upper classes. Since the redistributive efforts were directed at the black urban working class, the elite found a natural ally in the East Indian population. Added to this was lingering black animosity to the ruling party.

The problem for the ULF was that it was spawned in radical mobilization. Its campaign of class warfare alienated the country's middle and upper classes. Without significant support from the country's elite, it quickly collapsed, falling victim to the anti-radical bias in national discourse. In 1977, however, the ULF was re-established, purged of its more radical members. This was a telling replay of the PNM's decision to reject radical politics in its successful campaign to gain control of the post-colonial state. It underscored the strategic power of the elite in the power dynamics of governance. The new party entered into a loose arrangement with two other opposition parties. One, the Democratic Action Congress (DAC), had its support organized within the predominantly black population of Tobago. Its leader was a former heir apparent to Eric Williams in the PNM who had resigned his Cabinet portfolio during the Black Power revolt. He came with considerable black working-class legitimacy. The second party in the loose alliance was the Tapia House Movement headed by Lloyd Best, a black moderate intellectual who had begun to articulate concerns over the policies of the ruling party. This, in essence, represented a new elite alliance that relied upon the support of the surging East Indian population for its claim to power.

The anti-PNM alliance presaged a reconstruction of forces within the power relations of statist organization. It had profound implications for the future and anticipated the demise of Afro-Creole nationalism. In relative terms, the strategic position of Hindus in the power equation of governance was on the ascent as their leaders began developing politically strategic alliances across racial boundaries. The emergence of Tapia was a distinct indication of the onset of black middle-class alienation from the governing party. Opposition to the PNM intensified after 1978 as the economy began to experience a significant decline in export earnings from petroleum production, the mainstay of the Trinidadian economy. In 1982 government revenues went into deficit for the first time since 1973 and public debt began to escalate (see Bobb 1983; Hintzen 1989; *Trinidad Guardian,* 30 June 1983, 3). Economic decline provided the catalyst for the cementing of a new political realignment. The business and professional elite began to oppose the continued distribution of racial patronage by the PNM and to place the blame for the country's economic woes squarely on the appropriation of state funds for such patronage. With challenges mounting against the governing elite, the strategic importance of the Hindu opposition increased dramatically.

In national elections held in 1981, two new political parties, the National Alliance and the Organisation for National Reconstruction (ONR), mounted significant challenges to the PNM. This was the first clear and unambiguous indication of the erosion of PNM support among the middle and upper strata. The National Alliance was an amalgamation of the ULF, the DAC and Tapia, formalized in 1976; the ONR was the political organization of the country's business and professional elite, and it enjoyed significant support among the country's upper and upper-middle classes. While significant in absolute terms, support for the two parties was not enough, separately, to defeat the PNM in national elections held in 1981. Nonetheless, the indications were clear: a fundamental reformulation of political relations was threatening the PNM's continued ability to hold on to power. In attempts to cater to the interests of the black lower strata by developing an elaborate system of patronage, the PNM found itself in confrontation with highly politicized middle and upper strata.

The new constellation of elite interests and upper- and middle-class desertion of the PNM were aimed at preserving the position of these class groupings at the apex of governance. This reformulation of elite power was, in part, directed against the influence of the black working class and at limiting its access to the distributive resources of the state. In other words, it was an attempt to reduce its power. The middle and upper strata developed new political alliances with the rural Hindu social grouping and with the black population in Tobago in an effort to negate the role of black mobilization. The need for such alliances was dictated by the majoritarian impositions of Westminster democracy, which demanded the cultivation of a popular support base to legitimize elite domination. And the conditions of black popular support began to conflict sharply with elite accumulative and power interests. Rural East Indians were less predisposed to make demands upon the distributive resources of government under conditions of national marginalization. The representation in popular imagination of Tobago as a national backwater and of Trinidad as the engine of development combined with Tobago's small population to render insignificant any demands its population might make on state resources in exchange for political support. In other words, the redistributive claims by the elite's new mass base of supporters would be significantly reduced when compared with the massive demands made upon state resources by the black working and lower classes.

By 1983 a loose coalition, calling itself the Accommodation, was formalized between the Alliance and the ONR. Its effectiveness was tested in local government elections held that very year. The result was a resounding defeat for the PNM, with the Accommodation capturing 54.07 per cent of the popular vote to the PNM's 39.11 per cent (Ryan 1989, 43–45). The ruling party lost control of all but 3 urban municipalities and 1 county council, winning only 54 local government seats to the Accommodation's 66. With its demonstrated success, the leaders of the two political parties making up the Accommodation entered into a formal coalition called the National Alliance for Reconstruction (NAR). The new party contested general elections in 1986 in a campaign that mounted a frontal assault on "racial politics", a campaign that symbolized a rejection of the PNM's appeal to the country's black population.

The party won a landslide victory, capturing 33 of the 36 parliamentary seats and 67 per cent of the popular vote. This ended the thirty-year rule of the PNM despite continued strong support in black working-class constituencies (see Ryan 1989, 85). The defeat signalled the decline in the strategic influence of the black working and lower classes in electoral politics.

In its defeat, the PNM fell victim to its own successful strategy of creating opportunities for upward mobility for members of the black working class through its policies of redistribution and patronage. Many of its black supporters had become absorbed into reconstituted middle strata. Opportunities for their upward mobility were created through the use of massive earnings accruing to the state from oil-generated wealth between 1973 and 1981. These earnings supported policies of state expansion, which allowed increased employment of blacks in government services. They also supported, through massive liquidity transfers of state surpluses, the expansion of private sector business and professional activity. There was also considerable expansion in post-secondary education. Finally, state revenues supported an extensive system of racial patronage directed at the black urban and semi-urban population. When the economy collapsed, the response of black and coloured middle-class beneficiaries was to protect their newly acquired socio-economic status by supporting the opposition NAR. This stemmed as much from a desire by this parvenu to maintain its new-found socio-economic status as from a reflection of black ambivalence to the PNM spawned in the rebellion of 1970.

In effect, the NAR was nothing more than a reconstituted PNM. Its unabashed purpose as a governing party was to defend the relative position of the middle and upper strata against claims by the lower strata. Affinity with the black working class was jettisoned in favour of an alliance with the representatives of rural Hindus. When the Hindus began to make distributive claims on state resources, their political leaders were systematically marginalized. This caused the coalition to collapse in 1988 after five members of Parliament, all former members of the Hindu-based ULF, were suspended from the ruling party. The departure of the ULF membership left an elite representing the urban middle and upper classes and the predominantly Afro-Trinidadian Tobago constituency in control of the governing institutions of the state.

All this was occurring during a period of rapid economic decline that compelled the government to seek relief from international financial institutions. In 1988 foreign exchange assistance was sought from the International Monetary Fund (IMF). A regimen of structural adjustment was negotiated and implemented to ensure agreement by the country's international creditors to a program of debt rescheduling organized with the Fund's blessing. With the intervention of the IMF, the newly reconstituted government gave up much of its control of the economy to international financial institutions. IMF intervention paralleled the development of new technical and social conditions of international capital that favoured the interests of the domestic entrepreneurial, managerial and professional elite. Policies of structural adjustment undermine the economic and social interests of the salaried middle classes, particularly those dependent upon the state for employment, education, health, welfare and subsidies. The regime lost the ability to cater to the interests of this segment of its middle-strata supporters. The government was forced, inter alia, to embark on two rounds of devaluation, to cut back significantly on public spending, to divest itself of public assets, to abandon state-funded projects (particularly those in the energy-intensive sector), to cut public sector salaries, to retrench public sector workers, to curtail financial support for the private sector, to cut back significantly on patronage, to eliminate subsidies and to increase utility rates. As a result, real incomes plummeted, unemployment increased phenomenally and the level of poverty increased. The economy moved into severe recession (see Ryan 1989). This compounded the problem caused by the departure of the coalition's rural Hindu supporters.

By 1990 the government was facing an absolute crisis of legitimacy compounded by the loss of its Hindu mass support base and by the economic crisis. On 27 July 1990 a group of Afro-Muslims known as the Muslimeen, numbering fewer than three hundred and without any discernable support from any segment of the population, exploited widespread disenchantment stemming from the crisis of legitimacy to organize a bid to oust the government from power. Members of the group set off a bomb in the national police headquarters, invaded Parliament and took the prime minister, seven cabinet ministers and a number of other parliamentarians hostage. Its efforts almost succeeded, helped by an initial reluctance on the part of the military and police to intervene in support of the government. At the time of the attempted coup, the police had been engaged in acrimonious labour negotiations. Their membership had suffered significant cutbacks in wages, and work conditions were deteriorating badly. The force had lost much of its prestige and esteem. This reflected the general condition of the salaried middle class, particularly state employees and those in the private sector who were vulnerable to a decline in the relative wage rate. The desire by this segment of the population to see the regime out of office was matched only by its unwillingness to allow the Muslimeen to capture control of governance. The Muslimeen's anti-Western ideology, rooted in notions of black liberation, was anathema to middle- and upper-class interests. The attempted coup precipitated a total breakdown of law and order in the capital city and its environs and a near demobilization of the police force. The weakened regime was forced into negotiations with the rebels.

The response to the attempted takeover of government signalled a new divide in the country's political economy and the loss of the ability of the ruling party to sustain the strategic support that had brought it to power. To the loss of its Hindu supporters, necessary to ensure its democratic majority, was now added the loss of a significant segment of its middle-class support base. The general attitude of most was to support neither the rebels nor the ruling party. Indeed, a majority (60 per cent) supported the social agenda of the rebels while condemning their assault on democracy (Ryan 1991, 218). Some felt that the ruling party's insensitivity to the poor, its vindictiveness and its alliance with the white and near-white elite were principal causes of the rebellion (see Ryan 1991). After the attempted coup, a full 73 per cent of the public held negative views of the prime minister, and 32 per cent claimed that they had become less sympathetic to him after the rebellion; 71 per cent held negative views of the ruling party as a whole (Ryan 1991, 220). This left the governing executive politically isolated, apart from the support it continued to enjoy from the upper and upper-middle classes and from the Tobago constituency.

The NAR government was transformed into an arm of the international financial institutions. In doing so, it was forced to desert those of its strategic supporters whose interests were jeopardized by the dictates of new forms of capitalist globalization. The entrepreneurial, professional and managerial elite had every reason to support the new conditions of economic globalization imposed by international public policy. They were its beneficiaries. Apart from personal allegiance to the NAR leadership, there was every reason for the black lower-class population of Tobago to support international capitalist penetration. A history of economic neglect by the central government was forcing the smaller island to fall back upon its reputation as a tropical paradise in order to develop a tourist industry. Moreover, there was tremendous potential for the development of offshore oil and gas reserves. Both depended upon massive amounts of foreign investments and upon foreign assistance for the infrastructure development. The problem for the NAR was the loss of the majoritarian base needed to preserve the legitimizing fiction of democratic governance.

Elections were held in 1992, and the NAR was defeated in every constituency in Trinidad. It won only in the two Tobago constituencies, in the island stronghold of the prime minister and party leader. With some exceptions, the middle and upper classes returned to the fold of the PNM, adding their strategic power to the party's racial support among the black working class. Once again, rural Hindus were left out of the governing equation, returning to their former exclusivity and isolation. The Hindu elite had organized itself into a new party, the United National Congress (UNC), which won in all of the rural East Indian constituencies. While the new party lost the election, its support base presaged a new constellation of power interests that had all the ingredients necessary for capturing control of state governance. The new social and technical conditions of global capital had catapulted the East Indian elite into the most strategic sectors of the domestic political economy. The East Indian domestic business class owns and controls a significant share of the country's economic capital, and East Indian professionals and intellectuals are heavily represented in technical and managerial professions and disciplines. Significant numbers of East Indian salaried and wage workers are migrating to the urbanized areas of the country, formerly the exclusive preserve of the Creole segments of the population (blacks, coloureds, whites and so on). They have changed voting dynamics in a number of urbanized constituencies. In addition, the UNC can count on the solidary support of East Indians in Hindu rural constituencies.

The increasing urbanization and urbanism of East Indians is accompanied by the cultural creolization of the population. In the past, such creolization has lessened the racial and ethno-religious appeal of its political elite. As a result, in its heyday, the PNM enjoyed substantial support from urban Muslim and Christian East Indians. But with the growing prominence of the East Indian elite, creolization has gone hand in hand with the growth and retention of Hindu religiosity. Pressures for creolization have been most evident upon the East Indian middle class. These pressures derive from their functional insertion into Trinidad's political economy and the postcolonial benefits of nationalism that have accrued to their Creole counterparts. Such benefits have propelled many Hindus to incorporate more universal Western forms into their religious practice, signalling some measure of creolization without sacrificing their Hindu identity (see Klass 1991). The middle and upper classes have managed an accommodation of the two, particularly through the practice of new forms of Hinduism that are distinguished from the more traditional forms practised by rural agriculturalists (see Klass 1991).

At the same time, there is mounting resistance to creolization among the Hindu cultural elite. In their campaign, they are employing resources of symbolic power to petition for inclusion in the nationalist space *as East Indians*. The theme of "douglarization" emerges persistently in East Indian narratives of purity. It has become emblematic of the polluting consequences of sexual contact with Africans. Douglarization, therefore, is the process of transformation of East Indians into racial Creoles through miscegenation. Hindu purity is being deployed as a symbolic resource by these leaders to de-legitimize the representations and practices of what they present as a "polluted" Creole discourse. Their challenge is organized around narratives of Creole cultural degradation directed, particularly, at the cultural ascendance of Afro-Creole forms in nationalist discourse. The campaign is accompanied by mounting contestation of the claims made by Afro-Creoles of a central role in nation building.

In their self-representations, East Indians are beginning to present themselves as the true builders of the nation and as the nation's saviours from Afro-Creole degradation (Yelvington 1995). Theirs is not merely a quest for nationalist inclusion – it represents a claim to the nationalist space that is legitimized through a redemptive counter-discourse to Afro-Creole nationalism. In this regard, it presents a fundamental challenge to Trinidadian *créolité* through a rejection of notions of hybridity and of "blending and impurity" as its fundamental values (Yelvington 1995, 77). While the Hindu elite is at the forefront of the challenges to Afro-Creole nationalism, what has emerged is a growth in the sense of East Indianness, independent of religion, in which both Christians and Muslims participate. This process of "re-Indianization" of the creolized Indo-Trinidadian has been attributed to the upward mobility of Hindus, which has produced a levelling effect upon the population, and to a growing sense of Afro-Creole domination of the national social, cultural and political arena (see Premdas and Sitahal 1991). The twin themes of Hinduism and purity have become new bases for East Indian solidarity, upon which disciplinary power is exercised on the East Indian electorate. Each, by itself, guarantees the support of the urbanized and socially creolized East Indian population, which otherwise might have been resistant to racial and ethno-religious appeals.

In 1995 support by these strategic segments of the population combined to produce a victory by political representatives of the Hindu elite, organized in the UNC under Basdeo Panday, in national elections. For the first time, a party identified with rural East Indians was able to take exclusive control of the governing institutions of the state. Like the PNM before them, leaders of the party employed the idioms of race and ethnicity to assure themselves of majoritarian support. And like the PNM before them, the leaders quickly accommodated the reconstituted interests of a new elite, organized around business, the professions and a managerial class, in their exercise of governance. This assures the ruling party of the strategic support necessary to remain in power. The willingness of the black population to accept an "East Indian" government, and of many of the black elite to serve in its executive and legislative branches, underscores both the weakening association of the nation with its Afro-Creole population and the loss of racial legitimacy by the PNM.

But changing social and economic conditions of capitalist production are creating a new role for the PNM. The conditions of globalization, favouring a new managerial, professional and business elite, provided opportunities for the party to attract segments of the black and coloured salaried middle class away from the coalition of elite interests that catapulted the NAR into power during the 1980s. The social and economic capital of elite interests has been significantly devalued in the new political economy. By combining its version of populist welfarism with a resuscitated racial appeal, the PNM has been able to rebuild a strong support base to challenge the UNC. In elections held in

December 2000, the UNC barely managed to hold on to power against a strong electoral challenge mounted by the PNM. The success of the PNM's revived racial appeal was signalled by a win in one of the two predominantly black constituencies of Tobago. The NAR, with its Tobago base, won in the smaller island's second constituency by a very thin margin. The UNC won nineteen seats against a sixteen-seat total for the PNM, helped significantly by a movement of East Indian wage and salaried workers and small-scale businessmen into the urbanized former strongholds of PNM's black supporters. This, and the solid support it received in the rural Hindu constituencies, assured the party of victory at the polls.

In all of the domestic political contentions, the changing dynamics of international globalization is hardly noticed, despite the profound consequences it has for the domestic political economy. The new terms of social and economic organization are accepted as necessary for "development". There is growing inequality between a privileged class that has become absorbed into a global elite of producers, managers and skilled professionals, on the one hand, and the lower-middle and lower classes, which are losing social and economic ground, on the other. This is explained in a discourse of modernity that rewards and valorizes those individuals possessing the prerequisites for developmental transformation of their countries into clones of the industrialized political economies of the North Atlantic. The organization of this type of formal democratic practice that is devoid of representative governance legitimizes the role of an international elite and a globalized domestic elite at the apex of state power while rendering invisible the true nature of its exploitative authoritarianism. In the process, all semblance of sovereignty and self-determination has disappeared.

In Trinidad, the struggle for control of governance occurs within the context of the majoritarian demands of democratic political organization. The elite is not this organization's only beneficiaries. The mobilization of lower-class Afro-Trinidadians forced a PNM regime that was dependent upon their support to create conditions for their upward mobility. Black Tobagonians were able to exploit alliances with the regime to secure resources for economic growth. Ultimately, however, it is elite interests that prevail. Without elite support, the PNM lost power. And despite the challenge mounted by the PNM in the elections of 2000, it is the support of the strategic elite segments of the political economy that continues to determine electoral outcomes. This has to do with the ability of this elite to use race symbolically in its exercise of disciplinary power over the masses while sustaining solidary support from among its various segments. In the new constellation of elite interests, the wage and salaried segments of the lower middle strata have been sloughed off in the new globalized political economy. Their support for a populist PNM provided the party with an electoral boost. It was not enough, however, to ensure control of governance.

Conclusion

Democratic organization can be manipulated in the service of the interest of a dominant social grouping. In Trinidad, it has produced reconstruction and reformulation of relations among racial and socioeconomic groupings over time. In a regulating discourse of political identity, subjectivities rooted in notions of belonging are politicized in support of elite interests. Trinidad's democracy is characterized by such regulation as an elite comprising bureaucrats, professionals, managers, intellectuals, businessmen and large-scale farmers employs race as an instrument of its own power. The importance of racially defined organization in Trinidad is the role it plays in creating and sustaining the conditions for political domination, irrespective of the democratic nature of political organization.

Notes

1. These figures are taken from the 1990 population census reported by the Central Statistical Office of Trinidad and Tobago (Central Statistical Office 1993).
2. See Harris (1987) for a discussion of the characteristics of this reconstructed social grouping.

References

Anderson, Benedict. 1983. *Imagined Communities: Reflections on the Origin and Spread of Nationalism.* London: Verso.

Bobb, Euric. 1983. "The Oil Industry: Impact on the Local Economy. Review 1982/Forecast 1983". Central Bank of Trinidad and Tobago, *Quarterly Economic Bulletin* 2, no. 1: 90–98.

Central Statistical Office. 1993. *1990 Population and Housing Census: Institutional Report.* Port of Spain, Trinidad: Central Statistical Office.

Chatterjee, Partha. 1986. *Nationalist Thought and the Colonial World: A Derivative Discourse?* London: Zed; New York: United Nations University.

Dryfus, Hubert L., and Paul Rabinow. 1983. *Michel Foucault: Beyond Structuralism and Hermeneutics,* 2nd edition. Chicago: University of Chicago Press.

Foucault, Michel. 1979. *Discipline and Punish: The Birth of the Prison.* Translated by Alan Sheridan. New York: Vintage/Random House.

Fraser, Cary. 1994. *Ambivalent Anti-Colonialism: The United States and the Genesis of West Indian Independence, 1940–1964.* Westport, Conn.: Greenwood.

Harris, Nigel. 1987. *The End of the Third World: Newly Industrializing Countries and the Decline of an Ideology.* Harmondsworth, UK: Penguin.

Hintzen, Percy C. 1989. *The Costs of Regime Survival: Racial Mobilization, Elite Domination, and Control of the State in Guyana and Trinidad.* Cambridge: Cambridge University Press.

Klass, Morton. 1991. *Singing with Sai Baba: The Politics of Revitalization in Trinidad.* Boulder, Colo.: Westview.

Oxaal, Ivor. 1968. *Black Intellectuals Come to Power: The Rise of Creole Nationalism in Trinidad and Tobago.* Cambridge, Mass.: Hall and Schenkman.

Premdas, Ralph, and Sitahal, Harold. 1991. "Religion and Culture: The Case of the Presbyterians in Trinidad's Stratified System". In *Social and Occupational Stratification in Contemporary Trinidad and Tobago,* edited by Selwyn Ryan, 337–49. St Augustine, Trinidad: Institute of Social and Economic Research.

Ryan, Selwyn. 1972. *Race and Nationalism in Trinidad and Tobago: A Study of Decolonization in a Multiracial Society.* Toronto: University of Toronto Press.

———. 1989. *The Disillusioned Electorate: The Politics of Succession in Trinidad and Tobago.* Port of Spain, Trinidad: Inprint Caribbean.

———. 1991. *The Muslimeen Grab for Power: Race, Religion, and Revolution in Trinidad and Tobago.* Port of Spain, Trinidad: Inprint Caribbean.

———. 1993. *Pathways to Power: Indians and the Politics of National Unity in Trinidad and Tobago.* St Augustine, Trinidad: Institute of Social and Economic Research.

Segal, Daniel A. 1992. " 'Race' and 'Color' in Pre-Independence Trinidad and Tobago". In *Trinidad Ethnicity*, edited by Kevin A. Yelvington, 81–115. London: Macmillan.

Stewart, Taimoon. 1994. "Introduction: Caribbean Entrepreneurship in Historical Capitalism". In *Entrepreneurship in the Caribbean: Culture, Structure, Conjuncture,* edited by Selwyn Ryan and Taimoon Stewart, 1–35. St Augustine, Trinidad: Institute of Social and Economic Research.

Yelvington, Kevin A. 1992. "Introduction: Trinidad Ethnicity". In *Trinidad Ethnicity*, edited by Kevin. A. Yelvington, 1–32. London: Macmillian.

———. 1995. *Producing Power: Ethnicity, Gender, and Class in a Caribbean Workplace.* Philadelphia: Temple University Press.

[16]

Democratic Transition and Authoritarianism
The Case of Haiti

Fred Reno

Introduction

An analysis of the political transition in Haiti can hardly be based on the sole observation of the passage from authoritarianism to democracy. When assessing the implementation of particular techniques and procedures in a given country, one needs to measure beforehand the extent to which these techniques and procedures have been assimilated. If the country in question neither fabricated those practices nor grew accustomed to them, there is a risk that appearances will be mistaken for reality. Should the idea of the fragility of democracy need any exemplification, Haiti could easily provide it.

The recent democratization process in the world has gone through four phases. The first occurred during the 1970s in southern Europe, with Portugal, Greece and Spain adopting political models in keeping with their history and their culture. The second phase started at the end of the same decade in Latin America and stretched over a longer period. As early as the nineteenth century the countries of this region of the world adopted representative government and endowed themselves with constitutions. The third phase, which began at the end of the

1980s, concerned the countries of Central and Eastern Europe. It developed convulsively, causing nationalisms long kept at bay by authoritarian states to emerge again. The last phase is African, involving mainly the French-speaking countries of that continent. National conferences were held, with the various political and social sectors getting involved.

While these changes constitute important steps forward, they cannot be regarded as definitive. For them to be significant there needs to be a basic consensus on their meaning. As Guy Hermet has written, "Democracy is not firmly rooted anywhere unless ordinary people and elites alike regard it as the unique legitimate only and possible form of government" (Hermet 1993, 186; my translation). Such is not the case in Haiti for the moment. The current geopolitical context does not favour potential dictators, as the "red threat" can no longer be dangled in a bid to justify domestic human rights violations and extort financial support from the West. The US action aiming at the restoration of democracy in Haiti in 1994 is an illustration of this new trend which makes foreign intervention decisive in the defeat of local authoritarian resistance and in the setting up of a freed space, the latter being most often controlled – at least at the beginning – by those who conquered it. The intervention in Haiti comes within the framework of a wider plan, which had been initiated and implemented before. The "invasion" of the island of Grenada in 1983 and the kidnapping of General Manuel Noriega in Panama, though not similar in their development, both resulted in the implantation of liberal regimes faithful to the United States and compliant to the requirements of the market.

Transition experiences are increasingly numerous and have been encouraged since the end of the bipolar world. Countries engaged in them have been getting democratic assistance from the West. What is sought now is not just the triumph of the liberal model, but its consolidation in an international context with new constraints and tensions. Democratic assistance is one of the ways the West intervenes in these countries politically, allowing technology and liberal values to spread. In countries with a deeply rooted autocratic culture and in which democracy is regarded as an exotic product, democracy becomes a challenge for its advocates as well as for those who are in charge of its implementation.

Besides the social and humanitarian actions carried out by nongovernmental organizations, international actions by Western national bodies are directed towards the exportation and maintenance of the democratic product. For example, in the 1980s two American institutes were set up in order to promote the American "political way of life" abroad. The National Democratic Institute for International Affairs (NDI) and the International Republican Institute (IRI) receive an annual budget of US$15 to $25 million from the US Agency for International Development (www.usaid.gov). This shows Washington's interest in the generalization of its model in spite of the reservations expressed by the George W. Bush administration. Running parallel to the American initiatives is the recent creation in 1992 by the British of the Westminster Foundation for Democracy, whose objectives are similar but whose means are more limited. The Netherlands' initiative towards South Africa is equally noteworthy. The Foundation for a New South Africa (SNZA) is a branch of the "Dutch development assistance", which is anxious to lend a hand in this country's democratization process by means of technical assistance from Dutch political parties to their African counterparts.

All these initiatives are based upon common philosophical values and political expertise. Their promoters require that such principles as consent, legitimacy and responsibility be complied with by all parties (Faber and de Jong 1966). From the nature of the programmes implemented to the political conditions developing countries must meet for the economic aid to be granted, everything points to the wide regard of the democratic model as universal.

The bodies and experts designing the international relations programmes often have an institutionalist approach to democracy. Democracy is referred to as "a political system in which sovereignty is deemed to rest with citizens of a country who express their wish in periodic and free elections for the selection of representatives who will legislate on their behalf" (Faber and de Jong 1966, 3).

Such an approach makes elections the tool par excellence to measure the level of democracy in a given country. This much the elites in developing countries have understood. Aware of the advantages that can be derived from the importation of the model, in particular the financial aid that goes along with it, they mimic the paraphernalia of democracy. But how effective is that when the principles themselves are not fully adhered to? The fairness of the ballot is supposed to prevail over the results themselves – the democratic character of the game is determined by that very fairness. In complying with those principles and practices, the West makes the electoral scene the functional forum in which potential conflicts are defused. A long electoral tradition officializes, as it were, the social function of the vote.

Conversely, the electoral process in developing countries is often meant as a way of giving a democratic garment to the domination of those who have managed to silence their opponents one way or another. South America is a case in point: "Many coups occurred in the wake of elections because the results had to be in keeping with the established order. But at the same time the legitimate power was the one obtained by force, elections being a mere formality whose object was to present the international community with a fait accompli" (Dabène 1992, 224; my translation). Elections can thus be used to betray democracy even while their object is to be a tool for its expression.

In addition to the political context proper, socio-economic variables are sometimes determining in the choices of public policies or political systems made. In this respect experts regard the democratization process as closely correlated to growth and development. While a cause-and-effect relationship should not be played up, the African and South American examples are evidence that democracy stands little chance of thriving in situations of deep social division. Sluggish economies and weak states have been liabilities in the political development of these countries. This does not mean that democracy is possible only in economically developed societies. The examples of India and the former British colonies of the West Indies show that democratic culture can be imported in special historical situations. Still, it is hard to deny that deteriorating living conditions sometimes result in backward phenomena of authoritarianism that alter the initial democratic course and jeopardize the support the transition entrepreneurs had enjoyed previously, as the cases of Guatemala, Peru and Venezuela indicate.

The Haitian case can also be read in this light. The 1990 overthrow of President Jean-Bertrand Aristide by General Raoul Cedras a few months after Aristide's election shows how fragile these institutions are and how important it is for the social actors to share the basic principles of a democratic culture. In countries which initiated political change, consent, legitimacy and responsibility are not collectively shared values even though lip service is constantly paid to them. In periods of transition, the meanings given to political actions and to the procedures derived from them are probably more reliable clues to the rootedness or vulnerability of the democratic game. In this respect, the weight of the cultural factor in the tension between genuine acceptation and utter rejection should be given more attention. Experts are too often prone to underrating the cultural factor or setting it aside altogether in their belief that recipes and procedures can be applied without the "web of significance" that validates, legitimates or, conversely, disqualifies them. Fair elections, the relations between populations and political structures and the prevailing attitudes and values within the society, notably in the economic sector, are paramount in the experts' eyes (Faber and de Jong 1966). It is my contention that while these elements are important in that they describe attitudes and are essential prerequisites to the analysis of representations, they fail to take into account or underestimate the semiotic dimension of the social action through which actors assign meaning to their behaviour (Geertz 1973).

The notion that the places where democracy seeks to implant itself are different from the places it originated in, and that the recipient countries may reject the graft from the Western donor, is accepted by certain organizations which export liberal structures. An example of this is the National Endowment for Democracy (NED), a US organization created in 1983 which

> is guided by the belief that freedom is a universal human aspiration that can be achieved through the development of democratic institutions, procedures and values. Democracy cannot be established through a single election and need not be based upon the model of the United States or any other particular country. Rather, it evolves according to the needs and traditions of the diverse political cultures.[1]

While the structures and attitudes adopted in developing countries can be those of democratic countries, this should by no means lead to the conclusion that the democratic game is durably rooted. Heuristically, that reality proves the necessity to integrate the cultural and sociohistorical variables in our analysis of developing countries. Culture and history both offer the advantage of informing us of continuities and discontinuities and consequently of the invariant political trends at work in the society under scrutiny.

This chapter sets out to shed light on the Haitian democratic experience in this twofold perspective. The recurring political instability and the paradoxical (to say the least) attitude of the champions of democracy leads to an interrogation into the resilience of autocracy in the period of transition we are witnessing, and hence into the resources available to the democratic process in such a context.

The Authoritarian Roots of the Democratic Transition

His term coming to its end in 1996 and the constitution not allowing him two terms in a row, the Haitian president stepped down in favour of his duly designated successor. René Préval thus became, after a presidential election with a low turnout, the second president of the post-Duvalier era.

For the first time in its history, Haiti was experiencing one of the rites of Western democracy in conditions deemed fair by the international community. Five years later Préval's predecessor, Jean-Bertrand Aristide, was to return to power after elections contested by both opposition parties and international bodies, this time with reservations about the fairness of the vote. After denouncing the ruling party's control of the political life, Aristide's opponents asked the population not to vote. The low turnout should not be interpreted by the opposition as a victory, though, when one knows that the tensions which built up during the elections period most likely caused constituents to stay away from the polling stations. The tragic retrospective images of voters shot down while lining up in front of the polling stations and of ballot boxes being smashed open presumably deterred them.

On 26 November 2000, Jean-Bertrand Aristide was elected at the end of a one-choice election. Once again doubts were rekindled about the solidity of Haiti's democratic roots. In the years that followed the fall of the dictatorship, Haitians had not managed to bring about the necessary conditions for change. Democratic institutions had been set up, but authoritarianism was still deeply rooted, as the political and social history of Haiti shows.

The republic officially installed on 18 December 1806 was a liberal regime of sorts. It borrowed from internationally available political models. Its institutions could hardly depart from the former colonial power's models or from those of the American neighbour whose revolution against England fascinated the elites of Santo Domingo. The new state was inspired by the French political structures of that period, but it disregarded the importance of the cultural environment that was part and parcel of those structures. While it cannot be denied that culture is a construct that does not export easily, the English-speaking Caribbean countries illustrate the fact that under certain historical circumstances, particularly in colonies with non-indigenous populations, certain features of the metropolitan political culture could be imported. In Haiti the implantation of the political values and procedures associated with the French model proved complex, if possible at all, because of the conditions in which the state had emerged in the colony. The result was an adulterated version of the original, whose artifices are well depicted in Aimé Césaire's *La tragédie du Roi Christophe*. The political emerged from an extremely violent background with a mass of freshly emancipated slaves having no better political traditions than the ones inspired by life on the plantations and by centralizing Jacobinism. Emancipation by a plantation's white master or by the white rulers overseas first meant imitation of them. The Haitian case is no different in this regard from those of the European possessions in Africa or South America. The political structures of the new state were similar to those of the former colonial power – they differed mainly in the way they functioned.

In the first years, the Senate was the dominant institution in the political life: "It was a regime of Assembly. . . . The president of the Republic was the head of the executive power, but in fact the Senate devised and led the nation's general policy" (Michel 1990, 18; my translation). The bicameralism often favoured the lower chamber, which was more prestigious and endowed with important prerogatives. Since most senates are in fact upper chambers, with an elected lower assembly, the upper chamber in this case is the assembly or *assemblée nationale*. In 1816, for example, its members being designated through indirect universal suffrage, the Senate sat permanently and elected the Executive. This unbalanced bicameralism departed from the parliamentarian regime to the extent that the classical checks-and-balances mechanisms of reciprocal pressure between the legislative and the executive could not be engineered.

The Haitian founding fathers were also inspired by the American institutions, but that did not help provide the long-term legal framework the attempts at democratization require. Indeed, before the 1987 Constitutional Act, only two constitutional texts were of democratic inspiration. The first one was adopted in 1843; the president was elected by universal suffrage, his powers were limited and the bicameralism was egalitarian. The paradox in this legal construction was in the limitations on the prerogatives of the head of state, who at the same time enjoyed strong legitimacy. The system was short-lived. Political instability seemed to be the rule, a permanent phenomenon with a string of coups for the control of the executive and the economic resources it provided.

Twenty-four years after the first trial, Haiti again tried to shake off the autocratic evil by curbing the president's powers. Unlike what the 1843 Constitution provided for, the president was not elected through direct universal suffrage under the 1867 Constitutional Act. The 1867 Act took a more realistic approach to the socio-political context with the possible drifts a designation by the people could have led to. As in the other constitutions, the reference to the US model is obvious, notably in the impossibility of dissolving the chambers. For more than ten years, the country enjoyed a relative institutional stability, which was broken by the 1879 civil war.

The longest stable period began in 1889 and lasted until the US occupation (1915–34). Now controlled by Washington, the Haitian state had its bicameral parliament amputated in retaliation for the legislative body's refusal to declare war against Germany. The State Council which sat in lieu of Parliament had no autonomy. Appointed by the president, it could also be revoked by him. In the 1918 Constitution, the Parliament was re-established and the Senate was designated directly by the people. But after two periods of relative stability, authoritarianism was to resume. In 1934, within months of the end of the occupation, the head of the executive, Stenio Vincent, revoked ten senators, and the following year, a referendum was held which was to provide the constitutional basis for Vincent's power.

The 1946 liberal-inspired constitution was in turn to be swept aside by a coup on 10 May 1950. Once again, authoritarianism assumed the form of an excessive increase in presidential power, which became even more so when the representatives and the senators voted to eliminate the Senate in 1957, committing, as it were, institutional hara-kiri. The suicide of the high chamber, scheduled for 1963, was to be expedited: François Duvalier did away with it himself in 1961.

Many things have been said on the Duvalier period which fit into the main features of totalitarianism as delineated by scholars. The Haitian society found itself fragmented under the Duvalier family's twenty-nine-year iron-fisted rule. Fear and mistrust were rampant. *Noirité*, a race-based ideology, became a national ideology in order to mask the social exploitation of the people. This period was characterized by dehumanizing violence.

What Hannah Arendt (1972) and Raymond Aron (1965) write could easily apply to Haiti. Individual or collective liberties were not just limited, they were purely and simply negated. Through its propaganda, the power structure cannibalized all the social spheres, in particular the religious, which was used as a mere instrument of its policy. The popular voodoo religion was integrated into the particular system, with its priests becoming the faithful intermediaries of the regime. It was an Orwellian world of sorts in which "Big Papa Doc" was *watching you* and the truth was Duvalierian. The opposition was systematically eliminated. People began to leave the country. Emigration was a derivative of idleness and poverty, but it also meant tragedy for the boat people who risked their lives trying to reach Miami on board makeshift rafts. The conjoined effects of such a system on the society have been long-lasting on attitudes and behaviours. The words of former president of the Senate Raymond Eudrice speak volumes about the rift within the country: "Being on one's guard when one speaks in the presence of a stranger is still a reflex today because the spies, the informers and the low-paid detectives that the peaceful citizens feared and made efforts to spot in the streets or under the benevolent features of a relative are still vivid images of the past" (1992, 14; my translation). The end of the dictatorship did not bring about a reconstruction of the social fabric, although certain elements in today's situation point to a will to root out the evil – the wounds of the past are still festering underneath. Arguably, Haiti's hectic history has fostered an intolerant political culture, though any pathologic approach to the Haitian question must be taken with more than a pinch of salt. The situation is not irreversible. An autocratic culture does not preclude a passage to democracy, but the transition is all the more difficult as the period of dictatorship has been long and deep.

The events that occurred after the dictator was gone are evidence that its initiators and its die-hard defenders need not be present for authoritarianism to manifest itself. Certain democrats drew inspiration from it and changed their attitude when coming to power, which shows that the system of referents is well rooted and could still mobilize the political actors in the period of transition, a violent and cathartic phase characterized by the so-called *déchoukage* (uprooting) of the institutional and social hallmarks of the dictatorship.

One of the first ambitions of the anti-Duvalier revolution was to wipe out the living and visible symbols of the dictatorial era. A society which for years had been crushed under the juggernaut of the state stood up against its oppressor in a spontaneous and massive reaction that caught observers unawares. But symbols, just like myths, die hard. Their resilience comes from their immaterial nature. Democratic transitions prove all the more difficult to achieve as the hidden roots of the evil are strong.

In a second phase of the anti-Duvalier revolution, certain actors endowed with material and symbolic resources set out to build up "strongholds" in various sectors of the social life, which resulted in the elites' being divided between antagonistic factions. President Aristide's attitude and obstruction by the majority party in Parliament are examples of this phenomenon. One of the legal weapons of the democratization process was the 1987 Constitution, which in many respects did not fit the context. Allegedly, "it was enacted to prevent attempts at the domestication of the Haitian Parliament, coups, and other wrongdoings that were at their peak with the 1983 pro-Duvalier Parliament, which had become a mere registration chamber, a mock Parliament of sorts" ("Parlement et Démocratie", 31; my translation). The controversial debate over the 1987 Constitution has more to do with power strategies than with genuine constitutional law issues. Some monstrous provisions of the 1987 Constitutional Act make it similar to the 1843 Constitutional Act, which had in fact been nicknamed "the little monster". The comparison is relevant to the extent that the 1987 Constitution has proven ineffective in sorting out the institutional crisis the country has been going through and has yet to fill the expected structuring role.

In reaction to the executive's acting *ultra vires* under Préval's presidency, Parliament again became the blocking force it had been at the very beginning of its history. The head of state was denied his right to appoint the prime minister as provided for by the Constitution. The consequences were serious enough for a modification of the constitutional text to be considered. The 1987 Parliament was the most powerful one Haiti had known since 1806, and to cap it all, it could be neither dissolved nor adjourned ("Parlement et Démocratie", 31; my translation).

Such a situation is all the more detrimental to the democratic process since the conciliation commission set up to settle the disputes arising between the chambers, and between the latter and the head of state, did not play its role. "Parliament exercises a strict and tight control of the executive so as to prevent dictatorship and the abuses of personal power," a member of Parliament was proud to write ("Parlement et Démocratie", 33; my translation). The same argument was developed by the majority political group in the Assembly (the Organisation of the People in Struggle [OPL]) to ground their rejection of the prime minister chosen by the president. Besides the scope of the problems and the length of what has been called "the crisis", the question of the investiture of the head of government threw into relief the deep-seated divergences between the OPL and the Lavalas organization, which have less to do with economic programmes than with the desire to conquer power and to cling to it like grim death. Curiously enough, the two groups, which formerly constituted the single organization Lavalas, are rivals today and keep bandying the same arguments at each other under different forms. The government party accuses the opposition party of not complying with the rule of law. Conversely, the members of the opposition fear that the political strategies of the new administration might favour a return to dictatorship. Each one sees the weed of authoritarianism growing on the other side of the political fence. The prime minister's dispute had a negative impact on the country both domestically and externally, impairing the integration of Haiti into CARICOM.

The prime minister is the only person entitled to negotiate with the party to define the country's national policy. Political regulation is made difficult, if not impossible, without him. Under such conditions the president does not have much leeway. He can either wait and pray for the cat to jump on the right side of what he thinks is the country's best interests, or he can bypass the law and face trouble with the legislative. If it is to persist, such an attitude from the Parliament cannot fail to undermine the function of prime minister, thus confirming the inefficient character of the Constitution. This attitude would then go against the wishes of the drafters of the Constitution by actually reinforcing the authority of the head of state. The result would therefore be a paradoxical situation in which the contested traditional power representation would be re-established by the very people who fought against it. Without being pessimistic and without precluding the possibility of a normalization of the relations between the assemblies and the new executive, it seems to me that President Préval's petition to the members of Parliament anticipates this evolution. "Please," he said, "do not give me more power than does the Constitution." Those who are critical of the presidential regime are the same people who urge the president to encroach on the prerogatives of the prime minister (Agence Haïtienne de Presse, 27 April 1998).

As one can see, excessive formalism and ill-adapted provisions in the fundamental law harbour dangerous threats to the country's public life. Indeed, the paralysis of the institutions comes from the action of a political party. But the stability of the country, and to a certain extent democracy, itself are potentially endangered by the capacity of these groups to block the system. The provisions concerning the parties contained in the Constitution have not proven efficient. Before being an instrument for structuring and mobilizing opinion, partisan organizations are in the hands of people whose rational and individualistic calculations prevail over the programmatic function of their structure. When elected representatives are members of a party or become so after being elected, they sometimes dissociate themselves from their group to adopt more individual strategies: "Most of the time they intervene like ordinary citizens and even when the laws are being voted, one does not feel a real party member reflex in them" ("Parlement et Démocratie", 31; my translation). Still, it is less the individualistic rationality than the democrats' anti-democratic reflexes that are worrying in the Haitian context.

Democrats against Democracy

The reality of Toussaint L'Ouverture's nation is that of an originally and permanently broken society. This idea is conveyed through a popular saying which traces the feelings of animosity between men back to the time when they still lived in Guinea ("*Dépi nan Guinen Nèg pa lé wè Nèg*", "Back in Africa, Niggers already hated Niggers"). Of course, this myth, worded differently, can be found in other contexts. But it takes on a particular dimension in the eyes of the Haitian Protestant Federation. "It is hard to contest how rooted this saying is and the importance it must have had in the formation of the collective psychology and in the way Haitians see each others", says a representative of this religious structure which militates in favour of reconciliation (Fédération protestante d'Haïti 1994, 10).

This latent fatalism could lead to the belief that there is a "Haitian curse". The truth of the matter is that the question of change poses the parallel interrogation of the relationship the Haitian community has historically maintained with its institutions – in particular the state. The country has seemingly known two consensual parentheses: the first one, in 1804, led to independence from France, while the second, on 7 February 1986, saw the uprooting of the Duvaliers. In between, "conflicts of interests drove Haiti back to a status quo which was as dehumanising as that of the colonial period. After the uprooting, tribalism and divergent interests took over" (*Forum Libre*, no. 4 [1990]: 27). These statements reinforce the idea of a structural difficulty in applying consensual rules that exist but cannot be implemented.

The impossibility of the head of state's appointing the prime minister he choose is probably a case in point. "As for the appointment of the Prime Minister, I did what the Constitution provides for in article 137," said President Préval, "I did it twice. I continue to do my duty. The Haitian people will judge."[2]

Still, on several occasions, the Parliament dominated by the OPL, which is in favour of a democratic change, rejected the propositions made by the executive on the grounds that there had been no previous negotiations for the designation of the prime minister. "Our institutions are learning democracy and this means teething troubles," said the former president Préval laconically (Agence Haïtienne de Presse, 4 May 1998). An incursion into the constitutional history of Haiti reinforces the idea that this "learning of democracy" is all the more difficult as the society has been fragmented by years of dictatorship and is steeped in violence. This is illustrated by the place the army has occupied in the emergence of the state. The military institution set up by Toussaint during the period of colonization came prior to the state which it was supposed to serve.

With the exception of the heroic struggles against the French troops and the deep incursions into neighbouring Dominican territory, the enemy of the army was essentially an internal one. A coalition was made between politicians and the army, the latter's main role being to serve as a police force against the opponents. That fusion of the two roles limited the chances for the emergence of a true democratic culture. Contrary to the *idée reçue,* authoritarianism is not limited to violent appropriation of power by the head of the executive. The attitude of the members of Parliament, who have repeatedly refused to have the prime minister appointed, is an example of the tendency of personalities or parties to conceive of power relations as a mere struggle without compromises. It is a different, less violent consequence of the anti-democratic behaviours of a certain section of the political class throughout history. Authoritarianism brings about a strong politicization of society. This does not contradict the fact that the latter is turning its back on politics to protect itself from the exactions and the violence provoked by the rivalries between competing factions. The weight of politics on Haitian society can be explained by the resources it provides to those who have made it their livelihood in a hard economic context.

As with many countries confronted with the growing shortage of resources, the control of the state has contributed to the emergence of something like a bourgeoisie whose main resources are less the economic wealth of the country than the control of power. "Politics in Haiti", Eudrice writes, "has always been an instrument of domination for an ambitious and power-hungry oligarchy which has taken over the state apparatus to better enrich itself" (Eudrice 1992, 18; my translation). In developing countries, the middle class gets its local economic basis through the privatization of public resources and the representation of foreign interests (see Fanon 1965). The embezzlement of international aid and the appropriation of the state's funds in Haiti have been denounced on several occasions. Today, the threat of an authoritarian exercise of power could resurface. While this does not necessarily coincide with patrimonialistic practices, it could favour them. The conditions in which the May 2000 and November 2000 elections took place are not reassuring signs.

On 21 May 2000, nineteen seats were to be filled in the Senate; eighteen of them went to the Lavalas party, ten of them because of fraud. To proclaim the victory of these candidates close to President Aristide, the people legally in charge of the vote count attributed to the first four the votes of the other candidates, thus avoiding a second ballot and validating the election of candidates who lacked the required number of votes.[3] The fraud was all the more serious as the president's partisans stood a fair chance of winning at the end of the second ballot. Obviously, victory was not the only objective of those who committed the fraud. The adversaries also had to be crushed, and to do this, the basic principles of the democratic game had to be trampled. The democratic game requires some formalism, which is a guarantee of respect of opponents as well as of the efficiency of the game. The delusion has never been so big as in this context of transition in which the elected representatives of the universal suffrage, including those who rule the state, are nipping democracy in the bud.

The epilogue to the conflict which opposed the chairman of the Provisional Electoral Council (CEP), Leo Manus, to the authorities during these elections illustrates this:

> The problems began with the very first steps of the council. There were technical problems of administration and finances owing to the inherent weaknesses of the electoral institution structure, which caused us to fall behind schedule. Also, even though the CEP is an independent organisation, it must have the active cooperation of the state to carry out an important part of its mission, namely budget support, access to state-run media, and security arrangements for the voters and candidates. In reality the CEP had to face incomprehension of our mission from some, bad faith from others, and often a lack of cooperation from the administration including at the top level. Even the international assistance sought by the council was viewed with suspicion by the government. So the environment in which the CEP had to work was often plagued with traps and attacks. The slanders and threats came in profusion, some overt, others hidden, most often orchestrated by the state-run media.[4]

Refusing to condone the fraud perpetrated by the "democrats", the chairman denounced it:

> The twenty-first of May was for the CEP and the whole country a reason for great satisfaction. Against all predictions everything happened calmly and despite certain delays and logistical problems caused by the ponderousness or newness of certain parts of the electoral machinery, even the harshest critics, both national and foreign, had to acknowledge that the day and the vote of May 21 was a success.
>
> This was all the more so because the challenges were in a good number of cases legitimate, in particular when they dealt with the active role of ele-

ments of the police in certain acts of fraud, in the theft of ballot boxes or falsification of tally sheets during the night and the day after the vote. . . .

So the final senate tally saw only five senators elected in the first round. The majority of those in the lead at the time of the partial count had to go to the second round. This is what was shown by the final vote count and tabulation of the results in accordance with the electoral law. These are the results which as president of the CEP I intended to make public, in conformity with the provisions of the Haitian constitution, with ethical principles and with the equity which should be the compass of government servants. . . . As soon as my decision was made known to the executive branch, the pressures began to be exerted ever more insistently to turn the partial results into final ones. This despite all considerations of justice and respect for the electoral law.

As he thought his life was threatened by the state authorities, the chairman sought asylum in the Dominican Republic, then in the United States:

Moreover, my safety was seriously endangered because I would never agree to certify the last incorrect electoral results which did not conform to the electoral law. At the top governmental level unequivocal messages were transmitted to me on the consequences that would follow if I refused to publish the false final results. Also groups of individuals claiming to belong to one political party began to threaten to engulf the capital and provincial cities in fire and blood, destroying everything in their path. They gave me an ultimatum for the immediate announcement of the results which I considered illegitimate and incorrect. I was incapable of such an act of betrayal of my country at this decisive turn in its history. I understood that this conflict between my legal and constitutional position and the arbitrary intransigence of state power and the fury orchestrated by certain so-called "popular" organisations was inevitable.

This situation left me no other choice but to temporarily leave the country to avoid the worst and restrain the storm. . . .

I continue to believe in democracy which conquers dictatorship and provides liberty, the spirit of sharing and dialogue, well-being and development.

This long testimony from the person in charge of the institution for the regulation of the elections illustrates one of the features of the state in Haiti. Far from being a universalistic structure, the political centre remains an instrument in the hands of partisans. Under the pretence of defending national interest, they use symbolic and physical violence to retain power. Once again, in Haiti as in other economically disadvantaged countries, the conquest of political positions and of the state is an opportunity for middle-class ascension in a context in which poverty limits the chances of social promotion. Thus, "official violence" is not restricted to governmental functions. It is first an instrument of pressure and domination at the service of those who are in power. The history of Haiti and the recent developments in the country illustrate this phenomenon.

The events described by the person in charge of the CEP took place in a climate of quasi-violence detrimental to the exercise of liberties. The assassination of journalist Jean Dominique must be regarded as the event which symbolically jeopardized democracy the most. His murder, which was denounced by the international community, is in line with the will to gag those who like him have chosen freedom of expression. The moment of mourning and recollection at his funeral was disturbed by groups of people who also attacked the head office of the opposition. After the assassination, several radio stations discontinued their political news programmes for fear they might become targets for the *Chimères* (the Chimeras), the ruthless militia whose acts of violence are similar in some respects to those perpetrated by the *Tonton macoutes* of the Duvalier era.

Elected on 26 November 2000, the new president pledged to lead his country to democracy. In an article published in 1997 in the United States, he expressed his thoughts on what democracy means in a deeply non-egalitarian world in which 20 per cent of the population captures 85 per cent of the wealth of the planet, international institutions have a growing influence on local decision-making processes and neoliberal policies narrow the state's room to manoeuvre. What does "making democracy triumph" mean for a poor person? Jean-Bertrand Aristide asked. According to the president, there is a risk today of the most destitute looking at democracy as a set of merely formal structures (Aristide 1997). It is necessary to add to this analysis that a shared belief in a minimum set of rules is necessary for the democratic game to take root. The sabotaging of the electoral machinery by Aristide's partisans and Aristide's own reluctance to condemn the violence lead the observer to wonder whether he is really committed to the rules of the game. The opposition gathered in "the Group of Convergence" did not wait for the government to be appointed to form a parallel government in the name of democratic principles. Headed by Mr Gourgues, a lawyer well known for his commitments to human rights in Haiti, the group's objective is to contribute to "the awakening of the people's consciousness, the democratic consciousness and also the participative consciousness" (Agence Haïtienne de Presse, 6 Feb. 2001).

The international community, notably the European Union, also reacted by freezing the aid granted to the country. The new text regulating the relations between the European Union and the African, Caribbean and Pacific (ACP) countries, which was signed in Cotonou, Benin, on 26 June 2000 to replace the Lomé agreements, was offered one of its first opportunities for implementation in Haiti. The Cotonou agreement toughens the democratic requirements for aid applicants and provide sanctions against the contravening countries. In a February 2001 communiqué, the EU Council considered that the basic provisions of Article 9 of the Cotonou agreement have been violated by the non-compliance with the Haitian electoral law and with democratic principles.

The United States has adopted a more moderate attitude. The US State Department's representative, Philip T. Reeker, acknowledged, along with the foreign observers present in Haiti, that there had been low voter turnout. He also adopted the European viewpoint that the rule of law was absent from the country: "Low voter turnout and pre-election violence are strong indicators of the need for reconciliation among all sectors of the Haïtian society. We urge all Haïtians to respect the rule of law and to work together to strengthen democracy" (Gonzalez 2000a, 1). Unlike the Europeans, the Americans were present when the president was sworn in. The apparent moderation of the United States was certainly motivated by geopolitical considerations.

The support they had given to the successive dictatorships was grounded on anti-communism. In a depolarized world, the choice of democracy is motivated less by moral reason than by the awareness of the effects a non-democratic situation can bring about, such as larger waves of boat people and immigrants on US soil. The US intervention in the domestic affairs of the fragile republic also has to do with the fear that Haiti might become a "narco-state" since it is already a transshipment board for a substantial part of the Colombian cocaine destined for the US market.

The promises Jean-Bertrand Aristide made to Bill Clinton before taking office are a good illustration of Washington's expectations. Aristide pledged to call new and fair elections in order to designate ten senators, thus acknowledging the fraudulent character of the 21 May 2000 ballot. He also promised that a new electoral council would be set up after consultation with the opposition, which would take part in the conduct of government's business. The Organization of the American States would be called in to monitor the human rights situation in Haiti. Drugs and immigration would be among the front-burner issues of the new administration. The Haitian head of state closed his letter in the following terms: "I confirm my commitment to the points made therein . . . confident that they will help strengthen ties between our two nations where democracy and peace will flourish" (Gonzales 2000b, 1).

The US aid is allegedly aimed at securing the democratic process. On a strictly political level, it had already assumed the form of an intervention whose open ambition was to "restore democracy" and to harness a state that many citizens regarded as "a profit-oriented private business" (see Reno 1998).

The choice made by the Haitian elites, including the most anti-American among them, to relinquish a part of their national sovereignty is indicative of a change in representation and strategy with regard to dependence on the United States in a context in which a return to the old days is a constant threat. Dependency on the United States affects local life dramatically. Still, it is less a subjugation to a foreign power than a relationship of a clientelistic nature in which Haitians make up for the decline of the state and of society at large thanks to the resources granted. The clientelistic relationship manifests itself through a form of multidimensional exchange. The US boss grants its protection, its financial aid and asylum to some migrants in exchange for varied symbolic and material goods. The alienation of the client's sovereignty, notably in the obligation to toe the line traced by its partner in the international game and to adopt the US model, is a key element of the exchange. In today's Haitian situation, dependency is not mere subjugation, it is a resource.

Dependency: A Way to Democratization

Toussaint L'Ouverture's motherland is part of the zone of US influence and is heavily dependent in this respect on the White House's foreign policy. The history of the relationship between Washington and Port-au-Prince is primarily one of control by the White House of the Haitian elites and society. Heads of state who did not pledge allegiance to the United States are few and far between. The 1915–34 US occupation and 1994's Operation Restore Democracy, though different in many respects, are both reminders of the power struggle in the region and of the nature of the relations between the two countries. The still dubious democratization process in Haiti largely hinges upon the attitude of the Americans.

It may sound surprising and even illogical that dependency should constitute a resource for a state and might even be one of the means of its progress. Indeed, the literature dealing with Third World politics and sociology has striven to teach us just the contrary. Building notably on the centre-versus-periphery paradigm, this literature convincingly argues that North–South relations develop within a framework of unequal exchange between an international bourgeoisie and economically subjugated societies, politics being nothing more than the reflection of the subjugation of the periphery by the dominating class (Smith 1979; see also Henke 2000).

The Haitian case hardly fits that paradigm, though. While not disqualifying the dependency approach altogether, it nevertheless points to one of its impasses. When inferring domination from dependency, one is led to disregard the fact that in certain situations dependency can be a strategy for development. Haiti depends heavily on international money transfers, as evidenced by all the economic and social indicators. Agricultural output is low, the number of jobs in the industrial sector has decreased, and living conditions, the number of homeless poeple and people living in substandard housing have reached inhuman proportions. The situation is made bleaker still by unemployment, which affects 60 per cent of the population unemployed. The rural masses are in dire straits as they can no longer rely on the back country to alleviate their plight. More than just a real livelihood, dependency is a means for many Haitians to keep body and soul together.

The growing place the international community and an impressive range of non-governmental organizations occupy in the country is revealing of the importance of the external aid in the average Haitian's daily life. The large number of NGOs is an indicator of the level of poverty. In fact, the activities of NGOs go beyond addressing situations of poverty or participating as experts in the implementation of aid programmes. Through these activities, the local elite cashes in on the country's poverty. It is difficult to assess international aid in terms of figures as it goes beyond the financing of programmes. Foreign intervention is now so ingrained in the Haitian reality that it determines the strategies of many local agents, who are prone to regarding the aid as their own rather than as a resource for the destitute.

Dependency is obviously widespread, feeding an integrated system through which international financial and economic actions are massively diverted. Arguably, the diversion of the aid will not be substantially affected by the new political conditions required by the international community for the aid to be granted. The authorities may just be paying lip service to democracy while maintaining undemocratic practices underneath. The emergence of Aristide as "Titid", the priest of the poor, the charismatic leader who controls both the executive and the legislative powers after contested elections, is mind-boggling. After threats of sanctions, he promised a return to democracy as well as some amendments to the process that had made him the head of the state, but he did not consider stepping down. Presented with a fait accompli, international bodies have been exercising pressures that are all the more toothless as the alternative solutions are limited, the various democratic currents having proven neither their popularity nor their capacities for innovation. Political life in Haiti today is divided between two factions. One builds upon the charismatic legitimacy of the head of state while the other desperately seeks the support of the people and of the other nations. The feud between the members of the elite is detrimental to the interests of the population, particularly the most destitute, who bear the brunt of international sanctions.

The authorities have nevertheless secured the support of that part of the population by redistributing a portion of the aid and by holding an ambivalent discourse on the subjugation of the country to foreign interests. The head of state uses a double-standard strategy that consists in seeking the support of foreign states while criticizing them at home for domestic purposes. Reaching out to the opposition parties, Aristide urged them to make the country "the world champion of resistance" (Agence Haïtienne de Presse, 7 February 2001). President Préval before him had recalled the role played by France in the dismantling of the economy. This sort of reaction runs parallel to the development of demonizing discourses against political opponents, who are also held responsible for the stagnation of the first black republic.

In truth, democracy and the state appear as imported products in a society ruled by communitarian rationales and a political class with a plundering mentality. In adopting, if only fictitiously, the liberal model, a portion of the Westernized elites seeks to cash in on recognition by the international community in order to deploy their self-centred strategies of appropriation of foreign aid.

Dependency results from a tormented history whose marks result from more than colonization and economic imperialism. The construction of the Haitian nation and political centre was a violent process which often assumed the form of the personalization of power. Authoritarianism has been a constant feature in the history of the country. Democracy, which is now emerging, stumbles over behaviours difficult to understand short of questioning the Haitian political culture carved by over a century of autocratic power.

Principles such as secularization, differentiation and the universalistic orientation of politics emerged in the history of Europe, notably through the mutation of the links between the church and the political sphere proper, the social crisis of the agrarian society and the consequential limitation of the powers of the sovereign. But these features of the process of political institutionalization are not universal; they are the result of a culture which gradually took root in the societies that generated it. The Haitian trajectory has been different. The relative failure of the democratic transition reveals the difficulty of the invention of politics and the limits of mimetism.

The difficulties encountered in setting up a performing administration point to the gap between the Weberian model of regulation and the Haitian socio-political reality regulated by patrimonialism and clientelism. Far from being impersonal and rational, the Haitian administration is at the service of "bosses" and families who instrumentalize it. The civil servant, whose situation is unstable, finds it hard to be dedicated to his function and is lured into particularistic exchanges. Obviously, personal dependency supersedes the rational and legal functioning of the state. When confronted with this problem, the authorities fall back on experts' missions, as if an immediate technical solution were enough to address a question which is embedded not only in the culture but first and foremost in the nature of the relations that the state has historically maintained with the civil society. This discrepancy between the adopted European institutions and their chaotic functioning has led Haiti to be widely regarded as a country in crisis.

The Relevance and Irrelevance of the Idea of Political Crisis in Haiti

When on 6 February 2001, the opposition gathered in the Democratic Convergence Movement symbolically appointed Gérard Gourgues provisional president for a twenty-four-month mandate, it called upon the nation "to form a security belt around the convergence government and work for the consolidation of the institutions and of the conditions for the rule of law to emerge" (Agence Haïtienne de Presse, 6 February 2001). It thus refused what it regarded as a *coup de force* by the rulers in office and the Fanmi Lavalas party for the benefit of Aristide, whose legitimacy it contested. Such a move can hardly be more than symbolical short of support from other social sectors. Given the nature of the Haitian situation, the alternative proposed is fragile and consequently stands little chance of success.

Similar complaints were voiced by another group of political opponents: "Two individuals are directly responsible for the catastrophes our country suffer from today," says a representative of the Espace de Concertation ("Forum of Exchange").

> Their names are René Préval and Jean Bertrand Aristide. . . . It must be clear to everyone that in the post-electoral dispute that opposes Lavalas to the democrats of this country, the issue for the opposition leaders is not to fight for a seat of senator or a ministerial portfolio. The fight goes far beyond that since what is at stake is the future of the country and of democracy itself. (*Espace de concertation,* October 2000)

Haiti is still in a dubious battle after the operation which reestablished a democratically elected government and after the successive elections that took place afterwards. The enthusiasm of the beginning has turned into disenchantment. There still is a long way to go for the institutions to be firmly consolidated. The army has been dissolved, and though organized insecurity is losing ground, violence is still rampant. The visible signs of the dictatorship are less conspicuous but its roots are still solid. What is clear, however, is that democracy is far from being the only game in town. Everything is possible.

This situation shows the depth of the population's despair and of the Haitian crisis. The very notion of crisis is recurrent in the discourses, and it seems that people who study the Haitian trajectory are unanimous on the term. The following statements from politicians illustrate this point. Préval's statement "Let me repeat it again: Haiti is a bankrupt country"[5] reminds one of another just as revealing made at the presentation of the programme of a political party: "The situation is serious, we are sinking" (Panpra 1987, 2). These quotations sum up the fragility of the democratization process in a deeply fragmented society whose revolutionary past has so far been on the wrong side of the process.

Can we seriously consider that today's situation is a departure from the traditions of the past? Judging from the permanent instability and the involutions that Haiti has known, can we possibly say that Haiti has entered the democratic age? These questions are implicit in the analyses that historian Michel Hector (1998) dedicates to the four "big systemic crises", the most recent being the one that unravelled from 1986 to 1994. Characterized by strong popular mobilization, a gradual deterioration of living conditions and the weakening of the regime, these crises did not bring about any democratic change. The argument put forward to account for this failure is that the coalition of the dominating classes allegedly managed through these very alliance strategies to maintain a relative stability favourable to their interests. In fact, it can be argued that these crises only marginally disturbed a system whose origins can be traced back to the pre-independence period and whose resilience has kept postponing the entry into democracy.

Other scholars contend that the first breaking point dates to the government of Toussaint L'Ouverture, before the accession to independence. A social contract allegedly took form and substance with the 1801 Constitution (Célius 1998). While it was a short-lived experience, it assumed a foundational value in that it *delivered* the nation. The experience is even said to have had an international dimension. Judging from the features of the political relations that Santo Domingo set up with its French metropolis, Toussaint, it is suggested, invented the associated state.

Without denying or playing down the importance of the action taken by the man whom Aimé Césaire regards as "the central figure in the history of the West Indies" (1981, 345; my translation), one may question the impact of this contract on the development of the country. It did not stop the black general from becoming governor for life even though one may accept that the socio-political context of the time required that undivided form of power. But the contract helped in no way to avoid the subsequent drifts, particularly the institutional mimetism, which is yet another form of dependency through which the successive heads of state were to give constitutional garment to their self-interests.

Thus, socio-historical parameters do account for the failure of the social contract and for the difficulties in institutional regulation. If a social contract is the mutual recognition of social groups and agents in the public space and the subsequent compliance with the rules of the public game, the question is whether such a contract has ever existed in Haiti.

The Republic of Haiti was born of the determination of inexperienced "black Jacobins" with no political tradition other than the one forged in the adamant struggle against white slavery and the real or imaginary greed of the so-called mulattos.

The troops which fought the slave owners were in place prior to the state they were supposed to serve. They transformed themselves into a domestic police force, thus reinforcing the authoritarian penchants of their political relays or of those who promised them the permanence of the privileges they had gained in the course of history. This army was instrumental in carving the vision Haitians have of politics. The following comment on the 1991 coup by which the military, whom the democratically elected authorities trusted, ousted President Aristide illustrates that view:

> One must seek to understand the rationale that inexorably drives the government to rule despotically and to spread death and terror around in a terribly tranquil way. Indeed, in the crisis triggered by the coup, one could witness the spectacle of an explicit adhesion to despotism on the part of a certain number of political leaders and intellectuals who called themselves activists of the Democratic Left hours before acceding to power. (Hurbon 1993, 9; my translation)

The agents' strategic paradigm is a bit flimsy as a possible explanation for the phenomenon with respect to recent developments which point to the deep-seated character of the anti-democratic referents. A glance at the country's constitutional history is enough to grasp the resilient character of that autocratic political culture.

The idea that Haiti does not have a political culture is put forth by those who are prone to confusing political culture with democracy. While it cannot be gainsaid that the democratic state has yet to materialize in Port-au-Prince, it would be equally wrong to deny the existence of a political culture in this country. Developmentalist theories keep examining the modernization process in non-Western societies using the models developed by European societies.

In Haiti, just as in any other country, political culture is closely linked to the history of the country. Haiti has inherited from a dictatorial past. The impasses in the democratic process show an embedded arbitrariness and the prevalence of confrontation over compromise. If political crisis is a break in continuities (Dobry 1986), one must wonder whether the Haitian case fits in the crisis paradigm.

Indeed, the Haitian problem is less the re-establishment of democratic continuities than their *real establishment*. To consider this problem as one of re-establishment would imply that democratic continuities have existed in a significant manner, as in the South American countries, which experienced political regimes based on national sovereignty and representation as early as the beginning of the nineteenth century.

Democratization is not a recipe. It hinges upon miscellaneous historical, political, cultural and economic factors whose comparative weight is difficult to evaluate beforehand. In the case of Haiti, it is too early to talk of a consolidation of the process. For the fragile democratic flower to blossom durably, the vivacious seed of civic culture must take root. Unlike other nations – not as poor, it must be said – Haiti has benefited from exceptional aid programmes. It consequently needs time, perhaps a long time, to separate the wheat of democracy from the chaff of its garment. Democracy needs to plunge deep into its feeding soil; it requires mystical accumulation for the civic culture to take root (see Hermet 1993).

Acknowledgements

The author gratefully acknowledges the assistance of Bernard Phipps, who provided the translation of the original text.

Notes

1. For information about the NED, see http://www.ned.org/about/about.html (accessed 31 October 2002).
2. Exposé général sur la situation du pays présenté par le Président de la République devant le corps législatif, Port-au-Prince, Haiti, 12 January 1998.
3. James Morrell, A vouloir toujours plus voilà ce qui arrive. Aristide avait les voix pour une victoire, mais il a triché et a perdu sa victoire légitime, Peacenet-info@igc.apc.org
4. Déclaration de Léo Manus à l'étranger, 21 juin 2000, Haïtionline.com
5. Exposé général sur la situation du pays.

References

Arendt, Hannah. 1972. *Le Système totalitaire.* Translated by Jean-Loup Bourget, Robert Davreu and Patrick Lévy. Paris: Seuil.

Aristide, Jean Bertrand. 1997. "Turn Formal Democracies into Living Ones". *Ethical Spectacle,* March. Available at http://www.spectacle.org/397/aristide.html

Aron, Raymond. 1965. *Démocratie et totalitarisme.* Paris: Gallimard.

Célius, C. 1988. "Le Contrat social haïtien". *Pouvoirs dans la Caraïbe* (Centre de Recherche sur les Pouvoirs Locaux dans la Caraibe, Université des Antilles et de la Guyane), no. 10: 27–70.

Césaire, Aimé. 1970. *La tragédie du Roi Christophe.* Paris: Présence Africaine.

———. 1981. *Toussaint Louverture: la Révolution française et le problème colonial.* Paris: Présence africaine.

Dabène, Olivier. 1992. "Amérique centrale: transformer les régimes". In *Réinventer la démocratie: le défi latino-américain,* edited by Georges Couffignal, 221–43. Paris: Presses de la Fondation nationale des sciences politiques.

Dobry, Michel. 1986. *Sociologie des crises politiques: la dynamique des mobilisations multisectorielles.* Paris: Presses de la Fondation nationale des sciences politiques.

Eudrice, Raymond. 1992. "Rôle du sénat dans la Démocratie". Forum libre, no. 10: 12–24.

Faber, Doeke, and Karijn de Jong. 1966. *Democracies in Transition: The Model, the Factors, the Approach.* Maastricht: European Centre for Development Policy Management (ECPDM).

Fanon, Frantz. 1965. *The Wretched of the Earth*. Translated by Constance Farrington. New York: Grove Press.

Fédération protestante d'Haïti. 1994. *Urgence et exigences de la réconciliation*. Port-au-Prince, Haiti: Fédération protestante d'Haïti.

Geertz, Clifford. 1973. *The Interpretation of Cultures: Selected Essays*. New York: Basic Books.

Gonzalez, David. 2000a. "Aristide, Waiting for Tally, Delays Claiming Presidency". *New York Times on the Web*, 28 November.

———. 2000b. "Haiti's President Elect Pledges Reform in a Letter to Clinton". *New York Times on the Web*, 29 December.

Hector, Michel. 1998. "Mouvements populaires et sortie de crise en Haïti". *Pouvoirs dans la Caraïbe* (Centre de Recherche sur les Pouvoirs Locaux dans la Caraibe, Université des Antilles et de la Guyane), no. 10: 71–96.

Henke, Holger. 2000. *Between Self-Determination and Dependency: Jamaica's Foreign Relations 1972–1989*. Mona, Jamaica: University of the West Indies Press.

Hermet, Guy. 1993. *Culture et démocratie*. Paris: UNESCO/Albin Michel.

Hurbon, Laënnec. 1993. "Nationalisme et démocratie en Haïti". *Chemins critiques* 3, nos. 1–2: 11–27.

Michel, Georges. 1990. "Pourquoi le 7 février?" *Forum libre*, no. 4: 9–17.

Panpra. 1987. *Programme of Panpra: parti nationaliste progressiste révolutionnaire haïtien*. Port-au-Prince, Haiti: Panpra.

"Parlement et Démocratie: Des sénateurs et des députés parlent". 1992. *Forum libre*, no. 10: 31–33.

Reno, Fred. 1998. "Haïti, l'oraison démocratique". *Pouvoirs dans la Caraïbe* (Centre de Recherche sur les Pouvoirs Locaux dans la Caraibe, Université des Antilles et de la Guyane), no. 10: 7–24.

Smith, Tony. 1979. "The Underdevelopment of Development Literature: The Case of Dependency Theory". *World Politics* 31, no. 2 (January): 247–88.

Contributors

Holger Henke is Rockefeller fellow at the Institute for Research on the African Diaspora in the Americas and the Caribbean (IRADAC) at City College of New York (CUNY) and a senior fellow of the Caribbean Research Center at Medgar Evers College, CUNY. In addition, he is the assistant editor of the refereed journal *Wadabagei: A Journal of the Caribbean and Its Diaspora*. His research interests include various aspects of Caribbean studies and foreign relations, international political economy, migration, race relations and (political) culture. He has published three books and numerous articles in academic journals and magazines.

Fred Reno is professor of polical science and director of the Centre d'Analyse Géopolitique et Internationale (CAGI) at the Université des Antilles et de la Guyane. He has published numerous articles on the French West Indies. He is co-editor, with Richard Burton, of *French and West Indian: Martinique, Guadeloupe and French Guiana Today* (London: Macmillan, 1995) and, with Robert Hudson, of *Politics of Identity: Migrants and Minorities in Multicultural States* (New York: Palgrave Macmillan and St Martin's Press, 2000).

Anton L. Allahar is full professor of sociology at the University of Western Ontario, Canada. He is an economic and political sociologist who specializes in Cuba and Trinidad. He has written five books and over fifty refereed articles and book chapters on questions of economic development, politics, nationalism and ethno-racial identity in the Caribbean.

Hans-Jürgen Burchardt is professor in the Institute for Sociology at the University of Hannover, Germany. His research focuses on the processes of globalization and transformation in Third World countries. He has published numerous articles about Cuba in Europe, the United States and Latin America. His better-known publications are the monographs *Kuba: Der* *lange Abschied von einem Mythos* (Stuttgart: Schmetterling Verlag, 1996) and *Kuba: Im Herbst des Patriarchen* (Stuttgart: Schmetterling Verlag, 1999) and the edited books *La última reforma agraria del siglo* (Caracas: Nueva Sociedad, 2000) and *Mercados globales y gobernabilidad local: Retos para la descentralización* (Caracas: Nueva Sociedad, 2001).

Fred Constant is currently rector of the International University Léopold Sédar Senghor in Alexandria, Egypt, and a former professor of political science at the Université des Antilles et de la Guyane, Martinique. He has authored numerous studies about the political economy of the Caribbean, in particular on issues of race, ethnicity and citizenship.

Jacky Dahomay is professor of philosophy at the Lycée de Pointe-à-Pitre, Guadeloupe, and one of the leading intellectuals in the French Caribbean.

Edward Dew is professor and chair of the Department of Politics at Fairfield University in Fairfield, Connecticut. He teaches courses in Comparative Politics and International Relations, with a specialization in Latin America and the Caribbean. His work on Suriname was supported by the Ford and Rockefeller Foundations Program in Support of Social Science and Legal Research on Population Policy, the Netherlands Institute for Advanced Studies, and the Fulbright Program.

Obika Gray is professor of political science at the University of Wisconsin, Eau Claire. He is the author of *Radicalism and Social Change in Jamaica, 1960–1972* (Knoxville: University of Tennessee Press, 1991) and has written widely on social movements in Jamaica. His new book, *Demeaned but Empowered: The Social Power of the Urban Poor*, is forthcoming.

David Hinds is currently a visiting assistant professor of political science at Claremont Graduate University, California. His research interests include race and ethnicity, governance, party politics, political thought and pan-Africanism. He is a prolific writer and commentator in the popular media on these issues. His first book, *Race, Party Politics and Governance in Guyana: Power Sharing and Other Essays*, was released in 2000.

Percy C. Hintzen is professor and chairperson in the Department of African American Studies at the University of California at Berkeley. He is the author of *West Indian in the West* (New York University Press, 2001) and editor, with Jean Rahier, of *Invisible Others: Active Presences in US Black Community* (Routledge, 2002).

CONTRIBUTORS

Bert Hoffmann is assistant professor of political science at the Free University of Berlin's Latin America Institute. He has published widely on the political, economic and social transformations in Cuba, including *Cuba: Apertura y reforma económica: Perfil de un debate* (ed.) (Caracas: Nueva Sociedad, 1995), *The Cuban Transformation as a Conflict Issue in the Americas: The Challenges for Brazil's Foreign Policy* (Hamburg: Institut für Iberoamerika-Kunde, 1999) and *Kuba* (Munich: C.H. Beck, 2000). He is also co-editor of the yearbook *Lateinamerika Analysen und Berichte* (Münster: Westfälisches Dampfboot).

Perry Mars is associate professor in the Department of Africana Studies at Wayne State University. He is a former professor in the Institute of Development Studies, University of Guyana, and has held Fulbright professorships at the University of California at Berkeley and California State University, Los Angeles. His most recent book is entitled *Ideology and Change: The Transformation of the Caribbean Left* (Detroit: Wayne State University Press, 1998).

Brian Meeks is senior lecturer and director of the Centre for Caribbean Thought in the Department of Government at the University of the West Indies, Mona. He has also taught at Michigan State University and Florida International University. His recent books include *Narratives of Resistance: Jamaica, Trinidad, the Caribbean* (Mona: University of the West Indies Press, 2000) and *New Caribbean Thought: A Reader*, co-edited with Folke Lindahl (Mona: University of the West Indies Press, 2001). His first novel, *Paint the Town Red*, was published in January 2003.

Douglas Midgett is an associate professor of anthropology at the University of Iowa. He has conducted research over three decades in the Eastern Caribbean on topics that include language and expressive culture, politics and trade union history, land tenure and transfer, and migration.

Simboonath Singh is assistant professor of sociology at University of Michigan, Dearborn. His primary areas of interest are Caribbean studies, race and ethnic relations and social movements.

Anita M. Waters is associate professor of sociology at Denison University, Ohio. Her areas of interest include race and ethnicity, Caribbean society, cultural sociology, sociology of religion, political sociology, reggae music and education. One of her recent works has been published under the title *Race, Class and Political Symbols: Rastafari and Reggae in Jamaican*

Politics (New Brunswick, NJ: Transaction, 1985), and her articles appeared in the *Journal of Black Studies, Museum Anthropology* and *Caribbean Quarterly.*